balance its debts with its dreams, its powerful history with its uncertain future . . . What a treat we have in store' ***** Craig Brown's Book of the Week, *Mail on Sunday*

'His approach is distinctive . . . A skilful blend of statistical data, personal testimony and obscure but entertaining detail, it is remarkable for the freshness of the materials on which it is based. Alongside familiar sources like *Picture Post* and *Passport to Pimlico*, Kynaston has unearthed long-forgotten social surveys, radio scripts, local newspapers, and the unpublished diaries of "ordinary people" whose voices bring home the petty frustrations of everyday life during the "age of austerity". This is social history fashioned into narrative on the grand scale . . . *Austerity Britain* is an outstanding portrait of an age'
Paul Addison, *Literary Review*

'An engrossing and lively study of the post-war experience'
Sunday Times 'You Really Must Read'

'This wonderful volume is only the first in a series that will take us to 1979 and the election of Margaret Thatcher. When complete, Kynaston's skill in mixing eyewitness accounts and political analysis will surely be one of the greatest and most enduring publishing ventures for generations. It is very hard to praise the author too highly. He was born the year this first volume ends. Professional historians do not always feel under an obligation to write well and, in any case, writing about the immediate past is notoriously dangerous ground. But here it is very different. *Austerity Britain* is as supple as willow. For all its factual density, it reads wonderfully . . . What makes Kynaston's book unputdownable is the joyous recognition of an unalterable Britishness. These grey, unwashed, politically suspicious and often derisive shadows, their pockets bulging with ration books and permit applications, are not strangers to us but old friends. Read, but do not weep. Be grateful'
Brian Thompson, *Observer*

'As an evocation of an age that now seems as remote as the Renaissance, this is unsurpassed; as a portrait of the age which shaped much of modern Britain, it is also unsurpassed . . . It is a classic because its portrayal of that unheroic, slightly shabby yet formative era that was Attlee's Britain is utterly convincing – and more than that, evocative. No one born in this country between 1939 and 1959 will fail to recognise what is being described . . . Kynaston has selected his diarists with a sure touch. Autobiographies, articles, film scripts, reports of football matches, Hansard, political diaries, advertising slogans, all these are not just grist to the mill, they are carefully woven into the fabric of this fascinating book. Kynaston's eye for the telling quotation enables him to fix the spirit of the age with just the right one'
John Charmley, *Guardian*

'It is a different sort of history from the usual top-down view . . . The book is a marvel of organisation. Following a closely chronological structure, Kynaston wonderfully conveys the random simultaneity of great and small events while managing, by some deft links, to direct his spotlight in turn on different aspects of everyday life: crime, sex, education, shopping, entertainment, but above all the world of work . . . Drawing on a wealth of sources, Kynaston vividly evokes this vanished world of hard, hot, dirty physical labour . . . These varied voices present a wonderfully sardonic commentary on the familiar narrative of Westminster and Whitehall. If the succeeding volumes can sustain this quality, Kynaston will have written the fullest, deepest and most balanced history of our times'   John Campbell, *Sunday Telegraph*

'A magnificently refulgent take on the immediate post-war years . . . A couple of months before the Attlee landslide, Evelyn Waugh published *Brideshead Revisited*, that bestselling high-Tory paean to a lost age. A couple of years after Margaret Thatcher took office, a TV adaptation made Waugh's vision of a sweet and innocent past more popular than ever. Nearly 700 pages long, *Austerity Britain* is only the first in a projected series of books that will take us all the way from *Brideshead* to *Brideshead*. I, for one, can't wait'   Chris Bray, *New Statesman*

'Kynaston's book is an absorbing history with surprises for young and old . . . Kynaston's achievement is great, and the facts and views and values here will give us much to think about'   Rhoda Koenig, *Evening Standard*

'A nuanced portrait of the elastic ties between families and the variety of outlooks on an unpredictable new world'   *First Post*

'*Austerity Britain* calls on a dazzling array of contemporary voices, many of them writing in private diaries, to chart the emergence of today's Britain from VE day to 1979'   Martin Waller, *The Times*

'His aim is quite different. It is to recapture the popular mood following the rejection of Churchill and the election of Britain's first majority Labour government. *Austerity Britain* is stream-of-consciousness history, using not only the evidence of the Gallup polls, but also the more impressionistic surveys of Mass Observation, and of observers such as George Orwell, to build a picture of the period. The result is a glorious bran-tub of a book . . . full of miscellaneous information about the post-war habits of the British people . . . it is written with a wit and sparkle that makes it a pleasure to read'   Vernon Bogdanor, *Financial Times Magazine*

A WORLD TO BUILD

David Kynaston

BLOOMSBURY

First published in Great Britain 2007
This paperback edition published 2008

Copyright © 2007 by David Kynaston

The moral right of the author has been asserted

Cover image: © Hulton-Deutsch Collection/Corbis
Date photographed: 8 May, 1945
A Father and Baby Bicycle: a father cycles past a crowd outside Buckingham Palace with his
baby riding in a seat behind him during a patriotic tour of the West End on VE Day, 1945

Bloomsbury Publishing Plc
36 Soho Square
London W1D 3QY

www.bloomsbury.com

Bloomsbury Publishing, London, New York and Berlin

A CIP catalogue record for this book
is available from the British Library

ISBN 978 0 7475 8540 4
10 9 8 7 6 5 4 3 2 1

Typeset by Hewer Text Ltd, Edinburgh
Printed in Great Britain by Clays Ltd, St Ives plc

www.talesofanewjerusalem.com

Contents

This book is dedicated to Lucy

Preface

A World to Build is the first book of *Tales of a New Jerusalem*, a projected sequence about Britain between 1945 and 1979.

These dates are justly iconic. Within weeks of VE Day in May 1945, the general election produced a Labour landslide and then the implementation over the next three years of a broadly socialist, egalitarian programme of reforms, epitomised by the creation of the National Health Service and extensive nationalisation. The building blocks of the new Britain were in place. But barely three decades later, in May 1979, Margaret Thatcher came to power with a fierce determination to apply the precepts of market-based individualism and dismantle much of the post-war settlement. In the early twenty-first century, it is clear that her arrival in Downing Street marks the defining line in the sand of contemporary British history, and that therefore the years 1945 to 1979 have become a period – a story – in their own right.

It is this story that *Tales of a New Jerusalem* is intended to tell: a story of ordinary citizens as well as ministers and mandarins, of consumers as well as producers, of the provinces as well as London, of the everyday as well as the seismic, of the mute and inarticulate as well as the all too fluent opinion-formers, of the Singing Postman as well as John Lennon. It is a history that does not pursue the chimera of being 'definitive'; it does try to offer an intimate, multilayered, multivoiced, unsentimental portrait of a society that evolved in such a way during these 34 years as to make it possible for the certainties of '1945' to become the counter-certainties of '1979'.

Many of us grew up and were formed during that evolution. We live – and our children will continue to live – with the consequences.

———

'Unadjusted impressions have their value, and the road to a true philosophy of life seems to lie in humbly recording diverse readings of its phenomena as they are forced upon us by chance and change.'

Thomas Hardy
Preface to *Poems of the Past and Present*
1901

PART ONE

Waiting for Something to Happen

Eleven a.m. on Tuesday, 8 May 1945, overheard by a Mass-Observation investigator at a newsagent's somewhere in central London:

First woman: They played us a dirty trick – a proper dirty trick.

First man: A muddle it was. Just a muddle.

Second woman: People waiting and waiting and nothing happening. No church bells or nothing.

Second man: Yes – what 'appened to them church bells, I'd like to know.

Third man: (ironically) Heard that thunderstorm in the night? God's wrath that was!

Fourth man: Telling us over and over the church bells would be the signal. And then there was *no* signal. Just hanging around.

Second man: Well, I'm sick and tired – browned off of them I am. The way they've behaved – why, it was an insult to the British people. Stood up to all wot we've stood up to, and then afraid to tell us it was peace, just as if we was a lot of kids. Just as if we couldn't be trusted to be'ave ourselves.

Third man: Do 'em no good in the general election – the way they've gone on over this. People won't forget it. Insult's just what it was. No more and no less.

Third woman: (placatingly) Oh, well, I expect people will get excited enough later in the day.

Second man: It's not the same. It should of been yesterday. When you think of it – peace signed at 2.40 in the morning, and then people wait and wait all day, and then nothing but it would be

VE Day tomorrow. No bells, no All Clear, nothing to start people off.

First woman: That's just what they were afraid of, I reckon.[1]

Over a week after Hitler's death, and following the tardy radio announcement at 7.40 the previous evening, two days of celebration and good cheer were at last under way.

It took a while for things to warm up. Many people, not having heard the news, had arrived for work only to be turned back; quite a few stockbrokers, who naturally had heard the news, journeyed to the City anyway, just to make sure that the Stock Exchange really was closed; outside food shops the inevitable queues were even worse than usual; and in the north of England it rained steadily until lunchtime. Anthony Heap, a middle-aged local-government officer from St Pancras, found himself (with his wife Marjorie) in Piccadilly. 'Had some lunch at the Kardomah Café followed by ice cream at a Milk Bar in Leicester Square.' They did themselves better in Liverpool, where Beryl Bainbridge's parents took her to a celebratory businessmen's luncheon: 'The man who earned his living by having boulders broken on his chest in Williamson Square was standing outside the restaurant belting out the song "It's a lovely day tomorrow/ Tomorrow is a lovely day". My Dad gave him a shilling and shook his hand . . . like they were equals. My mother made him go instantly to the Gents, to wash off the germs.'

By early afternoon, huge crowds were gathering in all the main city centres, especially London. Gladys Langford, a middle-aged school-teacher, caught a bus from Islington to Knightsbridge: 'Piccadilly was already a seething mass of people. The hoarding around Eros was overcrowded with young people of both sexes, mostly of the Forces. About 1/3 of the people were wearing paper-hats, many of them of very attractive design. People were everywhere – on shop-fronts, up lamp-standards, singing and shouting.' Harold Nicolson, walking through Trafalgar Square and down Whitehall after his lunch at the Beefsteak, was less enamoured of what he called 'paper caps' – 'horrible, being of the comic variety' – and regretfully observed 'three Guardsmen in full uniform wearing such hats'. At 2.20 a bus managed to get through Whitehall – 'HITLER MISSED THIS BUS' chalked across it – and soon afterwards, down at the jam-packed Parliament Square end, three middle-aged women were overheard uttering their thoughts: 'I bet Churchill's pleased with himself.' 'So he should. He's done a grand job of work for a man his age – never sparing himself.' 'Pity Roosevelt's dead.' A 50-year-old man butted in: 'It was just like this after the last war and twelve months later we was standing in dole queues.' But after cries of 'Shut up', another middle-aged woman had, for the moment, the final word: 'Nobody's going to make me miserable today. I've been waiting for it too long.'[2]

At 3.00 the flags stopped waving, the bells stopped ringing, and the tumult briefly died down as everyone paused to hear Winston Churchill's short speech, delivered from 10 Downing Street and heard across the land not only on radios but from innumerable loudspeakers, including in Whitehall itself. He announced that the war in Europe would formally end just after midnight but that hostilities had in effect ceased; declared with a characteristic flourish that 'the evil-doers now lie prostrate before us' (a gasp from the Whitehall crowds); and near the end almost barked out the words 'Advance Britannia!' 'There followed,' Nicolson recorded, 'the Last Post and *God Save the King* which we all sang very loud indeed. And then cheer upon cheer.' Gladys Langford, sitting on a chair just inside Green Park and hearing the speech 'broadcast thro' loudspeakers in the trees', was unsure whether it was the King or Churchill speaking, but few others had doubts. A notably unenthusiastic member of the dense throng around Westminster was Vera Brittain, a pacifist throughout the war and now returning to the spot where she had been on Armistice Day, 1918. She generally found the mood of the afternoon 'all so formal and "arranged"' in comparison with the 'spontaneity' 27 years earlier – but it was Churchill specifically whom she could not bear. She felt his appeal to crude nationalism all too 'typical'; condemned him for having in his speech 'introduced no phrase of constructive hope for a better society which renounces war'; and even 'caught a glimpse of him standing in his car as he went from Downing St. to the H. of Commons surrounded by cheering crowds, waving his hat, with the usual cigar & self-satisfied expression'.

As soon as his speech was over, the Heaps, who had joined the multitude in Parliament Square, managed to beat a temporary retreat home (a top-floor flat at Rashleigh House, near Judd Street) for 'a much needed wash and cool off' on what was becoming 'a sweltering hot day'. But for Langford, who had no intention of returning to the fray, escape was far more difficult:

> Queued for a bus but none came – contingents of marchers – officers, men, girls, lads in rough marching order. Walked back to Piccadilly but couldn't negotiate the Circus. Solid mass of people (St John's Ambulance men and nurses behind Swan and Edgar's). A policeman advised me to work my way along by the wall – but I couldn't get near the wall. Followed a tall American soldier and made my way to Wardour St. but Leicester Sq. was impassable. Dodged thro' Soho side streets and finally reached Tottenham Court Rd – a 19 bus and home.

Between 3.20 and 4.00, about a third of the adult population was tuned in to *Bells and Victory Celebrations*. Happily for BBC Audience Research, the 'great majority' of its listeners' panel 'found this broadcast exactly fitted their mood and taste – it was vivid, noisy and inspiring; it brought invalids, and those who lived in remote corners of the country, in touch with the spirit of festivity in the capital and other cities visited'. Even so, 'some wished that the noises – of merry-making, bells and sirens – had been left to speak for themselves, without the constant flow of "patter"' – and 'the commentator at Cardiff who spoke through the Hallelujah Chorus was thought particularly tiresome.' Frank Lewis, a young man from Barry, might well have been in Cardiff that afternoon but in fact was in Manchester, where he had been studying at the university and had just started a job in a warehouse. At 3.15, having listened to the Prime Minister's address, he left his suburban lodgings and caught a tram to the city centre: 'Town was full of people, all lounging about doing nothing . . . I went in Lyons, by the Oxford cinema (where there was a queue) and got a cup of tea.' Lewis, definitely a glass-half-empty diarist, then went to the crowded Albert Square: 'Everybody seemed to be waiting for something to happen. I stayed for only 10 minutes, then came home; there was nothing doing. These so-called celebrations seem so useless, – people hanging about "doing nought".'[3]

Lewis was no doubt more curmudgeonly than most participants, or indeed non-participants. But it is clear from the findings of the pioneering sociological-cum-anthropological organisation Mass-Observation – which had begun in 1937 and relied largely on volunteer diarists and observers – that riotous abandon was the exception rather than the rule:

> Mostly, the crowds are concentrated in the few focal points of Central London. Away from these, people are restrained and orderly; the excitement seems to be almost entirely a result of the stimulus of crowds and group feeling . . . There was little gaiety in Central London away from the thickest of the crowds, and correspondingly little in the suburbs. People had put great efforts into decorating their houses, but seemed to anticipate little further in the way of celebrations . . . Bonfires, street tea-parties and fireworks, activities meant in the first place for children, were the chief features of provincial celebrations.

Adeline Vaughan Williams (the composer's first wife) was struck by how 'very sedate' Dorking in Surrey was, while Cecil Beaton found Kensington 'as quiet as a Sunday'. And he added, 'There is no general feeling of rejoicing. Victory does not bring with it a sense of triumph – rather a dull numbness of relief that the blood-letting is over.' Even young people could find it hard to celebrate with a full heart – 'I felt most depressed which I felt was very naughty considering how long we have worked and fought for this' was the downbeat diary entry of Joan Waley, who after school and a year's domestic-science course had joined the WRNS and worked near Bletchley on the Enigma code-breaking machines – while for those who had lost loved ones, a heavy tinge of sadness was inevitable.

Nevertheless, the probability is that *most* people were neither depressed nor ecstatic. Rather, they took the two days in their stride, reflected upon them to a greater or lesser extent, and above all tried to have a good time while enjoying the spectacle. '*V.E. Day*,' noted Alice (known to all as Judy) Haines, a youngish married woman living in Chingford, with a firm underlining in her diary, 'and we are due to go to the Westminster Theatre, Buckingham Gate (!) to see Cedric Hardwicke in "Yellow Sands". Decided to chance it by 38, which indicated "Victoria" as the destination anyway. Yes, but we dodged

Piccadilly, travelling via Oxford St.' The exclamation mark was a nod to Buckingham Palace, where from soon after Churchill's speech the Royal Family had started to make a series of balcony appearances to the delight of the massed subjects below. But Haines's main concern, especially as she was accompanying her husband to the show, was to look the part on this special day: 'I wore my blue silk frock with red, white and blue (mountain rose, edelweiss and gentian flowers) brooch and red coat, and felt right in the fashion.'[4]

Many in the course of the evening went to thanksgiving services. 'In the quiet of that tiny country church we found the note we really had been seeking,' the Cotton Board's Sir Raymond Streat, one of whose sons had died in action the previous autumn, wrote to another son about attending Nether Alderley Church. 'Manchester business men and Cheshire farm labourers joined in a crowded service. References were made to those whose lives had gone into the purchase of victory. Your lady mother took this stoically.' Ernest Loftus, headmaster of Barking Abbey School, attended the church in the village near Tilbury where he lived: 'A full house – largest congregation I've seen for years. I read lesson as usual. Villagers had bonfire & social afterwards. We went home & listened to B.B.C.' He was probably in time to hear the Home Service's *Tribute to the King*, running from 8.30 to 9.00 and listened to by 36 per cent of the adult population. Representatives from different walks of life were lined up in Studio 8, Broadcasting House to pay their particular live tributes. 'I speak for the men and women of the British Police,' an anonymous policeman announced. 'The war brought us many new tasks: we've faced them not only as officers of the law, but as the friends and protectors of your Majesty's subjects.' The not yet unmistakable voice belonged to John Arlott, still an acting patrol sergeant based in Southampton but starting to get some radio work.

The royal tribute was the prelude to George VI's address to his people, broadcast live at 9.00. The King's stammer made it a somewhat nerve-wracking occasion for all concerned, but in fact his longest-ever broadcast (some 13 minutes) did not go too badly – the ultra-royalist James Lees-Milne even describing it as 'perfect, well phrased, well delivered in his rich, resonant voice' and 'expressed with true feeling'. Just before it began, one of Mass-Observation's investigators slipped into her local pub in Chelsea, where she joined three young Marxist neighbours ('two M22B, twin brothers, and F25B', in other words two 22-year-old middle-class men and a 25-year-old middle-class woman):

> They say the pub has sold out of everything but gin, so Inv. gets four gins, and a few minutes later – a little late for the start – the King's speech is turned on. Several women at the back of the lounge stand up, assuming reverent attitudes. There is a sense that people have been waiting all this time for something symbolic and now they have got it: the room is hushed as a church. M22B puts his feet on the table, leans back in his chair, and groans ... At 'endured to your utmost' there are deep cries of 'Hear hear!'. Whenever the King pauses, M22B says loudly, Ts, Ts, and becomes the centre of looks of intense malevolence from all corners of the room ... When the King says 'Of just (long pause) – of just triumph' several women's foreheads pucker and they wear a lacerated look. At 'strength and shield' Marxist unaccountably removes feet from table. When *God Save the King* is sung, the whole room rises to its feet and sings, with the exception of the Marxist twins, who remain sullenly seated. F25B, the wife of one, gets up.

Afterwards, the investigator asked her why she had stood up. 'Was it sheer politeness? She says yes, she supposes so – she felt like being in harmony with everyone else.'[5]

The news bulletin that accompanied the King's broadcast included the welcome return of the weather report (Stuart Hibberd referring jocularly to 'news of an old friend – the large depression'), though for Nella Last, a middle-aged, middle-class housewife living in Barrow-in-Furness, not even this made her 'fully realise things' as she continued to have 'that curious "flat" feeling' through the evening. Thirty-nine per cent of adults then stayed tuned to *Victory Parade*, though by the time the programme ended at 10.45 the audience had dropped by more than half as even the unadventurous left home to see the flood-lights and the bonfires. 'A grand team of voices', as one grateful listener put it, included Stewart MacPherson describing the scene in Piccadilly, Richard Dimbleby in Whitehall and Howard Marshall outside Buckingham Palace. There was praise for 'the choice of Tommy

Trinder to give the running commentary from Lambeth', while 'listeners were much moved by the final sequence of Ralph Wightman [the countryman broadcaster] from Piddletrenthide', which was 'even described as "a stroke of genius"'. The programme also featured the recorded voices of Eisenhower, Montgomery, Air Chief Marshal Tedder and men of the fighting units, as well as descriptions of the celebrations in Dover, Birmingham and several American cities. 'Made me think,' ruminated Frank Lewis in his digs at 233 Upper Brook Street, Manchester 13. 'Pretty picturesque and patriotic picture as a whole; especially descriptive were the crowded scenes, Piccadilly etc, and Mr Churchill speaking to a crowd from a roof top in Whitehall, with his cabinet'. Even so, he ended his diary entry on a far from gruntled note: '"On this most memorable of all days," to quote the radio, I have spent the enormous sum, I don't think, of 1/11d.'[6]

Of course, the image we have of that warm Tuesday night is very different and predominantly takes its cue from the events in London's West End. 'There was wild excitement in Trafalgar Square, half London seemed to be floodlit – so much unexpected light was quite unreal,' wrote Joan Wyndham, having taken time off from her WAAF mess in the East Midlands. 'There were people dancing like crazy, jumping in the fountains and climbing lamp-posts.' Or take Noël Coward: 'I walked down the Mall and stood outside Buckingham Palace, which was floodlit. The crowd was stupendous. The King and Queen came out on the balcony, looking enchanting. We all roared ourselves hoarse . . . I suppose this is the greatest day in our history.' The iconography is understandably imperishable: of Churchill making the 'V' sign from a floodlit Ministry of Health balcony as the jubilant crowd below sang 'Land of Hope and Glory'; of the Old Etonian trumpeter (and young Guards officer) Humphrey Lyttelton playing 'Roll out the Barrel' as he lurched on a handcart from Buckingham Palace to Trafalgar Square and back followed by a long, swaying line of revellers doing the conga; of young women in confident groups on their own; of even the two princesses (Elizabeth and a 14-year-old Margaret Rose) being allowed to mingle with the crowds after midnight.

Certainly Anthony Heap had no complaints, or at least no complaints bar the absence of live music and 'the fact that the pubs, though allowed to keep open till midnight, were nearly all closed'.

He and his wife returned to the West End at 7.30, saw one of the Royal Family's 11 balcony appearances and made a typically painstaking tour of the main floodlit buildings. 'One small incident we witnessed in St James's Street – a dozen or so young revellers dancing "ring-a-ring-a-roses" round Philip Page, the gouty and arthritic dramatic critic of the *Daily Mail*, as he slowly hobbled across the road – was typical of the hundreds of smaller manifestations of high spirited gaiety that we saw tonight.' For many, Heap noted, that night was still young:

> No one seemed to bother much about getting home, for though the last trains to the suburbs had left the West End at the ridiculously early hour of 11.15 or thereabouts, there were still as many sightseers about when we started to walk home just before midnight as there were when we arrived on the scene in the early evening. While outside Leicester Square station was a queue extending all the way up to Cambridge Circus waiting for the first trams in the morning! A sight which made us truly thankful that we were able to walk home, footsore and weary though we were as we trudged through Bloomsbury, so dark and drear by comparison with the brightly illuminated West End.

The couple finally flopped into bed at 1 a.m. 'It had been a grand day and we'd savoured it to the full. We were, in fact, VE Day-drunk!'[7]

The West End, though, was not London, let alone Britain. 'Usually, crowds were too few and too thin to inspire much feeling,' reckoned Mass-Observation, 'and on V.E. night most people were either at home, at small private parties, at indoor dances or in public houses, or collected in small groups around the bonfires, where there was sometimes singing and dancing, but by no means riotously.' Most contemporary accounts confirm this rather low-key feel to proceedings. 'The town was thronged but the crowds were orderly' was how Colin Ferguson, a pattern-maker working for Babcock & Wilcox in Glasgow, found that city's George Square shortly before midnight. 'Most of those walking about evidently just out to see what was going on.' So, too, in the Birmingham suburb of Erdington, where after the King's broadcast 'the "bonfire" in Mr Swinnerton's field in Marsh

Lane' was the attraction for Mary King (a retired teacher), her husband and a group of friends: 'It was a tremendous scene. Many people gathered to enjoy the sight. Everything quiet and orderly & enjoyable.' Raymond Streat was at a big bonfire in Wilmslow, built by the Boy Scouts: 'What curious people are we English? There was no cheering or rowdying. About two thousand folk stood there silently watching flames lighting up the dark skies . . . We were all content, apparently, to stand still and to stare. One or two attempts to launch a song died away.' Judy Haines and her husband, meanwhile, had heard the King's speech relayed at the Westminster Theatre before setting out for home: 'Quite easy to get on the bus (though we changed at Leyton) and we had a front seat and good view of the bonfires and merriment. Met Mother H. waiting for Dad, at Chingford. Went in to spam and chips, etc. After that we were invited to a party at the Odeon, which we refused. Mrs Telford had thought we would have loved it, but I explained we had just done a show and had a meal.' She noted, as any sensible person would, 'It was twenty to twelve, by the way.'[8]

Not all the bonfires were quiet, meditative affairs. Certainly not in deepest Herefordshire, where the local paper described what it was pleased to call 'A Country Village Celebration':

Passing through the village of Stoke Lacy early on Tuesday afternoon one was startled to see the effigy of Hitler hanging from a gibbet in the car park of the Plough. That evening, a crowd began to gather, and word went round that Hitler was to be consumed in flames at 11 pm. At that hour excitement was intense, when Mr W R Symonds called upon Mr S J Parker, the Commander of No 12 Platoon, of the Home Guard, to set the effigy alight. In a few minutes the body of Hitler disintegrated as his 1,000-years Empire has done. First, his arm, poised in a Heil Hitler salute, dropped as smartly as it was ever raised in life. Quickly followed his German hat; then a leg fell off, and then the flames burnt fiercely to the strains of 'Rule Britannia', 'Land of Hope and Glory', 'There'll always be an England' and 'Roll out the Barrel'. Then the crowd spontaneously linked hands, and in a circle of 300 strong sang 'Auld Lang Syne'. Mr Parker then called for cheers for Mr Churchill, President Truman, Marshal Stalin, and our serving boys and girls.

The ceremony was followed by the singing of 'God Save the King'.

There were similar scenes elsewhere. In the West Midlands, where streets in the working-class districts of Wolverhampton 'vied with each other in the number of streamers and flags they could produce', Hitler was 'burned many times over'; in a Coventry suburb a self-appointed 'Mayor and Wife' – both men, with a builder, 'the fattest man in the street, and the jolliest', as the Mayoress – conducted a mock funeral for the effigy. 'Preparations for these affairs were elaborate and careful and they were well-organised,' the Mass-Observation survey found. 'The whole performance seems to have been charged with a deep satisfaction for most of the people who watched it.'[9]

But for Gladys Langford – 55 years old, married in 1913, deserted by her husband in 1914, living on her own at the Woodstock Hotel, N5 – the escape from central London on a number 19 bus did not presage a happy evening:

> Miss Sweeney invited me to the bar [ie at the hotel] and I said I would go after the King's Speech. When I arrived and saw a semi-circle of people all 'put' so to speak, I just fled. I remembered what Lil used to say at parties at home, 'They don't really want you – they are only being polite', so I fled! Miss Sweeney & Miss Gilman both followed me but I refused their welcome and decided to go to bed early. However, Miss Stevens, Mrs Polley and Mrs Mobbs came about 11 pm to call me from the drive, inviting me to go to Highbury Fields where there was a concert – of sorts – and flood-lit dancing spaces. Crowds there with dogs and children much in evidence. Came back to find everyone almost in the bar and was persuaded to join the throng. Peter Gurney bought me a light ale and Mr Burchell a double gin. People were dancing on a space the size of a handkerchief, sentimentalising and singing – all in different keys and often different songs. Mafoot [?] insisted on kissing me and holding my hand – and I detest him. 18 year old Gurney took me on his knee and put his arm round my neck and Burchell wanted me to do 'Boomps-a-daisy' with him. My inhibitions made me refrain from doing more than laugh at less restrained people.

Writing up her diary some hours later, she added with grim satisfaction, 'there are some sore heads here this morning.'

Henry St John was also on his own and living in a hotel, in his case the Westbourne in Bristol. In his mid-30s, he had been educated at Acton County School, and his parents had run a confectioner's in Chiswick High Street. He had joined the Civil Service straight from school and seems by the mid-1940s to have had a fairly itinerant role, going to different regions and auditing the accounts at their labour exchanges. For him, rather as for Philip Larkin, the war had essentially been a personal inconvenience, and his diary entry for VE Day was entirely in character. It read in toto: 'It was learned that the cook, who had been living at the Westbourne, went out yesterday and had not come back.' Nor did St John's next entry, recording the events of the Tuesday night, quite take the big view: 'A party in a nearby house went on until 2 a.m., with music, dancing, singing, and shouting, so that I could not sleep until well past that hour, and as I slept badly the previous night I felt good for nothing today.' St John seems to have been a man of virtually non-existent human sympathies but was not wholly exceptional in apparently having zero interest in this historic event. Another sleepless diarist was perhaps more typical. 'Far into the night there was the noise of singing and shouting at the pub and fireworks going off, and in the sky the glimmer of some huge bonfire, or was it the illumination of London?' The writer Denton Welch, living in Hadlow in Kent, then felt – as surely so many did – the discomfort of imminent change from a condition that, for all its inconveniences, had become familiar: 'There were awful thoughts and anxieties in the air – the breaking of something – the splitting apart of an atmosphere that had surrounded us for six years.'[10]

VE+1, the Wednesday, was inevitably a bit of a let-down, not helped by most pubs (in London anyway) having run out of beer. 'This VE business is getting me down with fatigue' was how Lees-Milne bluntly put it. A certain amount of normality returned – for example, the senior Labour politician Hugh Dalton took Michael Young from his party's research department to lunch at the Marsham Restaurant and found him 'not particularly sympathetic, but quite capable' – but there were still plenty of festivities, including a plethora of street parties for children. These were mainly jolly affairs, as innumerable photographs show, though not without their tensions. 'Half our road where all my friends lived had semi-detached houses and detached bungalows while at the bottom end the houses were small and terraced,'

Michael Burns later recalled about growing up in Tolworth just off the Kingston bypass. 'We had a street party that our parents were insistent should not include the children from the terraced houses, so there were two parties in Southwood Drive divided by about two hundred yards.' In Islington one of the children's street parties was organised by a maid from the Woodstock Hotel. 'She obtained a Nazi flag and took it into a pub and let people pay 6d a time to spit on it,' Gladys Langford recorded. 'She finally sold it for 10/-, having made a total of £2 15s od.' Frank Lewis once again tried the centre of Manchester and once again was unimpressed: 'Big crowds everywhere, especially Albert Square, still doing nothing, apparently just hanging about.'

As for Anthony Heap, he more or less repeated his 'programme' of the day before, this time on his first leg getting a glimpse of the Royal Family as they set out for their tour of the East End. In the evening it was 'once more unto the West End', where he found 'the same good humoured crowds, the same high spirited skylarking, the same awe inspiring floodlighting', though it 'wasn't perhaps *quite* so overwhelming an occasion'. He finished with 'a last enchanting eye-full of the floodlit splendour of St Paul's Cathedral, Houses of Parliament etc from Waterloo Bridge' before catching 'what must have been the last 68 bus to Euston Rd which was completely illuminated from end to end with its full pale-blue peace-time lighting'. After seemingly interminable blackouts and no street lighting, this did indeed 'seem the most amazing thing – this prodigality with light', as Alan Bennett would express it when describing his VE memories (improbably enough of Guildford, to where his parents had moved briefly from Leeds). Heap concluded his diary entry without ambiguity: 'And so we came to end of two perfect days. They couldn't have furnished a happier set of memories to look back on in my old age.'[11]

Kenneth Tynan might not have agreed. A precocious schoolboy in his last year at King Edward's, Birmingham, Tynan had spent VE night watching his girl (Joy Matthews) go off with someone else, only not coming to blows because he realised that his rival was stronger. 'But Wednesday night capped everything,' he wrote to a friend. 'I have never felt nearer to murder than I did then and do now.' Ken and Joy were among a party – of fifty to a hundred strong – that spent most of the evening first at a 'Jazz Jamboree' at the Midland Institute and then at the Birmingham University Students' Union, before heading towards Moseley:

> We walked along in a colossal line spread out across Bristol Rd – all except Joy and Bernard, who walked ecstatically in front, embracing each other every few yards. Then I got mad. I went completely berserk and walked bang into the headlights of a car approaching along Priory Rd. I was utterly, utterly despondent . . . I dashed off after Joy, croaking in a reedy hoarse treble that I was taking her home and that I would slit both their throats if they didn't stop. Of course, they didn't. They stopped, *laughed at me* (O Christ) and proceeded to neck in front of me in the middle of the road.
>
> It took eight of them to stop me from strangling the filthy bitch and that low bastard.

A provincial wannabe being laughed at: a terrible moment, but he would soon enough be on the fast track to exact cosmic revenge.

About the same time as Tynan's humiliation, the Chelsea-based Mass-Observation investigator was returning home. She had spent the evening in the West End, mainly outside Buckingham Palace watching the crowds waiting for a balcony appearance and eventually getting it at about 10 p.m.: '"Doesn't the Queen look lovely?" says F35C. "The princesses were among the crowd last night, only nobody recognised them," says somebody else.' The gates were closed at both Piccadilly Circus and Green Park stations, so she walked home. Her report finished with a post-midnight vignette: 'On a piece of waste ground in Flood Street ten or twelve children are silently gathered round a bonfire. They look tired but happy and absorbed. One says in a low voice, "It'll last a long time yet." A man at the end of the street is striking matches and says he is looking for a shilling he has dropped. Throws match away angrily, saying, "They don't last long enough."'[12]

2

Broad Vistas and All That

Britain in 1945. No supermarkets, no motorways, no teabags, no sliced bread, no frozen food, no flavoured crisps, no lager, no microwaves, no dishwashers, no Formica, no vinyl, no CDs, no computers, no mobiles, no duvets, no Pill, no trainers, no hoodies, no Starbucks. Four Indian restaurants. Shops on every corner, pubs on every corner, cinemas in every high street, red telephone boxes, Lyons Corner Houses, trams, trolley-buses, steam trains. Woodbines, Craven 'A', Senior Service, smoke, smog, Vapex inhalant. No launderettes, no automatic washing machines, wash day every Monday, clothes boiled in a tub, scrubbed on the draining board, rinsed in the sink, put through a mangle, hung out to dry. Central heating rare, coke boilers, water geysers, the coal fire, the hearth, the home, chilblains common. Abortion illegal, homosexual relationships illegal, suicide illegal, capital punishment legal. White faces everywhere. Back-to-backs, narrow cobbled streets, Victorian terraces, no high-rises. Arterial roads, suburban semis, the march of the pylon. Austin Sevens, Ford Eights, no seat belts, Triumph motorcycles with sidecars. A Bakelite wireless in the home, *Housewives' Choice* or *Workers' Playtime* or *ITMA* on the air, televisions almost unknown, no programmes to watch, the family eating together. Milk of Magnesia, Vick Vapour Rub, Friar's Balsam, Fynnon Salts, Eno's, Germolene. Suits and hats, dresses and hats, cloth caps and mufflers, no leisurewear, no 'teenagers'. Heavy coins, heavy shoes, heavy suitcases, heavy tweed coats, heavy leather footballs, no unbearable lightness of being. Meat rationed, butter rationed, lard rationed, margarine rationed, sugar rationed, tea rationed, cheese rationed, jam rationed, eggs rationed, sweets rationed, soap rationed, clothes rationed. Make do and mend.

For the policy-makers, the planners, the intelligentsia, the readers of Penguin Specials, everyone with an occupational or emotional stake in 'the condition of the people', there was no shortage of problems to be tackled.[1] Some flowed directly from the war – three-quarters of a million houses destroyed or severely damaged, huge disruption to public services, Britain's debt a record £3.5 billion – but others were of longer standing. Life expectancy had increased from some 50 years in the Edwardian era to about 65, and classic killer diseases like tuberculosis, scarlet fever and typhoid were almost under control; yet access to the medical services remained for many far from free or equitable, and considerable suffering resulted from an unwillingness or (more usually) financial inability to use them. Despite a reasonably energetic slum-clearance programme between the wars, there were still many appalling Victorian slums in the major cities and large pockets of overcrowded, inadequate-to-wretched housing almost everywhere. About seven million dwellings lacked a hot-water supply, some six million an inside WC, almost five million a fixed bath. Above all, there was the profound emotional as well as practical legacy of the economic slump between the wars – at its worst from the late 1920s to the mid-1930s, causing widespread poverty and destroying or at best stunting millions of lives. The resonance of 'Jarrow', the 'murdered' north-east shipyard town that famously marched against unemployment, or indeed 'the thirties', would last for half a century. Even a Prince of Wales had once murmured that something had to be done; it had become a less than revolutionary sentiment to agree.

Wartime developments had – at least in retrospect – a seemingly irresistible momentum. As early as January 1941, while the bombs were falling, *Picture Post* outlined in a celebrated special issue (complete with six naked, presumably impoverished small children on the cover) 'A Plan For Britain'. The magazine recalled the sudden end of the war in November 1918: 'The plan was not there. We got no new Britain . . . This time we can be better prepared. But we can only be better prepared if we think now.' Accordingly, a series of articles (including 'Work for All', 'Plan the Home', 'Social Security', 'A Plan for Education', 'Health for All' and 'The New Britain Must be Planned') offered an initial blueprint for 'a fairer, pleasanter, happier, more beautiful Britain than our own'.[2]

Over the next 18 months or so, the concept began to be accepted that the British people, in return for all their sufferings in a noble cause, deserved a new start after the war. December 1942 saw the publication of the Beveridge Report, drawn up by the eminent economist and civil servant Sir William Beveridge. In it he set out proposals for a comprehensive post-war system of social security, in effect laying the foundations for the 'classic' welfare state – an attack upon what he memorably depicted as 'the five giant evils' of want, disease, ignorance, squalor and idleness – and in so doing caused such a stir that an extraordinary 630,000 copies of the report (mainly the abridged, popular edition) were sold. Then, in 1944, as the war began to draw to a close, there were two major 'reconstruction' moments: in May the publication of a White Paper that committed the British government to the pursuit of full employment as the highest economic objective; and in August the arrival on the statute book of R. A. ('Rab') Butler's Education Act, which, among other things, created free, non-fee-paying grammar schools.

To all appearances the reforming, forward-looking tide was running fast. *Who Else Is Rank* was the symptomatic title of an unpublished novel co-written the following winter by a 22-year-old Kingsley Amis and a fellow Signals officer. 'We must see to it after we're demobilised,' the Amis figure (a sensitive young lieutenant) says at one point, 'that these common men, from whom we're separated only by a traditional barrier – we're no more than common men ourselves – benefit from the work that has been done, and if the system won't let that happen, well, we shall just have to change the system.'[3]

In April 1945, as Hitler made his last stand in Berlin, the Labour Party issued its manifesto for the election that was bound to follow the end of the war. Called *Let Us Face the Future*, it demanded decisive action by the state to ensure full employment, the nationalisation of several key industries, an urgent housing programme, the creation of a new national health service and (in a nod to Beveridge) 'social provision against rainy days'. The tone was admirably lacking in bombast but distinctly high-minded. 'The problems and pressures of the post-war world,' the fairly brief document declared, 'threaten our security and progress as surely as – though less dramatically than – the Germans threatened them in 1940. We need the spirit of Dunkirk and of the

Blitz sustained over a period of years. The Labour Party's programme is a practical expression of that spirit applied to the tasks of peace. It calls for hard work, energy and sound sense.' The manifesto's principal author was Michael Young, not long before his lunch with Hugh Dalton. Aged 29, he had been educated at the progressive Dartington Hall and been director of a newish organisation, Political and Economic Planning (PEP), before in February 1945 moving to the Labour Party's research department. Young in later life was self-deprecating about the manifesto: 'The mood was such that second-class documents were going to be thought first-class with a star.'[4]

Two crucial questions suggest themselves, however. How by 1945, at the apparent birth of a new world, did the 'activators' – politicians, planners, public intellectuals, opinion-formers – *really* see the future? And how did their vision of what lay ahead compare with that of 'ordinary people'? The overlaps and mismatches between these two sets of expectations would be fundamental to the playing out of the next three or more decades.

There would be no fly-pasts in its honour, but arguably 1940 was the British state's finest hour, as the nation – under the iron-willed direction of Ernest Bevin as Minister of Labour in Churchill's coalition government – mobilised for total war more quickly and effectively than either Germany or Russia. The state, in other words, proved that it could deliver, as it also did by introducing wide-scale rationing in a way generally seen as equitable. Simultaneously, the first half of the war saw the creation of a plethora of new ministries: not only Labour but Economic Warfare, Food, Home Security, Information, Shipping, Aircraft Production and Production. By 1943 there were, not surprisingly, well over a quarter of a million more civil servants than there had been before the war. It was soon clear, moreover, that all the work of these ministries, as well as of the traditional ones, was now predicated upon assumptions of co-ordinated central planning – an utterly different mindset from Whitehall's customary approach and propagated by some exceptionally talented temporary recruits there, often operating at a very high level.

How, if at all, might this translate into peacetime economic policy? Relatively early in the war, the great economist John Maynard Keynes had more or less won the battle within the Treasury to persuade that deeply conservative institution to accept at least a substantial measure of demand management as the principal way of regulating the economy in order to keep the level of unemployment down. Thereafter, the real intellectual conflict among radically minded 'activators' was between Keynesians and those whose ideal was wartime-style (and Soviet-style) direct physical planning. For the former, there was still a significant role – at least in theory – to be played by the price mechanism of the market; for the latter, that role was fairly surplus to requirements. By the end of the war, it seemed that the force was with the out-and-out planners, with their emphasis on investment planning and, through direct controls over labour, manpower planning.

Indeed, such was the temper of the times that even most Keynesians had, in a visceral sense, little real faith in, or any great intellectual curiosity about, the possible economic merits of the market or of supply-side reforms. Hence the largely stony academic-cum-intellectual reception accorded in 1944 to *The Road to Serfdom* (dedicated 'To the Socialists of All Parties') by the Austrian economist F. A. Hayek, who was based at the London School of Economics (LSE). 'His central argument was that a modern economy was a vast system of information flows which signal to everyone indispensable facts about scarcity and opportunity,' a latter-day follower, Kenneth Minogue, has helpfully summarised. 'The vitality of modern Western economies, and the best use of scarce resources, rested upon the workers and entrepreneurs having these signals available to them. No planning committee could possibly plug into them. Central direction could lead only to poverty and oppression.'[5] Such was the loss of confidence among economic liberals following the events of the previous 20 years – the inter-war slump, the lessons of the war (including the apparent Russian lessons) – that it would be a long time before a critical mass of politicians began to make a full-bloodedly coherent or attractive case on Hayek's behalf.

Unsurprisingly, then, the inescapable necessity of a substantial portion of the economy being in public ownership was hardly questioned for many years after 1945. Indeed, such had arguably become the prevailing activator consensus from well before the war. The BBC (1922), Central Electricity Board (1926) and BOAC (British Overseas Airways Corporation, 1939) were all examples of important new organisations being set up on a public rather than private basis, while Harold Macmillan, the rising force on the Tory left, called in *The Middle Way* (1938) for a programme of nationalisation at least as ambitious as that then being advocated by the Labour Party. To many, the arguments seemed unanswerable: not only were there the examples of major, palpably enfeebled industries like coal mining and the railways as clear proof that private enterprise had failed, but in economies of scale, especially as applied to utilities (the so-called natural monopolies), there was an even more powerful siren call, very much reflecting what the political economist John Vaizey would term the prevailing 'cult of giganticism'. During the last year of war, a quite sharp leftwards shift in the Labour Party – identifying public owner-ship with both economic efficiency and, in an ominously fundamen-talist way, socialist purity – resulted in a fairly ambitious shopping list in *Let Us Face the Future*, featuring the Bank of England, fuel and power, inland transport, and (most contentiously) iron and steel, though with the high-street banks, heavy industry and building all excluded.

What sort of nationalisation would it be? The key text was the 1933 treatise *Socialisation and Transport* by the leading Labour politician Herbert Morrison, creator of the London Passenger Transport Board and, in due course, grandfather of Peter Mandelson. Notably short of hard economic analysis, Morrison's paper nevertheless put forward a plausible enough public-corporation model that envisaged publicly appointed managers running monopoly industries in the public interest, though in a more or less autonomous way. Morrison did not have any truck with the notion of democratic control over these nationalised industries – certainly not democratic control as exercised from the shop floor. 'The majority of workmen are,' he insisted, 'more interested in the organisation, conditions, and life of their own work-shop than in those finer balances of financial and commercial policy which are discussed in the Board room.'[6] The assumption was that the managers of these public corporations would be exemplars of scrupulous, objective professionalism – and that the workers in them should know their place.

A similar faith in the beneficent, public-minded expert underlay the creation of the modern welfare state. There was in December 1942 no greater expert than Beveridge himself, who summarised his Report as 'first and foremost, a plan of insurance – of giving in return for contributions benefits up to subsistence level, as of right and without means test'. This last point was crucial, given the widespread detestation that had developed between the wars of the many forms of means testing. And this in practice meant that the social insurance provided – essentially against loss or interruption of earnings due to unemployment, sickness or old age – would be *universal*. Beveridge's proposals engendered serious consternation on the part of Churchill, most Conservative MPs and some top Whitehall officials. But by March 1943 it was clear, following a clutch of by-elections, that there was an unignorable head of steam behind them. That month, Churchill – in a broadcast called 'After the War' – solemnly promised 'national compulsory insurance for all classes for all purposes from the cradle to the grave' – not the first use of that striking phrase but the one that made it famous. There were still plenty of debates and committees to go through, but by the time the war in Europe ended, family allowances – the first of the Beveridge-inspired pieces of legislation, providing 5s a week (more than 5 per cent of the average male wage) for each child from the second onwards – were virtually on the statute book.

From the perspective of more than half a century later, three of Beveridge's central assumptions are especially striking, starting with what one might call the 'Nissen hut' assumption. Beveridge's insistence that contributions be levied at a flat rate, rather than in the earnings-related way that tended to be adopted in other advanced industrial economies, was perhaps appropriate in an age of austerity. But that would change in an age of affluence with its inflationary implications and, above all, financially onerous concept of *relative* poverty. Secondly, there was Beveridge's assumption that married women would – following their wartime experience – return to and stay at home, given that their prime task was to 'ensure the continuation of the British race', which at 'its present rate of reproduction . . . cannot continue'. In administrative terms this meant that a married woman would be subordinate to her husband, with benefits to her coming only as a result of his insurance. Beveridge's third, equally Victorian assumption, befitting a Liberal who was already in his teens when

Gladstone had been Prime Minister in the 1890s, was that in the post-war world enhanced rights would be matched by enhanced responsibilities. Not only did he insist that his social-security system be contribution-based rather than tax-based, but he was also determined that his ultimate safety net of means-tested national assistance would be pitched at such an unattractively minimalist level that it would 'leave the person assisted with an effective motive to avoid the need for assistance and to rely on earnings or insurance'. And he added sternly that 'an assistance scheme which makes those assisted unamenable to economic rewards and punishments while treating them as free citizens is inconsistent with the principles of a free community'.[7] Beveridge's welfare state – a term not yet invented but one that he would come to loathe – was not, in short, to be a soft touch.

Integral to the Beveridge vision of the future was a free and comprehensive national health service. The key propagandist, in terms of preparing the intellectual ground for such a development, was undoubtedly Richard Titmuss – a remarkable person who would become (in Edmund Leach's words) the 'high priest of the welfare state'. Titmuss was still a young man, the son of a failed farmer-turned-haulier, when he researched and wrote *Poverty and Population* (1938), which he somehow managed to do while holding down a full-time job as an insurance actuary. In it he examined the depressed areas of industrial Britain and showed in irrefutable detail the appalling human wastage resulting there from poverty and inequality. Other books followed, including (soon after Beveridge) *Birth, Poverty and Wealth* (1943), which put infant mortality under the microscope of social class and found that each week almost 2,000 lives were lost unnecessarily. 'The writings of Titmuss set a new standard,' the historian of the NHS has written. 'Their influence was extensive and immediate. His method of demonstrating inequalities found its way into popularisations aimed at various classes of reader.'

In February 1944 the Conservative Minister of Health in Churchill's coalition government, Henry Willink, issued a White Paper that spoke of 'the need to bring the country's full resources to bear upon reducing ill-health and promoting good health in all its citizens' – in effect making it clear that a post-war Conservative administration would bow to Beveridge's wishes and introduce a national health service.

Nevertheless, 'there is a certain danger in making personal health the subject of a national service at all,' the document added. 'It is the danger of over-organisation.' One way in which Willink intended to minimise that danger was through combining free, universal access on the one hand with diversity of provision on the other – above all through not nationalising the hospital stock as a whole, maintaining instead a mixture of voluntary and municipally run hospitals.

The attitude of the medical profession to all this was ambivalent. It broadly accepted the case for a free and universal health service, but it was understandably reluctant to abandon its profitable private work, feared political interference (whether at a local or at a national level) and – on the part of GPs, who usually operated solo – saw in the increasingly fashionable nostrum of the health centre a dastardly socialist plot. 'We have entered a new era of social consciousness,' the Spectator – hardly noted for left-wing views – observed in the spring of 1944. 'Some of the doctors seem not to have realised that fully, and it is desirable in everyone's interest that they should.'[8] A year later there was still a significant degree of consciousness-raising to be done.

If in health there was still much to play for by 1945, the same was rather less true in education, where in outline anyway the post-war settlement had already taken shape. In a flurry of wartime action, it had three main elements: the Norwood Report of 1943, which examined what should be emphasised in the curriculum at secondary schools and (to the private satisfaction of the President of the Board of Education, Rab Butler, in theory a reforming Conservative) plumped for the time-honoured virtues of PE, 'character' and the English language, as opposed to anything more technical or modern; the Butler Act of 1944, which vastly expanded access to free secondary education; and, from the same year, the Fleming Report on the public schools, which in retrospect represented the spurning of a realistic chance to seek the abolition of the independent sector.

Relatively few people at the time appreciated the negative significance of Norwood and Fleming, amid a general preference for concentrating on provision and numbers, whereas even at its outline stage the Butler legislation was widely seen as historic. 'A landmark has been set up in English education,' the Times Educational

Supplement declared. 'The Government's White Paper promises the greatest and grandest educational advance since 1870.' The paper's editor, the progressive-minded Harold Dent, claimed that the government now accepted two key principles – 'that there shall be equality of opportunity, and diversity of provision without impairment of the social unity' – and boldly prophesied that 'the throwing open of secondary education, of various types, to all' would 'result in a prodigious freeing of creative ability, and ensure to an extent yet incalculable that every child shall be prepared for the life he is best fitted to lead and the service he is best fitted to give'.

Did that innocuous phrase 'of various types' catch some eyes? Quite possibly, for although Butler's subsequent legislation would have nothing specific to say about different types of secondary school within the state sector, the fact was that at the very time of his White Paper the Norwood Report was not only enshrining as orthodoxy a tripartite system of grammar schools, technical schools and secondary moderns but explicitly avowing that 'in the Grammar School the pupil is offered, because he is capable of reaching towards it, a conception of knowledge which is different from that which can be and should be envisaged in other types of school'. A former headmaster of Bristol Grammar School, Marlborough College and Harrow School, Sir Cyril Norwood had no qualms about pecking orders. In fact, there was an incipient movement under way in favour of the comprehensive school (or the 'multilateral', as it was then usually called), a movement in which Dent cautiously participated; yet even in one of English society's more egalitarian phases, such a concept was far removed from practical politics. Significantly, when Dent in early 1944 wrote a pamphlet entitled *The New Educational Bill*, he neither questioned tripartism nor mentioned the comprehensive alternative.

There seems, moreover, to have been a similar lack of concern about the inevitable selection implications of a tripartite structure. 'The Government hold that there is nothing to be said in favour of a system which subjects children at the age of 11 to the strain of a competitive examination on which not only their future schooling but their future careers may depend,' wrote Dent about the White Paper in wholly sanguine mode. 'In the future, children at the age of 11 should be classified, not on the results of a competitive test, but on assessment of their individual aptitudes largely by such means as school records, supplemented, if necessary, by intelligence tests, due regard being had to their parents' wishes and the careers they have in mind.' Just in case anyone was worried, he added that there would be arrangements for children to transfer at 13 in the unlikely event of a mistake having been made two years earlier.[9]

If for Keynesians, social reformers and educationalists the war provided unimagined opportunities for influencing the shape of the future, this was even more true for architects and town planners and their cheerleaders. In their case a momentum for fundamental change had been building inexorably between the wars, and now the heady mixture of destruction and reconstruction gave them their chance. That gathering impetus was perfectly encapsulated as early as 1934 by a young architectural writer answering the question 'What Would Wren Have Built Today?' After diagnosing the City of London as overcrowded, badly lit and generally impossible to work in either efficiently or pleasantly, he went on:

> We must give up the building rule which restricts the height of buildings, and we must not only do that, but we must build office blocks twice as high as St Paul's, and have green spaces and wide roads in between the blocks ... Two dozen skyscrapers, though they would obviously dwarf St Paul's, would not take away from its beauty if they were beautiful themselves. They would alter the skyline, certainly, yet we should not sacrifice health, time, and comfort to one skyline because we have not the courage to create another.

The author of this confident, uncompromising clarion call? John Betjeman, that future doughty conservationist.

Crucially, this rapidly swelling appetite for the new embraced not only the horrors (real and perceived) of the unplanned Victorian city – above all, understandably enough, the horrors of the industrial slums. It also addressed the much more recent blight, as received 'activator' opinion had it, of the suburbs, sprawling outwards through the 1920s and 1930s, especially around London, in a spectacular and apparently unplanned way. They were, declared the Welsh architect Sir Clough Williams-Ellis in 1928, full of 'mean and perky little houses that surely none but mean and perky little souls should inhabit with satisfaction', while ten years later, according to Osbert Lancaster (cartoonist, architectural writer and coiner of the derogatory term 'Stockbroker Tudor'), the certainty that the streets and estates of the suburbs would 'eventually become the slums of the future' unless they were obliterated did much 'to reconcile one to the prospect of aerial bombardment'. Even George Orwell could not see their point. In his last pre-war novel, *Coming Up for Air*, he wrote contemptuously of 'long, long rows of little semi-detached houses', of 'the stucco front, the creosoted gate, the privet hedge, the green front door', of 'the Laurels, the Myrtles, the Hawthorns, Mon Abri, Mon Repos, Belle Vue', and of the 'respectable householders – that's to say Tories, yes-men, and bumsuckers who live in them'. To someone like Thomas Sharp, a planning consultant as well as a university lecturer in architecture and town planning, 'suburbia' – where by the end of the 1930s about a quarter of the population lived – was complete anathema; without compunction he condemned 'its social sterility, its aesthetic emptiness, its economic wastefulness'. In short: 'Suburbia is not a utility that can promote any proper measure of human happiness and fulfilment.'

Sharp had been implacably anti-suburb through the 1930s, but this particular broadside was published in *Town Planning*, an influential 1940 Pelican paperback. 'However little can be done in wartime towards the achievement of the ideals I have tried to set out, it is essential that we should get our minds clear *now* as to what we are going to do when the war is over,' he stressed. 'The thing is there for us to do if we will. We can continue to live in stale and shameful slum-towns. Or in sterile and disorderly suburbs. Or we can build clean proud towns of living and light. The choice is entirely our own.' Two years later, *When We Build Again* (a documentary focusing on Bournville Village in Birmingham) was even more ideal-istic. 'There must be no uncontrolled building, no more ugly houses and straggling roads, no stinting of effort before we build again,' declared the film's narrator, Dylan Thomas, who also wrote the script. 'Nothing is too good for the people.' The Beveridge Report did not concern itself specifically with town planning, but in February 1943 – the same year that a bespoke Ministry of Town and Country

Planning was set up – it was Beveridge who opened a notable exhibition, Rebuilding Britain, at the National Gallery. 'How can the war on Squalor be won?' asked the accompanying catalogue, referring to one of the five evil giants that Sir William's report hoped to slay. The answer was sublime in its certainty: 'The very first thing to win is the Battle of Planning. We shall need to have planning on a national scale, boldly overstepping the traditional boundaries of urban council, rural council, County Council. Boldly overstepping the interests described so often as vested.'

The following year's Town and Country Planning Act did indeed give far-reaching powers to local authorities for reconstruction and redevelopment, and by the time the war ended it was almost a truism that the future lay with the planners. Entirely characteristic was the plan published in March 1945 for the future of Glasgow, with the most stirring of mottoes on its front cover: 'The Voice of Time Cries out to Man – ADVANCE!' One old man, though, was unconvinced. 'Ah, yes,' said Churchill, as towards the end of the war he looked round the Cabinet and considered his minister's favourable assessment of the latest town and country planning reports. 'All this stuff about planning and compensation and betterment. Broad vistas and all that. But give to me the eighteenth-century alley, where foot-pads lurk, and the harlot plies her trade, and none of this new-fangled planning doctrine.'[10]

Among those actively seeking a new and better post-war environment for the British people there were two main camps: baldly put, those who did not believe that the future lay in the big cities, and those who, broadly embracing modernism, did believe just that. They were, with on the whole unfortunate results, almost diametrically opposed to each other.

To-morrow: A Peaceful Path to Real Reform was the title of Ebenezer Howard's influential 1898 treatise, a utopian vision (heavily influenced by William Morris) of dispersal of population from the huge industrial cities and the creation of new, self-supporting towns of some 30,000 residents of mixed social background, living in light, airy surroundings and surrounded by a 'green belt'. The first 'garden city' was established five years later at Letchworth, in Herfordshire, and it was followed in 1920 by Welwyn Garden City. During the war, the Howardian agenda entered the political mainstream, as a series of reports and plans, culminating in the *Greater London Plan* published in 1945, recommended a less populous inner core, a suburbia contained by a substantial green-belt ring and, beyond that ring, the building of environmentally favoured new towns.

Howard's direct successor, and a formidable but in many ways attractive figure in the planning world, was Frederic Osborn, kingpin by the 1940s of the Town and Country Planning Association and an indefatigable propagandist as well as administrator. 'It is not a passion for order, or even for harmony (desirable as they are in measure) that has produced the demand for town planning,' he wrote shortly before the end of the war. 'The thing that has produced the dynamic for planning – the really big and fundamental thing that is wrong with our cities – is congestion: too many buildings and too many people in too little space.'[11] Osborn, though just about willing to concede that suburbanites might actually enjoy living in the suburbs, never really faced foursquare the possibility that life in a high-density, imperfectly planned city might have its positive attractions. But unlike many planners, he was well aware that planning did not automatically fit the crooked timber of humanity.

The other camp comprised architects as much as town planners, with many (but not all) looking to the alternative utopia set out in the pronouncements and example of the charismatic French architect Le Corbusier. His *La Ville radieuse* had been translated in 1929 and *Vers une architecture* in 1931; in them he demonstrated his belief in the future of great cities – but great cities entirely transformed along ultra-modern lines. 'Men can be paltry,' he declared, 'but the thing we call Man is great ... What gives our dreams their daring is that they can be realized.' There were also his four famous, increasingly verbless propositions: 'Architecture has for its first duty that of bringing about a revision of values. We must create the mass production spirit. The spirit of constructing mass production houses. The spirit of living in mass production houses.'

Le Corbusier's English followers had established the MARS (Modern Architectural Research) Group in 1933, with the young Maxwell Fry as one of its most active members. 'Courts and alleys are swept away' ran part of the caption to the visual plan of Fry's ideal city published in the *Picture Post* special issue in 1941. 'New flats stand in a park.' These high-minded, modern-minded, well-intentioned men – who for a mixture of pragmatic and more or less socialist reasons tended to look to public housing (as yet the Cinderella of the British housing stock) as the likeliest opportunity for making an impact – took few prisoners in either their drawings or their writings. Another such individual with high ambitions and limited tolerance was Ernö Goldfinger: born in Hungary in 1902, a student in Paris until moving to England in 1933, a larger-than-life presence with a frightening temper. Writing in 1942 in the *Architectural Review* (one of modernism's strongholds), he gave a hostile appraisal of a clutch of publications in Faber and Faber's 'Rebuilding Britain' series, masterminded by Osborn and including Osborn's own *Overture to Planning*. After noting that all the publications 'state as axiomatic truths the one-sided arguments of the Garden City Movement', Goldfinger went on: 'The problem before the re-planners of the country can be neatly and precisely defined by saying that *it is to create a frame for human life*, liberated as far as possible from the drudgery of material need. Modern technology enables this to be done. But this aim will not be furthered by the introduction of sentimentality.' Justifying this charge by picking out phrases from Osborn's pamphlet like 'values of our civilisation' and 'sacred fires', Goldfinger then put his modernist cards on the table:

> In all these publications the problem of the size of cities is treated again and again with an unrealistic and sentimental bias. The tendency to industrial concentration is brushed aside as one of the evil consequences of modern ways and not as it should be treated, as one of the basic means of efficient production ... All the authors seem to be smitten by a kind of agoraphobia and a tendency to animize at the same time. The small, the child-like, seems to haunt them, they transpose their feelings for persons to geographical units.

He added, with a final put-down from a considerable height, that such infantilism was 'noticeable not only in Garden City circles, but in a large section of well-meaning, so-called progressives'.

Fundamental to Le Corbusier's vision was the high-rise, with his ideal city featuring at its centre towers of as many as 60 storeys. However, even though a fair number of new blocks of flats (rarely above four or five storeys) were built in the 1930s, that aspect of his vision elicited relatively little enthusiasm before the war, with even a modernist like Fry somewhat sceptical. The real flats versus houses (or, as they were often called, 'cottages') controversy only seriously flared up during the war. 'It is eventually undeniable,' insisted Sharp in his 1940 Pelican, 'that the flat, if its own particular problems of design are sufficiently studied, *can* afford the pleasantest possible conditions of living for a very considerable proportion of the inhabitants of our towns.' And although he conceded that flats were not ideal for everyone, there were 'hosts' of people who 'could live far more happily in a block of flats, among all the communal facilities and advantages which that form of dwelling can offer, than in the social isolation of the small house, burdened with a private garden which they have neither the time nor the inclination to cultivate'.[12]

Two key documents produced during the second half of the war tilted the balance towards flats. The first was the 1943 *County of London Plan*, the work of Patrick Abercrombie (the leading town planner of the day, with a foot in both camps) and J. H. Forshaw. They concluded that if even six out of ten former inhabitants of bombed-out inner London (above all of the East End) were to be rehoused in their own familiar districts, this would entail a density of 136 people per net residential acre – which in turn meant that only a third of these resettled residents would be in houses and almost two-thirds would be in flats of eight or ten storeys. A deeply disappointed Osborn was convinced that Abercrombie had been nobbled by the London County Council (LCC), to which Forshaw was Architect. He was probably right. The LCC, which unlike the subsequent Greater London Council did not include the new outer suburbs, was dominated by inner-London Labour boroughs; and their councillors were naturally fearful that excessive dispersal would not only play havoc with rateable values but significantly diminish their reliably loyal working-class electorates.

The other pivotal document appeared a year later, with the Dudley Committee's report *The Design of Dwellings*, which for 'large concentrated urban areas' recommended a maximum density of 120 per acre – again, in other words, with significant high-rise implications. Importantly, the submissions that seem to have pushed the committee towards this conclusion were not from zealous architects but from thoroughly 'sensible' organisations like the National Council of Social Service, which argued that most of the low-rise housing estates built between the wars by the LCC had lacked adequate communal facilities, something that well-designed blocks of flats could provide, thereby obviating social problems. Between them, with fateful consequences, the plan and the report went a long way towards making the flat officially acceptable as a standard form of housing, especially public housing.

What gave such matters a new urgency was the Luftwaffe. 'Hitler has at last brought us to our senses,' declared Max Lock, a young architect and planner. 'We, the British public, have suddenly seen our cities as they are! After experiencing the shock of familiar buildings disembowelled before our eyes – like an all too real surrealism – we find the cleared and cleaned up spaces a relief. In them we have hope for the future, opportunities to be taken or lost.'[13] It was apparent from soon after the worst of the Blitz that the government was broadly backing, albeit with considerable financial nervousness, major reconstruction in the most badly affected cities, so that by the end of the war a series of plans for the future of those cities had been published and/or exhibited.[14] Southampton was to have a wholly new road system and city centre; Portsmouth a rather more modest redevelopment; Bristol a heavily zoned new city centre, including an ambitious new shopping precinct in the Broadmead area; and Hull (through the joint efforts of Abercrombie and Lock) a fairly ambitious redevelopment that included segregated industrial zones and a new, semi-pedestrianised shopping area.

Abercrombie – in his mid-60s, exceedingly well connected, author of the hugely influential textbook *Town and Country Planning* (1933) that saw virtually no role for preservation, even in the most historic cities – was also persuaded, for a not especially generous fee of 250 guineas, to submit a plan for Plymouth. The doyen of town planning did not disappoint. 'The outworn street pattern was totally abandoned, the old Devonport shopping area was swallowed up, and the precinct principle was applied to the civic, business and shopping areas' is how the planning historian Gordon Cherry has aptly summed up

Abercrombie's 1943 vision for a city where less than a tenth of its pre-war housing stock was irrevocably beyond repair as a result of enemy action. 'Unified architectural treatment would be introduced. A new central area road system was decided. One monumental feature was provided: a garden parkway from the station to the Hoe constructing a backbone to the whole of central Plymouth.' It was, Abercrombie himself insisted, the only possible way 'out of the disasters of war to snatch a victory for the city of the future'. There was little or no local consultation, with all objections overruled.[15]

In one blitzed city, even more than Plymouth, the man and the hour came together. 'Every town should have in its architect's department a group of town planners . . . Building science is advancing so rapidly that we have no right to build for a thousand years . . . A house should be regarded as permanent only for about thirty years and should then be replaced by an up-to-date one . . . For the good of the community private interests must be subordinated to public ones.' The speaker was Donald Gibson, City Architect of Coventry, addressing the Royal Society of Arts in early December 1940, less than three weeks after a night's intense bombardment had destroyed or seriously damaged most of the medieval city centre. Since his appointment a year before the war, he had been working on radical, more or less modernist plans for the city's future, culminating in May 1940 in a MARS-influenced exhibition on the 'Coventry of Tomorrow'; but the devastation only six months later created a wholly new opportunity.

As early as February 1941, the city council was able to make the choice between two competing plans for the centre's redevelopment. One plan (by Ernest Ford, the City Engineer) emphasised continuity and traditional street patterns; the other, Gibson's, envisaged an entirely new centre that, set inside an inner ring road, would boast not only impressive – and culturally improving – municipal facilities (including library, civic hall, museum, adult educational institution, and school of art and art gallery) surrounded by large open spaces but also a largely pedestrianised shopping precinct of six- or seven-storey buildings. Perhaps emboldened by Gibson's appeal – 'Let it not be said by future generations that the people of Coventry failed them, when the ideal was within their reach' – the Labour-controlled council voted 43 to 6 in his favour.

The decision immediately attracted considerable national attention, and in a visit about a year later the King himself made approbatory noises and 'expressed the opinion that in all schemes of re-planning towns and cities which had been badly bombed, the future amenities for the citizens were of supreme importance'. During the rest of the war, despite concerns from Whitehall about cost and precedent, the City Council held firm to Gibson's plan. 'A cauldron in which experiments were taking place' was how the Bishop of Coventry proudly saw his city early in 1945. Speaking to the local Rotary, he added, 'England was watching to see if the city was going to do its job and allow a full life to the people.'[16] Given Coventry's unique pre-war place in the national psyche as the hub of the thriving British motor industry, the cutting edge of the second Industrial Revolution, this was perhaps not an absurd claim to make.

But would the new, rebuilt, reconstructed Britain enjoy – as Gibson in his plans clearly hoped it would – a new, more democratic, more socially concerned, more politically conscious culture? 'When Work is Over' was J. B. Priestley's contribution to *Picture Post*'s 1941 'Plan' for Britain and, apart from 'real holidays for all', his main vision of leisure in the post-war age seemed to involve more facilities to study the arts and the setting up of civic centres of music, drama, film and talk. Increased leisure as such, he emphasised, was not necessarily a boon: 'We do not want greyhound racing and dirt track performances to be given at all hours of the day and night, pin table establishments doing a roaring trade from dawn to midnight, and idiotic films being shown down every street.' Priestley himself kept his distance from the Labour Party, but during the war there was a comfortable, almost automatic assumption on the part of Labour politicians and activists that the conflict was producing a more egalitarian society and thus a more serious-minded, socialist people. Herbert Morrison, for example, was apparently convinced by the spring of 1944 that there now existed a 'genuine social idealism', reflecting the 'altered moral sense of the community', and that accordingly the British people were 'moving into an altogether different form of society, working in an altogether different atmosphere of ideas' – a revolution of outlook, shifting from the values of private enterprise to the values of socialism, that meant that the people would never again 'be content with limited and material aims'.[17]

These were not assumptions shared by Evan Durbin, the Labour Party's most interesting thinker of the 1940s and arguably of the twentieth century. Durbin – born in 1906, the son of a Baptist minister – was an attractively paradoxical figure. He once remarked that his three greatest pleasures were 'food, sleep and sex' but accused D. H. Lawrence of 'shallow abstractions' in relation to 'freedom in sexual relations'; politically, he defined himself as a 'militant Moderate'; and, as a trained economist who had lectured through the 1930s at the LSE, he combined a strong belief in economic planning with the conviction that the price mechanism was indispensable if the liberty of consumers in a modern democracy was to be ensured. During the 1930s, Durbin became close to the young psychiatrist John Bowlby, and the influence of Bowlby ran through much of his major work, *The Politics of Democratic Socialism*, published in 1940. As for economics itself, Durbin made a brave gesture towards the 'sound money' school – its citadel the City of London – that had wrecked Ramsay MacDonald's 1931 Labour government, by declaring that 'it is not wise in the long run to expect to live upon golden eggs and slowly to strangle the goose that lays them'.

Towards the end of his book, an arrestingly bleak passage shows how far removed Durbin was from the average political or economic thinker:

Although wealth, physical health and social equality may all make their contributions to human happiness, they can all do little and cannot themselves be secured, without health in the individual mind. We are our own kingdoms and make for ourselves, in large measure, the world in which we live. We may be rich, and healthy, and liberal; but unless we are free from secret guilt, the agonies of inferiority and frustration, and the fire of unexpressed aggression, all other things are added to our lives in vain. The cruelty and irrationality of human society spring from these secret sources. The savagery of a Hitler, the brutality of a Stalin, the ruthlessness and refined bestiality that is rampant in the world today – persecution, cruelty and war – are nothing but the external expression, the institutional and rationalized form, of these dark forces in the human heart.

Among the many phrases that stand out is 'the brutality of a Stalin' – language not yet much heard (as George Orwell had already lamented) on the left.

In 1944, by this time seconded to Whitehall and contemplating standing as a candidate in the next general election, Durbin locked horns with Hayek after the latter's *The Road to Serfdom* was published. Planning, Durbin insisted, was used by socialists to 'indicate a principle of administration and not an inflexible budget of production'; and he emphasised anew that 'the centrally directed economy can be, and should be, instructed to adapt its programme to the changing wishes of the consuming public and the changing conditions of technical efficiency.'[18] It was the characteristically assured, with-the-grain response of a man seemingly poised for the most glittering prizes.

———

How in fact *did* all these noble aspirations for a better post-war world strike the much-invoked, less often consulted and still heavily (about 75 per cent) working-class British people?

Some observers as well as politicians were convinced that the plates had shifted not just in terms of the formation of an elite progressive consensus (though with hindsight one can see how the extent of that consensus was possible to exaggerate) but also in terms of opinion and sentiment at large. 'At every period,' reflected a Political and Economic Planning (PEP) broadsheet in the winter of 1941/2, 'there have been idealists who have wanted to reform the world; only at rare moments has the demand for the assertion of new principles and new liberties surged from the bottom of society upwards with such overwhelming force that serious opposition is not possible. Now is one of those moments.' The well-informed journalist and author James Lansdale Hodson, in the overall 'ledger of war' that he drew up in February 1945, might not have disagreed: 'Glancing, if one may, at the minds of our people, I think we have moved Leftwards, i.e. turned more progressive in the sense that not many would wish to go back to where we were in 1938–9. The love of books and good music has grown. Our A.B.C.A. [Army Bureau of Current Affairs] and other discussion groups in the Forces have encouraged a number, at all events, to enjoy arguments and the methods of democracy, and our production committees have worked similarly in factories.' Such was also the conviction of Richard Titmuss, who in 1942 was commissioned to write an official history of the wartime work of the Ministry of Health.

The eventual magisterial account, *Problems of Social Policy* (1950), would make canonical the interpretation that there had indeed been a sea-change in the British outlook – first as the mass evacuation of women and children from the main cities brought the social classes into a far closer mutual understanding than there had ever been before, then as the months of stark and dangerous isolation after Dunkirk created an impatient, almost aggressive mood decrying privilege and demanding 'fair shares' for all. Between them, according to the Titmuss version, these two circumstances led to a widespread desire for major social and other reforms of a universalist, egalitarian nature. The Beveridge Report and the rest of the reconstruction package followed. Tellingly, in his treatment of the Blitz, Titmuss noted that 'there was nothing to be ashamed of in being "bombed out" by the enemy' and that 'public sympathy with, and approval of, families who suffered in the raids was in sharp contrast to the low social evaluation accorded to those who lost material standards through being unemployed during the 1930s'.[19] In the round, such a Whiggish, feel-good reading – unity forged through adversity, irresistible pressure from below leading to longed-for change, human nature actually improving – would, not surprisingly, take some shifting.

And of course, there were plausible grounds for it. In August 1942, a year and a half after Orwell in *The Lion and the Unicorn* had detected a 'visible swing in public opinion' towards socialism and a planned economy since the fall of France, Mass-Observation asked working-class residents of Holborn and Paddington what changes they hoped to see after the war. 'Well, I can't say I'm sure,' was the rather helpless reply of one middle-aged woman, but others were more forthcoming. 'C' in M-O annotation referred to 'artisan and skilled workers', with 'D' being 'unskilled workers and the least economically or educationally trained third of our people':

There'll have to be more equalness. Things not fair now. Nobody can tell me they are. There's them with more money what they can ever use. This ain't right and it's got to be put right. (*M65C*)

I think the biggest change of all should be security for the ordinary people; I mean, nothing like the depression that followed the last war. I think a lot could be done to avoid that. (*Inv. asked how*). I'm afraid that's too big a question. (*M30C*)

I think I'd like a lot of changes. (*What particularly?*) I don't know. (*F50D*)

I do feel that the schooling of children should be a sort of pooled schooling; every child should be allowed to have the same chance; not because a mother has more money she should be allowed to send her child to one school – the class distinction in the schools, I think that should be wiped right out . . . (*F30C*)

Oh, lots. (*asked what*) Much better living for the ordinary working man. (*Anything else?*) Better housing and everything. (*F25C*)

There'll have to be changes. Did you read about that old bitch Lady Astor? She's one that'll be changed, if I had my way. It's the likes of her that causes revolutions. (*M45C*)

Later that year, in early December, the publication of the Beveridge Report caused a sensation. One London diarist noted that it had 'set everybody talking', and Beveridge himself conceded that 'it's been a revelation to me how concerned people are with conditions after the war'. Among 'my friends and colleagues', stated an engineering draughtsman, 'the publication of the Report caused more discussion and interest than any war news for a long time,' and he added that 'the tone of *all* the discussions was favourable.' From Mass-Observation's national panel of some 1,500 regular correspondents (from 'all walks of life, living in all parts of the country', though in practice almost certainly with a middle-class bias), more than 300 wrote in to express their views, with only a handful against. Reconstruction hopes seemingly remained high and widespread later in the war. Debates in 1943/4 in the Forces 'Parliament' in Cairo saw strong support for bills to nationalise the retail trade and restrict inheritances; a poll by Gallup in July 1944 found 55 per cent welcoming the idea of a national health service (and 69 per cent preferring the prospect of health centres to the normal doctor's surgery); and shortly before Christmas that year almost one in four of the adult population listened to a series of eight Home Service programmes about full employment.[20]

One activator who had no doubt that things were going the right way was Mrs Madge Waller, who in March 1942 chaired a meeting at the Housing Centre in London. In her introductory remarks she assured the audience that 'there seemed to her to be a fairly general opinion that after the war everything was going to be better, especially among young people'; remarked that 'she had come in contact with several who were thinking and talking about planning for post-war Britain'; and declared that after 'an almost wasted quarter of a century – muddled thinking and mere talking about planning, without any real plan – we would probably not be allowed to "muddle through" again'. She then introduced her main speaker, Tom Harrisson, co-founder five years earlier of Mass-Observation.

Almost certainly the audience, including Mrs Waller, sat up in their seats as Harrisson at the outset stated bluntly that the growing assumption 'that everyone wanted a better Britain in future' was 'rather a false one':

> There was quite a striking number of people who were thinking not in terms of helping to make this country better to live in, but of getting out of the country after the war and going to America, Australia, etc. A strong feeling was growing up that people should have less planned and ordered lives and could be themselves more. Certain types of people were in favour of more co-operation in planning, but a very large number of people of the working-class population were so appalled by what would have to be done after the war that they felt rather hopeless about the task.

For elaboration, Harrisson then turned to the study that Mass-Observation had been making of what people wanted after the war compared with what they expected:

> What were most hoped for were equality of opportunity, better housing and education, socialism, security, abolition of unemployment, and a mass of other things which might be lumped together as town planning, but was not consciously thought of as such. Their expectations were far inferior to their hopes ... People had the right hopes, but the feeling that these hopes would not or could not materialise was very strong.

Overwhelming emphasis was laid on what had happened after the last war. Disappointment then had created a kind of neurosis that seemed unconquerable to a lot of people.

He ended this section of his talk with his killer facts: 'It had been found that five people were pessimistic to every one that was optimistic about reconstruction plans in general after the war, and that proportion increased to nine to one in certain heavily-raided areas.'[21]

The evidence suggests that Harrisson was broadly right – that although in 1940/41 there was at least some popular, largely positive engagement with post-war reconstruction issues, from 1942 the trend was (apart from a blip at the time of the Beveridge Report) the other way. Indeed, some qualifying remarks even need to be made about Beveridge. Before it appeared, a wide-ranging survey (supervised by G.D.H. Cole, a leading socialist intellectual) into popular attitudes to welfare found that, in the words of its Manchester investigator, 'some seemed to be quite satisfied in an inarticulate sort of way' and 'the majority just *did not know*'. At the time of the report's celebrated publication, there was a significant minority of dissenters ('If people here stand for the trades unions putting this bloody Beveridge scheme across they deserve to lose the sodding war' was how one middle-aged man, who called himself a 'Jack of All Trades', put it to an Mass-Observation observer in London), and it is far from clear how many outside the middle class were among those who bought the report in either of its forms. Moreover, from soon afterwards there was widespread cynicism about whether it would ever be implemented, typified by a 55-year-old woman of the 'artisan class' telling an interviewer that 'soon as it's over and they've no further use for you, they'll have a general election and apologise that they can't stand by the promise of the war government – it'll happen just as it did last time'.[22]

A Gallup poll taken in April 1943, asking people whether they would like to see 'any great changes' in their way of life after the war, probably captured accurately enough the popular political mood. Of the 57 per cent who agreed with that proposition, 35 per cent had 'no comment' on what changes these might be; 16 per cent hoped for 'better working conditions, better wages, work for everybody, no unemployment'; 15 per cent nominated a 'better standard of living all round, pension and security when old'; a bare 3 per cent mentioned 'socialism' or a 'changed economic system'; and only 1 per cent plumped even more idealistically for 'no more wars, better international understanding'. The widespread middle-class feeling that the focus on reconstruction was premature may well have been shared instinctively by at least some in the working class. 'Meeting many people in various occupations daily, I find, with my own opinion, too much is being broadcast by the BBC, and circulated in the newspapers, re post-war plans,' wrote a correspondent styling himself 'Commercial' to his local paper in Wolverhampton later that year. 'It is generally agreed that these plans could be arranged without all this prattle, because it definitely tends to make everyone certain that our Government know just when this war will finish, and encourages people to sit easy, instead of getting on with the job.'[23]

In the workplace there was (in the context of full employment in a wartime economy) an undeniable new self-assertiveness – Hodson in his 'ledger of war' complained that 'the working-classes, feeling their power, have often shown some ruthlessness, manifested by bus drivers refusing to stop at halts, transport workers striking on Christmas Day, coal-miners refusing sometimes to do a decent day's work' – but this was far from automatically translating into any enhanced political radicalism. *War Factory*, Mass-Observation's 1942/3 study of a Gloucestershire factory producing radar systems where the workers were mainly women, revealed resentment, boredom and alienation as the predominant sentiments, including predictably little interest in the progress of the war. Soon after Beveridge, an engineer from Dudley told M-O that, as far as his fellow-workers in an electrode factory were concerned, the prevailing atmosphere of each man for himself had 'dulled the mind to all except personal problems'. Nor were the armed forces quite the radical hotbed they have sometimes been depicted as. Analysis of the Army Bureau of Current Affairs suggests that their debates were seen more as an opportunity for a welcome respite from military duties than as an occasion to engage in serious political discussion; the future novelist Nicholas Monserrat wrote of the sailors under his command that 'there is no time and, in effect, no occasion for political interest'; or as Hodson heard an officer with the 79th Armoured Division in Germany put it just before the war's end, 'in fifteen months in the ranks I never heard politics mentioned'.[24]

Was there perhaps widespread popular anticipation of a future national health service? Those who have scoured wartime diaries report remarkably few sightings, and indeed the 1944 Gallup poll revealing 55 per cent approval also showed a not inconsiderable 32 per cent in favour of the status quo. Polling evidence demonstrated that approval towards the end of the war for Labour's nationalisation plans was reasonably broad (usually in the 40–60 per cent range) but invariably shallow, with few people seeing it as a high-priority issue. As for education, a poll in early 1945 found less than half those questioned had heard of the recent Education Act and a mere 13 per cent were aware of its provision to remove fees from grammar schools. Under-standably, Orwell's earlier optimism about a newly radicalised people had by this time completely vanished. 'I overhear very little discussion of the wider issues of the war,' he told his American readers in autumn 1944. 'Everyone expects not only that there will be a ghastly muddle over demobilization, but that mass unemployment will promptly return.' And he added, 'Everyone wants, above all things, a rest.'[25]

There was plenty of further statistical underpinning available for these and similar assertions. In the autumn of 1943, for example, more than 500 interviews by Mass-Observation across the country found that 43 per cent expected heavy post-war unemployment, 46 per cent another war after the present one, 50 per cent uncertain or without an opinion as to whether the government was paying too much or too little attention to post-war reconstruction, and 49 per cent (up from 19 per cent a year earlier) saying that their main priority after the war was to 'relax or have a change'. But in the end, over and above the figures, we need to listen to the voices, as in the cynical, mistrustful, rather truculent tone of four young tradesmen in an army unit – reminiscent of Rudyard Kipling's 'Tommy' – describing their expectations of demobilisation:

It'll be the same old story, those who can pull the strings will be all right, the other poor buggers can look after themselves.

Just the same mess as last time.

Personally I don't trust the Government and I don't suppose they're likely to worry much about us. We're heroes while the war's on, but we can look after ourselves afterwards.

I can't see they can afford to unload everybody at once, or there'll be a lot of trouble. Chaps aren't going to stand for it.

In August 1944, with the long war clearly drawing to an end, an M-O team was in Gloucester. 'What do you feel the next ten years of your life will be like?' it asked a group of working-class mothers. 'Are you looking forward to them, or aren't you looking forward to them much?' The replies have a wonderful – and revealing – authenticity about a world where the big picture was infinitely more local and immediate than any of the activators ever imagined:

> Oh God! I'm not good at answering questions.
>
> Well, yes and no. As long as I don't have any more kids I shall be all right.
>
> Don't know. Really I don't.
>
> Why, yes.
>
> Well, I suppose I am – we like to think the future's going to be better.
>
> Oh yes, I don't want to die yet!
>
> Am I? I'll say I am. I want to buy my own house if I can. But it won't be in Alma Place – the row here is terrible, and they keep the kids up till 11 and 12 at night, yelling about the street.
>
> Oh, well, of course I am, hoping for the war to end and things to improve.
>
> Well, it's all according. It all depends on if it's any better than the last two or three.

One of the women was the 'worn and dirty' 43-year-old mother of fourteen 'filthy and ragged' offspring aged between twenty and eight months. 'Well,' she answered when she found a moment, 'I hope I live to see 'em all grow up to look arter theirselves.' She was also asked whether she was religious. 'Well, I believe in God but I can't say I'm religious. You get a bit hasty when you've so many children.'[26]

These were the sort of people whom Harrisson surely had in mind when in March 1942 he turned specifically to his lecture's title, 'Propaganda for Town Planning', and let rip:

> The idea that places really were going to be rebuilt and better new houses constructed had not penetrated down to the large masses of the population. While there had certainly been much talk and propaganda

about town planning, about 95 per cent of it had been quite above most people's heads. Mr Harrisson said that he was worried most by the way that planners and others associated with the matter talked as if they were winning over the general public when really they were only winning over each other. He had never met any group of people who 'scratched each other's backs' more than planners did.

For those in the audience bitten with the planning bug there was worse to come:

> The planning conferences were only for those who knew about the subject; the talks on the wireless probably did not reach the people for whom they would be most use; the majority of the planning exhibitions seemed to mean little to any of the general public who saw them. The people needing planning propaganda are those who are used to thinking in concrete terms – who could talk for ages about things connected with their own house, but could not frame a single sentence about planning.

'Planning will have,' Harrisson concluded bluntly, 'either to find out what people want and design propaganda that will have an immediate appeal, or educate people to appreciate how their own lives could be improved by putting into practice the theories held by the planners.'[27] The record of the meeting does not, sadly, include any ensuing discussion.

Was Harrisson being unfair to the planners? Significantly, only a few months earlier, the editor of the *Architectural Review*, J. M. Richards, had strongly criticised organisations like Mass-Observation ('a phenomenon very typical of recent years') as tending to block properly visionary town planning. 'The needs of society are a fit subject for scientific study, but they cannot be elucidated by a gigantic piece of consumer research' was the Richards line. 'It is a fallacy that the needs of society are the aggregate of as many individual demands as can be ascertained.' In practice, many planners, exemplified by Max Lock at Middlesbrough, did try quite hard to initiate and then sustain a dialogue with public opinion at both a local and a national level, in order to try to keep that opinion broadly on side with their plans; any view that sees the planners (of the 1940s anyway) as crazed, tinpot dictators is simply a caricature. The fact that there were so few opportunities during the war, and indeed afterwards, for those being planned for to express an explicit democratic verdict on the plans was less the fault of the planners than of local (and arguably national) politicians.

Nevertheless, to read Thomas Sharp's presidential address in 1945 to the Town Planning Institute is still to be struck by his profession's ultimately top-down assumptions. He did not deny that people had 'the inalienable right to know fully what is being planned for them' – including 'the right to comment on the plans, to require alterations in them, and, if necessary, to reject them'. What Sharp explicitly repudiated, however, was 'actual participation in the act of planning', in other words before draft plans had been drawn up; the notion that the planner should essentially be the servant of the people, putting their wishes into technical form, he castigated as nothing other than 'sheer demagogy, rather than a manifestation of the working of a true democracy'.[28]

That the language of the Rebuilding Britain exhibition in 1943 was so notably circumspect and reassuring presumably reflected the lack of popular enthusiasm for town planning. 'Don't get the idea,' it insisted in almost hurt tones, 'that the planner is a robot of a man without sentiment or good manners, whose *idée fixe* is to tear out the ancient core of our towns in the cause of traffic-flow or Brave New Worldliness. The truth is the exact opposite. The move for planning in England has come largely from those who loved old buildings and could see no other way of saving them than by getting "building development" controlled. It is not the dream of the planner to recondition towns until nothing of their personality remains.' They did not see it quite that way in Bristol, where in the last two years of the war a sustained, unavailing campaign (mostly waged by traders but not entirely) sought to reverse the planners' decision to create a large new shopping centre in the 'off the beaten track' Broadmead area at the expense of the city's traditional shopping core. Nor did they in Wolverhampton, where in early 1945 what response there was to the plan for thoroughgoing redevelopment was typified by the view of one correspondent to the local paper: 'I think Wolverhampton people's best interests will be served in the preservation of much that is old in the town, rather than the sweeping away of familiar landmarks in a fetish or orgy of modernising that is almost an obsession today.'[29]

The same, crucially, may well also have been the case in Coventry, or at least on the part of the middle-aged and elderly suddenly finding themselves living in the middle of the new symbol of the new Britain. Barely a week after the decisive vote by the city council in February 1941 in favour of Gibson's radical plan, a local paper published a cry from the heart by 'An Old Citizen': 'It is to be hoped that the citizens as a whole will have the opportunity of expressing their views before any irretrievable step is taken, for the views of local government officials are not necessarily those of Coventry people who, after all, may want to live here after the war. We should like the new Coventry to be something of the old Coventry, and not merely a fourth-rate provincial city on futurist lines.' Over the next three years there seems to have been relatively little expression of popular feeling either way, as local traders tried unsuccessfully to persuade the City Reconstruction Committee that, in the words of the President of the local chamber of commerce, 'the old idea of street shopping was much better than "cloistered precincts"'. But in December 1944 the issue did briefly if obliquely break cover after the pro-plan *Coventry Evening Telegraph* reported Gibson's talk on 'The New Coventry' to a meeting of Armstrong Siddeley workers. After stressing the need for 20,000 new houses in the city, Gibson had 'pointed out the need for a departure from tradition in building methods' before remarking in conclusion that 'the people themselves would decide how they would be housed in the future'. This brought a double negative response: from 'Coventrian', arguing that 'the people will decide that it is bricks and mortar they require, and perhaps a few less planners,' and from 'Longview', who was 'certain that if a referendum could be taken there would be an overwhelming majority in favour of the orthodox brick and mortar house'.

But for most Coventrians in the years after their devastating Blitz, the top priority was not to take part in controversies about a nebulous future. Rather it was to regroup, to retrench and to try to get back as soon as possible to something like normality, which in essence meant life before the war. 'For the majority of the city's population,' the historians of this strong trend have noted, 'abstract ruminations were simply irrelevant.' By 1944 local cinemas were attracting record attendances, organised cricket and football were once again being played on Saturday afternoons, the Coventry Amateur Operatic Society was

meeting for the first time since 1939, and the National Federation of
Anglers was choosing Coventry as the venue for its AGM, reflecting
the city's almost 7,000 members of that decidedly non-reconstructionist
body. Perhaps most telling of all was the behaviour of Coventry's
gardeners. Amid warnings from civic leaders that the proper business
of horticulture was still the cultivation of vegetables, they quietly and
privately during the last fifteen months of the war grew flowers and
shrubs – potent, non-utilitarian reminders of a peaceful way of life
that perhaps had not been irretrievably fractured.[30]

Above all, across the country, it was on the home that most people's
hopes and concerns were really focused. 'Home means a place to go
to when in trouble,' a female Mass-Observation panellist declared in
1943. 'A place where bygone days were happiest. A place sadly altered
by the war. A place where you can do as you like without landladies
to consider . . . A place to glorify when away and rely on always.' The
same year M-O published *People's Homes*, a comprehensive survey of
working-class attitudes to housing. 'One often hears planners argue
that ordinary people have no idea of what they want in housing,' the
survey's introduction noted. 'This is a satisfactory argument when you
are planning for others without knowing their hearts and minds. The
many verbatim remarks in this report put that tale out of court once
and for all.' Among those quoted was a 50-year-old working woman
who lived in an upper tenement flat 'with a husband, two children
working and two children still at school'. She was asked about her
dream home:

I'd like a sitting-room-kitchen, so that you could have meals in it, and
a nice garden at the back for vegetables and chickens, and a flower garden
in front. A nice bathroom all done with lino . . . Coal fire in the living
room and none in the bedrooms, I don't think fires in a bedroom are
healthy. I'd like a sort of sunshine paper, if you know what I mean,
with just a little beading round the top, flowers or fruit. That for the
sitting room, and blue for the bedrooms. I like boards in the bedrooms,
not polished or anything of that, but scrubbed, so that they come up
lovely and white. Just scrub them with a bit of soap. The same in the
kitchen unless we had a bit of lino there. I don't like the stone floor in
the kitchen. It's so cold and damp.

On the basis of this and much other evidence, the survey concluded that 'the "dream home" of the majority is still the small modern suburban house, preferably possessing all modern conveniences, such as a labour-saving kitchen, hot and cold water laid on to a sink in the scullery, and a bathroom with a separate lavatory'. It would also have 'small but light windows, built-in cupboards, coal fires for warming, electric points in most rooms – these and a hundred other things would be appreciated'. Inevitably, 'the range of personal wants is immense – but happily the elasticity of true democratic planning can offer an almost infinite variety, and so satisfy the healthy, contradictory categories of human need and hope and hate.'

This was not good enough for one of the book's reviewers, the economist P. Sargant Florence. 'The most that can be deduced is that some people like one thing, some another' was his unenthusiastic response, and he argued that the book once again pointed 'to the moral that standards it is desirable to achieve cannot safely be left to housewives who are not equipped with the necessary knowledge of what lies within the realm of possibility'. Accordingly, 'architects and planners must give the lead and the target must be placed higher than the inarticulate yearnings of the average working-class housewife, if the same ill-defined sense of dissatisfaction is not to be perpetuated'.[31]

Over and above 'all mod cons', what people wanted – and clearly, unambiguously wanted – was privacy in their homes. 'A garden that is overlooked, windows into which neighbours can see, balconies visible from the road or from houses opposite are all deplored,' the report noted. 'But above all, people dislike sharing a house with another family or even with one person, as many have to do.' The unashamedly unemancipated Mrs Michael Pleydell-Bouverie, who by 1944 had spent three and a half years on behalf of the *Daily Mail* talking to 'the Women of Britain' about present and putative homes, agreed: 'Speaking generally the people want to breathe and move, to be rid of neighbours' wireless, and the clatter of early-risers and late-bedders ... The community life of which everyone has had experience to some degree or other in this war, has not endeared or recommended itself as a permanent state of affairs.' This strong desire for greater privacy was hardly a new phenomenon – historical demographers have shown that the 'privatised', home-centred domestic unit, founded on the nuclear family, goes back to pre-industrial England – but undoubtedly the war's more or less enforced communal sociability sharpened such instincts. 'Emphatically, no' and 'We prefer to wash our dirty linen in private' were two typical, highly symptomatic contributions to discussions in 1943 by almost 300 Townswomen's Guilds about the desirability of developing communal laundries.[32]

There is evidence, moreover, that if having to move some distance (usually out of a city centre) was the only way in which the desired mixture of greater privacy and more amenities-cum-space (including a garden) could be achieved, then most people were prepared to do that. A cross-class survey in 1943 of 2,000 women in their teens and 20s found that over half wanted to live in a suburb or small town and nearly a third in the country; while a study the same year by the Society for Women Housing Managers discovered that 'an overwhelming majority plumped for a suburban house' if given the choice between different types of modern housing. Nevertheless, the very understandable wish for modern conveniences far from implied an unambiguously positive attitude towards the modern as a whole. An official survey carried out in the closing weeks of the war saw a random sample of 1,727 housewives being shown four photographs of bedroom furniture. Number 1 was 'plain and fairly modern', number 2 'the most old fashioned', and numbers 3 and 4 'extremely modern'. The preferences respectively expressed were 27, 45, 13 and 12 per cent. Significantly, in terms of the breakdown of these preferences, 'the upper economic group tend towards modernity rather more than the lower economic groups' and 'the younger age groups like modern furniture more than the older age group'.[33]

It was the overwhelming desire for privacy that pervaded what was nothing less than a mass aversion towards the whole idea of flats – despite, as Frederic Osborn caustically put it in 1942, 'the most persistent propaganda by architectural playboys who want larger boxes of plasticine with which to indulge their creative fancy'. A year earlier, the *Picture Post* special (including Maxwell Fry's modernist vision) had prompted congratulatory letters (with a fair sprinkling from the great and the good), but Margaret Blundell dissented: 'Your Brave New World plan is all very well in some respects, but will "the workers" be satisfied even if it is put into practice?' asked this gasfitter's wife from Sirdar

Road, Wood Green, N22. 'I doubt it. Your flats would never be home to me. You can clear away whole towns of ugly old houses in one sweep, but you cannot change human nature so quickly. Slow change is better in the long run.'[34]

Over the rest of the war, a series of surveys showed how far from unusual Blundell's dislike of flats was – a dislike, it must be remembered, at a time when 'flats' meant in most people's minds a handful of storeys, not a high-rise in the modern sense of the term. Whereas 49 per cent of those asked in the *People's Homes* survey wanted ideally to 'live in a small house with a garden', only 5 per cent of the sample 'would by choice inhabit a flat, and even among flat dwellers only 28 per cent would not prefer to move to some sort of house, if they had the choice'. Soon afterwards, a submission made to the Dudley Committee by the Women's Advisory Housing Council similarly asserted that only 5.7 per cent of its respondents preferred flats to houses, with drawbacks of the former including not only lack of privacy but noise, fears over children's safety, 'gangsterism' and problems of coal deliveries and refuse disposal. And Pleydell-Bouverie confirmed that 90.2 per cent of the women she had polled had expressed a preference for a house or a bungalow, a preference partly explained by one of her more graphic chapter titles, '99% Want a Garden'. Still, as the *People's Homes* report had wryly concluded about working-class people and such apparently firm wishes, 'Happily for the planners, they will make the best of a bad lot or a good little.'[35]

What about 'community'? That bewitching, tantalising word would be the subject of many facile generalisations and much mental anguish in the years ahead but was not yet on the lips of every social investigator. Probably the closest to a 'community study' undertaken during the war was Dennis Chapman's survey of Middlesbrough (a town not short of slums and industrial pollution), based on interviews in the summer of 1944 with 1,387 'housewives', 971 'men workers' and 238 'women workers'.

Almost three-quarters expressed the wish to continue living in Middlesbrough after the war, with easily the most common reason being 'born here, used to it', followed by 'reasons connected with employment', 'friends and relatives here', and 'like it'. Predictably, it was younger people and higher earners who most frequently expressed the wish to live elsewhere. Asked about Middlesbrough's post-war problems, most people put unemployment and housing as their two main concerns; but although 'neither men nor women in Middlesbrough considered problems of physical planning to be of first importance', they were prepared to express views when asked what 'should be done after the war to make Middlesbrough a better place to live in', with 'improved roads and traffic circulation' seen as the top priority. Most people also wanted to see more libraries, theatres, playing fields, play centres, swimming pools and health clinics, but there was no majority support for more meeting places.

In answer to the question 'In what part of Middlesbrough and its neighbourhood would you prefer to live – why?', the most popular reason for choosing a particular district was 'healthier, better air, better for children', followed by 'like country, open', 'like the district' and 'better housing', with 'near relatives and friends' trailing badly behind. Asked if they wanted to move to a new house, in practice almost certainly in a suburb, more than two-thirds answered in the affirmative – with the desire for better amenities (including a garden) as the principal motive but with what Chapman called 'dissatisfaction caused by the social quality of the neighbourhood' also playing a part. He got closer to that factor by asking the pertinent question 'If you were entirely free to choose, would you want to live amongst the same kind of people that are in your neighbourhood now, or would you prefer to live amongst a different group of people?' In reply, 55 per cent said they did want to go on living among the same kind of people; 28 per cent would prefer to live among different people; and 17 per cent were 'unable or unwilling to express an opinion'. By far the most common reason given by the satisfied was 'like them, they are all right, etc', while among the dissatisfied a pervasive complaint was that 'people are noisy, rough, etc', though 'don't have much to do with neighbours – don't like people round here' was also popular.

Chapman further found that 'neighbourly relations are of considerable extent and play an important part in many fields of the daily life of the housewife', though he added the crucial qualifying point that 'the unit of neighbourly relations appears to be very small, a handful of families participating in each group'. Moreover, not only was it the case that 'the common social institution has so far been an insignificant source of "best friends" and even the common school is of very minor importance', but 'visits to common social institutions between neighbours who are friends are likewise seen to affect only a small number of people'. There were, accordingly, no strong grounds for 'centring a residential unit around a common social institution – a community centre or a school – from the point of view of creating social integration'. Put another way, 'the evidence is fairly conclusive that the idea of a neighbourhood unit [à la latest American town planning] which should be a microcosm of the social structure of the whole community is incorrect'.[36]

All in all, Chapman's report was sober, unsentimental stuff. It realistically portrayed people's strong desire for improvement in their personal conditions, preferably as part of a suburban lifestyle; their almost equally strong wish to live among those whom they perceived to be their own kind of people (whatever that kind might be); and their strictly limited appetite for the communal.

Was 'the Titmuss version' a complete myth, then? No, not quite. An official survey in late 1942 into public attitudes to plans for reconstruction located what it called a 'thinking minority' that was *actively* in favour of more state intervention in order to implement policies (in areas such as employment, welfare, housing and education) that would seek to benefit all – even if such policies involved higher taxation. The size of this 'thinking minority' was reckoned at between 5 and 20 per cent. Beyond that point it is difficult to salvage the myth. Indeed, the probability is that the size of this minority (inevitably disproportionately middle-class in composition) was actually shrinking towards the end of the war. Penguin Specials, originally launched in 1937, probably hit their peak in February 1942 with the publication of Archbishop William Temple's *Christianity and the Social Order*, which sought to marry faith with socialism and rapidly sold 140,000 copies. But by 1945 sales of the Specials had slumped to such an extent that the series was temporarily abandoned.

Fundamental social and cultural continuities remained – indeed, were arguably strengthened rather than lessened by the war. 'Class feeling and class resentment are very strong,' Harold Nicolson observed with foreboding soon after the European conflict ended. The Cutteslowe walls – built across and even along a north Oxford road in 1934 in order to separate private from council housing – stayed obstinately in place. The most-watched films during the war were Gainsborough melodramas, virtually without political or even social content, while the plots of the ever-popular Mills and Boon novels coursed along almost regardless of what was going on in the outside world. A culture that was still holding its own was that of the improving, intensely respectable, wanting-no-hand-outs working class. The gasfitter's wife Margaret Blundell spoke eloquently for it in her 1941 letter to *Picture Post:* 'What sort of men and women will the New World children turn out to be if they are to have no struggle? One must strive if one is to develop character. Your picture of Rich *v* Poor does not ring quite true. A considerable number of working-class manage a holiday every year, all the more enjoyable when one has struggled for it. You would make things too easy. Jealousy is the canker of our time. The rich will always be with us in one form or another and rightly so.' But within the working class the cultural future lay elsewhere – a future simulta-neously epitomised and hastened by the startling rise in the *Daily Mirror*'s popularity (beginning in the mid-1930s but accelerating from 1943, with circulation rising from two million that year to three million by 1946). Drawing inspiration directly from America, it successfully relied on a threefold formula: a brash irreverence (not only in peacetime) towards the authorities; a Labour-supporting politics of a far more populist, less heavy-duty type than that ponderously upheld by the Trades Union Congress-backed *Daily Herald*; and a very professionally assembled tabloid blend of cartoons, comic strips (the legendary Jane), human interest, sport and (often Hollywood) celebrities. 'Catering for short tea-breaks and even shorter attention spans', in the regretful but probably accurate words of one historian, it was a formula whose time had come.[37]

A final survey. *Patterns of Marriage* by Eliot Slater (a psychologist) and Moya Woodside (a psychiatric social worker) was not published until 1951, but its richly suggestive fieldwork comprised a detailed survey conducted between 1943 and 1946 of 200 working-class soldiers and their wives, mainly from the London area. Slater and Woodside's central focus was on courtship, marriage and sex – revealing in the last area an extensive amount of what the authors called 'passive endurance' on the part of the wives, typified by one's remark: 'He's very good, he doesn't bother me much.' But there was much else. Both men and women, they found on the class front, 'were dominated by the distinction that is expressed in "We" and "They", and, even in this war in which all were involved together, by the feeling of a cleft between the "two nations"'. Typical assertions quoted were: 'there'll never be much improvement so long as the country is run by people with money', 'the working class should be given a fairer do than they have had', and 'MPs have no worries, they've all got money in the bank.' The war itself had done little or nothing to broaden horizons. Nearly all the male conscripts, Slater and Woodside found, 'were bored and "fed up", took little interest in wider and impersonal issues, and were only concerned to get the war over and get home again'. As for their wives, 'the war was a background to daily life, irritating, endless, without significance other than its effects on their personal lives.' And for 'men and women alike patriotism was a remote conception, not altogether without meaning, but associated with feelings which were entirely inarticulate'.

For the husbands in particular, Slater and Woodside emphasised, one concern dominated above all:

> The spectre of unemployment is never very far away. Some have experienced it themselves; others remember its effect on their own childhood; and for still others it exists as a malignant bogy that must dog the steps of every working man. Again and again a preference is expressed for the 'steady job' as opposed to high wages, more especially by the older men. It is not likely that the lesson that England learned from the years of the trade depression will ever be forgotten ... There was a strong feeling that the fate of the individual under the capitalist system had little to do with merit, and depended on nebulous and unpredictable social forces. If only these could be controlled, a rich reward for personal ambitions was of secondary importance.

None of which guaranteed any more than a minimal interest in politics: 'Politics, it was felt, had nothing to do with their ordinary lives, in which other interests, sport and home, predominated. Politics was a special subject, beyond the understanding of the uneducated, or too vast and impersonal for any individual effort to influence.' A mere 21 out of the 200 men took 'an active interest in politics', but the attitude of the overwhelming majority was summed up by assertions like 'I'm not interested in politics, it isn't my job', 'politics are a pain in the neck, I've not the education to understand them', and 'me being an ordinary working-class man, politics is nothing to do with me; we're too busy with our families and jobs'. Politicians themselves, moreover, were generally seen in a dim light – 'all politicians are rogues', 'I'm against political parties, they're only out for their own gain,' 'no government is any good'.

The wives, meanwhile, were not sufficiently engaged with politics even to be cynical, with 'a serious and intelligent interest' being taken by only seven out of 200. 'The remainder showed an extreme apathy and lack of interest. Politics are felt to be remote from real everyday life, as incomprehensible as mathematics, the business of men. Preoccupation with personal concerns, the affairs of the home, children, leave little room.' Slater and Woodside quoted some of them: 'I married young, and had no time, with the children', 'I don't read papers much about the Government', 'After being on your feet all day, you just want to sit down and have somebody bring you a nice cup of tea.' With a note of palpable disappointment, the authors concluded about the wives that 'their effect as a whole is negative, conservative, a brake on any change from the established order'.[38]

It hardly took a Nostradamus to see that the outriders for a New Jerusalem – a vision predicated on an active, informed, classless, progressively minded citizenship – were going to have their work cut out.

Britain in 1945. A land of orderly queues, hat-doffing men walking on the outside, seats given up to the elderly, no swearing in front of women and children, censored books, censored films, censored plays, infinite repression of desires. Divorce for most an unthinkable social disgrace, marriage too often a lifetime sentence. ('I didn't want it,' my own grandmother would say to me in the 1970s when, making small talk soon after my grandfather's death, I said that at least he had lived long enough for them to have their Golden Wedding party. 'All I could think about was the misery.') Even the happier marriages seldom companionable, with husbands and wives living in separate, self-contained spheres, the husband often not telling the wife how much he had earned. And despite women working in wartime jobs, few quarrelling with the assumption that the two sexes were fundamentally different from each other. Children in the street ticked off by strangers, children in the street kept an eye on by strangers, children at home rarely consulted, children stopping being children when they left school at 14 and got a job. A land of hierarchical social assumptions, of accent and dress as giveaways to class, of Irish jokes and casually derogatory references to Jews and niggers. Expectations low and limited but anyone in or on the fringes of the middle class hoping for 'a job for life' and comforted by the myth that the working class kept their coal in the bath. A pride in Britain, which had stood alone, a pride even in 'Made in Britain'. A deep satisfaction with our own idiosyncratic, non-metric units of distance, weight, temperature, money: the bob, the tanner, the threepenny Joey. A sense of history, however nugatory the knowledge of that history. A land in which authority was respected? Or rather, accepted? Yes, perhaps the latter, co-existing with the necessary safety valve of copious everyday grumbling. A land of domestic hobbies and domestic pets. The story of Churchill in the Blitz driving through a London slum on a Friday evening – seeing a long queue outside a shop – stopping the car – sending his detective to find out what this shortage was – the answer: birdseed. Turning the cuffs, elbow patches on jackets, sheets sides to middle. A deeply conservative land.

3

Oh Wonderful People of Britain!

'Seventeen days since V.E. Day, and never have I seen a nation change so quickly from a war mentality to a peace mentality,' observed the diplomat-turned-writer Sir Robert Bruce Lockhart near the end of May 1945. 'The war [ie that was continuing in the Far East and was expected to last well into 1946] has disappeared from the news . . . Sport and the election now fill the front pages.' Sport included what was still the national game, and on 22 May the First 'Victory' Test ended at Lord's with Australia pummelling an ageing England attack to win by six wickets. For Gladys Langford there was a rare treat that day, in the company of Mr Burchell, a fellow-resident at her hotel: 'He took me first to the Saviours' Arms at Westminster where we had a substantial lunch – then we tried to get into a cinema but there were queues everywhere. We finally went to the Polytechnic after which, queues being in evidence, everywhere, we had fish & chips in a Soho "dive" where coloured men [probably American servicemen] were much in evidence. To be taken out at 55 is quite a triumph.' Anyone who had imagined that life would suddenly become easier in that first summer of peace was swiftly disabused. Judy Haines, however, took it all in her stride:

> *16 May*. Mother and Dad H. came to tea. Abbé [her husband, whose real name was Alfred] made the jelly and blancmange. Mother played and I sang – for 2 hours. The husbands seemed very happy about it. Then we became engrossed in KANUGO [a card game], till nearly 11 o'clock. Very satisfactory evening.
>
> *19 May*. As usual at holiday time [the Whit weekend], queues

everywhere in Chingford . . . The bread queue was the longest I have ever seen, and think many were disappointed. We had just about sufficient, and I have always Ryvita to help out.

26 May. Cleared out tallboy. Listened to *Pride & Prejudice*. The ration this week, of chops, contained some suet. Good! Chopped it and wrapped it in flour for future suet pudding.

For Henry St John, working a few days later in Midsomer Norton, there was as ever only frustration – 'I tried in vain to buy some Ovaltine, this being the 11th successive shop at which I failed to get it, although it continues to be widely advertised' – but there was some compensation when, on the train back to Bristol, an American soldier gave him a Camel cigarette. The American influence, and indeed anything that smacked of the modern, did not play well with Ernest Loftus in Essex. 'Mrs Williams [the French mistress] and I are taking joint action to stop our scholars attending Youth Clubs or, as I call them, Child Night Clubs,' noted Barking Abbey School's head in early June. 'So far as our type of school is concerned they are a menace. The world is sex-mad & they are the outcome of the sex-urge + the war + the cinema + evil books + a debased art & music + an uneducated parentage.'[1]

For one American, the writer Edmund Wilson, the experience of arriving in London later in June and putting up at the Green Park Hotel in Half Moon Street proved a salutary revelation of the Old World's post-bellum bleakness:

I was given a little room with yellow walls rubbed by greasy heads above the bed – little daybed with horrible brown cover that seemed to be impregnated with dirt – wooden washstand with no towel – brown carpet with rhomboidal pattern, stained and full of dust – piles of dirt in plain sight in corners – small shit-colored coal grate with dismal gas logs in corner. The dining room, with slovenly wretched waitresses – stains of soup, eggs, and jam on the table that seemed never to have been wiped off.

None of this, though, pierced Wilson's heart. But for Surrey's scholar-naturalist Eric Parker, driving through 'the Fold Country' (between Blackdown and Godalming) on the last day of May to see what had happened to his county's favourite corner since he had last been there in 1940, it was very different. 'The Fold Country was an aerodrome,' he found. 'Oak woods had been uprooted, engines of steel had torn out by the roots cottages and fields of corn.' Getting out of his car and wandering down a favourite lane, he suddenly found himself on a plain he had never seen before: 'The woods had gone. The lane had come to an end. Instead, in front of me stretched a vast flat space, a mile-wide level with a mile-deep highway broadening out to where I stood . . . There in the mid-distance were the huge noses of steel machines lifting into the sky, monstrous waiting insects.' Consolation came only when he reached Dunsfold and 'its green with the old black-smith's shop, and the Bricklayers' Arms, and a cottage on the green covered with white roses, and another cottage with scarlet geraniums climbing to the windows – all as it used to be, years ago, in the Fold Country'.

Even in May 1945 there appeared two books that in time would fuel a nostalgia industry: Evelyn Waugh's *Brideshead Revisited* (early reviews dominated by perceptions of the novel's snobbishness) and the Rev. W. Awdry's *The Three Railway Engines*. The latter was published by Edmund Ward, a fine-art printer in Leicester who was, as Awdry later put it, 'appalled at the lack of good quality literature for children available in the shops'. The irresistible size and format were almost certainly chosen with the aim of saving paper, and in 'The Sad Story of Henry' there featured the Fat Director ('My doctor has forbidden me to pull'). The first performance of Benjamin Britten's *Peter Grimes*, at Sadler's Wells on 7 June, struck an altogether more pioneering note, as the National Opera Company returned home from a war spent touring. 'After each curtain call,' a member of the audience recalled, 'people turned to one another excitedly while continuing to applaud; it was as if they wanted not simply to express their enthusiasm but to share it with their neighbours.' Grimes himself, a rough-hewn fisherman, was a rounded, ultimately tragic figure, far removed from the usual dramatic depiction of the lower classes as little more than buffoons. 'It looks as if the old spell on British opera may be broken at last!' Britten wrote soon afterwards in response to an appreciative letter.[2]

But some things never changed, or closed, and less than a week later

Henry St John, briefly up in town, was in the fourth row at the Wind-mill: 'The first scene included a sideways view of a nude, and a front view of a woman whose breasts were bare. I delayed masturbation until another para-nude appeared seen frontways, with drapery depending between the exposed breasts. Actually the most erotic scene was one featuring Jane Rock with a diaphanous scarf across her bosom, because during her dancing this flimsy covering jerked away to expose the white globes of her breasts and the nipples.' The Lord Chamberlain's rules insisted on statuesque poses, but for the diarist it was still enough to make him entitle the top of his page 'A GLIMPSE OF BEAUTY'. Shortly afterwards, a young would-be writer, working for the Leeds firm J. T. Buckton & Sons, had the thrill of seeing his first article ('Music Hath Charms') appear in print, in the July issue of *London Opinion*, but sadly for its author, Keith Waterhouse, 'my fellow-clerks were more interested in the tasteful nudes'.

Another young provincial had a rather more shattering experience. Dennis Potter, the ten-year-old son of a Forest of Dean miner, spent most of the summer lodging (with his mother and sister) in his grand-father's small terraced house in Hammersmith, while they waited for a council house in the Forest. He went to a local school, where he was mercilessly teased because of his accent, and spent many hours in the Hammersmith Gaumont, a huge Art Deco cinema complete with a gleaming white Hammond organ, transparent curtains and a projector that shed 'blue tobacco smoke' light. But what affected him most inti-mately were the attentions of his just-demobilised Uncle Ernie, also lodging at 56 Rednall Terrace and deputed to share a bed with his nephew. Years later, Potter was asked if he had told anyone about the drink-induced abuse that he had suffered during those weeks. 'I couldn't talk about it,' he replied. 'You don't know the circumstances, the house, and the sense that I had, that it would be like throwing a bomb into the middle of everything that made me feel secure. So . . .'[3]

It was also an election summer. Churchill's strong preference – shared by Clement Attlee, leader of the Labour Party, and his most important colleague, Ernest Bevin – was for the wartime coalition to continue until Japan was defeated. But at its party conference in Blackpool on 21 May, Labour's rank and file almost unanimously endorsed its National Executive's unwillingness to extend the coalition's life beyond

October, whether or not Japan was defeated by then. Churchill responded by dissolving the coalition, forming a caretaker administration and calling a general election for 5 July. The Blackpool mood was almost rapturously optimistic, with loud and prolonged ovations being given to speakers old and new. 'It is in no pure Party spirit that we are going into this election,' the Tredegar firebrand Aneurin ('Nye') Bevan told them. 'We know that in us, and in us alone, lies the economic salvation of this country and the opportunity of providing a great example to the world.' He went on, with his matchless, inspiriting, immoderate oratory:

> We have been the dreamers, we have been the sufferers, now we are the builders. We enter this campaign not merely to get rid of the Tory majority – that will not be enough for our task. It will not be sufficient to get a parliamentary majority. We want the complete political extinction of the Tory Party, and twenty-five years of Labour Government. We cannot do in five years what requires to be done. It needs a new industrial revolution. We require that modern industrial science be applied to our heavy industry. It can only be done by men with modern minds, by men of a new age. It can only be done by the fine young men and women that we have seen in this Conference this week.

Few finer than Major Denis Healey and Captain Roy Jenkins – both prospective candidates, both in uniform, though Healey in battledress, Jenkins in service dress. Cuffs turned back and all eyes on him, Healey won applause by invoking his own experience of Europe in the past three years, claiming that 'the upper classes in every country are selfish, depraved, dissolute and decadent', and boldly insisting that 'the crucial principle of our own foreign policy should be to protect, assist, encourage and aid in every way the Socialist revolution wherever it appears'. It was, his friend and rival Jenkins would recall with wryness as much as affection, a 'macho' and 'striking' performance.[4]

Churchill could hardly have made a more counterproductive start to his campaign. 'No Socialist Government conducting the entire life and industry of the country could afford to allow free, sharp, or violently-worded expressions of public discontent,' he rashly declared in his opening radio broadcast on 4 June. 'They would have to fall back on some form of Gestapo, no doubt very humanely directed in the first instance. And this would nip opinion in the bud; it would stop criticism as it reared its head, and it would gather all the power to the supreme party and the party leaders.' The immediate reaction of Judy Haines was almost certainly typical of middle opinion: 'I thought it was awful. He condemned the socialists and used the word "Gestapo" on their policy of continuing to direct people into jobs until the world is a bit more put-to-rights.' Twenty-four hours later her reaction to the latest broadcast was very different: 'Attlee spoke, and after Churchill's outburst of last evening, I found it pleasant listening. He dealt with Churchill's accusation, but didn't counter-accuse.' Nevertheless, there remained a widespread assumption that Churchill's indisputably fine record as a war leader would be enough to see the Tories home. 'I think this election is going to be alright,' their licensed maverick, Bob Boothby, wrote to the press magnate Lord Beaverbrook on the 8th, 'and that the P.M. will pull it off. Without him I would not give the Tories two hundred seats.'

Churchill's three subsequent election broadcasts did improve some-what – though even so, Vita Sackville-West thought them 'confused, woolly, unconstructed and so wordy that it is impossible to pick out any concrete impression from them' – and towards the end of June he undertook a three-day tour of the north and Scotland in which, amid high levels of enthusiasm, he addressed no fewer than 27 meetings. In London, however, his appearances met with a less positive response. In Chelsea, as he drove down Royal Avenue making the inevitable but now anachronistic 'V' sign, 'nobody cheered, and the silence was dire'; in Islington it was the same, reducing the great man to taking off his hat to a passing bus, bowing to it and saying, 'Good night, bus!'; in Camberwell he was booed, and in Southwark he even had to be rescued by police from a crowd turning ugly. He continued to trust to the tunes he knew best. 'A glib and specious policy may have unpleasant booby traps attached to it,' he wrote in the *News of the World* the Sunday before polling. 'That is my view of nationalisation and socialism. History has shown – and this war has confirmed it – that the genius and greatness of our race lie in the encouragement and development of free enterprise and the spirit of adventure and self reliance which go with it.' But deep down he perhaps knew that this time around those tunes would not be enough. 'I've tried them with pep and I've tried them with pap,' he confided at one point (reputedly to Attlee of all people), 'and I still don't know what they want.'[5]

As in any general election, there was a patchwork of local colour. In Preston the young Tory candidate Julian Amery disconcertingly discovered in his canvassing that it was 'quite common to find eleven or twelve people sleeping in a single room'. In Dundee one of the Labour Party's leading left-wing theorists, John Strachey, made much of the fact that he was 'Wing Commander Strachey' and ensured that in his election address he was photographed in uniform. For another photo opportunity, Labour's candidate in Oxford, Frank Pakenham (later Lord Longford), hired a pony and cart, installed his many children in the back and set out holding aloft the placard 'A NON-STOP DRIVE FOR HOUSING'; unfortunately, the pony soon came to a halt and refused to be budged. In Grantham an Oxford chemistry undergraduate, Margaret Roberts (later Thatcher), spent the early weeks of her summer vacation supporting the Tory candidate, Squadron Leader Worth; she declared, in her capacity as a warm-up speaker at his meetings, that 'it is the people of my generation who will bear the brunt of the change from the trials of the past into calmer channels' and insisted that 'just punishment must be meted out' to the defeated German enemy. In Kettering the writer Naomi Mitchison, whose husband Dick was standing for Labour, noted of the Tory candidate John Profumo that 'when asked questions he runs away into the car', but that 'he has got the small shop-keepers frightened'. In Blackburn the young Barbara Castle, one of only 87 women candidates in the whole election (out of almost 1,700), told a packed, smoke-filled, almost entirely male hall to forget that she was a woman – 'I'm no feminist. Just judge me as a socialist.' In Plymouth the Labour candidate Michael Foot (still in his early 30s but, improbably enough, already a former editor of the *Evening Standard*) met his future wife Jill Craigie, who was making a documentary for Rank about the Abercrombie Plan. With complete confidence he told the electors, 'We really can have the most beautiful city in the world.' In feudal Northumberland, where Sir William Beveridge was standing for the Liberals at Berwick, the young Durham miner, Methodist preacher and tyro writer Sid Chaplin, on holiday in Alnwick, told a friend that 'the shadow of Percy Hotspur still hovers over the town – the Politics of the Duke are the Politics of the Town – Transport House is a rash dream, the *Daily Herald* a red rag! and Communism a nasty nightmare.' Accordingly, he added, 'when the Duke spoke for the Tory nincompoop that settled the interloper Beveridge!' And in Edmonton the Labour candidate, Evan Durbin, told the electors in his best LSE manner that 'we shall only win the battles of peace against unemployment, poverty and ill-health if we bring to the service of our common purpose the latest inventions of economic and political thought', while nevertheless emphasising at another meeting (held on Edmonton Green) that he 'was not asking for the votes of the people because he, or his Party, could produce a new heaven and a new earth in one day or in the lifetime of one Parliament'.[6]

As emblematic as anywhere of the bigger picture was Luton, home of the Vauxhall car plant. 'Electors Losing Apathy: Political Warming Up Beginning in Luton: First Assembly Hall Meeting Draws 2,000 Audience' ran the local headlines after the legendary journalist Hannen Swaffer had come to the town on 19 June to support the Labour candidate, William Warbey. 'There is tremendous enthusiasm within the ranks of our Party, an enthusiasm such as we have never seen before,' Warbey told those gathered. 'I firmly believe that for the first time in history we are going to win Luton for Labour on July 5.' As for Swaffer, he directly targeted Churchill: 'You haven't got a house? The reason is because there is no plan. He doesn't understand plans – a magnificent man of war, but he doesn't understand planning.' A week later, Warbey's star speaker was none other than Harold Laski, the Labour Party Chairman and LSE professor, who had been the object of sustained attack from Churchill and the Beaverbrook press following various indiscreet remarks. To a packed hall, requiring loudspeakers to be fitted outside for the overspill, Laski insisted, reasonably enough, that the election was not about him. Meanwhile, Warbey (in normal life a press officer living in Barnes) and his Tory opponent Dr Graham Brown were busy addressing an array of meetings, including lunchtime congregations of workers in canteens. Warbey visited the Vauxhall works, but it was in the heavy-machine shop of Hayward-Taylor & Co. that he got his most enthusiastic reception, as workers 'banged out a welcome with hammers and other tools'.

On the campaign's final day, 4 July, both candidates held meetings at the Assembly Hall. Brown went first, telling a women's meeting that 'the Socialists were making a determined attack to win Luton but, if elected, their programme would mean the end of a democratically-elected Parliament', while to a later, more male gathering, Warbey summed up the Labour case:

> The people wanted to make sure that the war in the Far East would be speedily and successfully concluded and that the men and women in the Services would return to a country in which we had a Government which knew how to plan for jobs for all; for the four million houses required; for all-round social security and for world peace. They were determined not to return to the bad old days of poverty and unemployment which was all they could get if Labour's opponents were returned to power.[7]

It was the case – plausible, direct, appealing – that in a pre-television age Labour candidates were making all over the country on that culminating, momentous, pregnant Wednesday evening.

Was it an enthused electorate? Certainly the legend of 'the spirit of '45' would be a powerful one. 'The packed eve-of-poll meeting in Canning Town Public Hall, scene of many famous trade union meetings, was tremendous,' a Labour Lord Chancellor, Lord Elwyn-Jones, recalled about his fight for Plaistow in London's East End. 'None of us who took part will ever forget it – the rows of intent, uplifted faces – dockers in their caps and white mufflers, the wives and children and old men and women who had been through so much.' So, too, Castle, who remembered the 3,000 people at her eve-of-poll meeting in St George's Hall, Blackburn, and 'a sort of unbelievable buoyancy in the atmosphere, as though people who had had all the textile depression years, the men and women who had suffered in the forces and the women who had been working double shifts, making munitions and the rest of it, suddenly thought, "My heavens, we can win the peace for people like us."' Or take a non-politico memoirist, the writer Nina Bawden, who as a member of the Oxford University Labour Club went with others to campaign for Ian Mikardo in Reading; there they found themselves 'caught up in an extraordinary atmosphere of political excitement that everyone seemed to share – soldiers on home leave, old men in pubs, tired women in bus queues'.[8]

Clearly, then, there were pockets of high excitement, perhaps especially on the Labour side. But the contemporary evidence suggests an electorate that was essentially jaded and sceptical. 'The war's got us down, what with the bombing and the blackout, and the worrying about coupons and queues, women like me haven't the mind to take to politics,' a Fulham resident told Mass-Observation early in the campaign. 'We want to be left alone for a bit – not worrying about speeches.' A woman from Bayswater agreed: 'I don't take any interest in it. Not a scrap. To me it's an awful lot of tommy rot, what with each party running the other down, and when they get in, they'll be bosom pals.' A Chelsea man was the most succinct: 'Dunno who I'll vote for. I don't like politicians anyway – they're all crooks.' In mid-June an M-O survey of Londoners as a whole found that only one in seven was 'happy or elated', that a third 'felt no different from during the war', that a quarter 'felt worried', that 15 per cent 'felt depressed', and that several 'simply said that there ought not to be an election yet'.

There is no doubt that the general interest did increase somewhat as the campaign went on – so that by the end only 24 per cent (as opposed to 57 per cent at the outset) admitted to taking no interest in the local outcome – but when George Orwell went looking in London in the closing weeks for signs of popular interest, he failed either to overhear 'a spontaneous remark' in the street or to see 'a single person stopping to look at an election poster'. Edmund Wilson, meanwhile, escaped from his squalid hotel on the penultimate Sunday before polling and went to watch Laski do his stuff at Southbury Road School, Enfield, on behalf of the local Labour candidate. Wilson's notebook jottings evoke a quintessentially English scene, in a quintessentially English suburb: 'Enfield – little bay windows and brick doorways – gray sandy-looking sides of houses (called rough cast or sprinkled ash) – meeting out of doors in noon sun – yellow bricks, dim or neutral red tiles: pale faces, quiet people – blue and gray, occasionally khaki clothes – all in Sunday clothes, the men wearing coats.' Even in Coventry, symbolic focus of post-war reconstruction hopes, there were few signs of election fever. Indeed, the only time the crowds there really came out, including no doubt many Labour voters, was to see Churchill – and thereby to be able to tell their grandchildren that they had done so.[9]

'This is not the election that is going to shake Tory England,' declared the *Manchester Guardian* the day before polling. Few pundits disagreed, even though that same day the *News Chronicle* published a Gallup poll giving Labour a six-point lead – a poll which the paper found so hard to credit that it ran the story as a low-key, single-column one full of caveats. Next day, polling began at 7.00 a.m. (except in 24 northern and Scottish constituencies where 'Wakes week' fell on the 5th, necessitating a week's, in one or two places a fortnight's, delay), and a quarter of an hour later the Home Service's *The Daily Dozen* gave all but the earliest voters a chance to exercise while they pondered their collective mind. We have a few glimpses from what turned out a pretty warm day. At Gladys Langford's Highbury hotel, another resident, Mr White, was 'furious' at breakfast when he read that a youth had flung a lighted squib in Churchill's face. '"*Very* reprehensible but NOT criminal," said I while *he* was advocating lynching.' In contrasting stages of life, H. G. Wells voted for the last time (unable to leave his car, he had to have the ballot paper brought to him for marking) while the five-year-old Patrick Stewart (many years later Captain Jean-Luc Picard in *Star Trek*) was briskly moved along by a policeman for marching with a placard and singing loudly outside a polling booth near his home in working-class Mirfield, West Yorkshire – a moment that turned him into a lifelong Labour supporter. For Durbin in Edmonton, standing in a truck all day touring the streets, these were tedious hours of what his wife remembered him calling 'just cheering and wasting time'. Ernest Loftus, down in Tilbury, exercised his democratic right after tea: 'I voted for the National Conservatives – that is Churchill. The least one could do for the man who has saved the country. His opponent here is a wretched Jew – the limit. Why can't we find English Gentiles to represent us?' Another diarist, St John, made no reference to voting but that afternoon travelled by train from Bristol to London, reaching Paddington by 6.20. 'I had to wait until after 6.35 for a train to Shepherds Bush, which came in packed. It stopped at White City, where many passengers alighted, presumably to attend a dog-racing meeting.'

The polling stations closed at 9.00 p.m., just as *Northern Music-Hall* was finishing on the Home Service and a quarter of an hour before Alistair Cooke's *American Commentary*. For those interested in the outcome, that left three weeks to wait before counting began, while the votes came in from the Forces abroad. 'If I may put down my forecast of the result,' the Tory-supporting Glasgow pattern-maker Colin Ferguson surmised, 'it is this: – For the Govt. 360; Labour 220; the rest 60.' Three days later, the *News of the World*'s jumping-the-gun headline was similarly sanguine: 'Mr Churchill Has Secured His Working Majority'. But whatever the eventual result, there was satisfaction in a general election successfully conducted, the first for almost ten years. Or, as the Pathé News commentator sententiously boomed out the following week to the cinema-going millions, over anodyne shots of the backs of people in polling booths, 'A good many European countries might learn a thing or two from the way a free people choose their government.'[10]

As ever, life's daily rhythms continued during those three suspenseful weeks before 26 July and the declarations in the constituencies. Royal Ascot may have resumed on Saturday the 7th for the first time since 1939 – 'It was something of a shock,' one report noted, 'to discover cloth caps, Panamas, and grey slacks in the Royal Enclosure, where peace-time etiquette demanded more formal clothes' – but for Nella Last in Barrow a week later it was an altogether more humdrum motif: 'Queues were everywhere, for wedge-heeled shoes, pork-pies, fish, bread & cakes, tomatoes – & emergency ration-cards at the food office.' Indeed, by this time such was the fed-upness with ever-lengthening queues that two determined London housewives (Irene Lovelock, married to a South London vicar, and Alfreda Landau, married to a Neasden rabbi) came together, following local campaigns, to form a British Housewives' League. Still, later on in the day during which Last gazed glumly at the queues, there was a major boost for all. 'The clocks are being put back tonight [marking the end of wartime double-summer time], and the lights are up!' Judy Haines recorded. 'I was very thrilled indeed to see Chingford lit up.' No longer the groping along with a torch looking for steps and obstacles, no longer either the windows of buses and Tube trains mainly covered by gauze netting, with only a little diamond slit to see where one was.

An impressed visitor was André Gide's translator, Dorothy Bussy. 'Everyone,' she wrote to him from London on 16 July, 'is extraordinarily kind and attentive and unselfish – bus conductors, the travellers in buses and trains and tubes, policemen of course, but food officials too.' She was also struck by 'London's ruins', which were 'now a garden of grass and wild flowers, green & pink and yellow, springing of their own accord in the wastes'. The following evening, some 27,000 kind and attentive Londoners packed into the Spurs ground at White Hart Lane to see Doncaster's Bruce Woodcock win the British and Empire heavyweight titles with a sixth-round knockout. 'For Jack Solomons, the promoter, the fight was a triumph,' the local Tottenham paper noted. 'The crowd paid from 5/- to 10 guineas to see it. About 5,000 came by cars which lined each side of 30 side streets around the ground.'[11] On the radio, clashing with a transmission of *Peter Grimes*, Raymond Glendenning's plummy, excitable commentary was complemented by the magisterial inter-round summaries of W. Barrington Dalby.

Nothing mattered more, though, than a roof over the head. 'In the country something stirs,' the Independent MP W. J. Brown observed in his diary on 12 July. 'A bunch of people at Brighton, calling themselves the Vigilantes, have set about solving the housing problem in their own way, by commandeering any house that is empty and installing in it a family in need of accommodation.' It was not a well-documented campaign, but later that month Frederic Osborn noted how in the past few weeks there had been 'organised squatting in empty mansions, with enough public approval to force the Government and the authorities into more active requisitioning'.

For those with a home or aspiring to one, there was the *Daily Herald* Post-war Homes Exhibition at Dorland Hall in London's Regent Street. 'They could just give me *any* of it, and I should think it wonderful,' a young middle-class married woman told Mass-Observation. 'Honestly I liked it *all*. I'm so desperate for a house I'd like anything. I can't criticise or judge it at all – four walls and a roof is the height of my ambition.' M-O found pessimism on the part of some of the working-class wives at the exhibition. 'I feel it's pretty hopeless,' one said. 'I'll never be able to afford to buy the fitments to modernise our kitchen. It would cost an awful lot to convert.' Asked what they liked best, more than three-quarters of those interviewed nominated the demonstration kitchens. 'The lovely kitchens, so fresh and clean,' said one woman. 'The kitchens, everything tucked away and all flush and it saves so much stooping,' replied another, and a third was yet more expansive: 'It was the kitchenette. I think that's what interests most women, all the cupboard room. It's a lovely idea, covered in under the sink. I've wanted that for years and we've never had it.'[12]

The members of the London Stock Exchange probably had no strong views either way about kitchenettes. What really mattered to those stockbrokers and jobbers, atavistically Tory almost to a man, was the outcome of the election. Their unofficial spokesman and bell-wether was a cheery, birdlike, veteran member called Walter Landells. Under the name 'Autolycus' – a snapper-up of unconsidered trifles – he had for years contributed a daily column to the City's pink bible, the *Financial Times*. 'That Mr Churchill and his party will be returned is practically taken for granted,' Autolycus declared on Thursday, 19 July; 'the point of uncertainty is the sum of the majority.' He was just as confident by the following Tuesday ('No sign exists in the Stock Exchange of apprehension'), while the paper's front-page headlines were similarly optimistic: 'Cheerful Market Tone Maintained' that same day, 'Market Steadiness Well Maintained' on the Wednesday, and 'Firm and Confident Tone of Markets' on the Thursday itself, the 26th. That, though, was merely the public face of the Stock Exchange. Were its habitués – widely if fallaciously assumed to have an unparalleled insight into the future – truly so certain there would not be a dreadful upset? Perhaps they were, but it is worth recording the remark to Mass-Observation by the manager of a London bookshop: 'Well, what's going to be the result on Thursday? I was told last week that the betting on the London Stock Exchange was 6 to 4 on Labour getting in.'[13] It is unlikely that Landells was part of the clever money and giving a deliberately misleading steer, but one never knows.

The Foreign Office, and Sir Robert Bruce Lockhart's pen, provide as good a vantage point as any for the crucial hours of a day of destiny: 'The election results began to come in as soon as I reached the office at about 10 a.m. The first returns showed Labour gains, but as they came from the industrial north no one was very excited. But as the morning approached midday, it was already clear that the tide was running strongly in favour of the Left. Early on, there were casualties among the ministers, Harold Macmillan being one of the first to fall.' All over the country, that morning and into the afternoon as the weather in many places turned wet, individual fates were determined. Durbin won comfortably in Edmonton; Castle was returned in Black-burn, Foot in Plymouth Devonport; Healey lost in Pudsey and Otley, Jenkins in Solihull; a promising young Tory, Flight-Lieutenant Reginald Maudling, went down in Heston and Isleworth. In Cardiff South exuberant Labour supporters carried the winning candidate, Lieutenant James Callaghan, shoulder high from the city hall; in Coventry there was only a sparse gathering to applaud the two winning Labour candidates, one of them the gifted intellectual Richard Crossman. In Abertillery (Labour majority over 24,000) a vengeful Labour agent insisted on a recount in an ultimately unsuccessful attempt to make the Tory lose his deposit; in Kettering, as it became clear that Naomi Mitchison's husband had won, 'Profumo himself was being very decent,' though later he 'made the gesture which was not really very tactful of giving Dick a sheet of House of Commons note paper'.

Bruce Lockhart, meanwhile, lunched at the Dorchester with the flour miller and film magnate J. Arthur Rank: 'There was a huge board (with results) in the hall. Many people were watching it, mostly with glum faces. Already Labour had gained over a hundred seats. When I came down from Rank's room, the faces round the board were even glummer. Labour had now over 300 seats with over 150 more results to come. A complete majority over *all* other parties was therefore certain.' The atmosphere was still gloomier at an election luncheon given by the press magnate's wife Lady Rothermere. 'Although the champagne was exiguous and the vodka watery, the spectacle of consternation as details of the massacre spread was a strong intoxicant,' Evelyn Waugh wrote home about a party 'full of chums dressed up to the nines and down in the dumps'. For Graham Greene, then literary editor of the *Spectator*, there was a purely private emotion involved. The writer Walter Allen met him for lunch at Rules, where as they sat down Greene's eye was caught by the dramatic *Evening Standard* headline 'SOCIALISTS IN'. 'Damn!' exclaimed Greene. 'Don't you approve, Graham?' asked Allen. Greene replied that he didn't care one way or the other, indeed hadn't even bothered to vote, but that on the assumption the Tories would win had been planning to make a telephone call at 3.00. 'There won't,' he added, 'be any point in doing so now.' It transpired that Greene had been intending to ring the Reform Club, where his magazine's editor Wilson Harris – a Churchill-supporting MP and detested by Greene – lunched every day. The message to be left was that Harris was to call at 10 Downing Street at 3.30.[14] Labour's first overall majority in its history had inconsiderately thwarted the practical joke.

Towards the end of the afternoon, after a family tea at the Great Western Hotel, the imperturbable Attlee arrived at Transport House in Smith Square. Among an excited crowd of Labour activists and others waiting to greet him was the 20-year-old Anthony Wedgwood Benn. A BBC man pressed a microphone in front of his face and asked, 'Will you shout, "Three cheers for the Prime Minister"?' but he was too shy and the honour passed elsewhere. At about 7.15p.m., having with Bevin's help thwarted an ignoble, last-ditch attempt by Herbert Morrison to wrest the party leadership, Attlee set out for Buckingham Palace, where Churchill was in the process of resigning. He travelled, as he had done throughout the election campaign, in a Hillman Minx family saloon, with his wife Vi driving. 'I've won the election,' he told the King, in a rather strained conversation between two decidedly non-loquacious men. 'I know,' was the reply. 'I heard it on the six o'clock news.' Vi then drove the new Prime Minister to Central Hall, West-minster. There were many other Labour celebrations that evening – including one at the Assembly Hall in Luton, where Warbey and his supporters celebrated a spanking majority of more than 7,000 – but this victory rally was the epicentre. The big words flowed freely. 'This great victory for socialism will bring a message of hope to every democ-racy all over the world,' Laski (mockingly calling himself 'the temporary head of the socialist Gestapo') told the faithful. Bevin promised that the new government would 'speak as a common man to the common man in other lands'. And Attlee himself announced, 'This is the first time in the history of the country that a labour movement with a socialist policy has received the approval of the electorate.' He then went on to the balcony to address briefly the crowd of cheering and chanting supporters outside. The rally ended with a rendition of 'The Red Flag', and as Attlee and his wife fought their way out, he told reporters, 'We are on the eve of a great advance in the human race.'[15]

If so, it was not an advance that many in the West End that evening looked forward to with much relish. Beaverbrook, whose *Daily Express* had led the demonisation of Laski and his colleagues, was in the unhappy position of having arranged to host a large party at Claridge's. 'This occasion was intended as a victory feast,' he stood up and announced to the assembled company. 'In the circumstances it now becomes a last supper.' At another of Churchill's favourite hotels, the Savoy, one lady diner was heard to say, 'But this is terrible – *they've* elected a Labour government, and *the country* will never stand for that.' The food turned even more to ashes in the mouth for the theatre critic James Agate, despite his best efforts after hearing the appalling news:

> I rang up the head waiter at one of my favourite restaurants and said, 'Listen to me carefully, Paul. I am quite willing that in future you address me as "comrade" or "fellow-worker", and chuck the food at me in the manner of Socialists to their kind. But that doesn't start until tomorrow morning. Tonight I am bringing two friends with the intention that we may together eat our last meal as gentlemen. There will be a magnum of champagne, and the best food your restaurant can provide. You, Paul, will behave with your wonted obsequiousness. The *sommelier*, the table waiter, and the *commis* waiter will smirk and cringe in the usual way. From tomorrow you will get no more tips. Tonight you will be tipped royally.' The head waiter said, 'Bien, m'sieu.' That was at a quarter-past six. At a quarter-past nine I arrived and was escorted by bowing menials to my table, where I found the magnum standing in its bucket and three plates each containing two small slices of spam!

Perhaps the most revealing detail, though, was Agate's rhetorical question: 'Who would have thought a head waiter to have so much wit in him?'[16]

That day and over the next few days, there were plenty of other reactions to Labour's stunning overall majority of 146. 'It's an amazing piece of ingratitude to Churchill,' asserted Loftus predictably enough, while once she had got over the 'severe shock' Mary King in Erdington declared that such ingratitude 'fills me with horror'. The diarist

Anthony Heap was yet more dismayed, anticipating 'the indefinite continuance of war-time controls, the incessant fostering of class-hatred, the stamping out of individual enterprise and initiative, the subjugation of everything and everybody to a totalitarian system of state control manipulated by a gigantic army of smug little bureaucrats'. Among Nella Last's fellow-sewers at the Women's Voluntary Service centre in Barrow, there was intense consternation as the news of the landslide percolated through: 'flushed and upset', Mrs Lord said that she *personally* feared riots and uprising' before Last calmed her down with 'two aspirins and a glass of muddy-looking liquid', purportedly sherry; and Mrs Higham said to Last, 'Don't you realise we may be on the brink of revolution?' Judy Haines's reaction was quite different – 'Labour in with a great majority, and I am thrilled!' – but significantly she added, 'People generally quiet – though it is the people who have done it.' One public schoolboy in Sussex, Bernard Levin, was positively ecstatic, hanging a red flag out of his window and braving the consequences. Two Oxford philosophers concurred: Isaiah Berlin danced a jig at hearing the news, while Iris Murdoch wrote with Wordsworthian fervour to a friend abroad, 'Oh wonderful people of Britain! After all the ballyhoo and eyewash, they've had the guts to vote against Winston! . . . I can't help feeling that to be young is very heaven!' Dylan Thomas was rather more understated. 'The rain has stopped, thank Jesus,' he wrote a few days later from a Carmarthenshire valley in his only apparent reference to the election result. 'Have the Socialists-in-power-now stopped it?' And soon afterwards, the poet W. S. Graham, Scottish but living near Marazion in Cornwall, was studiously indifferent: 'Yes I notice we have changed the government. It doesn't mean much though it's called Labour. Labour is now quite respectable.'[17]

Perhaps the most interesting response, however, came from the popular, ultra-patriotic historian Arthur Bryant. One might have expected indignation or anxiety to be the dominant note, but a letter that he wrote during August was very different in tone:

We can't return, even if we wanted to, to the social and economic frame-work of 1939, for it no longer exists, and the task of our rulers now is to create a new framework without causing social chaos in the meantime or saddling us with a totalitarian system. Without holding any exaggerated belief in the wisdom of Socialists, I believe the latter are more capable at the moment of doing this than the Conservatives, who are under the domination not only of vested interests but of something a great deal worse – vested ideas! And unlike the Conservatives, the Socialists do understand the discomfort and inhuman conditions under which so many people today are living and working.

It was a flexible, pragmatic reaction echoed by that of an underwriter at Lloyd's in the City of London. 'To my astonishment,' the future journalist John Gale would recall about returning to England after the election, 'I found that my father welcomed the Labour victory. "There might have been trouble if they hadn't got in," he said. I never asked how he voted.' But arguably, in terms of prophecy, the palm went to an old trouper. 'It may not be a bad idea for the Labour boys to hold the baby,' Noël Coward, no friend to the people's party, reflected. 'I always felt that England would be bloody uncomfortable during the immediate post-war period, and it is now almost a certainty that it will be so.'[18]

Why had it happened? Only two days after becoming Prime Minister, Attlee found himself at Potsdam being verbally strong-armed by Stalin, that electoral innocent, to account for Churchill's inexplicable defeat. 'One should distinguish between Mr Churchill the leader of the nation in the war and Mr Churchill the Conservative Party leader,' he answered. 'Many people looked upon the Conservatives as a reactionary party which would not carry out a policy answering to peace requirements.' For Beaverbrook, as for many contemporary analysts of the election, the current leader was not to blame. 'The unpopularity of the party,' he wrote soon afterwards, 'proved too strong for the greatness of Churchill and the affection in which he is held by the people.' Fortunately there were some, including one young reform-minded Tory, Cub Alport, who were able in their post-mortems to transcend the Churchill question. 'I think the election is a vote for the people who are least likely to involve us in foreign adventures, or bring us up against Russia,' he told Rab Butler. 'It is a vote for domestic security.' For a few intellectuals, that sort of interpretation was altogether too tame. 'It was not a vote about queues or housing,' declared Cyril Connolly in the September issue of

Horizon, 'but a vote of censure on Munich and Spain and Abyssinia . . . The Election result is a blow struck against the religion of money.' As usual, the views of his friend from prep school and Eton were more pertinent. 'No one, I think, expects the next few years to be easy ones,' Orwell wrote at about the same time, 'but on the whole people did vote Labour because of the belief that a Left government means family allowances, higher old age pensions, houses with bathrooms, etc., rather than from any internationalist consideration. They look to a Labour government to make them more secure and, after a few years, more comfortable.'[19]

Of course, there were plenty of other causal factors adduced then and subsequently.[20] The widespread belief that a Labour government would ensure a speedier demobilisation; the unusually even balance of political allegiance on the part of the press; the absence during the war of the familiar drip, drip of anti-Labour propaganda on the part of the fourth estate; the way in which that war had turned leading Labour politicians into familiar and trusted figures as senior ministers; the party's high degree of unity; above all, the general feeling that the number one immediate issue of housing could best be met by Labour's energetic message of can-do fairness: all these things contributed to the outcome. A significant minority of the usually Conservative-voting middle class switched to Labour and probably just as many abstained, often to decisive effect; for once, Disraeli's 'angels in marble', the working-class Conservatives, failed their betters; and across the classes, the young voted Labour in large numbers.

What about Churchill? In the eyes of a nation still hugely grateful for what he had done to help win the war, he was almost certainly still an electoral asset. But at the same time there can be no evading his prime culpability, as Tory leader from 1940, in the party's failure to develop and start to propagate realistic policies in response to people's understandable domestic concerns, above all in relation to housing and unemployment. 'Before the Election,' one Tory MP would recall, 'the Post-War Problems Committee's numerous reports, the "Signpost" booklets, the various pamphlets of the Tory Reform Committee, were all good, but they were not authoritative. They did not bear the *imprimatur* of the Prime Minister. There was no evidence that he had read them.'[21] Yet it is arguable that so powerful and pervasive was the mythology that had developed about the bleakness and inhumanity of the inter-war years – years dominated by Tory politicians and Tory policies – that no amount of domestic engagement by Churchill would have made much difference. Labour, after all, did not manage a decisive victory *during* those years, and indeed suffered three crushing defeats, culminating in 1935. Ten years and one arduous conflict later, a conflict which for an insular people had required an insular purpose, there was a strong desire not to return to the 'bad old days' – even though that desire paradoxically co-existed with a near-universal longing in other respects (above all the rhythms of everyday life) to get back to how it had been 'before the war'.

It would be both perverse and an error to exaggerate the revisionism. To take '1945' out of 1945 leaves a barren historical landscape indeed. The electorate may well have been voting more negatively against the Tories than positively for Labour, there may well have been relatively little popular enthusiasm for 'socialism' as such (as opposed to immediate material improvements), Orwell may well have been right when he asserted soon after the results that 'the mood of the country seems to me less revolutionary, less Utopian, even less hopeful, than it was in 1940 or 1942' – yet at some level most people realised that a rather amazing thing had happened, in effect marking off 'pre-1945' politically from 'post-1945'. 'My man,' called out a blazered, straw-hatted 14-year-old public schoolboy, John Rae, as he stood on Bishop's Stortford station with his trunk that late July. 'No,' came the porter's quiet but firm reply, 'that sort of thing is all over now.'

Even so, if there was such awareness, however inchoate or subterranean it may have been in many cases, it still had to fight for its place in the daily consciousness of the daily human round. Take a wonderfully revealing diary entry for Sunday, 29 July:

Weather has been lovely – such a difference from this time last year when we ran so often to shelter. The streets look so bright at night now, with all the lamps lit. We went to Kilburn & it was so nice to sit & chat & not have to listen for the warning. The election result is still creating talk – I wonder where this Labour Government will lead us to. I heard that Ladies shoes are going to 9 coupons on the new books. I expect it is true. I still don't believe Hitler is dead – & how much longer before the German war criminals are brought to trial. About time they were all shot else they will get off & start another war.[22]

Rose Uttin – mid-40s, married, living in Wembley, husband Bill in charge of stationery at the Royal Exchange Assurance, daughter Dora a clerical assistant at Harrow Education Office, elderly mother living upstairs in the back bedroom – had, like virtually everyone else, much else on her mind besides electoral earthquakes.

———

The pleasures of peace returned with a vengeance that weekend, as on the Saturday the trains of the London, Midland and Scottish Railway carried a record 102,889 holiday-makers to Blackpool's stations. On Sunday the new 'Light' Programme superseded the wartime 'Forces' Programme, and though Anthony Heap's immediate reaction was that 'there is precious little difference in the type of fare provided', there did take place on Monday afternoon the first episode of *The Robinson Family*, featuring 'the day-to-day adventures of a London family and their friends'. It is unlikely that there were any listeners among those present that evening at the dinner party given by Hugh Dalton (the new Chancellor) in a private room at the St Ermin's Hotel. The line-up was more or less the cream of Labour's up-and-coming talent, including Christopher Mayhew, Woodrow Wyatt and John Freeman, as well as Durbin, Crossman and Hugh Gaitskell. Also present were Harold Wilson, an archetypal grammar-school product who had made his name as an academic high-flyer helping Beveridge and who was already viewed by Harold Nicolson as 'brilliant', and the only non-university man, George Brown. Predictably, Wilson 'made me simply gape as he talked' (Mayhew wrote home afterwards), while Brown (according to Gaitskell) 'kept rather quiet'.[23]

Two days later, the new House of Commons met for the first time to elect its Speaker. 'When Churchill came in for the show he was greeted by the singing of "For he's a jolly good fellow" by the Tories,' recorded W. J. Brown (who had got back as an Independent). 'The Labour masses retorted by singing "The Red Flag" – which I thought was very bad tactics, doing no good and calculated to frighten all the retired Colonels in Cheltenham and Leamington Spa.' It was reputedly George Griffiths, a miner MP from South Yorkshire and member of the Salvation Army, who had started singing the socialist anthem; that evening Bob Boothby boasted at a London party that he was the sole Tory to have joined in. Strikingly, only 38 per cent of the Labour MPs came from a working-class background – compared with 72 per cent after the 1935 election.[24] Griffiths may have got them singing, but it was the lawyers, teachers, journalists, doctors, managers and technicians who would principally be calling the tune.

Monday the 6th – the day after the Giles cartoon 'Family' first appeared in the *Sunday Express*, on their way to the seaside – was the August Bank Holiday. There were large crowds at most seaside resorts (as many as 35 relief trains leaving Liverpool Street station) and the usual cultural preferences expressed at the main attractions (31,440 people at London Zoo, 4,553 at the V&A). At Lord's, where 10,000 were locked out ten minutes after the start of the Fourth Victory Test, play was interrupted at 1.00 by a terrific storm of hail and thunder – unluckily for listeners who, in an era before ball-by-ball, had been waiting patiently for Rex Alston's description of 'the closing overs before lunch'. Over at the White City stadium, some 100,000 tried, but only 52,000 managed, to watch a memorable athletics meeting. The stars were the two great Swedish middle-distance runners Gunder Hägg and Arne Andersson, the latter taking on Britain's pre-war record-holder Sydney Wooderson in the one mile and just winning. Wooderson, in the RASC, had reputedly travelled down from Glasgow by train and, not wanting to make a fuss about the fact that he was due to represent his country the next afternoon, had stood in the corridor all night. After the thunderstorm, the weather was cool and unsettled. 'Obviously no day for Hampstead [ie Heath] or anywhere like that,' noted Heap. 'So after an afternoon stroll round Bloomsbury and an early tea hied us round to the Regent to see "National Velvet".' He enjoyed it on the whole but despite Elizabeth Taylor's presence regretted that 'the essential English atmosphere is missing'.[25]

Meanwhile, some 25 per cent of the adult population had, as usual, been listening to the Home Service at 6.00:

Here is the News.

President Truman has announced a tremendous achievement by Allied scientists. They have produced the atomic bomb. One has already been dropped on a Japanese army base. It alone contained as much explosive power as 2,000 of our great ten-tonners. The President has also foreshadowed the enormous peace-time value of this harnessing of atomic energy.

Hiroshima ('it's been an army base for many years') was identified as the target; but even on the nine o'clock bulletin, which included an official account of Britain's role in the development of the bomb, there was still 'no news yet of what devastation was caused – reconnaissance aircraft couldn't see anything hours later because of the tremendous pall of smoke and dust that was still obscuring the city of once over 300,000 inhabitants'.

The impact, nevertheless, was immediate. 'My husband looked at me across the lounge of the London flat, and I looked at him,' the writer Ursula Bloom remembered. 'Horror filled us both, and to such a degree that for a moment neither of us could speak.' Elizabeth Longford was sitting alone in her Oxford home when she turned on the wireless. 'For the first time in my life I had a strong presentiment about the future: that a brilliant scientific discovery would bring a balance of evil to the human race.' Later that evening, Joan Wyndham, standing around with WAAF colleagues at their Nottinghamshire air base waiting for transport to take them to the late watch, noticed Flight Sergeant Kelly hurrying towards them:

First she walked a bit, then she broke into a run and walked again. It seemed odd because she wasn't late for the transport.

When she came up to us she said, 'There's a terrible bomb been dropped on Japan – the worst ever! It's to do with re-directing the energy from the sun, or something. Everybody thinks the Japs will surrender any minute!'

She probably expected a barrage of questions – or even cries of 'Good show!' – but there was nothing, only a shocked silence . . .

I think I was stunned, not so much because of the bomb as at the thought of the war ending. Later, when the meaning finally sank in, I felt the strangest mixture of elation and terror.

For the Rev. John Collins, Dean of Oriel College, Oxford, the news marked the moment when 'I finally decided against the whole concept

of the Just War.' Within minutes of the bulletin ending, he was rung
by the left-wing publisher Victor Gollancz, who persuaded Collins to
call at once his friend Sir Stafford Cripps, the ascetic, high-minded
Christian who had just become President of the Board of Trade. Collins,
as he later recalled, got through without difficulty, to be told by Cripps
that 'the Cabinet had not been informed about what was to happen',
though he 'went on to assure me that no more atomic bombs would
be used against the Japanese'. Still that same evening, Collins rang
Lambeth Palace in the hope of speaking to the Archbishop of Canterbury, Geoffrey Fisher. However, he got only a chaplain, who told him
'that His Grace had "gone into hiding" – a favourite posture of the
Church in moments of moral crisis'.[26]

Over the next week or so – which included, notwithstanding Cripps's
assurance, an atom bomb being dropped on Nagasaki – most people
reacted in characteristic ways. Randolph Churchill, son of Winston,
was reported by Evelyn Waugh as 'greatly over-excited'; Joyce Grenfell
declared herself 'all for the Atomic Bomb, but not to drop it much';
Noël Coward reckoned that a bomb that was going to 'blow us all to
buggery' was 'not a bad idea'; and Vanessa Bell, writing to her daughter,
spoke for the Bloomsbury Group: 'What a to-do about the atomic
bomb . . . I wish they'd get to the stage of labour-saving devices instead
of destroying whole cities.' J.R.R. Tolkien was even prompted to make
a rare pronouncement, albeit private, on a public matter. 'The utter
folly of these lunatic physicists to consent to do such work for war-
purposes: calmly plotting the destruction of the world,' he wrote to
his son. 'Such explosives in man's hands, while their moral and
intellectual status is declining, is about as useful as giving out firearms
to all inmates of a gaol and then saying that you hope "this will ensure
peace".' He concluded, 'Well we're in God's hands. But He does not
look kindly on Babel-builders.' The pattern-maker Colin Ferguson,
writing his diary in Glasgow on the 8th, concurred: 'The papers are
still full of the Atomic bomb and what it may mean for the future.
They hope it will have beneficial effects & not a diabolic outcome. I
say, before they place any "hopes" on the future they'll have to get
men changed – not "political systems" . . . And in that they're hoping
against hope: there is *no hope* in *man*, and he is credulous who believes
there is. The end is near – maybe some years only.' As the news of

the appalling human and material destruction filtered through, perhaps most people felt like that at some level, even if less starkly. Yet the observation of Gladys Langford was telling. 'Everybody very proud of the Atomic bomb *we've* dropped on Japan,' she noted on the 7th, 'and yet those same people cursed the Germans for *their* cruelty when *they* bombed *us*.'[27]

The day after Hiroshima found Henry St John, briefly on secondment in the north-east, working in Spennymoor: 'I tried in vain to buy cigarettes. The public lavatory had some fixtures missing, and an unusual wealth of scribblings on the door of the water closet. "I know a little girl of 11 who can take a man's prick. I broke her down in the woods, and did she enjoy it. I fuck my sister – she's 14," were specimens. A drawing showed a nude woman beside a bed, with a caption, "I'm ready, dean".' Two days later, the urban anthropologist returned to the scene 'to see if I could masturbate over the mural inscriptions', but vexingly, 'there was no lock on the door'. There was no such anticlimax for Nella Last and her husband on Saturday the 11th, when, having got 'the extra petrol', they set out from Barrow for the day, taking with them their next-door neighbours the Atkinsons:

> The thought that peace would soon be here, that mothers and wives could cease their constant worry, and anxiety, that people could begin to live their own lives again, seemed all mixed up with the warm sunshine and the fields of cut golden corn and the sea sparkling over the golden sands – a feeling of 'rightness'. We walked round Morecambe, *marvelling* at the tons of good food – things in Marks & Spencer's like brawn and sausage, thousands of sausage-rolls and pies, including big raised pork-pies.
>
> We went on to Heysham Head – surely the best shilling's worth in the whole world! Lovely surroundings, a show in the Rose Gardens, a circus, concert party, marionette show, little menagerie, dance board with relayed music, seats for everyone, either in the sun or the shade – all included! . . . We sat on the slope of the Head to watch the circus, and I saw a group sitting near in very earnest conversation, with their heads together. I'd have loved to go and butt in. I love being in an argument, and thought, 'Perhaps they are talking about the atomic bomb – or the result of the Election.' I've very good hearing, and when I'd got used to the different sounds around, I could hear what they *were*

discussing – the new 'cold perm'! Every woman I know is interested in
it – another revolution, when curly hair can be assured by a method so
simple that it can be done at home.

'We felt in a real holiday mood' as, coatless, they drove home. And
Last thought: 'It will be a good month for getting in the crops, for the
moon rose fair when it came in.'[28]
Negotiations had dragged on for several days after the Japanese
surrender on the 10th, but by Tuesday the 14th there was a general
expectation that the end of the war could be only hours away. 'Crowds
of small boys keep going by with packing cases for burning,' Gladys
Langford tut-tutted that day. 'I think it is a great pity in view of necessary
economy in fuel this coming winter.' The suspense mounted. 'We listened
eagerly to the six o'clock news – still nothing tangible,' noted Last. 'I
thought of a remark I'd heard: "Perhaps Japan, too, has a mystery bomb
and is playing for time."' Later, 'when there was nothing on the nine
o'clock news, I said that I was going to bed, as my back ached badly.'
But finally, as Ernest Loftus near Tilbury succinctly recorded, it came:

At 11 p.m. – summary of news – we were told to stand by at 12 for an
important announcement.

At midnight, therefore, I switched on and Attlee the new Prime
Minister announced PEACE. The Japs had accepted our terms. Even
while Attlee was speaking the sirens began to sound on the ships in the
river & some of them are still at it at 12.55 as I write this.

The *Merthyr Express* described the memorable scenes and noises that
ensued in South Wales – as in many parts of Britain – almost straight
after the typically clipped announcement:

The streets in all the towns and villages in the Merthyr Valley, the
Rhymney Valley and the West Monmouthshire area were thronged with
singing and cheering people. Dancing and singing took place from soon
after midnight until the small hours.

Those who did not hear the Premier's broadcast were awakened by
their neighbours, and many left their beds, donned dressing gowns or
overcoats and joined the ever-increasing crowds.

'The war is over' was a cry frequently heard, and for many the news was almost unbelievable at first. Many women were in tears at the thought of again seeing a husband or son soon to be released from prisoner-of-war camps.

Large buildings in many districts were floodlit – red, white and blue 'V' signs being very prominent. All our South Wales colliery hooters, train whistles, detonators, fireworks and rattles were used to swell the great chorus of celebration. Many bonfires were lit in the streets and on the mountain-sides, and shone out as symbols of Peace and Freedom.

Nella Last in Barrow was woken from her half-sleep by shouting and the noise of ships' sirens and church bells. For the next hour, as she looked through her bedroom window but could not quite bring herself to get dressed and go out, there were 'cars rushing down Abbey Road into the town', an excitable neighbour 'half-screaming "God Save the King"', from all directions 'the sound of opening doors and people telling each other they had been in bed and asleep', dogs 'barking crazily', ships' hooters 'turned on and forgotten', and 'the sound of fireworks coming out of little back gardens'. By 1.00 she had had enough. 'I feel no wild whoopee, just a quiet thankfulness and a feeling of "flatness",' she scribbled before returning to bed. 'I think I'll take two aspirins and try and read myself to sleep.'[29]

Attlee had announced in his broadcast that the next two days were to be public holidays, and as it happened Wednesday the 15th – VJ Day – had long been booked for the state opening of Parliament and the King's Speech. 'It was like old times even though there was no gold coach,' reflected one of the Tory survivors, Sir Cuthbert Headlam. 'The new Labour M.P.s are a strange looking lot – one regrets the departure of the sound old Trade Unionists and the advent of this rabble of youthful, ignorant young men.' Not everyone, to judge by Judy Haines's report, had been aware of the midnight revels:

We got up as usual and were breakfasting and listening to the 7 o'clock news, when we realised a V.J. day was on. People had started out for work and hardly knew which way to turn when it was conveyed to them today and tomorrow are holidays. Some had evidently been given instructions to join the bread queue in the event of VJ, for that is what

they did. I have never seen so many people in Chingford. The queues
were more like those of a football match. The queue for bread from
List's stretched round to the Prince Albert. I was very glad Dyson's
opened as it is my shopping morning and I needed my rations.

It was no better in Wembley. 'Women grumbling & arguing in the
queues,' noted Rose Uttin, '& then it started to rain – everybody with
heavy bags of shopping got soaked.' Elsewhere, once the shopping was
in and with the weather brightening up, there were the familiar street
tea parties for children, followed by victory dances and bonfires in the
evening. 'All day long,' observed Langford in less disapproving mode,
'children have been passing with doors, window frames and other wood-
work torn from buildings.' Anthony Heap and his wife, on holiday in
Somerset when they heard the news, decided to 'dash up to London
for the celebrations', catching the 10.35 from Frome. For a time, as they
made 'a preliminary tour of the West End', he half-regretted their
decision: 'Not quite so thrilling as we expected. The inevitable crowds
gathered en masse in Trafalgar Square, Piccadilly Circus & Buckingham
Palace listening to tinned music emanating from loud speakers. But
otherwise the rejoicing seemed to be rather subdued. Just thousands of
weary-looking people wandering round the streets or sprawling on the
grass in the parks.' Sticking to their VE ritual, they went home for some
tea before 'embarking on the evening excursion':

Had to walk there and back this time, but as it turned out to be so much
more lively and jubilant a jaunt than the afternoon one, we didn't mind
that so much. We waited among the multitude outside Buckingham Palace
to hear the King's Broadcast speech at 9.0 and see the Royal Family appear
on the balcony afterwards. We stood among the crowds in Whitehall and
saw Attlee, Morrison and Bevin on the balcony of the Ministry of Health
building, though we couldn't hear what the former was saying for his
speech was continually drowned by shouts of 'We want Churchill' . . .
We saw the floodlighting, we saw the fireworks, we saw the town literally
and figuratively lit up – despite the deplorable dearth of drink – as it's
rarely been lit up before . . . So far as revelry by night was concerned, VE
Day had nothing on VJ Day. It was London with the lid off!

VE Day celebrations in Lambert Square, Coxlodge, Newcastle upon Tyne

The Tory candidate addresses an election meeting in Bethnal Green, June 1945

Aneurin Bevan in Ebbw Vale during the 1945 election

Above: The Haymarket, Sheffield, 1946

Right: Museum steps, Liverpool, 1946

Mrs Francis, Christmas Street, off the Old Kent Road, 1946

The Gorbals, Glasgow, 1948

'Mr Browning's Winning Team': West Sussex, 1947

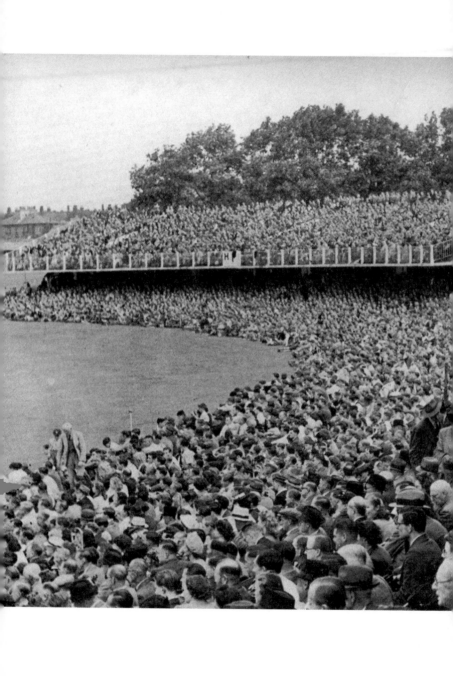

England versus South Africa at Lord's, June 1947

Margate, June 1948

So no doubt it was, but for many people one day of celebrations was quite enough, even more than enough. 'Another V.J. day spent quietly at home,' wrote Haines on the 16th. 'So glad of the rest.'[30]

The election, the atom bomb, the end of the world war: all within a matter of weeks. It was a moment, inevitably, for taking stock. Frederic Osborn, starting on the 14th a long letter to the great American urban prophet Lewis Mumford, pondered the political upheaval:

What has happened is a very big step in the British revolution – a shift of power to meet new conditions and new ideas. Britain will not willingly go far towards Communism; it will remain at heart a free-enterprise nation . . . It does not accept the state-monopoly solution, despite Laski and Aneurin Bevan; and sooner or later it will revolt against the facile solution of state ownership and be driven to expedients of entirely new kinds, which Labour philosophy at present scornfully scouts.

Next day, amid the happy junketings, he turned to his obsession:

I don't think philanthropic housing people anywhere realise the irresistible strength of the impulse towards the family house and garden as prosperity increases; they think the suburban trend can be reversed by large-scale multi-storey buildings in the down-town districts, which is not merely a pernicious belief from the human point of view, but a delusion. Many of our 'practical' people, including our Mr Silkin [Lewis Silkin, the new Minister of Town and Country Planning], share the delusion . . . I am inclined to think the multi-storey technique will have to have its run . . . It is a pity we can't go straight for the right policy. But it takes a long time for an idea, accepted theoretically, to soak through the whole of an administration; and the conflicting idea of good multi-storey development has enough enthusiasts to claim a trial in some cities on a fairly large scale. Damage will be done to society by the trial; but probably all I can do is hasten the date of disillusion. If I have underestimated the complacency of the urban masses, the damage may amount to a disaster.

Few of any persuasion imagined that the end of the war meant the end of Britain's problems. 'We have a lot in front of us in reconstruction,'

Grantham's Mayor-elect, Alderman Alfred Roberts, explained on VJ +1 to the local paper. 'When you have won the war you have to heal the wounds of war, and that is our next job.'[31]

PART TWO

4

We're So Short of Everything

The sporting highlight of the first autumn of peace was a far from peaceful British tour by the Russian football champions Moscow Dynamo. Amid much mutual suspicion and misunderstanding, four matches were played – draws against Chelsea and Glasgow Rangers, a narrow win over Arsenal and a 10–1 demolition of Cardiff City. The ill feeling that characterised at least two of the matches provoked George Orwell, writing just before Christmas in the left-wing magazine *Tribune*, to launch a full-frontal attack on professional football and its followers: 'People want to see one side on top and the other humiliated, and they forget that victory gained through cheating or through the intervention of the crowd is meaningless.' In short, 'serious sport . . . is war minus the shooting'. This was too much for E. S. Fayers of Harrow, Middlesex. 'George Orwell is always interesting,' began his riposte. 'But he does write some bilge.' And after defending football as a game to play, he went on:

> As to the spectators, with the greatest possible diffidence, I suggest that George is in danger of falling into the error of intellectual contempt for the 'mob'. These football crowds, if only he got among them, he would find are not great ignorant mobs of sadistic morons. They are a pretty good mixture of just ordinary men. A little puzzled, a little anxious, steady, sceptical, humorous, knowledgeable, having a little fun, hoping for a bit of excitement, and definitely getting quite a lot of enjoyment out of that glorious king of games – football.

The good-natured rebuke finished unanswerably: 'I'm sorry for George. He's missed a lot of fun in life.'[1]

There was no resumption of the Football League proper until the 1946–7 season, but happily for 'ordinary men' the FA Cup did take place in 1945–6, on a two-leg basis. Less than glamorous Accrington Stanley found themselves pitted in the third round against Manchester United, with the first leg at Peel Park. Two down at half-time, Stanley then, 'in as plucky a come-back as I have ever seen' (in the words of the local reporter 'Jason'), 'drew level with two minutes to go to the accompaniment of an almost hysterical roar of triumph from the crowd'. Predictably, United won the return 5–1 – but 'the game might have taken on a different aspect if two cruel pieces of ill-fortune had not come Stanley's way.' Three rounds later, at the Bolton Wanderers versus Stoke City match, there was disaster when 33 of the Burnden Park crowd were crushed to death. It could have been worse. 'I think I had a pretty narrow escape and it was because of the kindness of the men,' Audrey Nicholls recalled years later. 'That was typical of the spirit of the times that they were concerned for me, a girl, and they just lifted me up and off I went down. They were marvellous.' On 27 April 1946 the first post-war Cup Final, featuring Charlton Athletic versus Derby County, took place in front of almost 100,000 at Wembley's Empire Stadium. As an occasion it had everything: an intensely emotional singing of 'Abide with Me'; the appearance of King George VI in a grey overcoat ('Blimey, he's been demobbed too,' shouted a spectator through the cheering); Bert Turner managing within a minute to score for both sides; a burst ball (reflecting the prevailing leather shortage); three goals for Derby in extra time as they ran out 4–1 winners; and, in the absence of champagne, ginger beer celebrations in the victorious dressing room.

Almost everyone, it seemed, was hungry for escapism. 'The biggest entertainments boom ever known is now in full swing,' Anthony Heap noted in October 1945 against a background in the shops of an almost completely inadequate supply of goods for people's disposable incomes. 'Anything goes – good, bad or indifferent. Every theatre in the West End is packed out every night and to get reserved seats, one has to book weeks ahead.' A patriotic hit that autumn was *Merrie England*, enjoyed by a thoroughly sensible, suburban, church-going young woman, Erica Ford:

I put on scarlet & black jacket, black skirt, shoes & hat & bag. Went to N. Ealing Station & met Dumbo [an older man, called Harry Bywaters] 5.35. Went to Piccadilly & walked right up Shaftesbury Ave to Prince's Theatre ... Had two stalls. Very bright show & lovely music. Heddle Nash as Raleigh sang 'The English Rose' superbly ...

Went to Princes Restaurant 10.0 & had 4/6 dinner. Soup, plaice & chips & pears. Very nice. Bussed to Piccadilly & train to N. Ealing. Walked up Hanger Lane. Lovely night.

Elsewhere during these immediate post-war months, the dance halls were heaving (cementing the star status of band leaders like Ted Heath and Joe Loss); the country's 4,709 cinemas were almost invariably packed out (attracting in 1946 an all-time peak of 1,635 million admissions); and favourite programmes on the radio continued to draw huge listening figures, above all *ITMA*, the surreal yet warm Tommy Handley comedy vehicle which successfully relocated in peacetime to Tomtopia, a Utopia with Tommy as Governor. Colonel Chinstrap ('I don't mind if I do!') was still going strong, while new characters included Nurse Riff-Rafferty, Big Chief Bigga Banga and his daughter Banjoleo, according to Tommy a 'smashing portion of passion fruit, well worth a second helping'.

Not everyone appreciated these radio days. Mary King, impeccably middle-class but servantless in her Birmingham suburb, grappled one Monday in April 1946 with a particularly big wash load: 'Miss Newton, a young woman about 30 years of age living apart from her husband, had her wireless on in her bedroom with windows wide open (next door) from 9.30 to 2 p.m. All the jazz & what nots – a continual stream. It did not go in rhythm with my mangle, or aching arms ... I heard her mother ask her to shut it off – and her answer made me feel I should like to throw several of my buckets of suds right over her wireless. What a day!!!!' The disapproval, though, could go the other way. The middle-class cinema-going public may have lapped up *Brief Encounter*, but shortly before its official premiere in November 1945 its director, David Lean, had tried it out on a distinctly working-class audience in Rochester, where he was filming *Great Expectations*. The cinema, as Lean soon discovered, was full of sailors from the nearby Chatham dockyards. 'At the first love scene one woman down in the front started to laugh. I'll never forget it. And the second love scene it got worse. And then the audience caught on and waited for her to laugh and they all joined in and it ended in an absolute shambles. They were rolling in the aisles.'[2]

The high cultural mood, accurately reflecting the prevailing sense of fatigue even amid the pleasure-seeking, was one of isolation and retrenchment. A symptomatic episode was the enforced departure in October 1945 of William Glock as music critic of the *Observer* on account of his excessive enthusiasm for the difficult moderns, culminating in an obituary of Bartók which declared that 'no great composer has ever cared how "pleasant" his music sounded'. Two months later an exhibition at the V&A of Picasso and Matisse achieved notoriety. An outraged visitor threatening the paintings with his umbrella had to be forcibly removed; the elderly daughter of William Holman Hunt clapped her hands for silence and announced that the pictures were rubbish; Evelyn Waugh informed *The Times* that Picasso had as little artistic merit as an American crooner; and a columnist on the art magazine *Apollo* not only confessed that 'for me this stuff means precisely nothing' but compared Picasso and Matisse as artistic leaders to 'the more enterprising of the Gadarene Swine'.

Relatively few would have demurred, least of all the upper class, uneasily finding its feet after the war and the trauma of the Labour landslide, and now also unwittingly finding its Boswell – albeit a Boswell with a deeply imbued sense of what could be tastefully printed and what could not. On 7 November the *Tatler* introduced a new column, 'Jennifer Writes Her Social Journal'. 'Jennifer' was the redoubtable Betty Kenward, recently divorced by her Hussars husband and left financially high and dry. In her first entry she gave a detailed account of the wedding at St George's Chapel, Windsor, of Lord Kimberley to Miss Diana Legh, daughter of the Master of the Royal Household. 'The King of the Hellenes was among those present, and Lady Patricia Ramsay was there, as tall and good-looking as ever. Lady Grenfell, who is the bride's step-sister, was wearing a small cap of green cock's feathers, and it was amusing to note how popular feathers have become, ostrich being first in the running . . .' At times it was as if nothing had changed. 'At the fashionable, carefree Carcano–Ednam wedding reception,' the Tory MP, assiduous party-goer and cracking diarist Sir Henry 'Chips' Channon noted in early 1946, 'I remarked to Emerald [Cunard] how quickly London had recovered from the war and how quickly normal life had been resumed. "After all," I said, pointing to the crowded room, "this is what we have been fighting for."'[3]

Life was rather tougher for the men who had done most of the actual fighting. More than four million British servicemen were demobilised (too slowly, according to many) between June 1945 and January 1947, and probably for most the transition from war to peace was far from easy. Advice or support was not always available (partly because of the war in the Far East having ended so precipitately), previous jobs were often no longer open, the returnees were seldom treated as heroes by a deeply war-weary society, and the prosaic realities of peace frequently came to seem less attractive than the relative glamour (and male bonding) of war. 'Thoughts and plans begin to turn inwards in an unhealthy manner,' warned the *British Legion Journal*. 'This can lead to all sorts of pitfalls, not the least of which is self-pity, and should be shunned like early-morning PT.' The strains on marriages were severe. A couple might not have seen each other for several years; he expected to return to his familiar position as the undisputed head; she had become more independent (often working in a factory as well as running the home) – the possibilities for tension and strife, even when both were emotionally committed to each other, were endless. Inevitably, the number of divorces (in England and Wales) rose sharply: from 12,314 in 1944 (itself almost a doubling of the 1939 figure) to 60,190 by 1947.

Even if a marriage held together, as the great majority did, the experience for the children of a stranger's return home could be deeply bewildering and even damaging. 'I did not like this tall, weird, cold man,' Wendy Reeves remembered about the return of her POW father: 'After such a close relationship with my lovely warm, kindly grandad and uncle Colin, whom I worshipped, as they adored me. Of course, I did not understand at the time – but it became clearer as I became older – that Dad had become quite mentally unbalanced by his incarceration. He used to sleep in a separate room from Mum, was unkind to me – I received the first smack I had ever known, from him – and I became frightened of him.' It was little better in the case of

Brenda Bajak's father, a regimental sergeant major during the war:

> He was a total stranger to me and I didn't like him! He was moody
> and very demanding. He ordered us about as though he was still in the
> Army. He and my mother argued a lot and I wasn't used to grown-ups
> arguing. He had *no* idea how to behave with daughters. He shouted a
> lot and insisted things were done immediately. He told us little of his
> war. His moods were dreadful – he was great when out at work or with
> other people, but dreadful at home. He never participated in a 'family'
> life. He just worked and slept. My mother did everything for him and
> was the 'peacemaker'.[4]

Many such discordant stories were played out in these immediate post-
war years – the malign, destabilising legacy of a just conflict.

————————

Was the woman's place still, as it had been before the contingencies of
war, in the home? A sharp if short-lived anxiety about Britain's apparently
declining population proved a key 'pro-natalist' weapon for the home-
and-hearthists, even persuading two well-known progressives, Margaret
Bondfield and Eva Hubback, to argue publicly in November 1945 that
'domestic work in a modern home will be a career for educated women'.
Coming from a different standpoint, the psychiatrist John Bowlby
published in 1946 his first major work, *Forty-four Juvenile Thieves*,
which found that the one common denominator in a group of adolescent
London criminals was prolonged separation from their mothers. Also
in 1946, the eminent paediatrician James Spence gave a well-publicised
lecture entitled 'The Purpose of the Family' in which he emphasised the
welfare of children, argued that the benign family unit had come under
unprecedented pressure during the war, and insisted that only through
preserving the art of motherhood could the family be saved.

Unsurprisingly, women's magazines seldom deviated from
upholding the domestic status quo ante. 'If men and women fail to
take their traditional positions in the dance of life,' declared the *Lady*
in January 1946, 'only a greater dullness is achieved.' Soon afterwards,
a fictional heroine in *My Weekly* put it succinctly: 'I've spent a week
discovering I'd rather be Mrs Peter Grant, housewife, than Rosamund

Fuller, dress designer.' On the flickering screen, the message of *Brief Encounter* (set in the winter of 1938–9) was similar. 'It all started on an ordinary day in the most ordinary place in the world – the refreshment room at Milford Junction,' begins Laura's voiceover. 'I was having a cup of tea and reading a book that I got that morning from Boots. My train wasn't due for 10 minutes. I looked up and saw a man come in from the platform. He had on an ordinary mac, his hat was turned down . . .' But in the end she does not have an affair and returns to her dull husband: a vindication of restraint, domesticity and pre-war values.

By September 1946 the number of married women at work (including part-time) was, from a wartime peak of more than 7.2 million, down to 5.8 million – a total that no longer included Judy Haines in Chingford. Some seven months after gratefully leaving her London office job, she spent a peaceful but potentially disturbing evening with her husband on the first Sunday in March 1946:

Had Welsh Rarebit for tea. I must go to the Gas Company about the grill, the irons of which are missing, making it unusable. Welsh Rarebit isn't the same untoasted. Abbé washed up and I dried; we each read some chapters of 'The Outnumbered' and then listened to our serial, 'Jane Eyre'. I prepared our supper (cocoa and cakes) and put hot water bottles in bed while the news was on, to be in time for the speech by the Prime Minister, Mr Attlee. He was calling us all, especially women and the older people, to do a job of work [as] well. He added that he wasn't asking anyone to overwork. Oh dear! I don't want to go out working again. At the end of the speech Abbé said I had a job of work at home, and I was very happy. And I do do my own washing and make do and mend, which is all a help. I think Abbé deserves to be well looked after and a woman can't do this and go to work as well. If she does get through both jobs she cannot be much of a companion.

The nation's husbands agreed with Abbé. 'Am just beginning to appreciate some of the advantages that help to off-set the financial loss entailed by M's [ie his wife Marjorie's] change over from office work to house-wifery,' reflected Anthony Heap barely a fortnight later. These advantages included 'being able to have *all* my meals at home instead of going up to Mother's for breakfast and round to the British

Restaurant for lunch', as well as 'no longer having to do any housework, such as washing, wiping-up, sweeping, dusting, firelighting etc, etc'. In short, 'one certainly has a more comfortable time of it with a bustling wife around the house'. Or, as 'a solid trade unionist leader' in the north-east put it to the writer James Lansdale Hodson later in the year, 'Men hate their girls going out to work and impairing their own dignity as head o' the house.'[5]

Three women had contrasting destinies. Alison Readman (born 1922), daughter of a colonel of the Scots Greys, read PPE at Oxford before proving so efficient as R. B. McCallum's research assistant in his study of the 1945 general election that she finished up as co-author. Although their work was published in 1947 and immediately hailed as Britain's first book of psephology, that same year she married a White-hall civil servant and turned down an Oxford fellowship, believing that it would be incompatible with her future role of wife and mother. The first of five children was born in 1949, and in later years, in the words of her 2003 obituary, 'she worked on a book that was to combine a study of moral philosophy and contemporary ethics, but prolonged bouts of ill-health meant that it never came to fruition'. Margery Hurst (born 1913) chose another route. In 1946, with a £50 loan, a small room in Brook Street and a battered portable typewriter, she founded Brook Street Bureau of Mayfair Ltd, which soon became the Brook Street Bureau – by the 1960s a chain across three continents that was almost synonymous with the supply of secretaries and 'temps'. Marriage in 1948 and two daughters were successfully taken in her stride; a generally admiring obituarist in 1989, only a year after she stepped down as chairman of the plc, conceded that she could be 'infuriating, domineering, self-willed and insensitive to the effect that she had on others'; while as for her disinclination to stand up vocally for women's rights, at a time when the business world was almost wholly dominated by men, she would simply say, 'I can do more just by being me and letting it be seen what women can do.' For Judy Fryd (born 1909), the personal *was* the political. She married in 1936 and had four children, the first of whom had serious learning difficulties. Fryd encountered such problems and prejudice that in 1946 she was instrumental in founding the Association of Parents of Backward Children, from 1950 called the National Society for Mentally Handicapped Children, and now the Royal Society for Mentally Handicapped Children and Adults (MENCAP). 'My career was always going to be in politics,' she once remarked. 'I just didn't realise it was the mentally handicapped corner I would be fighting.' An obituarist in 2000 reflected that 'she taught us to help and learn from each other,' adding that 'Judy always reminded me of a cheeky little sparrow.'[6]

Still, even sparrows need nests. 'How I wish we'd a house to go to but still having my "main" piece of furniture will be "the best thing",' Muriel Bowmer, living with relatives in Sheffield, wrote to her soon-to-be-demobbed husband Fred in early October 1945. And a fortnight later, just before the great day, 'according to tonight's news they are going to "start at the bottom", & build houses to rent first – so it looks to me as though that dream of ours regarding "buying" is going to do a fade out. Perhaps it's as well we've got our name down at the Town Hall therefore.' Barbara Pym would have sympathised. 'Hilary [her sister] and I have taken a flat – in Pimlico, not a very good district, but perhaps we shall raise the tone,' the as yet unpublished novelist told a friend in November. 'It is on the corner of Warwick Square and really quite nice. Anyway we are so lucky to get anywhere at all, as it is practically impossible to get flats and you really can't choose at all.' Soon afterwards, Mollie Panter-Downes, another novelist but also the sender of a regular 'Letter from London' to the *The New Yorker*, noted that 'the personal columns of *The Times* are full of pathetic house-hunting advertisements inserted by ex-service men – the new displaced persons, who fought for the homes they are now desperately seeking, mostly, alas, without success'.

In March 1946 the housing shortage was just as bad, even in parts of leafy suburbia, as one rehousing officer, George Beardmore, privately recorded:

Two wretched families have moved into one of our requisitioned mansions in Marsh Lane [in Stanmore, Middlesex] and are shortly to receive an injunction to leave. Have twice visited them officially and once unofficially, under pledge of secrecy, to give them some clothes and blankets Jean [his wife] has found for them. A scene of squalor and misery rare even in these days. A bus conductor, two women, and three schoolchildren, driven desperate for somewhere to live, camp out in a large dilapidated room without light, water and (yesterday at least) without fuel for a fire. Sullen and dirty faces swollen with colds, an orange-box scraped dry of all but coal-dust, two saucepans on an unmade bed, a spirit-stove on which bacon was frying, and a green teapot shaped like a racing-car on a strip of newspaper many times ringed.

At about the same time, Glasgow Corporation commissioned a film, to be shown in Glasgow cinemas and called *Progress Report, No 1*, about what its housing department was doing. 'People everywhere are clamouring for houses,' the commentary declared. '94,000 names comprise the waiting list in Glasgow alone. Of these 40,600 are the names of people who are actually houseless. To provide more and more new homes in the shortest possible time is the aim of the Municipal Representative at George Square.'[7] Put another way, the numbers game was – for the best of reasons – now under way.

For a time, an important part of that game involved the construction of temporary homes using prefabricated materials – 'prefabs'. Churchill in 1944 had promised a programme of half a million new such homes, but in the event only 156,623 of these temporary bunga-lows – each with a similar two-bedroom layout and mainly occupied by young couples – were built between 1945 and 1949. 'You know we were offered the choice of a prefab?' a youngish working-class woman was overheard remarking to her female friend at the Modern Homes Exhibition at Dorland Hall in London in March 1946. 'Well, I wouldn't have it. They're nice inside but they look dreadful from the road. You don't like to feel ashamed every time you get near your own home.' The friend agreed: 'Those prefabs are awful – when you see a lot together they look like pigsties or hen-houses, I always think.'

Architects and other commentators were similarly dismissive – 'fungus-like outcroppings of those tin huts called "pre-fabs"' was how one saw them – but all the evidence is that those who lived in them were highly appreciative of having a fitted bath, constant hot water and a built-in refrigerator. 'I think everyone really felt they liked being in the prefabs,' one 1946 investigator, Peter Hunot, found after talking to almost thirty of the families in Clarence Crescent, a London County Council (LCC) run estate of prefabs in Wandsworth. No one wanted to live in a flat, 'many expressing a dislike of them', while 'hours and days had been spent on many of the gardens', with each prefab (as with prefabs generally) having one. Perhaps inevitably, Hunot's overall worry was that 'this contentment seemed to be individualist', though on hearing one man say that he had been among other people in the army for five years and was now glad to be on his own for a bit, the Hampstead-dwelling investigator 'felt sympathetic and not so certain that the lack of community was a fatal deficiency'.[8]

But of course, one word above all characterised life in immediate post-war Britain: austerity. Less than a fortnight after VJ Day, Panter-Downes outlined the grim implications of 'the sudden termination by the United States of Lend-Lease', the financial support that had got Britain through the war:

> The factories, which people hoped would soon be changing over to the production of goods for the shabby, short-of-everything home consumers are instead to produce goods for export. The Government will have to face up to the job of convincing the country that controls and hardships are as necessarily a part of a bankrupt peace as they were of a desperate war. Every inch of useable English soil will still have to be made to grow food. People are suddenly realising that in the enormous economic blitz that has just begun, their problems may be as serious as the blitz they so recently scraped through.

Writing to her absent Fred at about the same time, Muriel Bowmer in Sheffield was already sounding a somewhat pessimistic note:

> Everybody here aren't very thrilled by the news of the latest rationing hit, & also by the prospects of still more tightened belts. We did think that once Japan was beaten we should do away with queues, but it doesn't seem like it. Yesterday I queued 1/2 hour in Woolworths for some biscuits – & I was under cover. The fish problem seems to be a bit better here – it isn't quite so rotten although the queues are there still. As for me, I'm O.K. for coupons, as it happens, & well stocked for clothes also – so I shan't bother with much new this winter. I shall perhaps get a frock, & a new hat – I don't know yet. However once the new fashions start coming in there will be a new style of things I think ...

Over the next few months there began to grow a pervasive sense of disenchantment that the fruits of peace were proving so unbountiful. 'No sooner did we awake from the six years nightmare of war and feel free to enjoy life once more, than the means to do so immediately became even scantier than they had been during the war,' Anthony Heap reflected in his end-of-1945 review. 'Housing, food, clothing, fuel, beer, tobacco – all the ordinary comforts of life that we'd taken for granted before the war and naturally expected to become more plentiful again when it ended, became instead more and more scarce and difficult to come by.' He concluded, 'I can remember few years I've been happier to see the end of.'[9]

In terms of everyday shortages, the greatest concern – and source of potential flashpoints – was undoubtedly food. This was clear as early as October 1945, when an unofficial dock strike, lasting several weeks, proved signally unpopular. 'Dock Strike Threatens Rations' warned the front-page headline of the strongly anti-Labour *Daily Express* (the most widely read daily paper) just as the Ministry of Food was about to announce that if the strike continued it might become impossible to distribute the full bacon ration. 'Meat And Eggs May Be Off Next Week' warned Beaverbrook's crusader a few days later, by which time Mass-Observation was conducting a series of interviews in Chelsea (then rather more downmarket) and Battersea. Both men and women were predominantly critical of the dockers, but whereas men tended to look at the political aspect, including the damage being done to the Labour government, women concentrated firmly on the food situation:

> The rations are bare enough as it is, without having to do without the bacon . . . They should be satisfied with the wages and appreciate the fact that they're able to work without the Fly-bombs around.
>
> It's very selfish, I should say, making everybody suffer, instead of waiting a bit longer . . . It's the food is going to be the worry; it's disgusting when we're so short of everything.
>
> I think it's very unfair – all the food going to waste. It's not right at all.

All those three (aged between 35 and 50) were working-class; but a more middle-class woman of 30 did not disagree: 'I think it's simply disgusting, stabbing the whole community in the back, just at this moment too when everything is so difficult; food's so short. The one way to stop it would be to take away their ration books!'

The strike was eventually called off in early November, but the grumbling about food was unabated. 'I had to hunt for bread,' Gladys Langford in her north London hotel noted on Saturday the 3rd. 'After mid day it seems well nigh impossible to get a loaf. Wandered around Seven Dials, also thro' Chapel St. market where I saw two raddled old hags telling fortunes and a queue of working-class women waiting to consult each one of them.' Five days later, another hotel resident, Henry St John in Bristol, went by train to Minehead and found that 'a small sandwich which had a smear of sardine inside it cost me 3d at Taunton station.' And the next day, in Birmingham, Mary King managed to get near to the car of the visiting King and Queen: 'She looked a little too matronly for her age. Considering the rationing of the people she certainly looked well fed.' In the House of Commons, meanwhile, the only meat on the menu was whale or seal steak – 'both disgusting', according to one new Labour MP, Aidan Crawley – while even a 'white tie and tails' banquet could disappoint. 'Of course the meal was terrible,' noted Raymond Streat in the New Year, down from Manchester for the *News Chronicle*'s big centenary beano at Dorchester House. 'A speck of hot lobster: an impossibly tough and exceedingly small leg of chicken: a tiny bit of not very sweet, sweet and a cup of coffee.'[10]

It is unlikely, though, that Streat or any of the other 424 guests often did the household shopping. Judy Haines did, and the third Tuesday of 1946 was probably no worse than most days:

Got ahead with ironing and then felt I must go in quest of meat as that little chop left over from our Sunday joint will not make a very nourishing Shepherd's Pie. Dyson's very empty. I enquired tenderly if the van had called and they informed me 'no' and there should be some rabbits. I have had my hopes raised like this before, falsely. But I went home out of the cold, made myself a cup of cocoa and when half way through it saw the van. Hastily finished my drink and set off again. Yes, there were some rabbits but they weren't ready just yet. O.K. I'll come back again. Met Mother H. [her mother-in-law] who told me List's had some nice

Mince Tarts. I hardly liked leaving Dyson's, but she said she would wait
there, which seemed a help though Dyson's would only let their
registered customers have rabbits. Wondered if all the tarts would be
gone, but I was lucky, and this will make a nice sweet with some custard.
No sign of rabbits, so I went into the Post Office to draw my allowance,
cash money order and buy National Savings Stamps. Crowds in there
but I thought Dyson's couldn't sell out of rabbits very quickly. When
I returned to the shop there was a queue and only about three rabbits
visible. However, I waited and more came up. I was lucky.

'This shopping!' she added. 'All housewives are fed up to the eyebrows
with it.'

Austerity took a new twist on 5 February when the Minister of
Food, Sir Ben Smith, announced cuts in the bacon, poultry and egg
rations – the last cut made much worse by the simultaneous decision
to end the importing of dried eggs. The next few weeks saw a housewives' revolt, fuelled but not initiated by the anti-government press
and at its liveliest in the middle-class parts of Liverpool. Smith
eventually agreed to reintroduce dried eggs into the shops, but by then
the episode had given a major fresh impetus to the British Housewives'
League. In mid-March the appreciably more serious food shortage on
much of the Continent prompted Mass-Observation to ask a cluster
of working-class people, again in Chelsea and Battersea, 'How do you
feel about giving up some of your food for Europe?' The replies of
four men, followed by five women, were fairly typical:

No. I don't think we could do it at present, we're about down to rock
bottom.

I'd be against it, myself. It's Germany's turn to go without.

If it came to it, I suppose I'd do it as willingly as the next. But not
to help Germany – only the countries that's been overrun. I wouldn't
care what happened to the Germans – they've asked for it.

No, I definitely wouldn't – I think it's up to America – when you
read in the papers about what they eat – and it was just the same
when they were over here – they're the biggest gluttons in the world
now.

I wouldn't go short on half a loaf to benefit Germany.

Yes. Provided we still get something for every meal.

No, definitely not – if they were in our position they wouldn't help us, so why should we help them?

I think the Germans *ought* to go short, after all they've done.

I suppose we'd do it if we had to. I hope it won't come to that.

There was the occasional silver lining. The day after those interviews, on the 13th, Marian Raynham – middle-aged, living in Surbiton, mother of two – recorded a long-awaited moment: 'Bananas. Yes, bananas!! The first for 6 yrs. They are Robin's [her son's] really, as they are only allowed for under 18's . . . Robin says the boys are bringing the peel to school & putting it down for others to slip on. The monkeys.' Two days later, 'Robin came in to room with banana & wanted to know which end to start peeling it from!! . . . We told him from stem end, & later I wondered if that was right.' In early April things got even better: 'The milkman brought mustard, semolina, & sultanas *asking* if I wanted them!! "Do you want" not "you can't have"! War *is* over.'[11]

But overall, the food situation was becoming a source of considerable and understandable discontent. An authoritative British Medical Association report in the late 1940s, based on studies between 1941 and 1948 about the availability of food for a family comprising a husband, wife and three children suggests a significant deterioration:

Throughout the war the 'housewife' of the 'standard' family would have had little difficulty in obtaining the 'human needs' diet . . . The picture changed somewhat in Spring 1946, for although the diet could still be obtained without much difficulty, the shortage of fats made it difficult for adults to obtain a sufficient calorie intake without considerable strain on the digestion, this being the cause of the 'recurrent complaints' that 'people have not enough to eat' . . .

After the end of the war the difficulties facing housewives in obtaining a sufficient and appetising diet for their families were increased, owing not so much to an actual shortage of food as to an insufficiency of the more palatable foods. Those especially affected were families who could not afford to spend much on food.

There was also an increasing concern about bread – in terms not only of quality (Panter-Downes referred in early March to the recent 'reversion to the darker, more nutritious, but obstinately disliked loaf') but also of quantity, given that bread had never been rationed at any point during the war. The war itself was still sufficiently recent for the principle of food rationing in general to be widely accepted – fair shares, etc – but a Gallup poll found that half of the public disapproved of the prospect of bread rationing; accordingly, bread and its waste now became something of a national obsession.

It was an obsession fully shared by Florence Speed. Aged 50 and unmarried, she had at various times worked as a commercial artist and also for her family textile business in the City before it was destroyed in the Blitz, as well as having had two novels published. By 1946 she was living with a sister and brother in a solidly middle-class part of Brixton (59 Vassal Road) and struggling with the twin problems of ill health and genteel poverty. A real writer, albeit in a sometimes indecipherable hand, her diary has a particular vividness:

> 7 April. Took a book into the walled garden at Kennington Park but had only read a couple of pages when a chatty lady came and sat down beside me. 'Disgusting that children are allowed in here. They're so noisy & destroy everything.'
>
> 10 April. A pleasanter day than usual as we [her sister Ethel and herself] spoke to one or two strangers. First as we passed a hotel at Victoria, a girl on the bus. Outside was a van loaded with buns, piled high with crusts cut from sandwich loaves. Ethel exclaimed at the waste & the girl joined in. 'Good crusts, fresh crusts. It's wicked, they should be eaten.'
>
> 11 April. Going thro Kennington Park this morning, I saw three parts of a loaf thrown down under a tree. What sort of mentality have these food wasters?
>
> 26 April. Owing to wheat shortage the 2lb loaf is to be cut to 1¾lbs, but price is to be 4½d just the same![12]

The Ministry of Food seems to have hoped, in a flash of Baldrickian cunning, that people would continue to consume the same number of loaves, even though those loaves were now significantly smaller.

It is not fanciful to argue that within a year of VE Day there had set in not only a widespread sense of disenchantment – with peace, perhaps even with the Labour government – but also a certain sense of malaise, a feeling that society, which broadly speaking had held together during the war, was no longer working so well, was even starting to come apart. To an extent it was an inevitable reaction. 'No one feels well or happy just now,' the novelist Sylvia Townsend Warner, living in Dorset, wrote to a friend in January 1946. 'No one in wartime can quite escape the illusion that when the war ends things will snap back to where they were and that one will be the same age one was when it began, and able to go on from where one left off.' Hauntingly, she added, 'But the temple of Janus has two doors, and the door for war and door for peace are equally marked in plain lettering, No Way Back.' A few weeks earlier, more prosaically, the *Barry Dock News* had identified a mood of 'anti-climax' in the South Wales town and described how Barry, like elsewhere, 'struggles on, a little bit war-weary and depressed, but accepting the situation with stoicism'. Few felt the anti-climax more keenly than Quentin Crisp. 'The horrors of peace were many,' the defiantly open homosexual recalled in *The Naked Civil Servant*. 'Death-made-easy vanished overnight and soon love-made-easy, personified by the American soldiers, also disappeared . . . Even mere friendship grew scarce. Londoners started to regret their indiscriminate expansiveness. People do when some moment of shared danger is past. Emotions that had been displayed had now to be lived down.'[13]

How much of an oppressive cloud, post-Hiroshima, did the atom bomb cast? 'There is no sense of stability,' Dr David Mace of the Marriage Guidance Council observed in a September 1945 analysis of why the war was a key factor in accelerating family disruption and marriage breakdown. 'We are forced to live in the "here and now" because we just do not know about tomorrow. That mood still prevails. The atomic bomb "question mark" means that it is no good planning.' Two months later, after the government had announced that the Civil Defence Services would be merely suspended and should 'keep together', Panter-Downes overheard on a bus 'a seedy cockney matron' talking to a friend: 'It 'asn't 'arf put the wind up people. They can't seem to settle to things, and no wonder. Funny thing, even though I've taken every stitch off me back every night since VE Day, I can't seem to feel easy, either. It's peace, I tell meself, but some'ow it don't feel like peace ought to feel.' Panter-Downes reckoned that this woman 'spoke for most disturbed Londoners', but it is at least equally possible that most Londoners and their fellow-countrymen fairly soon learnt to put to the backs of their minds such cataclysmic thoughts – as people usually do about the great unpalatables.

Almost certainly a bigger source of oppression, on a day-to-day basis, was the unattractive mixture, certainly in peacetime, of not only a ceaseless preoccupation with ration books, vouchers and 'points' but also enforced exposure to frequent displays of petty authority. The writer Rupert Croft-Cooke, demobilised in the spring of 1946 and returning to what was still bombed-out London, was struck by how often he saw 'the feelings of gentle people, of naturally timorous people being trampled on by loud-mouthed bullies, frequently in uniform', such as policemen or public-transport officials or cinema commissionaires. Such behaviour was hardly the result of the new political dispensation but in difficult times could not but stimulate anti-government feelings. Happening in April 1946 to catch *Workers' Playtime* (the radio variety programme that began during the war to boost production in the factories and continued long into peace), Vere Hodgson, a welfare worker in west London and, like many Londoners, much disgusted by the peacetime determination of bus conductors not to allow standing passengers, was 'amazed' by the programme's criticism:

I do not listen very often, so it was all fresh to me. Much at the expense of Aneurin Bevan [the minister responsible for housing as well as health]. One comedian was going to Wales because a house had been built there last year! Then the song that struck me as being very remarkable was one called 'I'd Like To Be A Refugee From Britain'. All in rhyme it was . . . we were under fed and over taxed, and spent our lives in queues, etc, docketed and ticketed. But the most remarkable lines were the end . . . about they say they can do without Churchill, so they can do without me, I *want* to be a refugee from Britain.

'The factory girls,' she added, 'cheered to the echo.'

Crucial to the sense of malaise were the corrosive effects, in peacetime if not in war, of the overriding context of rationing, price controls and production controls. 'It's very easy to spot people who buy things without coupons in Barrow,' reflected Nella Last as early as September 1945. 'They have the Jewish stamp, over decorated & doll eyed bits & pieces of fur & tucks.' Ina Zweiniger-Bargielowska, historian of austerity, makes it abundantly clear that the black market and all its devices – including off-ration and under-the-counter sales as well as tipping and favouritism – were at least as extensive after the war as during it. Food orders, the Minister of Food noted in May 1946, were 'generally being ignored and evaded more flagrantly now than at any time during the war', while soon afterwards his ministry found that a 'substantial section of the agricultural community habitually disregard the Food Orders, adopting the attitude that they are just more regulations to be "got round" – at a profit – and not that such avoidance is fundamentally dishonest and unfair to the whole community', with farmers and dealers in Wales identified as the worst offenders. No doubt some of them had been partly responsible for the scandal that had done much to spoil the first peacetime Christmas (at least in London), with Panter-Downes reporting that 'most butchers refused to pay more than the legal prices for fowl and consequently had nothing but a nice row of empty hooks to show their customers'.[14]

It was about this time, moreover, that the black-market spiv really started to emerge as a well-known type: coat with wide lapels and padded-out shoulders, tight collar on shirt, big knot in tie, hair parted in middle with wave on either side, pencil moustache, he was grudgingly admired, essentially disliked. Yet the fact was that a significant part – perhaps even the majority – of the respectable middle class, and indeed of the respectable working class, simultaneously condemned *and* used the black market, without which they would have been hard pressed to maintain an even barely recognisable quality of life. Some even found themselves succumbing to the temptation of coupon fraud. 'I suspect there's more dishonesty in this country today than for many years,' Hodson reflected in May 1946. 'Rationing, controls of material, very high income tax [9 shillings in the pound], a feeling of despair at the state of the world – all these contribute to it.' Returning servicemen could, in this as other ways, find it particularly difficult. Thomas Hanley, 28 and just married, decided to try his luck in Devon. Half a century later, his memories were still sharp and painful:

I found business, even in a small seaside resort [probably Paignton], was run on chicanery and spivvery. I found that men, some not much older than myself, who had managed either by reason of age or health to miss a call-up, controlled all aspects of public life. In an atmosphere of rationing and shortages, interlopers like myself had a hard time. Helping hands were weighted by self-interest. Even persons of the utmost integrity, after six years of war, were motivated by self-preservation. It wasn't so much of 'dog eat dog', rather to make sure that no opportunity of easing one's existence was missed. I doubt if a single Englishman did not avail himself of the help of the 'black market'. Expedience was the name of the game.

In such a situation, Hanley reflected in retrospect, a returned serviceman's 'main attribute was the stoic acceptance of the inevitable, so much a part of his service life'. His formative years may have been taken from him, but 'at least he was alive'.[15]

There were plenty of other signs, big and small, of a society apparently out of joint. 'The trains are lighted now,' the headmaster Ernest Loftus conceded in October 1945, 'but the lighting is not always good & it is not easy to read unless one is lucky & manages to get a compartment with single lights behind the seats. People are awful vandals & some compartments are in darkness through the bulbs being pilfered – the window straps are also cut off – war disease – little sense of honesty.' That month was the busiest that Scotland Yard had ever known, and shortly before Christmas the Independent MP W. J. Brown considered in his diary the 'vast crime-wave in Britain today':

A most disturbing feature of it is the number of crimes with violence. In an effort to keep the thing within bounds the police have taken to large-scale raids on the public. Without warning they cordon-off a large area and make everyone produce his identity card [introduced during the war]. They take anyone who cannot satisfactorily account for himself to the police station for further enquiries. The first of these raids took place in the West End this last week. Many deserters were picked up and many clues found to gangs of robbers responsible for recent crimes. But it adds a new terror to pleasure-seeking in the West End . . .

It was also reported that one butcher in the pre-Christmas period, having managed by hook or by crook to obtain some turkeys, slept in his shop with a loaded revolver.

The crime wave, especially in the form of burglaries, did not abate in 1946; Panter-Downes that spring spoke for upper-middle if not middle England when she lamented the fact that 'practically nobody has a servant to leave on guard in the kitchen'. She then related the story of how a Chelsea householder had recently come home from the cinema one evening only to find that burglars had visited for the third time and taken his last overcoat, some tinned sardines, a pound of tea and two pots of marmalade. 'These are things,' she hardly needed to add, 'which are painful and grievous to lose nowadays.' The figures are patchy, but it seems that an appreciably higher proportion than usual of these burglaries were committed by juveniles – a fact that subsequent police reports not implausibly attributed to the way in which 'during the war years children have lacked fatherly control and restraint and in a large number of families mothers have obviously tended to allow too much freedom'.[16] What was indisputable was that a moral panic was brewing up nicely.

———

Reassuringly, during the spring and disappointingly poor summer, the old sporting rituals reappeared, apparently unscathed: not only the Cup Final but the Boat Race ('the Prime Minister was there, the swans were out, young men back from the services wore beards, folk picnicked on roofs, ate ice-cream, let off crackers,' noted Hodson), the Grand National (Captain Petre, on leave from the Scots Guards, winning on Lovely Cottage, very much the housewives' choice) and Wimbledon (the British players routed by the French, American and Australian ones). Then there was that traditional highlight of the social calendar, the Eton versus Harrow match at Lord's. 'There were only five tents in the usually close-packed stretch of turf,' reported Panter-Downes, 'and . . . the men looked an extremely shabby bunch. As a parade of the upper crust, valiantly pretending that everything was still the same, the occasion was a little saddening.'

Still, the cricket authorities made a fair show in this first peacetime season of pretending that nothing had changed. Although professionals were at last given their initials on the scorecards at Lord's, they were carefully put after the surname, with the initials for amateurs continuing to precede the surname; while the two classes of cricketer continued for the most part, though no longer invariably, to change in separate dressing rooms. Moreover, of the 17 first-class counties, only one was captained by a professional, Les Berry of Leicestershire. 'There has probably never been a better collection than those who have been appointed for this year,' the *Daily Telegraph*'s new cricket correspondent, E. W. Swanton, declared reassuringly on the season's eve. 'Better in the sense,' he explained, 'of having a truer notion of the essentials of a cricket match, of whatever kind.' Perhaps so, but the year's crop included not only at least three non-bowling amateurs who by no charitable stretch of the imagination were worth their places as batsmen but also Surrey's Nigel Bennett, an undistinguished club cricketer who got the job only through a case of mistaken identity. 'Want of knowledge of county cricket on the field presented an unconquerable hindrance to the satisfactory accomplishment of arduous duties' was the mild but telling verdict on him of *Wisden Cricketers' Almanack*, no friend of the open society.

Large crowds watched the run-stealers flicker to and fro. As usual, the final test (against India) was at The Oval, and on the first day 'rain that fell until one o'clock so affected the ground that it was doubtful if play would have been attempted even at five o'clock but for the crowds of people who waited around the walls from early in the morning'. Elsewhere, the wet summer did not hinder the pursuit of the poor man's opera – March 1947 would prove to be the peak of the post-war Bulge – and indeed 1946 set a new record for venereal infections. There was also the dream of the first proper summer holiday for at least seven years, but for many it remained a dream. In Coventry, when the factories closed in late July, the local paper described 'thousands of people, walking aimlessly through the streets or standing in queues for buses to take them a few miles away for a change from the every-day'. A 60-year-old working-class man, outlining his holiday plans to Mass-Observation at the start of August, was more enterprising or perhaps fortunate: 'We tried everywhere but we couldn't get in – they're so packed. People have booked up months ago, they're all full up. So in the end I told the wife to write to a place we stayed in Margate . . . We're very fond of Margate, it's lively and the air's good and we're going to make day trips to Ramsgate and elsewhere. It'll be a change.' For a 30-year-old more middle-class woman, waiting for her husband to be demobbed, common sense vied with natural yearnings:

> Well, we're going up North to Glasgow. We've gone up there every year for the simple reason it's cheapest and Mum and Dad are always glad to see us, and what with this rationing business and now the bread, well, it's too much bother going anywhere else. Besides think of the money it would cost to have a seaside holiday ... Oh, but I'd give anything to give Johnny a real holiday – one where he could make sand-pies on the beach. He's never been to the seaside ...

The Friday before the August Bank Holiday weekend (still then at the start of the month) saw huge queues for trains out of London, and at Paddington the railway officials for once relented and put up a notice: 'All platform tickets suspended'.[17]

The generally downbeat summer mood was epitomised by the lack of popular enthusiasm ahead of the full-scale Victory Parade in London on Saturday, 8 June. 'Are you going to put out your decorations?' Florence Speed asked a Brixton neighbour on the Thursday. 'No, things are worse,' was the gloomy reply. The same day a couple of Nottingham working-class women gave their reactions. 'I don't know what they want to have another V Day Parade so long after the war [for],' one said. 'People have had enough of it.' The other was even more negative: 'I don't agree with it at all. We haven't got much to celebrate about. The food is bad, the young fellows are still in the Forces – what will those women who have lost their sons in the war think?' On Friday afternoon, joining a queue of about 30 outside a baker's shop in London, a Mass-Observation investigator found the grumbling positively savage. '"I've been queuing ever since eight o'clock this morning, what with one thing and another," says F40D. "I'm about done for. I'd like to take that Attlee and all the rest of them and put them on top of a bonfire in Hyde Park and BURN them." "And I'd 'elp yer," says F65D. "Same 'ere," say several other angry women.'

On the day itself, marred by rain, some six million (by one estimate) assembled to watch the parade. 'The crowds were huge, Joyce, but really *huge*,' the well-bred journalist Virginia Graham assured her friend Joyce Grenfell soon afterwards. 'Most of the people had slept in the streets all night, & been rained upon, but there they were, paper caps & all, fainting like flies, cheering every horse or dog or policeman, as merry as grigs.' Certainly there was pride among the spectators and the many other millions who listened to it on the radio – the latter including Marian Raynham in Surbiton, who wondered 'what other country can make up such a varied performance' and marvelled at 'what organisation to do it' – but for the most part grig-like they were not. A note the following Tuesday by Mass-Observation's invaluable Chelsea-based investigator makes this clear:

> Almost everybody Inv met on the 10th and 11th, whether friends or tradespeople or strangers in shops, were saying loudly how utterly exhausted and washed-out they felt, not only those who had gone to see the procession but those who had stayed at home and merely heard it over the wireless. The remark incessantly repeated, both on Victory Day and afterwards, was: 'Well, it's the last of its kind – I don't suppose we shall ever see another'. Sometimes this was followed by 'The next war'll be short and sweet,' or 'We just won't be there at the finish, next time'.

One or two women did remark that there was still Princess Elizabeth's wedding to look forward to – but that 'it wouldn't be the same because there wouldn't be the troops'.[18]

The Victory Parade had – for relatively few, relatively well-off people – a side benefit. 'Remember me?' asked the announcer Jasmine Bligh on Friday the 7th, as BBC television began post-war broadcasting by showing the same Mickey Mouse cartoon that had been on the small screen when television had ceased in September 1939. That same day, the opening Variety Party featured Peter Waring, star of radio's *Variety Bandbox*. 'I must say, I feel a trifle self-conscious going into the lens of this thing,' ran his rather arch patter. 'But since I'm here I might just as well tell you a little about myself and my hobbies. I have one or two hobbies you know that Sir Stafford [Cripps, the famously austere Labour minister] can't control. No, I thought that now I'm being televised, you might see the jokes quicker.' Next day,

Freddie Grisewood was the main television commentator on the parade, with Richard Dimbleby (who had made his name describing the liberation of Belsen) as second string. 'You will forgive a man for saying that it is only a hat with feathers on it' was his surprisingly flip comment on Princess Elizabeth's elaborate headgear.[19] At this stage there existed only some 20,000 television sets (all pre-war), mainly within 30 miles of Alexandra Palace (from where programmes were transmitted), and as yet not many were inclined to take the new medium seriously as a force for the future.

The muted response to the Victory Parade was the first of three key symbolic events during the summer of 1946. The second was the imposition of bread rationing, announced four weeks in advance on 27 June by the new Minister of Food, the highly cerebral John Strachey. The generally negative reaction, especially on the part of women, was epitomised by a letter to her local paper immediately afterwards by E. Harris of 97 Cedars Avenue, Coventry:

> I am a housewife, and I wish to protest against this last burden which is to be put upon us. We have stood everything else, but this is the last straw. I have two menfolk. I cut up one large loaf every morning for packing, and my son can eat the best part of another for breakfast. How do they think we can live on the ration they are going to give us? Are we housewives to starve ourselves still more to give to those who go to earn our living for us? We give up most of our food to them now, and many of us are at breaking-point.

Over the next few weeks, much of the public protest was channelled through the Housewives' League, a largely middle-class organisation, which by mid-July had presented two petitions (one to the House of Commons, the other to the Ministry of Food), each with some 300,000 signatories. Judy Haines was probably not one of them. With the scheme due to start on Monday the 22nd, her approach was typically robust:

> *19 July.* How bakers are quibbling over bread rationing. I think Strachey is very patient with 'em. First they think it unnecessary (who should know?!), then they want it postponed! As if the Govt. are doing it

for fun! I welcome it. Probably see more cakes, and the ration is generous anyway. People will just be more bread conscious.

20 *July*. Housewives go 'bread crazy'. Shortages or queues everywhere. As if it will keep! Unfortunately I had my hair to rinse and set. Then tried Chingford, Walthamstow and Leyton for bread. Mum was able to buy rolls at Mrs Negus's and let me have half a loaf, which will do beautifully.

She was right. The amount of bread available on the Monday proved more than adequate; while as Grace Golden, a London-based commercial artist, perceptively put it in her diary, 'significant to see the patient tired faces of people queuing at Food Office, most of us too tired & apathetic to resist any stricture'.

Nevertheless, over the next few days not only did bread supplies often run out with dismaying speed, but there was the harrowing, widely publicised story of a girl of 19 who, fearful of a fine if she put six slices of bread in a bin, tried to burn them by pouring petrol over them and in the process burned herself to death. 'How do you feel about bread rationing?' Mass-Observation asked some working-class women in Kilburn and Finsbury Park in mid-August. One of the main reasons for the government's action had been to bring pressure on the Americans to do more to feed Germany, but the replies were unremittingly narrow in focus:

It's been good for us, we've got more points as a result.

Disgusting. If anything it's making people more discontented.

I'm well pleased with it. I haven't used all my bread units and so I get extra points.

Well, I think it's stopped a lot of waste.

It's a damned nuisance more than anything.[20]

Even if the bread ration was adequate, as most acknowledged it was, the very fact of peacetime bread rationing would remain a symbolic sore as long as it remained in force. This was especially so on the part of the middle class, and it was a straw in the wind when in a clutch of by-elections in July, two working-class Labour seats were held with only a small swing to the Tories, but in suburban, middle-class Bexley, captured by Labour in 1945, an 11 per cent swing to the Tories almost cost Labour the seat.

Of course, *everyone* apart from spivs and their suppliers became to a greater or lesser degree fed up with the inescapable reality of continuing rationing, shortages and all the rest of it. But broadly speaking, it does seem that the middle class lost patience more quickly and more conclusively than the rest. Clues lie in Florence Speed's Brixton diary entry about the baker's the day before the Victory Parade:

> Mrs Randall when Mabel [probably a friend or neighbour of Speed] went in for the bread about 10.30 said 'Sold out, & no more today'.
> Mabel replied 'Well I do think you might save a loaf for regular customers'.
> Mrs R. flared up & retorted, 'Don't you talk to me like that' . . .
> Mrs R. looked sick when Ethel [Speed's sister] went & paid the bill & said she wanted no more.
> 'I think you've treated me badly!' she told us. Treated *her*!!
> We've dealt at no other shop for 35 years despite change of ownership, & as Ethel said, 'It's like begging for your bread. We've never had to do that.'

A week later, forsaking Brixton, the two sisters observed the black market in something like close-up:

> While queuing in Regent Street, we watched a hawker with a barrow amply laden with peaches at 1/6d. In about 20 minutes he sold 25/6d worth. A boy with a whip, from a van, not more than 14 or 15, bought two & promptly ate them crossing the road back to his van. It is the most unlikely people who have the money! . . .
> Peaches imported from France are very plentiful, but much too costly for most people.

Gladys Langford was similarly struggling to hold her own in what felt like an increasingly alien, unfriendly world. On a Monday in August, mercifully on holiday from her miserable schoolteaching, she spent a day in the West End:

In D.H. Evans hordes of highly perfumed and under-washed women thronged the departments. Assistants ignored my presence – the only one I questioned announced she was not a saleswoman – so I walked out . . . No queues for ice-wafers and cornets since typhoid has been traced to ice-cream. By Piccadilly Tube Station – outside the Pavilion – a woman about my age was playing a piano-accordion. She was plastered with rouge and powder, wore a smart black costume and black peaked cap and a scarlet scarf was knotted about her neck. Another woman, also a beggar, one-legged and grimy, sat slicing a large peach!

Then came the poignant pay-off: '*I* cannot afford anything more tooth-some than plums at 4½d lb.'[21]

Two contrasting novels explored the middle-class predicament during these attritional times. *One Fine Day* (1947) by Mollie Panter-Downes was written during the spring and early summer of 1946 and set contemporaneously in a quiet part of the Surrey countryside. Laura and Stephen are learning to make do without domestic servants, a sympathetically depicted struggle in difficult circumstances, and contemplate selling up and moving somewhere smaller and more manageable. Revelation comes to the husband, the inevitable 'something in the City', in the penultimate chapter:

No, damnit, he thought, let's hold on a little longer and see if things improve. And it suddenly struck him as preposterous how dependent he and his class had been on the anonymous caps and aprons who lived out of sight and worked the strings. All his life he had expected to find doors opened if he rang, to wake up to the soft rattle of curtain rings being drawn back, to find the fires bright and the coffee smoking hot every morning as though household spirits had been working while he slept. And now the strings had been dropped, they all lay helpless as abandoned marionettes with nobody to twitch them.

There was no such mellowness in Angela Thirkell's *Private Enterprise* (1947), explicitly set in 1946, in this case among the minor gentry of 'Barsetshire'. Dissatisfaction with the present state of affairs ran through the whole novel, but it was bread rationing that really got Thirkell going:

> In addition to pages in the ration book called 'Do Not Fill In Anything In This Space', and 'Points' and 'Personal Points', and 'Do Not Write On This Counterfoil Unless Instructed', and large capital T's and K's and little things called Panels whose use nobody knew, and a thing called Grid General which meant absolutely nothing at all, the harrassed and overworked housewife was now faced with large capital L's and M's and small capital G's, each of which, so she gathered from the bleating of the wireless if she had time to listen, or the Sunday paper which she hadn't time to read, meant so many B.U.s. And what B.U.s were, nobody knew or cared, except that B seemed an eminently suitable adjective for whatever they were . . .

All in all, Thirkell shrilled on, there was after a year of so-called peace 'a great increase of boredom and crossness, which made people wonder what use it had been to stand alone against the Powers of Darkness if the reward was to be increasing discomfort and a vast army of half-baked bureaucrats stifling all freedom and ease, while some of the higher clergy preached on Mr Noël Coward's text of 'Don't let's be beastly to the Germans", only they meant it and he didn't'. Tellingly, Thirkell's hatred of what she saw as the destruction of old England struck a deep chord, and in the immediate post-war years her Barsetshire sequence of novels (begun in the 1930s) sold prodigiously. 'A clever though reliably conventional school friend rebuked me for never having heard of Angela Thirkell,' the future novelist David Pryce-Jones would recall of this time. '"At home we think she's the best living author. Everyone reads her." Home was in Camberley.'[22]

Yet even a Labour-supporting, mass-circulation paper like the *Sunday Pictorial*, in effect the Sunday version of the *Daily Mirror*, conceded that things were pretty grim when in July 1946 it launched its panel of '100 Families to speak for Britain' and give free rein to their many problems. 'I can't get shoes for my kiddies,' complained Eileen Lewis, a printer's wife of 246 Watford Road, Croxley Green. 'A couple of weeks ago I spent all day trying to buy two pairs of

shoes. I must have called at twenty shops.' Generally the women volun-
teers on the panel complained about food rations, while the men (more
than a third of whom smoked 100 or more cigarettes a week) were
especially put out by being unable to buy a new suit. The paper, though,
had no doubt about the headline story: '43 Families Out Of 100 Are
Wanting A New Home'. And it was the continuing housing shortage
that precipitated the third key episode that summer: the squatting
movement.

It began with the mass occupation of disused service camps – eventually
involving as many as 40,000 people in more than a thousand camps –
but really attracted attention when families, either homeless or living in
appalling lodgings, started occupying empty hotels and mansion blocks
in central London, most notably the seven-storey Duchess of Bedford
House just off Kensington High Street. Eventually, by late September,
eviction and a certain amount of rehousing had taken place. Although
they had been helped by the organisational skills of members of the
Communist Party, there is no evidence that the bulk of the squatters in
Kensington, and probably elsewhere, had any political motives other
than wanting somewhere decent to live. An observer, Diana Murray
Hill, asked one squatter what sort of house she would prefer if given
the choice. 'A prefab,' she replied. 'They look so neat and you can keep
them nice. With a garden in front and your own bath. Then you could
have the key to your own door and come in and go out as you liked.'

Arguably, though, the real significance of the episode was not the
additional spotlight it put on the housing question, with its accompanying embarrassment to the government, but rather the distinctly
mixed response of the public at large – partly in the context of most
of the press vigorously insisting that, whatever the human predicament
of the squatters, such flagrant breaking of the law was liable to open 'the
floodgates of anarchy' (as W. J. Brown put it in the *Evening Standard*).
On the day the Duchess of Bedford squatters departed, Murray Hill
listened to a young woman, apparently employed as a domestic at a
neighbouring block of luxury flats, chatting with a middle-aged friend:

Well, really, how anyone has the face to behave in such a silly way beats
me!
   Ridiculous, isn't it!

I wouldn't do a thing like that; not unless the Government told me to!

Well, I mean, just look at the Types!

Yes, it's only types like that'd do a thing like that. Some lovely kiddies though.

Poor little souls, fancy bringing your kids along to a place where there's no food! No electricity or anything! Poor little souls must be starving!

It's ridiculous! Why, these flats aren't fit to live in – they're in an awful state! They've got to have a lot done to them before they're fit to live in.

It's not as though doing a thing like this helps them at all, it only makes things worse in the end . . .

That's right. They should learn to be *patient* and *wait*.[23]

Being patient, waiting your turn, behaving with restraint, respecting the law: even in the difficult, disturbed conditions immediately following six years of war, these remained formidable codes to break.

The squatters were still in situ when on 16 September the Wilfred Pickles quiz show *Have a Go!* was broadcast nationally for the first time, radio's first real vehicle for ordinary working-class voices to be heard. Ten days later, the new series of *ITMA* began, soon introducing an all too expressive character, Mona Lott ('it's being so cheerful as keeps me going'), while on 7 October there was the debut of *Woman's Hour*, scheduled for 2.00 on the grounds that that was when women were doing the washing-up and thus had plenty of time to listen. For almost its first three months it was presented by a man, the journalist Alan Ivimey, and the opening of the edition on 7 November gives a flavour of its tone and contents:

Ivimey: Good afternoon. I have three ladies round the table to keep me in order today – Edith Saunders, who has been to a fascinating exhibition of Second Empire Styles at a big West End store –

Saunders: Good afternoon.

Ivimey: Marion Cutler, who's been looking into the working of that splendid service to housewives and mothers begun during the war, the Home Help scheme –

Cutler: Good afternoon.

Ivimey: And Marguerite Patten, who wants to save some of those tea-time tragedies when the lovely cake you've baked comes out of the oven with a hole in the middle instead of a nice brown bulge . . .

Four days later, the *Daily Mirror* condemned the programme as 'uninteresting, waste of time, full of old ideas', but the very next day Judy Haines was more charitable: 'Washing already damp and ironing quickly done. "Woman's Hour" does improve.' Soon afterwards, 61 members of the BBC's London Listening Panel attended meetings at the Aeolian Hall and were asked to evaluate extracts by different football commentators. Among them was one Wolstenholme, presumably Kenneth, but he fared poorly, with negative ratings for 'skill in giving a picture of play' and 'knowledgeability of soccer'.[24]

A new arrival this autumn was Franklin Birkinshaw (the future Fay Weldon), whose voyage from New Zealand ended as both dawn and her 15th birthday broke. 'Was this my mother's promised land?' she asked herself:

Where were the green fields, rippling brooks and church towers? Could this be the land of Strawberry Fair and sweet nightingales? Here was a grey harbour and a grey hillside, shrouded in a kind of murky, badly woven cloth, which as the day grew lighter proved to be a mass of tiny, dirty houses pressed up against one another, with holes gaping where bombs had fallen, as ragged as holes in the heels of lisle stockings. I could not believe that people actually chose to live like this.

'It's just Tilbury,' my mother said. 'It's always like this.'

Just Tilbury? The greyness was so vast, as far as the eye could reach.

About this time, Mass-Observation's Tom Harrisson returned from a lengthy spell in Borneo and was struck by 'the lack of dynamic enthusiasms, the apathetic mood of the moment, the decline in laughter'. There were moments of uplift – the Britain Can Make It (cruelly dubbed 'Britain Can't Have It') exhibition of industrial design at the V&A attracted one and a half million visitors, the 300,000 waiting list for private telephones started to come down ('I only want a footman and a large income to complete the picture,' observed a delighted Vere

Hodgson after getting hers), and the first British-made, American-style nylon stockings went on sale, albeit in tantalisingly small quantities. But overall Florence Speed's experience, lunching one Thursday with her sister at Fleming's in Oxford Street, was about par for the course. The fish, supposed to be plaice, was 'a horrible piece of fin' and the price of 2s 6d was exorbitant; altogether, she reflected, 'old Mr Fleming who took pride in quality & service must turn in his grave at the deterioration.'

It was also by December 1946 getting ominously chilly. 'Mr Thomson in particular is "blue" – says he is too cold to sleep altho' he has four blankets, an eiderdown, a travelling-rug and a great-coat on his bed,' Gladys Langford in her north London hotel was writing by the 8th of a fellow-resident. 'He has been buying socks at 3/6 per pair at WOOLWORTH'S!! Not the kind of place you expect the director of a big firm to use as a shopping centre.' It was not a great time to be having one's first baby. 'Sick,' scribbled an understandably frazzled Judy Haines in St Margaret's Hospital, Epping, on the 19th, two days before the birth. 'Had a bad night with Sister Hilton nagging me the whole time. I had pains every few minutes and she said I was all right till *she* came on. She told me to forget myself and think of babe and termed me neurotic. Said I was disturbing the patients who had *had* their babies.'[25]

Another rather cheerless Christmas was approaching. 'Prefab houses in Lottman Road have already hung up their Christmas decorations (paper chains, etc),' sniffed Speed in Brixton as early as 5 December. 'Anything less gala in appearance than the houses themselves couldn't be imagined.' Three days later, Henry St John in Bristol went to Sunday evensong, not a habitual occurrence, and found he was one of only 16 people in the congregation, that church's lowest figure in its 90 years of existence. 'Are we a pagan country?' asked James Lansdale Hodson on the 13th. 'Few of my friends go to church. I read in the report of an Archbishop's Committee on the Use of Modern Agencies for Evangelistic Propaganda that 90 per cent of our people seldom or never attend church. The church each week has five million attendances; the cinemas have 40 million.'

About this time, Mass-Observation conducted a survey of 500 residents of a semi-suburban London borough, 'Metrop', most probably Fulham; three-fifths of the sample did not belong to any sort of organisation, and predictably their favourite unorganised activities were the cinema and pub. The investigation, published as *Puzzled People*, found that two-thirds of men and four-fifths of women believed, 'or believed more or less', in the existence of a God. 'Yes, I think there is a God,' said a 20-year-old girl, 'but He seems a bit preoccupied at the moment.' Only 61 per cent of those believing in God also believed in the divinity of Christ; paradoxically, 25 per cent of those *not* believing in God *did* believe in the divinity of Christ. Only one person in 10 in Metrop went to church 'fairly regularly', and congregations had roughly three women to one man, with the women being mainly old and mainly educated. The survey threw up 'frequent' criticism of institutional religion and those who practised it, with double standards a favourite target:

> A lot of bloody hypocrisy, if you ask me. Go to church and then tear your neighbour's character to tatters, that's all it is. There's worse people goes to church than stays at home, I can tell you that.
>
> Going off to church on Sundays and bowing and scraping to others that does the same.
>
> Oh, the parsons and the churchgoing and all the setting yourself up to be better than ordinary folk.

But when asked their attitude towards religion as such, most people were tolerant enough, if hardly enthusiastic. As two women and a man replied:

> I dunno, I've not got any attitude, because I've not got any interest.
>
> It's all right for them as has time and inclination.
>
> Doesn't touch me much – it's all right for women, especially when they're getting on a bit – but I don't think I need it just yet, thanks.

A 40-year-old man captured the prevailing view – low-level tolerance of what was essentially an irrelevance – exactly: 'I think it's all right in a way, provided it's not overdone.'[26]

Ferdynand Zweig may or may not have visited Metrop, but between August 1946 and February 1947 he immersed himself in London's working-class districts and interviewed some 350 working men – interviews that this Polish-born economist (before the war a professor at Cracow University) conducted in pubs, cafés, parks, dog-racing stadiums or wherever he could get his subjects to talk freely. The inquiry began as a study of spending habits and poverty but rapidly broadened into a portrait of the English working class, that flesh-and-blood fodder for so many ambitious post-war plans. 'A working man is a great realist,' Zweig found in his eventual book:

> He sees life as it is – as a constant struggle, with its ups and downs. He has no illusions about life. He is little influenced by books or literature, and is more genuine and natural than people coming from other classes.
>
> If you ask working men about their views on life, in a large majority of cases you will get the invariable answer: 'Life is what you make it.' This English proverb is ingrained in every working man's brain. It is astonishing how many times they express this as their philosophy of life.
>
> The same meaning is conveyed by answers like this: 'I take life as it comes,' or 'I try to make the best of it' . . .
>
> The other view which is most common is to regard life as flux, and reality as a system of change. What is today is not decisive, and might change tomorrow. Tomorrow the lucky hour might strike or the conditions might improve.
>
> But the worker does not think about the future in the way of making provisions for it or worrying about what will happen next.

Zweig also found 'no class hatred or envy or jealousy'; an attitude to money defined in terms of 'beer, smokes and food'; and a far greater interest in sport than politics. 'What the working man dislikes most is preaching, moralising and edification,' he discovered. 'He has "no time for that", as he would say.'

The book includes a rich array of case histories. There is the blacksmith in a transport-maintenance shop whose wife is still suffering mentally from the Blitz and who knows, despite working incredibly long hours, that 'he has a bad time in front of him and needs all his will-power to get through'; the small-time decorator, divorced and living alone in a furnished suburban room, who goes each evening to the pub ('drinking six or seven pints') for want of anywhere else, chain-smokes and 'has no set purpose in life – he just drifts along'; the Irish building labourer who 'dislikes responsibility' and has stayed unmarried, 'goes in for football pools and lays out 5s or 7s 6d a week but has never won anything', and is happiest playing darts in the pub; the paper-picker-up in one of London's public parks who is paid so little that he tells Zweig frankly, 'I wish I were dead, because I have nothing to live for – I have no recreation, and can't even afford a glass of beer – you have no friends if you have no money'; the 'under-nourished' sandwich-board man who makes 'half an ounce of tobacco for cigarettes last him about four days'; the road-sweeper who has only been on holiday once in his life and insists, 'If a working man can't have a smoke and a drink, he might as well be dead'; the Red Line bus conductor who rolls his own cigarettes, who is fond of gardening and whose main complaint is that since the war 'the speed of the buses is greater, with greater stress on the body, so that you require more rest'; and so on.

Altogether, the seven months of intensive fieldwork proved (as he explained in his introduction) a transforming, deeply educative experience for Zweig. It was a lesson that he for one would try not to forget:

I approached the inquiry in the spirit of the traditional economist who knows everything about everything, who has neatly classified all things and put them into separate pigeon-holes. But I came to realise how little is really known about life itself. We can only catch a glimpse from time to time of real life with its constant changes, unexpected turns, enormous variety and richness, but how often do we content ourselves with outworn models, textbook patterns and artifice clumsily put together for certain analytical purposes which are taken as real. The renovation of economics and sociology can come only from the source of all being – i.e. from minute, conscientious and truthful observation of real life.[27]

5

Constructively Revolutionary

'Are you still a socialist?' the historian Raymond Carr asked his friend Iris Murdoch the first time they dined together after the war. She turned on him savagely: 'Yes. Aren't you?' That brusque Oxford exchange probably postdated the Fabian Society's away-weekend in September 1945 in the city of dreaming spires. A notable line-up assembled to discuss 'The Psychological and Sociological Problems of Modern Socialism', and presciently the most prestigious think-tank of the newly elected Labour Party was at least as much concerned with exploring how society at large might become 'socialist' as it was with analysing 'socialism' itself. Unlike their party leaders, most of the speakers did not assume that party and people were automatically in harmony.

The psychiatrist John Bowlby set the tone. 'In our enthusiasm for achieving long-sought social aims,' he argued, 'we should not overlook the private concerns of the masses, their predilections in sport or entertainments, their desire to have a home or garden of their own in which they can do what they like and which they do not frequently have to move, their preference in seaside resorts or Sunday newspapers.' Given the undeniable fact of these 'private goals', each of which had not only 'the attraction of being immediately and simply achieved' but also 'the sanction of tradition behind them', Bowlby asked how it would be possible to ensure 'the understanding and acceptance of the need for the inevitable controls required for the attainment of group goals such as, for instance, full employment, a maximising of production by reorganisation and increase of machinery, or a maximising of personal efficiency through longer and more arduous education and other social measures'. His solution was a mixture of democracy and psychology: 'The hope for the future lies in a far more profound understanding of the nature of the emotional forces involved and the development of scientific social techniques for modifying them.' In response, Britain's most venerated ethical socialist, R. H. Tawney, was relatively sanguine about the possibility of subsuming the private and pursuing group goals – 'the common people had enormous resources of initiative and ability that were hardly used at all' – but Bowlby's friend Evan Durbin, leading Labour thinker and now an MP, was deeply sceptical. 'People were far more wicked, i.e. mentally ill, than was commonly supposed,' he insisted, adding that 'as a whole we were all very sick and very stupid'. As for a solution, 'selective breeding was probably the answer'.

This was all too much for Frank Pakenham, the future Lord Longford: 'He failed to understand how virtue was to be promoted by psychologists, who, great as their therapeutic services had been, had as yet given little help in political matters. The conception of wickedness was very important and must be retained; our goal should be a race of *good* people.' Another rising star, Michael Young, principal author of Labour's victorious manifesto, agreed that he had not 'obtained much direct guidance from the psychologists'. Instead, 'his mental picture of the future was one of more planning at the top and more democracy at the bottom', and he explained what he meant by the latter:

As the result of the election, the idea of a ten-year plan had been accepted, but was not really understood by the bulk of people; the work of carrying it out must be publicised and dramatised, and progress must be clearly shown – even symbolic progress. It was dangerous to wait and hope for the best. Herein individual members of the Party must themselves get going and assist the process. He envisaged a whole host of local Advisory Committees in all subjects connected with the social programme of the new Government, for running health centres, for example; and, if the result of setting them up was to raise the minority of the population which actually took part in the work of government by 100% – from 5% to 10% of the total – it would be a great democratic step forward.

In the conference's final session, a characteristic contribution came from one of Labour's acknowledged intellectual giants, G.D.H. Cole. He 'did not agree with Mr Durbin that most people were either wicked or stupid'. Furthermore, he 'disliked the sharp separation which had been made by some speakers between leaders and led'. And as for what the aim should be, he posited a society in which 'a large proportion would participate in leadership in some field' – a fine aspiration which clearly not everyone present thought plausible.[1]

Different people, different visions. For a couple of particularly articulate workers, both of them miners, contrasting political futures were soon unfolding. 'What strange patient enduring brutes men are!' Sid Chaplin wrote in February 1946 to his friend John Bate. 'You can shepherd them to your will, but in their secret way they know and wait. And they are really brilliant at times, astonishingly awkward, but mostly devilishly stupid.' Chaplin, born in 1916 the son of a Durham pitman, had himself been in the mines since the age of 15, first as a blacksmith and then as an underground mechanic; he was now reflecting on his recent work ('taking in contributions, negotiating about ½ pensions and hunting out details of compensation') for the Durham Colliery Mechanics' Association. 'You get rid of all fancy illusions and ideals,' he went on. 'No, Jean Jacques R., man is not everywhere born free, he is born in harness, and you get so close in this work that you can see his nose twitch, the saliva dribble as he strains for the carrot that is always just beyond reach of his champing jaws.' Chaplin was also (though not for much longer) a Methodist lay preacher, and four months later he wrote again to Bate: 'I believe in God and I believe in human beings. I believe that human beings can make socialism work, eventually, as they have made other forms of society. But socialism as a panacea I take with a pinch of salt.' *The Leaping Lad*, Chaplin's first collection of stories, appeared in December 1946 and won warm reviews in the national press for its sympathetic, realistic, unforced depiction of life on the South-West Durham coalfield. 'Ferryhill Miner as Story Teller' was the local paper's front-page headline, and it quoted appreciatively from one of the stories, 'Big Little Hab': 'He lived close to all living and growing things. He was the most fascinating of companions although he was the most inarticulate of men.'[2] For Chaplin himself, who would never dream of voting anything other than Labour but no longer believed in a paradise on earth, the book's success stimulated him to try to become a full-time writer.

The other miner, Lawrence Daly, did believe in a heaven on earth – Soviet-style. He was born in 1924, the eldest of seven children of a miner who was an early member of the Communist Party of Great Britain. With his father being blacklisted by the coal owners and finding work hard to get, he had a tough Scottish upbringing before leaving school at 14 and going down the pit at Glencraig in Fife. Soon afterwards, abandoning his Roman Catholic faith, he joined the Young Communist League, and after two years the CP itself. 'The Communists were to the forefront in seeking to improve the low wages and terrible working conditions in the coal mine,' he recalled, 'and also in seeking to overcome the appalling social conditions in which we lived.' Daly was also through his teens a vigorous autodidact, taking correspondence courses (through the National Council of Labour Colleges) in economics, trade unionism, English and social history. Determined to expand his horizons, in November 1945 he attended the World Youth Conference in London, representing Young Miners of Great Britain; two months later, he was one of a British party (comprising parliamentary and non-parliamentary delegates) that visited Russia for several weeks. From Leningrad he wrote home describing the ballet at the Kirov Hall and its appreciative audience: 'It is only one of the many incidents I have seen which make an absolute mockery of the phrase "menace to Western civilisation". Here culture flourishes in its highest & finest form because it is used to elevate the whole people to the highest possible physical and moral plane.' Back at Glencraig, Daly became a National Union of Mineworkers (NUM) part-time lodge official and an increasingly active, committed member of the CP. Early in 1947, an episode involving a fellow-miner led to Daly being strongly criticised by some party members. Typically, in a long letter to the local area committee, he came out fighting: 'I have been taught by the C.P. to study *all* the factors in a situation taken together & in their movement. I knew *all* the local & personal circumstances – far better than Comrade McArthur did – & I believe that when the comrades consider these circumstances, as I have stated them, they will agree that my action was consistently Marxist.' Daly's mother may have once used her husband's copy of *Das Kapital* to kindle the fire, but the old man, who in letters to young Lawrence signed himself 'Comrade Pop', surely approved.[3]

In the country at large, there was still a considerable amount of understandable pro-Russia sentiment by the end of the war, and although in the 1945 election only two Communist MPs were elected (one of them in Fife), the British Communist Party's membership had tripled during the war to about 50,000 (including Iris Murdoch and Kingsley Amis). As for attitudes to Britain's other main wartime ally, the picture was distinctly mixed. There was an element of gratitude, certainly, and many personal entanglements, together with a largely frustrated longing for American material goods, but at the same time resentment of a newly risen superpower that seemed unpleasantly inclined to throw its weight around. 'Personally I'm sick of the sight of Yanks over here and will be mighty glad to see the back of them' was how Anthony Heap put it in September 1945.

Among the political class, on both right and left, these feelings were intensified by first the abrupt end of Lend-Lease and then the harsh terms, almost certainly reflecting distaste for the Labour government's nationalisation programme, of the proposed $3.75 billion American Loan. 'What is your alternative?' asked the Chancellor, Hugh Dalton, in the critical Commons debate in December 1945; he invoked the unappetising prospect of a dollarless Britain in which 'all those hopes of better times, to follow in the wake of victory, would be dissipated in despair and disillusion'. In effect there was no alternative but to accept the loan. 'It was extraordinarily unreal, even absurd, and shabby,' reflected Malcolm Muggeridge after two long days in the press gallery. 'Speakers took up their position, but the only reality was the fear which none of them dared to express – the fear of the consequences if cigarettes and films and spam were not available from America.'

Nevertheless, the 23 Labour MPs who voted against included not only predictable left-wing figures like Barbara Castle and Michael Foot (soon afterwards warning that American capitalism was 'arrogant, self-confident, merciless and convinced of its capacity to dictate the destinies of the world') but that future epitome of pragmatism and moderation, James Callaghan, who condemned 'economic aggression by the United States'. Callaghan and the others may have had good grounds for complaint – the American insistence on immediate multilateral trade was to prove as economically damaging to Britain as the other stipulation, that Britain by 15 July 1947 must allow convertibility, ie of sterling into dollars – but the bottom line, fairly or unfairly, was that beggars could not be choosers. A strong sense of grievance would persist on the part of the British left. 'It is clear,' complained the *New Statesman* in November 1946, 'that on the matters that most affect Britain today, the United States is nearly as hostile to the aspirations of Socialist Britain as to the Soviet Union.'[4]

None of which cut much ice with Ernest Bevin – creator between the wars of the Transport and General Workers' Union (TGWU), a crucial figure during the war as Minister of Labour, and now Foreign Secretary. 'His heavy, bullish frame, his rough and uncouth English, his blunt style of speech all combined to make a very powerful performance' – was how W. J. Brown admiringly described him in February 1946; more recently, one historian has made the bold, counter-Churchillian claim that 'this bullying, capricious, sasquatch of a politician, was also the most effective democratic statesman that this country produced in the twentieth century'. For Bevin, who had distrusted both Communists and the Soviet Union for more than 20 years, the fundamental premise of British policy towards Moscow had to be one of suspicion, or at best watchfulness. As for the alternative idea, broadly favoured by the Labour left, that Britain might pursue an even-handed path between the Russian and American power blocs, neither Bevin nor Clement Attlee saw it as a realistic possibility. It has been argued that the real instigators of a post-1945 anti-Russian policy, even before the Russians had unambiguously shown aggressive intent, were the mandarins in the Foreign Office. But that is surely to underestimate Bevin's considerable capacity for independent thought as well as his unrivalled force of character.

He also was well aware that his combative attitude would strike a chord among working-class patriots – so much so that George Orwell noted in the spring of 1946 that 'the public opinion polls taken by the *News Chronicle* showed that Bevin's popularity went sensationally *up* after his battle with Vishinsky [head of the Soviet delegation at the first meeting of the United Nations General Assembly, held in London], and went up most of all among Labour Party supporters'. Moreover, Bevin's strongly anti-Russian stance, typified by his statement to the UN that 'the danger to the peace of the world has been the incessant propaganda from Moscow against the British Commonwealth as a means to attack the British', also played extraordinarily well with his natural political opponents, possibly to his consternation but possibly not. Within a week of VJ Day, making his first major parliamentary speech as Foreign Secretary, he was, according to 'Chips' Channon, 'cheered and applauded by our side' for 'almost a Tory speech, full of sense'. Mollie Panter-Downes observed in October 1945 that 'people who three months ago were horror-stricken at the thought of Ernest Bevin negotiating England's foreign policy are now admitting, handsomely and unexpectedly, that they admire him'. Even high society welcomed the rough-tongued West Countryman, with 'Jennifer' recording how at a West End function a few weeks later Lord and Lady Rothermere had been spotted 'chatting to Mr Ernest Bevin, who was in great form with a fund of amusing stories'.[5]

Where Bevin and the rest of the Attlee government were less realistic was in their deep reluctance to accept that post-war Britain could no longer afford to enjoy great-power status. Admittedly there were retreats in these years from Greece, India and Palestine – with the granting of Indian independence a genuinely major if flawed achievement – but the illusion stubbornly persisted that Britain's rightful and permanent place was at the top table. Perhaps if Bevin had been at No. 11 (as Attlee had originally intended before being dissuaded by the King), fighting the financial battle for overseas retrenchment in a more tough-minded way than Dalton managed, it might have been different – but probably not. After all, assumptions of British superiority, and the rightness of large swathes of the globe being coloured red, were deeply rooted in the national psyche – and continued to be inculcated. 'The Empire Day celebration at school was absurd,' Gladys Langford noted disapprovingly in May 1946: 'Watts [presumably the headmaster at the north London school where she taught] had had posters made bearing names of Dominions and children held these aloft reciting doggerel rhymes – presumably of his composing – relating to their flora, fauna, and products. A few hymns were sung – quite out of tune – and we were exhorted to tell tub-thumpers to pack their bags and go away – that Russians were unpleasant people and Arabs

wicked slave-dealers.' In such a climate it seemed only proper that
Britain should have its own independent nuclear deterrent – in short,
a British bomb – an objective agreed by the government in January
1947. This very secret decision was 'not a response to an immediate
military threat', Margaret Gowing would write in her definitive study,
'but rather something fundamentalist and almost instinctive – a feeling
that Britain must possess so climacteric a weapon in order to deter an
atomically armed enemy, a feeling that Britain as a great power must
acquire all major new weapons . . .' Or as Bevin had put it a few months
earlier at a meeting of the relevant Cabinet committee, 'We've got to
have the bloody Union Jack on top of it.'[6]

What, in the generally difficult circumstances, was the economic
way ahead? 'I find myself,' John Maynard Keynes privately reflected
in April 1946, 'more and more relying for a solution of our problems
on the invisible hand [ie of the market] which I tried to eject from
economic thinking twenty years ago.' He died a few days later, but
Keynesianism – seeing that invisible hand as at best a regrettable, to-
be-circumscribed necessity – was poised to enter into its inheritance.
First, though, there was the playing out of the new government's
commitment, explicit in its election manifesto, to socialist planning.

For at least two years, the rhetoric that planning from the centre
was the key to a prosperous economy rarely faltered. 'Planning as it
is taking shape in this country under our eyes,' declared Herbert
Morrison, the minister responsible for co-ordinating the planning
machinery, in October 1946, 'is something new and constructively
revolutionary which will be regarded in times to come as a contribution
to civilization as vital and distinctly British as parliamentary democracy
under the rule of law.' Not long afterwards, there appeared a new
edition of Douglas Jay's *The Socialist Case*, first published in 1937.
Jay himself was now an economic minister, and he not only reaffirmed
the immortal maxim that 'the gentleman in Whitehall really does know
better what is good for people than the people know themselves' but
argued that, within the context of a properly planned, centrally run
economy, 'economic freedom – the freedom to buy or sell, to employ
or refrain from employing other people, to manufacture or not
manufacture – is a secondary freedom, often approaching a luxury,
which can and should be limited in a good cause'.[7]

Yet the reality was very different. 'Nebulous but exalted' was how one of the government's economic advisers, Alec Cairncross, would in retrospect caustically describe central economic planning during these immediate post-war years, while according to Kenneth Morgan, probably the most authoritative historian of the Attlee government, the 'attempt to plan private industry through the Treasury and the Board of Trade was half-hearted, indirect, and in many ways unsuccessful'. Indeed, he contended, 'so far as Labour had a strategy of planning it was largely to renew and continue the physical and financial controls of wartime, to help exports, to direct industry towards development areas, and to direct the use of vital raw materials' – in short, 'nothing that resembled the *dirigiste* economic strategy of de Gaulle's "popular front" government in France in 1945–6'. No output targets (even for industries identified as key), no way of fitting together manpower and cash forecasts, above all no powerful, autonomous institutional mechanism to give muscle to vague nostrums: the planning deficit was insurmountable.[8]

There were several main reasons for this anticlimactic outcome. The Treasury, not for the first or last time, gave a masterclass in institutional scepticism; there was much intellectual confusion as to what economic planning in peacetime actually meant and entailed, as epitomised by the muddle-headedness of Morrison, theoretically in charge of planning; and for more than two years there was the unwillingness of either the Ministry of Labour or the trade union leaders (for all their considerable goodwill towards the government) to countenance a wages policy, seen as a direct threat to the long, jealously guarded tradition of free collective bargaining – an unwillingness that more or less scuppered the chance of any meaningful manpower planning.

But ultimately, what really killed central economic planning was the lack of willpower on the part of government. In particular, the Labour Party's commitment to *democratic* socialism meant in practice an aversion to either new, unaccountable administrative mechanisms or any form of tripartism (ie government, management and labour) that seemed to threaten the sovereignty of the familiar parliamentary system. As for either the compulsory allocation of manpower or the planning of wages, neither was consistent with the traditional 'voluntarism' of the labour movement, with its deep distaste for outside interference, certainly in peacetime. 'If the maximum of persuasion and inducement fails to attract enough men and women into particular occupations to fulfil the plans laid down at the centre,' Durbin insisted as early as September 1945, 'then the plans must be changed.' Just over a year later, Sir Stafford Cripps at the Board of Trade was publicly accepting that no comprehensive plan could be carried out completely 'without compulsions of the most extreme kind, compulsions which democracy rightly refuses to accept' – which was why, he hardly needed to add, 'democratic planning is so very much more difficult than totalitarian planning'.[9]

Not that planning would have been easy, even if the iron political willpower had existed. Quite apart from institutional and labour difficulties, there would have been intense resistance on the part of privately owned industry, which was hostile enough anyway towards such government schemes as Development Councils, intended to stimulate co-operation between firms in specific sectors. Given, in the words of the economic historian Jim Tomlinson, 'the absence of a large cadre of potential industrial managers sympathetic to any form of socialism', it was hardly surprising that the charge was sounded so faintly. The 1940s may have been the least unpropitious decade in the twentieth century for peacetime economic planning, but that did not make it propitious.

Yet another reason why such planning failed to get off the ground after 1945 was the continuing existence of important physical controls exercised by the government, including controls on labour machinery, building and materials allocations. Such controls helped explain the almost complete absence of anything significant by way of investment planning, seen at this stage as superfluous. '"The City" in the middle of a socialist state is as anomalous as would be the Pope in Moscow,' Attlee had observed in 1931, just after (in instantly created Labour mythology anyway) a 'bankers' ramp' had destroyed Ramsay MacDonald's minority Labour government, but in practice, Attlee's own government did remarkably little to undermine the functions of the Square Mile and its inhabitants. In particular, the proposed National Investment Board, billed in the 1945 manifesto as the way to 'determine social priorities and promote better timing in private investment', was never established. Instead, in its place there was an almost wholly lame-duck, purely advisory National Investment Council, of nugatory achievement.

There was also, looked at from a socialist or planning point of view, the feeble, half-cock nationalisation of the Bank of England in 1946. The minister largely responsible was Dalton, who despite his acknowledged expertise on public finance had a sketchy grasp of the City and by the time he became Chancellor still did not understand the functions of the government broker, let alone the difference on the Stock Exchange between brokers and jobbers.[10] Certainly he did not strike a great deal: the Bank kept its essential institutional autonomy, quite unlike that of a government department; governors were to be appointed for a fixed term of years and could not be dismissed; and the Treasury failed to secure the power to issue directives to the clearing banks, effectively putting it at the mercy of the Bank's mediation. It is hard to resist the conclusion that the purpose of this particular piece of nationalisation was essentially symbolic – a way, in short, of appeasing the party's demons after the 1931 fiasco.

———

Of course, the taking into public ownership of a sizable chunk of the British economy was integral to the planning dream. The Bank of England was followed in fairly quick succession by Cable and Wireless, civil aviation, electricity, the coal mines, transport (including the railways and road haulage) and gas. Between them these newly nationalised industries employed some two million workers, with the majority either on the railways or in the mines. And, together with the postal and telephone services that were already in state ownership, these industries would for the next three decades form the core of the public part of the 'mixed economy'.

The principal architect-cum-draftsman of the 1946–9 wave of nationalisations was Herbert Morrison – usually depicted as the ultimate machine politician (especially in his capacity as leader of the London County Council through much of the 1930s) but also in fact a sincere believer in socialism's ethical dimension. 'Part of our work in politics and in industry must be to improve human nature,' he would tell Labour's conference in 1949, adding that 'we should set ourselves more than materialistic aims'. He believed, as did the party as a whole, that the nationalisation of several key industries would generate a wide range of economic, social and political gains. These included helping to co-ordinate production, distribution, investment and pricing policies within and across industries; encouraging economies of scale that in turn would provide opportunities for modernisation of plant and equipment; creating a virtuous circle of a more contented workforce, improved labour relations and rising productivity; and making it harder for the despised *rentier* class to prosper through unearned income (memories perhaps of Aunt Juley in E. M. Forster's *Howards End* and her tidy, predictable dividends from shares in Home Rails).

In May 1946, shortly after James Lansdale Hodson had noted, almost certainly accurately, that 'the nation isn't behind grandiose nationalisation to anything like the degree the Front Bench pretends', Morrison explained to the Commons, in the context of the Civil Aviation Bill, how it was to be done: 'Competent business people will be appointed to manage the undertaking, with a considerable degree of business freedom; on the other hand, it will be a public concern, appointed by public authority, and therefore, the spirit of the public interest must run right through the undertaking.'[11] Based to a large extent on the inter-war public corporation, this model for the post-war years was accepted with remarkably little debate – and with remarkably few realistic alternatives being put forward.

Over the years, though, there would be many criticisms of the way in which nationalisation took place. The financial and business guidelines were unduly restrictive, resulting in an unrealistic pricing policy and an inability to diversify into such areas as manufacturing; too many 'non-believers' were appointed to the nationalised boards, including not just businessmen but a motley crew of peers and retired generals; it was too easy for ministers to interfere or, according to some, too difficult; there was little coherent planning that related the newly nationalised industries to the economy as a whole; and so on. The criticism, though, that would resonate most through the years, at least from the left, was that a golden opportunity had been missed to institute a meaningful form of workers' control.

Yet at the time there were few who saw this as a runner. 'From my experience,' Cripps discouragingly told a Bristol audience in October 1946, 'there is not as yet a very large number of workers in Britain capable of taking over large enterprises.' He added that 'until there has been more experience by the workers of the managerial side of industry, I think it would be almost impossible to have worker-controlled industry in Britain, even if it were on the whole desirable.' Morrison did not disagree, and, more significantly, neither did the left-wing Aneurin Bevan. There is no evidence, moreover, that the workforces themselves, certainly in the form of their union leaders, wanted control or even a measure of control. When Emanuel (Manny) Shinwell, responsible for the nationalisation of the coal mines in his capacity as Minister of Fuel and Power, on two separate occasions in 1946 offered two seats on the National Coal Board (NCB) to the miners' leaders, he got nowhere. 'They refused, saying that administration was not their affair' was how he recalled the outcome. But it went down in the folklore of industrial relations that (in the subsequent words of the veteran industrial correspondent Geoffrey Goodman) 'the NUM President, Sir William Lowther, awkward and gruff as they used to chisel them in the Durham coalfield, told Shinwell to go to hell'.

Indeed, it is far from certain that the majority of workers in the relevant industries were especially keen on the prospect of nationalisation as such. Hodson, visiting South Yorkshire in May 1946, was told by a colliery managing director that his workers were about equally divided on the subject: 'Of those for it, 25 per cent are Socialists who accept it as they accept all the Government does, and the other 25 per cent believe it means more pay for less work. Of those against it, 25 per cent think these particular pits are well run and will be less efficient under the government and that they'll suffer; the other 25 per cent hate change of any sort.' It was a lack of enthusiasm that contrasted sharply – and ominously – with the scenes in Westminster a few months earlier, as old miners, now Labour MPs, shed tears as they passed through the 'aye' division-lobby to vote for the takeover of the coal mines and even burst into song. 'The strains of "The Red Flag" and "Cwm Rhondda" were heard clearly in the Chamber,' recalled one very socialist, already rather bored newish Labour MP, Tom Driberg, pre-war founder (as William Hickey in the *Daily Express*) of the modern gossip column.

Still, these were early days. Clause Four may have become the cornerstone of Labour's constitution back in 1918, but in his book-length tract *Labour's Plan for Plenty*, published in early 1947, Michael Young saw public ownership as only at the start of its journey:

No one in the Labour Party would claim that the last word has been said about nationalisation, or that the Party's views on the subject need not undergo further development... There is scope for variety in structure and for continuous experiment in methods of public administration. That is the way in which the organisation of nationalised industries can be steadily improved and the ground cleared for a rapid extension of public enterprise.[12]

6

Farewell Squalor

What really enthused the Labour Party and its supporters was welfare and the Attlee government's creation of the modern welfare state. Even *The Times*, daily organ of the British establishment, was strongly in favour of a national health service, seeing it as a desirable trade-off between state and citizen. 'The new social services will come to claim too large a share of the national income,' it warned in friendly rather than threatening fashion in May 1946, 'if the citizen, in pursuit of security, leisure, and comfort, fails to understand that what he expects of society can only be secured by the enterprise, diligence, and self-discipline with which he makes his personal contribution to the enlargement of the national product.'

The optimistic assumption that welfare and productivity would go hand in hand was not shared by the *Financial Times* and (presumably) its readers, still mainly in the City. 'Britain is piling up a large burden of social services in outlays on health, education, national insurance, family allowances and subsidies for housing and for food,' it had declared balefully a few weeks earlier:

> We are a nation of producers with an ever-increasing overhead of social charges ... With these extensive commitments, we shall have to meet the competition of the United States for the markets of the world, once the immediate famine for goods of all kinds has abated. When we have topped our potential wave of prosperity, how shall we deal with the challenge of reviving German and Japanese exporting industries, now temporarily out of commission?

Forty years later, the historian Correlli Barnett took up the charge, arguing forcibly in *The Audit of War* (1986) and then *The Lost Victory* (1995) that Britain during and after the war had made a profoundly mistaken choice by not giving economic reconstruction clear, unambiguous, unsentimental priority over social reconstruction. Instead, according to his pungent reading, the country fell victim to a hugely damaging and economically illiterate virus of elite-driven 'New Jerusalemism' – in his caustic words, 'the creation of that better, more equal Britain to be built when there were blue birds over / the white cliffs of Dover'.

Barnett's assessment of the existence of that mood, at least among the 'activators', is surely correct. Yet as others have pointed out, the notion that a long, arduous, ultimately victorious 'people's war' did not have to result in welfare improvements for that people, at least in the short term, is essentially ahistorical – flying in the face of the inescapable political realities of that time. If the Tories had been returned to office in 1945, they almost certainly would have created a welfare state not unrecognisably different from the one that Labour actually did create. Moreover, even within the strictly economic parameters of the debate, it is possible that Barnett has significantly overstated the cost of that welfare state. 'An austerity product of an age of austerity' is how one of his main adversaries, Jim Tomlinson, has crisply characterised it, showing in detail how, whatever may have happened later, the Attlee government could not be justly accused of extravagance in its welfare provisions. By 1950 the 10 per cent of British GDP that comprised public spending on social welfare may have been above the comparable proportions in Scandinavia, Italy and the Netherlands but was significantly below those of Belgium, Austria and West Germany. 'The welfare state was created,' Tomlinson gladly concedes, 'but in a context where it consumed a quite limited level of resources, and where it was continuously vulnerable to a resource allocation system which gave priority to exports and industry, and restrained both private and collective consumption.'[1]

Unsurprisingly, at a time when relatively few activators quarrelled with the assumption that a collectivised economy was not only more benign than a free-market economy but also more efficient, there was little debate about whether the *public* provision of health, education, housing and so on was the right road to be going down. Anyway, it seemed glaringly obvious to almost everyone that only if the state were actively involved as provider was there a chance of reasonable equality of outcome in the receipt of welfare services. Might the welfare state lead to a dependency culture? Barnett has written, in a notorious passage, of how the New Jerusalem 'dream' turned into 'a dank reality of a segregated, subliterate, unskilled, unhealthy and institutionalised proletariat hanging on the nipple of state maternalism'. To which one can retort that there were indeed many free lunches between 1945 and 1979 – but that it was not society's losers who ate most of them, let alone the best of them.

Instead, if there was a flaw at the heart of the classic social-democratic welfare state, it was the assumption that those operating it were by definition altruistic and trustworthy, together with the accompanying assumption that those receiving its benefits should be passive, patient and grateful. Or, as Julian Le Grand has put it, echoing the Scottish philosopher David Hume, it was a system designed to be 'operated by knights for the benefit of pawns', certainly not by 'knaves' on behalf of 'queens'.[2] That paternalist model may have seemed psychologically convincing in the 1940s – though even then it was questionable, given a realistic analysis of popular attitudes – but over the ensuing decades it would become ever less so.

———

'He is a big, heavy man, not very tall but thick set, with very powerful arms and shoulders, dark, round-headed, and beetle-browed with eyes, nose and chin all rather prominent and large, speaks with a lisp and a Welsh intonation' was how in August 1945 a Ministry of Health official, Enid Russell-Smith, described her new chief, Aneurin ('Nye') Bevan. Some months later, on a visit to Doncaster with him, she noted that 'here and there among the audience one sees that beatific expression on a worn old face which means that some pioneer in the Labour movement is seeing all Heaven in a Labour Minister in a Labour Government expounding a Socialist policy'.[3]

But if no one denied that Bevan was a fine, inspiring orator, capable also of considerable personal charm, what surprised many – friends as well as enemies – was the remarkably effective way in which he pushed through the creation of the National Health Service. Inevitably the scheme had many complexities, but at root there were seven key elements. Access to health care was to be free and universal; costs would be met from central taxation, not insurance; all hospitals – whether local authority or voluntary, cottage or teaching – were to be nationalised; the great majority of these hospitals would be run by regional hospital boards; the other two legs of a tripartite overall structure would be executive councils (overseeing GPs, dentists and opticians) and local authorities (still responsible for such miscellaneous activities as vaccinations, ambulances, community nursing, home help and immunisation programmes); NHS 'pay beds' would enable consultants to combine private practice with working for the NHS; and GPs would no longer be allowed to buy and sell practices but would not be put on a full-time salary basis, with the capitation (ie per patient head) element in their income making it easier for patients to move between doctors. There were plenty of dramas to come, but the NHS Bill that Bevan put forward in March 1946 more or less became actuality just over two years later.

Producing and implementing a broadly coherent, working scheme out of the medley of conflicting vested interests that he inherited was indisputably a virtuoso performance. There were, nevertheless, significant sacrifices involved. When Herbert Morrison, in a fierce Cabinet tussle, unsuccessfully fought for the continuing, even expanded, control of hospitals by local authorities, he was invoking not only his own faith and roots in municipal socialism but also, in the recent words of Rudolf Klein, 'a view of the world anchored in the values of localism: a view which stressed responsiveness rather than efficiency, differentiation rather than uniformity'. 'If we wish local government to thrive – as a school of political and democratic education as well as a method of administration – we must consider the general effect on local government of each particular proposal' was how Morrison himself put it. The regional boards, moreover, were appointed rather than elected and distinctly lacking in accountability. Apart from the almost statutory tame trade unionist, their social composition over the years would tend strongly to the upper-middle class; as for the NHS's foot soldiers, Bevan at the outset ruled out specific representation on either the regional boards or hospital management committees. 'If the nurses were to be consulted, why not also the hospital domestics? the radiotherapists? the physiotherapists? and so on,' he rather querulously asked the General Secretary of the Trades Union Congress (TUC), Sir Walter Citrine. Perhaps the most telling criticism of Bevan is that he succumbed to the consultants, not wanting to fight against them as well as the deeply suspicious GPs. Accordingly, the consultants had their fears of having to work for local authorities allayed; financially, had their mouths (as Bevan himself would later concede, or perhaps boast) 'stuffed with gold'; and generally saw their role exalted way above that of the GPs. 'The consultants ruled the new health service' would be the verdict 40 years later of David Widgery (East End GP and socialist intellectual), 'and they were bound to shape the health service, above all the new generations of doctors, in their own image.'

However, the biggest disappointment at the time, at least on the left, concerned Section 21 of Bevan's Act. 'It shall be the duty of every local health authority to provide, equip, and maintain to the satisfaction of the Ministry, premises which shall be called "Health Centres" . . .' – that was the promise. Long a socialist aspiration, these centres would not only house GPs, dentists, chemists and the local authority clinics but also receive visits from hospital consultants. Preventive and curative medicine would be equally emphasised, and in time all general practice would take place within them. Such aims inspired a young London doctor, Hugh Faulkner, demobilised in 1947. 'When I came into general practice and began to look at it,' he recalled, 'I found myself in conflict with the basic development of the general practice as basically a cottage industry, as very much a series of small businesses, which were quite openly in conflict with one another; the GPs that used to talk about the opposition, meaning the GP in the next road, and none of the GPs round here spoke to one another . . . It seemed to me that the isolation of doctors was perpetuating a very low level of medical care.' Faulkner, based in Kentish Town, responded by building up his own group practice, which focused on the social context of health and developed a team that included a health visitor, a midwife and a social worker.

But for a long time the larger trend ran the other way, with the British Medical Association (representing GPs) in particular dead set against health centres – so much so that after ten years of the NHS only ten had been built. For Rodney Lowe, a leading historian of the welfare state, the fate of health centres exemplified 'the balance of power enshrined in the new organisational structure', in that 'patients were expected to seek out professional care – doctors were not expected to make themselves readily available to patients'. Strikingly, there is no evidence of Bevan exercising any political will and trying to bring the apparently cherished concept to fruition; indeed, the probability is that, aware of the medical profession's widespread opposition, he deliberately sat on it. Virtually no health centres, municipal control eroded, the consultant as king – it is apposite to quote the bittersweet words of Sir Frederick Messer, a Labour MP and one of the minister's better-informed critics. 'I think his outstanding success,' Messer reflected after watching Bevan perform in the Commons, 'was the way he applied the anaesthetic to supporters on his own side, making them believe in things they had opposed almost all their lives.'[4]

―――――――

The natural complement to health was social security, and it largely fell to another Welsh ex-miner, James Griffiths, to implement Sir William Beveridge's celebrated wartime proposals, though building on the existing Family Allowances Act that took practical effect from the August Bank Holiday in 1946. There were two key measures.

The 1946 National Insurance Act, fully operational from July 1948 (as was the NHS), sought to protect the population, on a basis of universality, from the financial perils of sickness, unemployment and old age. Everyone from 16 to 65 (60 in the case of women), 'from the barrow boy to the field marshal' as Griffiths later put it, would be required to make flat-rate contributions to the state in return for flat-rate benefits. Whereas Beveridge had recommended old-age pensions to be phased in over a 20-year period, Griffiths was adamant they should be paid in full from the start. 'The men and women who had already retired had experienced a tough life,' he later explained. 'In their youth they had been caught by the 1914 war, in middle age they had experienced the indignities of the depression, and in 1940 had stood firm as a rock in the nation's hour of trial. They deserved well of the nation and should not wait for twenty years.'

The purpose of the 1948 National Assistance Act, the work of Bevan as well as Griffiths, was essentially to provide a safety net for the poor – non-contributory and paid out of central taxation. It was a measure formed by the long shadow of the 1930s. 'Let us remember the queues outside the Poor Relief offices, the destitute people, badly clothed, badly shod, lining up with their prams,' the robust Liverpool MP Bessie Braddock reminded the Commons in November 1947. 'They used to make soup every day and take it down to the central area of the city in a van and distribute it, and a piece of bread, to those who were hungry and waiting for it at a cost of a farthing a bowl. I have always remembered since then the terrible tragedy and horror on the faces of those in the queue when the soup was finished and there was no more to be sold.' Assistance was to be means-tested, but the fact that the much loathed whole-household means test had been abolished during the war, with the focus instead being on the means-testing of individuals and couples, meant that much of the old stigma had gone. 'I have spent many years of my life in fighting the means test,' Bevan declared. 'Now we have practically ended it.'[5]

But again, as with health, there were serious flaws amid the undeniable huge positives. For one thing, the flat-rate contributory basis to the National Insurance Act, as originally enshrined by Beveridge, was deeply regressive, though mitigated by the taxpayer's contribution through the Exchequer. For another, the accompanying benefits proved in real terms to be almost a third below what even the parsimonious Beveridge had calculated as necessary for subsistence. Analysis differs as to why this was so, but Tomlinson has convincingly demonstrated that a characteristic Treasury mixture of meanness and pessimism played a key role. There was a significant knock-on effect of these inadequate benefits. Griffiths and his senior civil servants had confidently assumed that a properly functioning national insurance scheme must irresistibly lead to the need for national assistance more or less disappearing. But the reverse proved the case, and over the years the numbers applying for national assistance (or supplementary benefit, as it was later renamed) would grow like Topsy.

There was also, once again, the whole question of the local and the national. The historian David Vincent has convincingly argued that 'Beveridge's greatest achievement may have been not to convert the Tories to the welfare state, but Labour to state welfare', given that historically Labour had tended to look to local authorities rather than the state for the relief of poverty. The practical consequence, following the wholesale shift of attitudes to the state as a result of the war, was an 'extensive indifference to the dangers of a system in which every official from whom claimants received money was controlled from Whitehall' – a system involving 'the creation of a huge new bureaucracy answerable to its clients only through the cumbersome mechanism of ministerial responsibility'.[6] A sometimes Kafkaesque trial – endured mainly by those least able to complain – was only just beginning.

Education, however, was where the left would really scent betrayal, in retrospect if not always at the time. Red-haired, diminutive Ellen Wilkinson, Minister of Education until her death in February 1947, may have been its feisty Jarrow heroine in the 1930s, but now she saw her prime task as the implementation of the essentially centrist 1944 Butler Act. Against a difficult background of very tight Treasury purse strings, not helped by the rising birth rate since 1942, she presided over the introduction of free school milk; managed against serious Cabinet opposition to push through the raising of the school-leaving age to 15, taking effect from April 1947; and was also able to get a modest school-building programme under way, exemplified by the prefabricated work in Hertfordshire of the modernist, socially concerned architect Stirrat Johnson-Marshall – a classic activator figure, 'Socratic in manner of discussion and intolerant of formality in any guise'. Structurally, Wilkinson followed the explicit line of the wartime Norwood Report, and the tacit line of Butler, by not only accepting but positively encouraging tripartism in secondary schools – that is, an overall mix of grammar schools, secondary moderns and secondary technical schools, each in theory enjoying parity of esteem.

The new secondary moderns, to which the majority of children went, 'were to be modern in aim as well as name and in no sense dumping grounds', Wilkinson assured her party conference in June 1946. But less than a fortnight later, the headmaster of a secondary modern in Middlesex publicly conceded that, given that his school's intake largely comprised pupils of 'under-average intelligence' who as adults would 'fill the more lowly positions in life', his object was 'not to get his children through the examinations but to make their school life happy and, at the same time, provide a background of interests and a balanced view that will serve them after they leave school'. Michael Young, charting *Labour's Plan for Plenty* soon afterwards, did not in essence dispute this analysis: 'The majority of children will go to the modern secondary schools . . . Many of those will unfortunately have to work in routine or semi-routine occupations which do not give them full scope for the expression of their personalities. Consequently, the curriculum will be designed primarily to equip the children to make full and creative use of their leisure time and to look after their own homes with skill and imagination.' By the time Wilkinson died, to be replaced by the stolid, commonsensical George Tomlinson, it was becoming crystal clear that the grammar schools enjoyed vastly more prestige, significantly greater financial resources and a far more middle-class intake than the secondary moderns. Moreover, few of the most able out of the 75 per cent or so of children allocated at the age of 11 to secondary moderns were subsequently given the chance to transfer to grammars.

As for the third leg of tripartism, the secondary technical schools, they proved almost a complete non-starter, never educating more than a small minority of pupils. Although launched with high hopes – 'work, and training for work, must be given an enhanced social significance, and general and vocational education fused into a purposeful whole', an advocate trumpeted in the *Times Educational Supplement* in February 1946 – they seem to have fallen foul of a mixture of parsimony (it being appreciably more expensive to equip a school training up engineers or technologists than one concentrating on arts subjects and pure science) and Wilkinson's instinctive opposition to narrow vocationalism, believing that it limited expectations and thus life chances. These technical schools would eventually take their place in the Correlli Barnett cosmology as the great white hope that 'might have fostered a technological national culture in place of a literary one' but were 'simply never to be built'.[7] Put in these terms, it is not absurdly Hampstead to feel only modified grief.

There was an alternative to tripartism – and, in particular, the division at 11 into sheep and goats. The movement for 'multilateral' (ie comprehensive) schools went back to the 1920s and had gathered momentum during the war, especially through the National Association of Labour Teachers, which had persuaded successive Labour Party conferences to accept pro-comprehensive resolutions. They found no echo at the Ministry of Education, whose pamphlet 'The Nation's Schools', published on VE Day, not only upheld a sharp distinction between the traditional grammar and the new secondary moderns (the latter being for working-class children 'whose future employment will not demand any measure of technical skill or knowledge') but made a four-fold case against multilateral schools: they would necessarily be very large, in order to have a viable sixth form, and that was intrinsically a bad thing; in practice, selection would continue within them; it was generally best if a school had one specific aim or function; and anyway, alternative plans for the future had already been formed. 'It would be a mistake,' in short, 'to plunge too hastily on a large scale into a revolutionary change.' Seven months later, in December 1945, the ministry's Circular 73 insisted that '*it is inevitable* for the immediate purposes of planning and in the light of the existing layout of schools, for local education authorities at the outset to think in terms of the three types'.

At this point, Wilkinson was the minister, and although not without sympathy for the egalitarianism of multilaterals – which, she told the Commons in July 1946, would 'mix all the children together in the corporate life of one community' and 'avoid snobbish distinctions between schools of different grades' – what truly stirred her was the prospect, in the wake of the 1944 Butler Act, of a new generation of bright, self-motivated, self-improving working-class children going to the traditionally elite, middle-class grammar schools and using that experience as a platform for future advance and fulfilment. 'The top few pupils were intelligent and could mop up facts like blotting paper,' she once recalled of her own non-grammar education in Manchester, 'but we were made to wait for the rest of the huge classes . . . We wanted to stretch our minds but were merely a nuisance.' Or as she told her party conference in 1946, 'I was born into a working-class home and I had to fight my own way through to university.' Put another way, socialism to her – and indeed to most of her Cabinet colleagues – was at least as much about equality of opportunity, for those with the brains and ambition to grasp it, as it was about equality of outcome.

Significantly, there had been no commitment to multilaterals in the 1945 manifesto. Anyway, the prevailing educational mood, not only in the ministry, was that immediate, on-the-ground reconstruction – finding enough teachers, finding enough decent buildings – mattered at this stage far more than the pursuit of alternative structures. Some local authorities (including by the spring of 1947 Coventry, Swansea and London) did submit plans with a greater or lesser multilateral component, but the majority, including Labour-controlled ones, were content to stick to tripartism. After all, it bore a reassuring similarity to the pre-war pattern of grammar schools, senior elementary schools and junior technical schools; neither educationalists nor laymen doubted the accuracy of intelligence testing; and the understandable bogey of hugeness had been instilled ever since the London County Council (LCC) in 1944 had first put forward 'a system of Comprehensive High Schools', each to have at least 2,000 children.[8] Nevertheless, a corrosive, long-running national (England and Wales) saga was under way.

There was another great educational might-have-been in these years. Labour was in with a thumping majority, a bewildered upper class had not yet had time to regroup, and there would never be a more plausible moment for seeking to abolish what was arguably the single most important source of political, social and economic privilege – the public schools. 'Attlee asked me what I thought of Geoffrey de Freitas who was there to be vetted as a candidate for Parliamentary Private Secretary,' Jock Colville (the Prime Minister's private secretary) recalled of a visit to Chequers the weekend after VJ Day. 'Charming, I said, and highly intelligent. "Yes," replied Attlee, "and what is more he was at Haileybury, my old school."' The following June, the PM returned to Haileybury to offer personal reassurance. 'He saw no reason for thinking that the public schools would disappear,' ran the report of his speech. 'He thought the great traditions would carry on, and they might even be extended.' A fortnight earlier, Wilkinson had sought to persuade her party's delegates that the right approach to the public-school question was 'to make the schools provided by the State so good and so varied that it will seem quite absurd to send children to these schools'. A noble aspiration, and undoubtedly there also existed in the Labour Party a widespread feeling that not allowing schools to exist outside the state system would be incompatible with prevailing notions of liberty; but it *might* have been a different story if there had been another figure at No. 10 than the deeply middle-class (son of a City solicitor), deeply respectable Attlee.

Nearly as much of a non-starter, moreover, was the Fleming Report's 1944 recommendation that public schools should voluntarily make available a quarter of their places to children from the state system. In practice there was a total lack of enthusiasm all round, whether on the part of the public schools themselves (once their fee-paying places started to fill up, as they quickly did), the Ministry of Education (which resisted the idea of state bursaries), the local education authorities (which had no wish to see their brightest pupils being creamed off) and working-class parents (naturally reluctant to have their children taken away to such an alien milieu). A 1946 play, *The Guinea Pig*, was soon afterwards turned into a successful film by Roy and John Boulting, starring the young Richard Attenborough as a 14-year-old cockney, Jack Read, sent to an ancient foundation. After early, heartrending scenes of bullying and unhappiness, the boy gradually adjusts and loses his accent, eventually winning a scholarship to Cambridge. 'Gosh sir, jolly good show' is his grateful response to the news.[9] The film portrays a triumph of social mobility, but in reality the Fleming scheme never got off the ground, and private and state education continued to co-exist as two utterly separate systems inhabiting utterly separate worlds.

The belief in 1945 that the public could match the private ran deep. Co-compiling that autumn a *Report on Luton* for the local council, Richard Titmuss ended the section on housing with a clarion call:

> There is evidence that the country is moving towards a wide acceptance of the principle that services provided by the people for themselves through the medium of central and local government, shall compare in standard with those provided by private enterprise. As it is with hospitals and clinics, so it should be with schools and houses. The council house should in the future provide the amenities, space and surroundings which hitherto have often been the monopoly of private building.

This was a vision fully shared by Bevan, perversely enough responsible for housing as well as health, two immensely challenging tasks. His unambiguous policy was severely to restrict private house-building and instead to pour as many resources as he could muster into new local-authority housing. Although there had been a significant growth of such housing between the wars, this policy marked the beginning of a fundamental and long-term step-change, so that by the end of the 1970s as much as a third of the national housing stock was in the hands of local authorities.

The most powerful historical critique of this strategy has come from Alison Ravetz. Noting that 'the weight placed on local councils as housing authorities – as developers, owners and managers – turned them, for several decades, into virtually unchallengeable landlords,' she particularly regrets Labour's lack of enthusiasm for such alternative housing agencies as housing associations, housing co-operatives and self-build societies. As a result, and aggravated by the lack of subsidy for private rented housing, the post-war British housing system had 'a distinctive, monolithic quality that set it apart from virtually all other European housing systems' – a system that 'befitted a centralised, collectivist, expertly advised and caring, but ultimately paternalistic, State'. To all of which one might add that there was also what now seems the glaring and obstinate refusal to admit that most people actually wanted to own their own homes. Yet was that true at the time? Tellingly, out of the *Sunday Pictorial*'s '100 Families' in July 1946, only 14 were reported as either owning or buying (ie from private landlords) 'the houses in which they lived'.[10] For most of the others, almost certainly, home ownership – in the middle of a serious national housing shortage – was simply not on the agenda.

At the heart of the new vision of public housing was quality as much as quantity. Typically, Bevan had no time for prefabs, not recognising their popularity and contemptuously dismissing them as 'rabbit hutches'. Instead, he wanted permanence and the highest standards possible, including lavatories upstairs and down as well as overall minimum room space increased from 750 to 900 square feet. 'We shall be judged for a year or two by the *number* of houses we build,' he declared. 'We shall be judged in ten years' time by the *type* of houses we build.'

Was Bevan's hope, as with Wilkinson in education, that if the quality was good enough in public housing, then there would be no demand for private? It is impossible to know, but certainly he placed much faith in mixing the classes together. 'You have colonies of low-income people, living in houses provided by the local authorities, and you have the higher income groups living in their own colonies,' he complained in October 1945. 'This is a wholly evil thing, from a civilised point of view ... It is a monstrous infliction upon the essential psychological and biological one-ness of the community.' Subsequently, he invoked the ideal community as one where 'all the various income groups of the population are mixed' – an ideal that had once existed in some English villages, 'where the small cottages of the labourers were cheek by jowl with the butcher's shop, and where the doctor could reside benignly with his patients in the same street'.[11] What this might mean in practice, though, was another matter. Building council houses in districts dominated by homeowners? Persuading the doctor to live in a council house? The contrast with health, Bevan's other responsibility, was painfully stark. In that area there was every chance of persuading the middle classes to embrace a nationalised health system, knowing that the medical-cum-financial benefits more than outweighed the temporary discomfort of a socially mixed doctor's waiting room or even, if the worst came to the worst, hospital ward. A socially mixed 24/7 was, for all concerned, a very different prospect.

In the short, quantitative term, faced by a daunting set of circumstances (including severe economic constraints, fiercely competing priorities for building materials which were in short supply anyway, and the immediate need for at least a million homes), Bevan made a patchy start, leading directly to the squatters' movement in the summer of 1946. But he recovered sufficiently well to be able to announce by September 1948 that 750,000 new homes had been provided since the end of the war – a mixture of new permanent houses (almost half the total), temporary housing (including the despised prefabs), repaired housing and house conversions. However, a huge problem of unmet demand still remained. It was estimated that several million new homes would be required by the mid-1950s and that was even before the slum-clearance programmes, halted at the onset of war, were restarted.

A survey of Willesden, conducted in late 1946 and early 1947, found 61 per cent expressing dissatisfaction with their present housing (dominated in that inner London suburb by decaying terraced houses), with 'overcrowding' and 'lack of privacy' as the most frequent complaints, followed by 'inadequate amenities'. Moreover, 62 per cent (especially younger people) said that they would like to move from their present home in the next two or three years; of these, 72 per cent did not want to stay in Willesden, with a majority expressing a preference to live either in an outer suburb or outside London altogether. The makings, in other words, were already apparent of a great, essentially voluntary exodus – one already begun before the war – from the streets upon streets of substandard, nineteenth-century inner-city and inner-suburb speculative housing, most of it privately rented, that Bevan understandably viewed as the spur to a golden age of public housing.

The Willesdenites were also asked what form their ideal new housing would take; as usual, only a small minority (15 per cent) opted for the self-contained flat. But by this time the government had already introduced new subsidy scales for local authorities that in effect gave them a significant financial incentive to build blocks of flats of four storeys or more, as long as they had lifts. 'People would not consent to live in the clouds if land was available,' complained one Labour MP in March 1946, describing the measure as 'so much flat-doodle'; but it still went ahead. Woodberry Down estate in Stoke Newington and Churchill Gardens estate in Pimlico, each including blocks of at least eight storeys, were early responses: high enough in comparison with the standard four-storey LCC blocks of the 1930s but not yet skyscrapers. Elsewhere in London, at East Ham, the attitude in 1946 of the local council mirrored that of several other Labour authorities in bombed-out districts, with a simultaneous reluctance to accept either blocks of flats or a significantly reduced population. In the end, firmly told by its experts (the Chief Housing Officer and the Borough Engineer) that these two policies were mutually exclusive, the council did agree in principle to allow flats, though only for single people or childless couples.[12] Overall, the majority of new council housing in the 1940s was along well-established 'cottage' lines, with (outside London anyway) few blocks of flats being built.

For most architects, eager to get involved in rebuilding Britain, the economic circumstances were such that they had no alternative but to bide their time. Ernö Goldfinger, ultra-modernist and left-wing, was lucky, receiving a commission just after the war to convert a bomb-damaged Victorian warehouse in Farringdon into new premises for the Communist Party's newspaper, the *Daily Worker*. A fractious process ensued – the builders objecting strongly to taking orders from someone palpably not English born and bred – during which Goldfinger stuck to his modernist guns by removing most of the Victorian mouldings.

The end result won many architectural plaudits, but the journalists who had to work there every day soon identified two major flaws: the unpleasantly noisy main newsroom, built in a pioneering open-plan style, and the very low toilets, unrepentantly justified by Goldfinger on the grounds that the nearer one got to squatting Continental-fashion over elephant's feet, the more complete the bowel evacuation. 'The journalists,' according to his biographer, 'were not convinced.'

'"Everybody" is talking Dispersal, Satellite Towns, Green Belts, Location of Industry, etc,' Goldfinger's old sparring partner, Frederic Osborn, noted with satisfaction in September 1945. That indeed was the spirit of the age – a planning zeitgeist that looked with dismay not just on the rundown inner cities but also on all the proliferating Acacia Avenues and Chestnut Groves. 'The suburbs have generally developed as an unplanned growth,' complained Coventry's mayor, Councillor J. C. Lee Gordon, in August 1946. 'In order to develop a social sense it is very necessary to divide the suburbs into definite zones, each with its own identity, and each with a social centre, or focal point, at which group activities may be carried on which are wider than the activities of a small family group.' What Gordon envisaged, he explained to a local paper, was 'a neighbourhood unit' – the increasingly popular town-planning concept, imported from America, which ignored Dennis Chapman's inconvenient Middlesbrough findings and argued that community spirit would be fostered through the creation of zoned, residential-only neighbourhoods that each had its own school, church, community centre and so on.

Later that year, J. M. Richards, editor of the *Architectural Review*, was broad-minded enough to put in a word for the much-maligned existing suburbs, pointing out that for all 'the alleged deficiencies of suburban taste', there was no denying 'the appeal it holds for ninety out of a hundred Englishmen, an appeal which cannot be explained away as some strange instance of mass aberration'. But Richards's short book, *The Castles on the Ground* (1946), was, he would recall, 'scorned by my contemporaries as either an irrelevant eccentricity or a betrayal of the forward-looking ideals of the Modern Movement'. The notable exception was John Betjeman, who found in John Piper's accompanying illustrations of 'the fake half-timber, the leaded lights and bow windows of the Englishman's castle' what he called 'a new beauty – the beauty of the despised, patronised suburb, the open heart of the nation'.[13]

The time, though, was far from ripe for Metroland nostalgia. Another book, also published in December 1946, caught much better the prevailing mood: 'Let us close our eyes on the nineteenth-century degradation and squalor, and let us only look with unseeing eyes on the sordid excrescences of the first decade of this century, let us blind ourselves to the septic and ugly building wens and ribbons perpetrated and planted on us between the wars, but let us open our eyes and look brightly forward and onward to the new town, the new living... Peterlee.' *Farewell Squalor* was the work of C. W. Clarke, Easington Rural District Council's Surveyor. Clarke called for a large development of new, better housing for Durham's miners, to be named after their legendary former leader, Peter Lee. They certainly needed it, to judge by James Lansdale Hodson's account shortly before of visiting a pit village near Bishop Auckland:

> Three long streets on a slight rise stood at right angles. We drove up one and down another, going very slowly, for the streets are unpaved, with small knolls of hard earth and cinders and runnels caused by rain. Patches of grass grew boldly. The streets were almost an unbroken line of miserable brick hovels, each street about 400 yards in length, most horrible and dreary. Our coming brought a few unkempt women and ill-clad children to the doors. Two hefty young men eyed us sullenly. It was nearer to hell, I thought, than anything I had seen since Belsen.

'Yet it exists in 1946,' reflected Hodson, 'and hardly more than an hour's journey from Newcastle-on-Tyne.'[14]

Peterlee was one of 14 New Towns designated between 1946 and 1950. In line with the wartime *County of London Plan*, more than half were for Greater London – in order of designation, Stevenage, Crawley, Hemel Hempstead, Harlow, Hatfield, Welwyn, Basildon and Bracknell. The other six were Corby in Northamptonshire, Newton Aycliffe and Peterlee in the north-east, East Kilbride and Glenrothes in Scotland, and Cwmbran in Wales. Developed partly to relieve the housing shortage but also with explicit brave new world ambitions, they would become emblematic of the whole 1945 settlement.

The essential guiding spirit of these new towns followed on from Ebenezer Howard's garden-city movement: they were to be economically self-contained and socially balanced communities that in national terms would stimulate decentralisation from the overcrowded big cities. Reporting in 1946 to the new Minister of Town and Country Planning, Lewis Silkin, the Reith Committee (with Osborn a prominent member) placed particular stress on the need for a strong sense of community and highlighted the potential benefits of the neighbourhood unit – which indeed was the model explicitly used in 11 out of the first 14 new towns. As with his inter-war stewardship of the BBC, Lord Reith did not really embrace popular culture. He hoped that each new town would have 'a civic cinema', thereby counteracting the commercial cinemas with their 'limited cultural range and American productions'; he did not mention commercial dance halls; and he specifically repudiated greyhound racing: 'While there may be a demand, it would bring in its train consequences likely to be specially objectionable in a new town because displeasing to a large proportion of the residents.'

How were these fun factories to be run? The Reith Committee canvassed various possibilities, but the New Towns Act 1946 which quickly followed its report came down decisively for government-funded, government-appointed public corporations, in the event called development corporations, with no directly elected element. It was a fundamental breach of the Howardian vision, which had involved the bottom-up creation of what have been called 'self-governing local welfare states'. Not that this worried Silkin, whose much greater anxiety, he told the Commons in May 1946 in the course of moving his bill's second reading, was that 'the planning should be such that the different income groups living in the new towns will not be segregated':

> No doubt they may enjoy common recreational facilities, and take part in amateur theatricals, or each play their part in a health centre or community centre. But when they leave to go home I do not want the better off people to go to the right, and the less well off to go to the left. I want them to ask each other, 'Are you going my way?' . . . Our aim must be to combine in the new town the friendly spirit of the former slum with the vastly improved health conditions of the new estate, but it must be a broadened spirit, embracing all classes of society.

A final burst of eloquence, perhaps helping to produce the notably bipartisan spirit that characterised the passage of his bill, reached for the sunlit uplands: 'We may well produce in the new towns a new type of citizen, a healthy, self-respecting dignified person with a sense of beauty, culture and civic pride.'[15]

By this time Stevenage had already been publicly identified as the first new town, with its population of some 6,000 expected to increase tenfold. 'How do you feel about it?' a Mass-Observation investigator asked some of the indigenous residents. 'It's time this town was woken up,' replied a 45-year-old signwriter. A 30-year-old coachbuilder agreed: 'It's progress, and it's what we badly need here.' So, too, a 50-year-old housewife: 'I think it will be a benefit myself. If you've got a family, well, it's a good thing to know there'll be work for them.' Those expressing definite opposition included a 60-year-old car-park attendant. 'My great grandfather was here, and his father before him,' he explained. 'We belong here, and I shouldn't like to see the beauty taken away . . . Have you seen the beauty of the place? That avenue of chestnuts up by the school and parish church? You should see it.'

A few weeks later, on 6 May, Silkin himself was in Stevenage, to address a packed, tumultuous meeting in the small town hall, with up to 3,000 locked outside listening to loudspeakers. 'I want to carry out in Stevenage a daring exercise in town planning,' he declared at one point. 'It is no good your jeering: it is going to be done.' Silkin argued that Stevenage was ideally placed to attract both people and light industry from overcrowded London; called on the existing residents to 'make some sacrifice' in order to 'provide for the happiness and welfare of some 50,000 men, women and children'; drew a picture of the new Stevenage recreating a village-like 'spirit of friendliness and neighbourliness, the sense of belonging to a large family, a community'; and once more insisted that there was no choice in the matter: 'The project will go forward, because it must go forward. It will do so more surely and more smoothly, and more successfully, with your help and co-operation. Stevenage will in a short time become world-famous. *(Laughter)* People from all over the world will come to Stevenage to see how we here in this country are building for the new way of life.' Amid cries of 'Gestapo!' and 'Dictator!', Silkin left the meeting and walked to his ministerial car, a 25 h.p.

Wolseley, only to find that some boys had deflated the tyres and put sand in the petrol tank.

Less than a fortnight later, a referendum was held: some 2,500 residents took part, with 52 per cent voting that they were 'entirely against the siting of a satellite town at Stevenage'. But it availed them little. Although considerable national publicity was garnered when Stevenage signs at the local railway station were temporarily replaced by Silkingrad ones, and although the High Court in February 1947 agreed with the Residents' Protection Association (mainly comprising the well-to-do) that Silkin had not properly considered the objections raised at the public inquiry the previous October, the government was not to be thwarted, with Silkin later in 1947 winning first at the Court of Appeal and then at the House of Lords. The juggernaut was rolling. Old Stevenage had been the setting for the house in *Howards End*; new Stevenage would, as an unsympathetic, non-connecting E. M. Forster now put it, 'fall out of a blue sky like a meteorite upon the ancient and delicate scenery of Hertfordshire'.[16]

Not surprisingly, given this sort of local opposition (apparent also in Crawley and elsewhere), it took several years to get the new towns up and running. Faced by an acute housing shortage, the LCC responded by expanding the programme of 'out-county' estates that it had started between the wars, notably in Becontree, St Helier and Downham, which by the end of the 1930s were three of the largest housing estates in the world. The LCC also between 1946 and 1949 built more than 31,000 dwellings (a mixture of unprepossessing but functional houses and low-rise flats) on new estates at Harold Hill, Aveley, South Oxhey, Borehamwood, Debden, St Paul's Cray and Hainault – all of them beyond the LCC's boundary and in several cases, as was often pointed out, in the green belt that it was wanting to protect. Harold Hill in Essex was the largest of the estates, but its near neighbour Debden, together with South Oxhey in Hertfordshire, would attract the most sociological attention. From the start, these out-county estates suffered, like their inter-war predecessors, from an image problem. Suddenly the new dwelling places for many thousands of working-class Londoners, entirely bereft of architectural distinction and often communal facilities such as churches and pubs, the estates were in effect, to quote the architectural historian Andrew Saint, 'lower-grade new towns without new town privileges'.[17] They were also the cause of considerable tension at the LCC. While the Valuer's Department under Cyril Walker got on with its job of achieving 'maximum output' in new housing, the Architect's Department (under Robert Matthew from 1947) was full of frustrated young graduate architects unable to implement their strongly modernist ideas about public housing. Not that this mattered much to the new residents of Harold Hill, Debden et al, happy enough to get on with their own lives with a roof over their head, an indoor lavatory, and hot and cold running water.

The new towns and out-county estates both reflected the widespread faith put in the 1940s on dispersal as the best way to relieve the familiar problems (overcrowding, congestion, poor health etc) of the modern industrial city. No city in Britain had worse problems – or a worse reputation – than Glasgow. 'It is a disgustingly ugly town, a huddle of dirty buildings trying to outdo one another and not succeeding,' Naomi Mitchison wrote in 1947. 'The population is as ugly as the buildings. Walk down the Gallowgate; notice how many children you see with obvious rickets, impetigo or heads close clipped for lice, see the wild, slippered sluts, not caring any more to look decent!'

Two competing visions were now set out for Glasgow's future. The first, the work of the City Engineer Robert Bruce, was essentially an urban one. The Bruce Plan advocated a radically new, high-speed road system, a geometrically planned city centre, the demolition of more than half the city's housing stock, and the decanting of the urban poor to developments on the city's periphery but within its boundaries. Ultimately, it was the vision of a Glasgow that would retain not only all its population but also its nineteenth-century heavy industrial base. By contrast, the Clyde Valley Regional Plan, appearing in interim form in 1946 and predominantly the work of the ubiquitous Sir Patrick Abercrombie, envisaged a depopulated, de-industrialised Glasgow, surrounded by a green belt and sending many of its ill-housed inhabitants to healthier, 'overspill' new towns beyond the city's boundaries. 'Whole districts are obsolescent and past the possibility of reconstruction to modern standards, alike for industry, commerce and housing,' Abercrombie would declare in his final report, published in 1949; all told, he expected that nearly half of Glasgow's 1.1 million population would move to outside the city.

This latter approach, seeing Glasgow as part of the region's problem rather than as part of its solution, naturally appalled Glasgow Corporation – above all its Housing Committee, which stood to lose many thousands of tenants as well as (through the green-belt provisions) much potential building land. It was as if Abercrombie was preparing to blow up one of the great municipal power bases. The gloom deepened when the government, attracted by the prospect of (in Miles Glendinning's words) 'a constellation of planned, Whitehall-controlled garden cities set within a Green Belt', plumped for Abercrombie, not Bruce.[18] The designation in 1947 of East Kilbride as Scotland's new town was an unmistakable signal of intent. Yet for the Corporation, and for all those who still believed in Glasgow as 'the Second City of the Empire', the game was far from over.

Overall, looking at town planning in the 1940s, it is easy to exaggerate the radicalism and modernism. For instance, in Portsmouth, where a redevelopment plan was accepted by the city council in February 1946, not only was the gutted Guildhall to remain the city's focal point, but the existing road pattern was to be kept, supplemented by a few new cross-routes. In Manchester, where a plan was formally unveiled in the first winter of peace, the City Surveyor and Engineer R. Nicholas accepted that some 100,000 of the city's slum dwellings needed to be pulled down but specifically repudiated the high-rise solution. 'It would,' he insisted, 'be a profound sociological mistake to force upon the British public, in defiance of its own widely expressed preference for separate houses with private gardens, a way of life that is fundamentally out of keeping with its traditions, instincts and opportunities.' Adding that 'the advocates of large-scale flat-building greatly overestimate the proportion of people now living in the congested areas who might thereby be decently housed on the site', he concluded bluntly, 'It is impossible to get rid of the effects of congested development by turning it on edge.'

Even in Coventry, epitome of the modern with its central area delineated by an inner ring road and containing zoned clusters of building types (shopping, entertainment, civic), Donald Gibson and his planning colleagues were far from slavish in the way they followed Le Corbusier's *City of Tomorrow*. 'We did not think that very high buildings were necessary for the centre of a smallish city which was unlikely ever to have more than 400,000 people,' Percy Johnson-Marshall (brother of Stirrat) recalled. 'We would have liked to have incorporated his dream of multi-level communications, but we were worried about expense, and felt that, anyway, our precinct form of development went a long way to bringing safety and convenience to the pedestrian.' As with some other badly bombed cities, including Bristol, Exeter and Plymouth, the outcome was indeed modern, in the sense of not following the familiar pattern, but it was – quite deliberately on Gibson's part – a generally restrained, unthreatening sort of modernism.

Nor were these immediate post-war planners as brutally unforgiving of the past as has sometimes been assumed. Thomas Sharp's declaration in 1946 that 'the watchword for the future should be – not restoration, but renewal' ran directly counter to the *Advisory Handbook for the Redevelopment of Central Areas* issued by Silkin's ministry the following year. This emphasised the importance of new buildings not swamping the old and pushed for retention of the 'existing main street pattern'. Moreover, as Peter Larkham has shown in a detailed study of urban-reconstruction plans up to the early 1950s, conservation played a surprisingly prominent role in them. Sharp himself, in his plans for Exeter, Oxford and Salisbury, was not entirely insensitive to their special architectural qualities, while plans for Edinburgh, Norwich, Warwick and Worcester all had a reasonably conservationist element, though in places only implicitly.[19]

Where there was virtually no call for conservationism was in the plans made for industrial cities and towns: there, the notion that the nineteenth-century industrial heritage might be worth preserving for aesthetic reasons did not feature. 'The city's buildings, with few exceptions, are undistinguished,' stated the plan for Manchester. 'Moreover, our few noteworthy buildings [identified as non-industrial] are obscured by the dense development surrounding them.' It was different, though, in the other great Victorian economic powerhouse. 'It would not be wise to adopt a new aesthetic and a new scale for building for the City of London until the old one has been definitely lost or outmoded,' asserted the architect Charles Holden and the town planner William Holford, the City Corporation's consultants for its rebuilding programme. 'The seventeenth-century scale should be preserved and

St Paul's Cathedral – the noblest in the City – should remain archi-
tecturally, as in other ways, its chief building.'

Yet despite all their relative moderation, the planners in these years
found it desperately slow going when it came to trying to put their
plans into practice. Most obviously, they and their local sponsors faced
a series of trying economic constraints, including patchy financial
support from central government and the severe rationing of building
materials – constraints which invariably led to delay and sometimes
to abandonment. Nor could they assume, however much they may
have tried to, that the popular will was always behind them. In Bristol,
for example, a poll organised in early 1947 by the local Retail Traders'
Federation found that only 400 people wanted the proposed new
Broadmead shopping centre, as against some 13,000 wishing to see the
old shopping centre reinstated. The planners, for their part, simply
ignored this unfortunate result.[20]

Regrettably, no comparable poll was taken in Coventry, where it
would have been fascinating to test empirically the generally prevailing
assumption that Gibson's plan was welcomed by the majority of
Coventrians. Admittedly an impressive 57,000 people attended the
Coventry of the Future exhibition held for a fortnight at the city's
Drill Hall in October 1945, but the *Coventry Evening Telegraph*'s
assertion on the third day that 'the public reaction appears to be that
the schemes outlined are on the lines along which they would like to
see the city developed' was somewhat belied by a letter it printed from
Herbert E. Edwards, who had visited the exhibition 'along with a party
of others':

> We were unanimous in our strong criticism of the central area lay-out
> as shown in the large model.
>
> The general feeling was that the hard, rigid lines of those monstrous
> buildings would utterly spoil Coventry's unique city centre, with its
> fine old churches, etc. The treatment seemed to us entirely foreign and
> out of touch with the traditional setting – which demands real harmony
> in its surroundings.
>
> The City Fathers must be blind indeed if they suppose this massed
> barracks-like ensemble could possibly appeal to citizens with a grain of
> artistic feeling.

Over the next week, other critical letters appeared. 'The general concept of the scheme is not in keeping with the characteristics of the Coventry people, who would not feel at home in it,' wrote C.S.P. 'They all say, "Give us Coventry back as we knew it". What is wanted is the old Coventry, restored with a new Sunday dress, but old Coventry nevertheless.' Other letters dissented ('We have,' affirmed one, 'a wonderful opportunity to rebuild a city in accordance with the spirit of our age'), but certainly the overall balance of the correspondence was not in favour of the plan.

Subsequent oral testimony similarly suggests mixed feelings. 'It showed the raised ring road, all where the Cathedral was and all the rest of it,' recalled one visitor, Basil Whitham, more than half a century later. 'And we thought that this was fascinating ... we were all into spaceships, you know ... Buck Rogers and so forth.' That, though, was a young person's perspective; among older people the rather jaundiced recollection of Celia Grew was probably more representative. 'Whatever they proposed to do in the rebuilding, you sort of went along with it in a sort of zombie-like fashion, at least I did,' she explained. ''Cause you see I had got things happening in my own life with my husband getting wounded and being brought to Bromsgrove Hospital and me going over there to see him and all that kind of stuff.' While as for those who *did* take an interest, the experience of Dorrie Glass, a council employee who one day saw in Gibson's department a model of the new Coventry, was illuminating: 'It was a proper model really. You were sort of looking down, you know, like an aerial view. But they were all buildings, it wasn't a picture it was models, you know. We went and had a look at that. You couldn't sort of visualise it really.'[21]

The relative lack of interest on the part of architects, planners and others in popular taste was neatly encapsulated by a snatch from a 1946 round table (convened by *Building* magazine) of some leading architects. 'The public generally have no knowledge of what they want,' declared one. 'The public generally are only concerned with their own house,' responded another. 'It is questionable if they have any views at all.' Unsurprisingly, the next year's Town and Country Planning Act had no mechanism for getting the public involved in the planning process, apart from the right to object to the development plan after publication. In practice, according to Alison Ravetz, 'probably most people were quite unaware of this right, and ... the Minister was not obliged to hold a public enquiry.'

The aspect of Silkin's measure that caused most controversy was the 100 per cent development levy on appreciating land values. It was a provision never destined to have a long-term life, being (again in Ravetz's words) 'universally blamed for putting a stop to development'. But the Act as a whole was a stayer. Above all, it enshrined the principle that all development was to be subject to planning controls – or, as a delighted Frederic Osborn put it, 'it gives effect to the supremacy of public control of land use, without abolishing private ownership'. A further plus in his and many other well-meaning, progressive, middle-class eyes was that the act did much to protect the countryside from the threat of creeping, unplanned suburbia, the dreaded 'bungaloid growth'. Agricultural land, it insisted, was to be for agricultural use, but there was silence about the high-rise implication of high urban densities as the population grew. This was an implication that would have particular resonance given that the act also sanctified the idea of 'comprehensive' redevelopment of the inner city, which would follow compulsory purchase of (again in the words of the act) 'any areas which in the opinion of the planning authority suffered from extensive war damage, conditions of bad layout, obsolete development, or were in need of the relocation of population or industry'. Thus were born Comprehensive Development Areas (CDAs), though an economic upturn would be required for them to take major effect. Quite what that effect might be, no one at this stage could realistically envisage.

For one Tory backbencher, Sir Cuthbert Headlam, it was a case of seeing through a dark glass very darkly. 'I don't profess to have read one word of this most important measure,' he reflected on the evening in May 1947 when the bill was guillotined in the Commons, 'but can only hope that it may not be as devastating in its effects as some people say that it will be. I have an instinctive distrust of planners and always feel that "planning" merely makes confusion worse confounded – but then I am out of date and prefer things to grow up in their own way.' The Times, however, was sanguine, reflecting much of middle opinion. 'The British people,' it declared on the day in 1948 that the act came into force, 'almost without knowing it, are embarking upon one of the greatest experiments in the social control of their environment ever attempted by a free society. In the process they are also putting old individual liberties in trust for the common good.'[22]

The Town and Country Planning Act was in many ways complemented by the Agriculture Act, also 1947. While the former was designed to protect agricultural land and the rural character of the countryside, the latter specifically addressed what was to done on that land, with the threefold aim – entirely understandable in the immediate context – of feeding the population, keeping down food imports and maximising production. The solution adopted by Tom Williams, a former Yorkshire miner who now found himself Minister of Agriculture, was to give the farmers guaranteed prices and assured markets for most of their produce, as well as grants for modernisation and ready access to a government-run scientific advisory service. Back in 1937, Attlee had declared that 'the Labour Party stands for the national ownership of the land', but that was now off the agenda. Instead, for many farmers it was jackpot time. The National Farmers' Union would play a pivotal role each February in the annual price review; Williams himself became known as 'the Farmer's Friend'; and on eventually leaving office, he was given a small dinner party at Claridges, organised by the Duke of Norfolk.

The farm labourers fared less well. Although the act gave them improved security of tenure and a wages board, the system of tied cottages remained widespread and the farm worker was still very poorly paid (roughly two-thirds of average earnings in manufacturing industries) for often punishingly long hours. For the consumer, there was a new, longlasting era of cheap food; for the government, the heavy subsidies to be paid were amply justified by the spectacular success story to be told as farm productivity increased by leaps and bounds, with output as early as 1950 reaching 146 per cent of the pre-war level. And for the environment? The remorseless goal, shared equally by farmers and the Ministry of Agriculture, of maximising production had serious consequences for wildlife and landscape; but in the immediate post-war climate, with the food-producing farmer still almost a hero after his efforts during the war, organisations like the Soil Association, set up at its end and pushing for what would later be called organic farming, were completely marginalised. A golden future for industrialised farming lay, in every sense, wide open.

The illusion at the heart of the 1947 acts, taken together, was that agricultural Britain could be modernised without this fundamentally affecting the character of rural Britain. Even as the acts were coming into force, John Moore was completing his 'Brensham' trilogy of novels, lovingly detailing a Cotswolds way of life (intimate, domestic, with a benign, semi-feudal social hierarchy) that he believed to be under threat from a mixture of bureaucracy and technology.[23] Yet from another, arguably less sentimental point of view, it was the very insistence of government planners that agriculture be the only activity allowed on agricultural land that, together with the attempted prevention of suburban encroachment, had serious employment implications once agricultural modernisation had begun to reduce sharply the number of farm labourers required. Simultaneously romanticising and destroying the existing way of life, the urban activators did to the countryside what they would soon do to the – real or imagined – communities in their midst.

7

Glad to Sit at Home

All new governments enjoy something of a honeymoon, in this case prompting Raymond Streat to reflect in December 1945 that there had been 'extraordinarily little fuss or resistance' to 'the first moves in a comprehensive revolution within the economic and political life of Britain'. But as early as the spring of 1946, against a background of painful austerity, whatever honeymoon there had been with the middle class was more or less over.

'We are the masters at the moment – and not only for the moment, but for a very long time to come,' the Attorney-General Sir Hartley Shawcross unwisely pronounced on 2 April – words soon truncated to the notorious catchphrase 'We are the masters now.' On 16 April, inspecting Kenwood House for National Trust purposes, James Lees-Milne was 'surprised a little' by the secretary there 'saying that she considered any infringement of a law passed by this Government was justifiable'; two days later, the novelist Elizabeth Bowen told the diarist that 'we must all fight against being state-ridden'; and in early May the architect Professor Albert Richardson insisted to Lees-Milne that 'without aristocracy of the higher and lower grades there could be no beauty' and that 'consequently it was our duty to oppose this Government at every turn'. About this time, the young J. G. Ballard arrived in Southampton, having spent most of the war in a Japanese civilian camp, and travelled via London to relatives in Birmingham. 'Everyone looked small and tired and white-faced and badly nourished,' he recalled many years later. But what most struck him was the prevailing mindset:

All these middle-class people, my parents, friends and relations and the like, were seething with a sort of repressed rage at the world around them. And what they were raging against was the post-war Labour government. It was impossible to have any kind of dialogue about the rights and wrongs of the National Health Service, which was about to come in, they talked as if this Labour government was an occupying power, that the Bolsheviks had arrived and were to strip them of everything they owned.

That kind of atavistic loathing, vividly caught in Angela Thirkell's 'Barsetshire' novels, was perhaps at its most intense in the City of London. When the young Colin Knock, straight from school, attended an interview at the jobbers Prior & Williams, he made the mistake of wearing a red tie. 'Does that have any political implications?' he was asked by a partner. None at all, he replied, and thereby got the position of office boy. At another Stock Exchange firm, the brokers Panmure Gordon, the senior partner Richard Hart-Davis insisted that the Prime Minister was Chinese and invariably referred to him as A. T. Lee. At Midland Bank, the newly knighted and unashamedly pro-Labour chief executive Sir Clarence Sadd came under severe internal pressure and was eventually forced out in 1948. Nor was a virulent animosity absent from the Palace of Westminster, once the Tories had regrouped and begun to recover their nerve. 'I have not forgotten,' a junior minister, John Freeman, recalled in the late 1950s, 'the tension of rising to answer questions or conduct a debate under the cold, implacable eyes of that row of well-tailored tycoons, who hated the Labour Government with a passion and fear which made them dedicated men in their determination to get it out of office and to limit the damage it could do to the world which they saw as theirs by right.'[1] All in all, though we cannot recover those lost conversations in saloon bars or at 19th holes or local Rotaries, it is pretty clear that a strong, almost tribal middle-class backlash was well under way within a year of Labour taking power.

Certainly the well-to-do believed they had been soaked (James Lansdale Hodson wondered in January 1947 whether the Cabinet was 'aware of the bitterness and cynicism expressed in clubs and the mood that it's no use making money because you won't be allowed to keep it'), but what was the reality? Under Hugh Dalton's fiscal stewardship (until

November 1947), both surtax and death duties were increased quite sharply, but the temptation to introduce either a capital-gains tax or a one-off capital levy was resisted, and in general the City of London, for all its grumbling, survived quite comfortably. Nevertheless, it does seem that the cumulative effect of war and the Labour government was for the middle class to lose out quite significantly relative to the working class: at the end of the 1940s, the Inland Revenue estimated that whereas salaries (after tax) had declined in real terms by 16 per cent between 1938 and 1949, wages had risen by 21 per cent. Yet the angst of the middle class might have been alleviated if there had been greater awareness of the extent to which it stood to gain from the Labour government's proudest achievement – the welfare state. Not only was there its underlying (though not total) universalism – including such attractive benefits in kind as free secondary education and a free health service – but, in Kenneth Morgan's words, summarising a mountain of research, 'the very extent and cost of the welfare state after 1945 meant that many of the new social reforms were financed by transfers of income within lower-income groups themselves, rather than by transfers from the rich to the poor'.[2] It was not, amid the clink of G&Ts, a point much made.

What about the much-vaunted, much-predicted, much-feared social revolution? 'The Stock Exchange will be pulled down, the horse plough will give way to the tractor, the country houses will be turned into children's holiday camps, the Eton and Harrow match will be forgotten' was how George Orwell, in his celebrated 1941 essay *The Lion and the Unicorn*, had keenly looked ahead to the post-war socialist future. If by the end of the war he was significantly less optimistic, he hoped at least for an assault on that symbol of social privilege seen everywhere on the railways – 'the First Class nonsense should be scrapped once and for all,' he thundered in October 1944. But by the spring of 1946, some eight months into the Labour government, he was frankly conceding that there would be no social revolution:

In the social set-up there is no symptom by which one could infer that we are not living under a Conservative government. No move has been made against the House of Lords, for example, there has been no talk of disestablishing the Church, there has been very little replacement of

Tory ambassadors, service chiefs or other high officials, and if any effort is really being made to democratize education, it has borne no fruit as yet. Allowing for the general impoverishment, the upper classes are still living their accustomed life.

Orwell was surely right. The House of Lords did eventually have its power to delay legislation halved from two years to one, but any prospect of more fundamental reform, let alone abolition, was explicitly squashed by Herbert Morrison, who in 1947 told the Liberal leader Clement Davies that 'we should not set up something new and different from the past'. The public schools, of course, remained out of radical bounds, as did the privileges of Oxbridge. Other key areas where there was no government appetite for real change included company-law reform and gender equality. In the former, where the real possibility existed of deep-seated reform along German lines, tepid political willpower proved no match for City and Whitehall opposition allied to trade union leaders who saw workers' representation as jeopardising free collective bargaining; in the latter, the Labour leadership simply ignored an overwhelming card vote at its 1947 party conference in favour of equal pay.

Irrespective of government policy, moreover, society at large remained riddled by petty snobbery and infinite gradations of class. 'Among both the upper and middle classes,' Frederic Osborn reflected in October 1945, 'the word "garden city" stands for a working-class housing estate, with perhaps just a touch of philanthropy. It has therefore been something to approve but on no account to live in.' The following year, faced by rising costs, the traditionally select North Hants Golf Club elected 30 new members. Unfortunately, three of them were, as various letters of complaint to the committee put it, 'engaged in trade in Fleet'. The storm died down only when the committee pointed out that all three had played on the course regularly during the war and that no permanent 'change of policy' was envisaged.[3]

There was also, as ever, the uncanny ability of 'The Thing' (as William Cobbett called the British establishment) to reinvent itself. Perhaps the prime example in these years was the National Trust, almost entirely run by Old Etonians. Historically, the Trust's prime purpose had been to preserve actually or potentially threatened tracts of countryside, but that now changed to the acquisition and upkeep of country houses which would otherwise probably have been demolished. Public access to the nation's new treasures was in some instances fixed at no more than 50 days in the year and at hours which were, as the Trust freely admitted in 1947, 'settled as far as possible to suit the donor's convenience'. In October 1946 the Trust's relevant committee, including Sir Robert ('Bertie') Abdy, met at Montacute House in Somerset to discuss arrangements there. 'Meeting quite a success,' noted Lees-Milne, 'in spite of Bertie's sole comment which electrified the others. He remarked that the public could not of course be admitted to the house because they smelt. There was two minutes dead silence . . .' Still, perhaps the point of the story *was* the stunned silence; maybe things were changing after all.

Either way, what mattered to much of the progressive intelligentsia was not so much redistribution of wealth or social egalitarianism, planning or welfare as cultural renewal – the spreading to the mass of the population of what Matthew Arnold had famously termed 'sweetness and light'. The enemy was easy enough to identify. 'Refuse with scorn the great dope-dreams of the economic emperors and their sorcerers and Hollywood sirens,' J. B. Priestley implored in his *Letter to a Returning Serviceman*, published in late 1945. 'Don't allow them to inject you with Glamour, Sport, Sensational News, and all the Deluxe nonsense, as if they were filling you with an anaesthetic.' There was so much to deplore. Labour Party memos in 1946/7 on the need for a 'Socialist policy for leisure' lamented the 'failure of the majority of Britain's citizens to enjoy a full life through their leisure pursuits'; labelled the cinema and gambling as two prime examples of regrettably 'passive' and superficial leisure pursuits; and drew the rather defeatist conclusion that 'all forms of escapist entertainment or recreation are encouraged by the drabness, insecurity and hopelessness of daily life'.[4] All the more cause, then, to attempt to inject a large and improving dose of cultural uplift. But unfortunately for the uplifters, as three examples all too graphically showed, the mass of the population was simply not interested.

The first example was the Arts Council, direct successor to the wartime state-sponsored organisation CEMA, which had brought high culture (especially in the form of drama and music) to thousands of captive audiences, whether in army camps or air-raid shelters or factory canteens. The new body's first chairman was John Maynard Keynes, who in July 1945 declared his intention of making 'the theatre and the concert hall and the art gallery . . . a living element in everyone's upbringing'. The initial strategy was to continue to take culture to the people, but in practice at least 80 per cent of the former wartime audience, now no longer captive, voted negatively with their feet. Activists, reported one regional office in 1947, were 'desperately worried' by 'their failure to establish contact with the ordinary folk in their towns'. Likewise, in a confidential report the same year, the Council concluded that its activities 'do not . . . touch the mass of the working-class, even to the extent they did during the war'. By the late 1940s a full-scale retreat was under way from regional outreach, and soon afterwards the Council's ambitious motto, 'The Best for the Most', was replaced by the more circumspect 'Few But Roses'. A similar lack of broad appeal proved the Achilles heel of the adult-education movement. The vaunted if overestimated wartime impact of the Army Bureau of Current Affairs prompted in peace a big increase in government funding, especially for the Workers' Education Association, but in the immediate post-war period the WEA was only able to attract fewer then 20,000 manual workers to its classes across England and Wales each year, barely a fifth of its students as a whole.[5]

Finally, almost notoriously, there was the Third Programme, the BBC's high-culture radio channel that began broadcasting on Sunday, 29 September 1946. 'Its whole content will be directed to an audience that is not of one class but that is perceptive and intelligent,' promised the director-general Sir William Haley – whose private goal was that in time so many listeners would migrate to it from the Light Programme and the Home Service that the two older channels would no longer be required. A glance, though, at the *Radio Times* for the first evening suggested that it would be a long route-march from *ITMA, Variety Bandbox* and *Grand Hotel* on the Light to such offerings as 'Reflections on World Affairs' by Field-Marshal Smuts, the BBC Symphony Orchestra conducted by Sir Adrian Boult and gramophone records of madrigals by Monteverdi. Quarterly figures soon revealed the average programme on the Third to be securing only a meagre share of the BBC's overall listening audience: 2.2 per cent in October–December 1946, and down to 0.9 per cent by July–September 1947, with one listener in three not even having made an attempt to tune in. Another 1947 audience-research report found that whereas 30 per cent of the upper-middle class had given a 'warm welcome' to the Third, only 4 per cent of the working class had.

'I would prefer the Third Programme to be a little more familiar ground,' complained one member of the BBC's Listening Panel, an unemployed miner, fairly soon afterwards. 'After all, we are not all University Students or even past students.' A housewife agreed: 'It bangs us right into the middle of things we really cannot understand.' And an accounts clerk frankly admitted that 'the great majority of items' did not attract him because they were 'too remote, too heavy, requiring mental powers which I simply have not got at the end of an ordinary weekday'. Such lack of engagement was consistent with Tom Harrisson's early warning, in January 1947, that there was 'a real danger in the Third Programme becoming somewhat "cliquey", a bit of a mutual admiration society'; among recent examples he cited 'the amazingly unreal, donnish utterances of A.J.P. Taylor on foreign affairs', 'the lack of topical controversy', 'the total neglect of sociology' and 'the exaggerated use of Dylan Thomas's vocal qualities'. Among those even willing to be engaged, perhaps the best advice came from the novelist Rose Macaulay: 'One should have a long but not debilitating illness and really get down to it.'[6]

Significantly, Priestley's returning serviceman had to do more than just raise his cultural game. 'I think we make too much of our separateness in this country,' the great man warned, and, after a dark reference to how the pre-war suburbs had been like 'tree-lined concentration camps', he went on: 'Beware the charmed cosy circle. Don't stay too long in that armchair . . . but get out and about, compel yourself to come to terms with strangers (who will not be strangers long), make one of a team or a group, be both worker and audience, and put a hand to the great tasks.'

Was Priestley knocking at an open door? The testimony of Raphael Samuel – that most eclectic of historians, here recalling the years of his childhood – might easily make one think so:

Organization was regarded as a good in itself; it was fetishized in the conduct of personal life quite as much as in the office or the factory; it extended to 'dancing in step' in the ballroom, to organized fun in the holiday camps, to the orderly queues at the football grounds and the orderly crowds on the terraces. The 1940s constituted, in Britain, a kind of zenith of mass society . . . In London there were no fringe theatres, except for 'Unity', our Communist theatre in St Pancras, no alternative food shops, except for some delicatessens in Swiss Cottage and a vegetarian grocer in Tottenham Court Road. Clothes were worn as an affirmation of social position rather than as a display of personal self, and they were regimented to a degree. Skirt lengths rose or fell uniformly, above or below the knee, according to the dictates of the season; a man who wore suede shoes was morally suspect.

Those of us too young to remember the 1940s indeed look at the photographs of the massed ranks of cloth caps on the terraces, or the respectable-looking men wearing hats, jackets and ties as they watch the cricket or even sit by the sea, and assume that a uniform, collective appearance signified a uniform, collective spirit. Perhaps sometimes it did, but it was not a spirit inclined to forsake what Priestley, in his stridently communal '1945' mood, lamented as 'that famous English privacy' responsible for 'the apathetic herd we were in the Baldwin and Chamberlain era, when we messed about in our back gardens, ran about in our little cars, listened to the crooners and the comics, while the terrible shadows crept nearer'. Those shadows, after all, had now been banished, and for most people their *reward* was to return to their gardens and cars – cars that in time might even be a different colour than black.

This was a truth that Frederic Osborn recognised. 'In Welwyn, where everyone has a house and a garden, we find a moderate desire for social and communal life,' he wrote to Lewis Mumford in August 1946 from his garden city. 'The demand has definite limits; I am more communal in my habits than most people are. I find many women dislike the idea of nursery school and crêches; they want to look after their own children. And young men and women prefer lodgings to hostels.' How, then, was a more communally minded society to be encouraged? With great difficulty. In their pioneering account of the

Labour Party and popular politics in the 1940s, Steven Fielding, Peter Thompson and Nick Tiratsoo chart the post-war development of such largely *de haut en bas* initiatives as neighbourhood units, socially mixed housing, municipal eating facilities, popular participation in urban planning and joint production committees in the workplace, with in each instance only chequered progress being made at best. In terms of voluntary organisations like Co-operative societies, friendly societies and community associations, all their evidence points towards an essentially 'divi-minded', instrumental use of them (whether for benefits or facilities) on the part of members, as opposed to a more socialist or ideological motivation.[7]

Contemporary surveys flesh out the picture. In Willesden in the winter of 1946/7, more than twice as many preferred to live in a single-class street than in a mixed street; most drew a very careful distinction between 'friends', 'acquaintances' and 'neighbours'; and 75 per cent of housewives were not on visiting terms with their neighbours, let alone going out together. Soon afterwards, a survey of Watling, an inter-war LCC estate near Edgware, found that only 30 per cent of adults answered 'Yes' to the question 'Do you belong to any clubs, sports associations, guilds, etc., for leisure time activities, including those connected with politics and the social life of churches?' – a figure apparently *above* the national trend. And in August 1947 an investigator in Bethnal Green heard explanations from working-class people about why they preferred to give a wide berth to clubs, societies and suchlike:

I don't like mixing, I like keeping myself to myself.

I'm a married woman and I prefer staying in my home. I don't want to go and mix with other people, I've too much to do in the house.

I've got too much to do in the house, I'm glad to sit at home in the evening.

No, I don't want anything to do with that kind of thing. I just don't like it that's all.

I'm just not interested I suppose, there's plenty to do without joining one of those.

Well I like going out with the hubby, and I don't bother to mix much with others.

I've got these three kiddies, they take up all my time.

By now even Priestley was reluctantly coming to accept the sovereignty of the individual. 'There seems to be far less kind and neighbourly co-operation than there was a few years ago, during the worst of the war years,' he told his Light Programme listeners (presumably waiting impatiently for the next crooner) two months later. 'People are harder, more selfish, more intent upon looking after Number One. They are more likely to snatch, grab, lose their temper.' And, like a thousand intellectuals before and (especially) after him, he added, 'Now why is this? What has gone wrong?'[8]

Over the years, the '"we wuz robbed!" tendency within British Labour historiography', as the historian Dilwyn Porter has termed it, would exercise huge influence. If only there had been more systematic economic planning, if only there had been more extensive and full-blooded nationalisation, if only private education had been abolished – in fact, if only the Attlee government had been more *socialist*, and thereby engendered an irresistible moral and political force of popular enthusiasm for its policies – then the story of post-war Britain would have been fundamentally different and fundamentally happier. That was not how the *New Statesman*'s resident versifier, 'Sagittarius' (a pseudonym for Olga Katzin), saw things. In 'Let Cowards Flinch,' a brilliant long poem imitating Byron's ottava rima and published in October 1947, she surveyed Labour's first two years in power. Two verses had a special piquancy:

> But while they speed the pace of legislation
>   With sleepless ardour and unmatched devotion,
> The lower strata of the population
>   Appear to have imbibed a soothing potion;
> Faced with the mighty tasks of restoration
>   The teeming millions seem devoid of motion,
> Indifferent to the bracing opportunity
>   Of selfless service to the whole community.
>
> It is as if the Government were making
>   Their maiden journey in the train of State,
> The streamlined engine built for record-breaking,

> Steaming regardless at a breakneck rate,
> Supposing all the while that they were taking
> Full complement of passengers and freight,
> But puffing on in solitary splendour,
> Uncoupled from the carriages and tender.

Yet one can exaggerate the degree of uncoupling and indeed the breakneck steaming ahead. Precisely because the Attlee government was essentially practical and moderate in its approach, faithfully reflecting Attlee himself, it managed to create a settlement that in operational practice had – above all on the welfare side – considerable direct appeal. Crucially, it was an appeal not only to the working class, thankful (more or less) to consolidate its wartime gains, but also to significant elements of the middle class, who for all their lack of political gratitude were understandably reluctant to look an apparent gift horse, albeit a rather threadbare one, in the mouth. People may not have been as communally minded as Priestley and Labour's other cheerleaders might have wished, but they were for the most part perfectly willing, at this stage anyway, to look to collective provision in order to satisfy individual needs and wants. Put another way, the fact that BUPA started in 1947 did not mean that the majority of people were not welcoming the prospect of a national health service free at the point of delivery.

Moreover, for many of those who had lived through the worst of the inter-war years – the bleak 'Jarrow' version of those years rather than Margaret Thatcher's more upbeat 'Grantham' version – there was a deep satisfaction in the very fact of a government no longer run by the old gang. There might be serious economic problems, there might be miserable austerity, but at last the awful spectre of mass unemployment had seemingly been banished. One afternoon in April 1946, Florence Speed, an inveterate Conservative voter, was gazing at a shop window in Brixton:

There were lovely fabrics on display & streamlined wooden carvings & furniture which doesn't appeal to me.

As I looked a friendly little man in a cap, but neat & respectable, said to me, 'Beautiful stuff there'.

'Yes,' I agreed slightly sardonically.

'But it *is* good.'

'Yes it is, but I like curves, not all these straight lines.'

'I like Victorian mahogany,' he said then. 'More homely. But this stuff is good.'

'British craftsmen are the best in the world – if they'd work.'

'Digging that old one up' the man retorted contemptuously, & in a few seconds the friendliness had changed to fanaticism as bottled up hate, poured out in a spate of sing song Welsh.

He had been a miner . . . 'Won't work? I'd have walked from Land's End to John o'Groats to get work. Every man's entitled to a job. I've had nothing in a day but a cup of tea . . .'

He had no teeth & spoke so vehemently, & rapidly, that he sprayed my face with spit.

He told me of a friend who had fought in World War I . . . On his return he could find no work, & died from malnutrition. When he was dying he called his sons, & told them, 'If there's another war, don't fight. I did & I've starved.' Two of his sons were conscientious objectors in the last war.

The Conservatives in a 100 years had done nothing but keep down 70% of the population & let them starve. There had been starvation in every town in the country. They would never be in office again. In fifty years time there would be no bloody dukes & no parasites. Everyone would have to work.

A mild pleasant sociable old man, no one would have guessed at the deep-down burning hatred. The Labour Government are doing fine of course! – at least they haven't had time yet . . .

He had so obviously suffered that I couldn't help sympathising with him.[9]

PART THREE

8

Christ It's Bleeding Cold

New Year's Day 1947 was a red-letter day. 'The MINES HAVE BEEN NATIONALISED TODAY,' noted a somewhat sceptical Vere Hodgson in west London. 'All is fun and games at the pits . . . The worst of it is these remedies for the troubles of life never turn out so well as you expect!' Certainly that Wednesday and over the next few days there were some stirring scenes at Britain's 970 pits, employing some 692,000 miners. The National Coal Board (NCB) flag was hoisted (often by the oldest employee at the colliery), speeches were made, songs were sung, banners were unfurled, brass bands played. They were all now 'one family', declared the NCB's chairman Lord Hyndley at celebrations at Murton Colliery on the Durham coalfield, adding that 'if they all worked hard and worked together they would make nationalisation a great success'. At nearby Thornley Colliery the main address was given by Hubert Tunney, former chairman of Thornley Miners' Lodge and now assistant labour director of the coal board at Newcastle:

Thirty years ago a lot of us saw in a far distance a dream of the public ownership of the mines. Now we have realised that ownership we have the important duty of making that venture a success. You are now privileged to work for a model employer. You have had holidays recently with pay and without conditions attached to them, the Board taking the view that there is a value in stressing and expressing the human side of the industry. The responsibility is now upon the management and the men to recognise that they must also play their part as far as production is concerned. Absenteeism must be reduced, lightning strikes must be cut out. There is no necessity for these things.

Fine words, and at one Durham colliery they duly celebrated Vesting Day by burying a symbolic hatchet. But for Sid Chaplin, at the Dean and Chapter Colliery that dominated Ferryhill, it was a case of sitting in the canteen and hearing the sound of music in the distance, as lodge and colliery officials marched behind band and banner. 'We had been working all night to install a new conveyer,' he recalled. 'It had been a long shift and we were tired. But the conveyer was ready for coal-work, and we were satisfied.'[1]

For a glimpse of the distinctive mentality and culture of the miners in the immediate post-war years, our best guide is the indefatigable Ferdynand Zweig, who travelled around the main English and Welsh coalfields between July and October 1947. 'While talking to the miners,' he found, 'one is continually struck by the fact that the past is deeply ingrained in their minds' – above all the 1926 coal strike. 'Twenty years in the miner's life,' he added, 'is probably like a year for others.' Events between the wars had also led to a widely shared, deeply ingrained pessimism, which full employment and better wages since the early 1940s had done little to remove. 'The great majority of miners are not politically minded,' Zweig reckoned, 'but all of them have an enormous – I would say an overwhelming – class consciousness.' Outside working hours, miners' favourite pastimes included watching games (especially football), going to the cinema, going dancing and gambling (dog and horse racing, football pools, sweepstakes). 'In a village in West York-shire the people could name me nine bookies with their offices, and on racing days those places are simply besieged by the patrons, who want to know the latest results coming in on a teleprinter.' As for reading habits, Zweig noted how 'lately a great wave of cheap, rubbishy stories has invaded the mining villages, and at the stalls in any market you can see these booklets in exciting paper covers with glaring titles, changing hands like hot cakes . . . mostly second-hand, and very dirty.' *Dangerous Dames, Moonlight Desire, White Traffic, The Penalty is Death, Corpses Don't Care, The League of the Living Dead*: 'glaring' indeed.

Inevitably, to Zweig's silent but still palpable regret, 'some welfare institutes and clubs have closed their reading and library rooms because they were not used and turned them into games rooms', while 'even in South Wales, where the traditions of cultural interests cultivated by the institution of "Eisteddfod" were very high, I was told that the choirs, dramatic societies, poetry and musical clubs are not as popular as they used to be.' Zweig enquired why. "The buses have done that," someone told him. "You can move freely for a few pence and get any amusement you want outside the village." Zweig also went into miners' homes, finding 'a great contrast between the unpleasant appearance of the houses from outside and the nice appearance inside':

> The rooms are kept very tidy and clean, and the housewives take immense pride in keeping their houses spotless. Most miners go to considerable pains to have a yearly re-decorating of their living-room, which is always larger than any of the others. The living-room is often furnished with a leather suite, including an armchair and a couch. In general, miners prefer brass fire-irons to wooden or other modern ones, and they still have very large fire-places of the metal type, with large set-pots. Another noticeable sight are the gaily decorated mantel-pieces, with brass and other ornaments. Hand-made rugs and carpets are the feature in nearly all mining houses . . .[2]

For all the gambling and lurid paperbacks, for all the enhanced physical mobility, the pit villages were still deeply respectable, ultimately home-centred worlds of their own.

What at the start of 1947 did their inhabitants really expect from nationalisation? Clearly it was a moment not without high hopes. 'Nationalisation appears as the final and the only all-embracing security,' a Mass-Observation investigator had concluded in 1942 after lengthy stays in Blaina and Nantyglo on the South Wales coalfield; on Vesting Day itself that coalfield saw many scenes of excitement and enthusiasm, including more than a thousand miners gathering at Park Colliery to sing 'Cwm Rhondda'. Yet did the rank and file, as opposed to some union leaders and activists, truly see nationalisation as ushering in, either actually or potentially, fundamental changes in working conditions and employer/employee relationships? Unfortunately, we have no contemporary surveys, ie at the point of nationalisation. But Ina Zweiniger-Bargielowska's 1980s interviews with a range of retired miners from four collieries (Oakdale, Park and Dare, Penrhiwceibr, Seven Sisters) in South Wales – significantly, a more radical coalfield than most – broadly confirm the low-key assessment that a South

Yorkshire colliery manager had offered to James Lansdale Hodson some seven months before the event. The recollections she heard were of a solid but essentially narrow, pay-oriented trade unionism in these early post-war years. Bob Crockett 'never took it into [his] head' to go to union meetings, and 'once I came out of that pit I came home and I never thought about the pit . . . until I had to go back there'; Cliff Price frankly conceded that he was 'only interested in things appertaining to myself, my own work'; and according to Eddie Bevan, the men were solely interested in union affairs 'when it hit their pockets, when something within the pit happens'. Few recalled the work itself with any fondness. 'The worst occupation in God's earth,' declared Stanley Warnes; 'as long as I was getting a wage at the end,' was Bevan's view; or, as Glan Powell put it, 'wages, that's what everybody is going down the pit for, to earn money'. Perhaps inevitably, such men tended to see the prospect of nationalisation as something which in itself did not particularly concern them. A 'pie-in-the-sky sort of thing,' remembered one, another that he 'didn't much think about it, to be honest', a third that '[I]wasn't really bothered myself.' If it brought tangible, bread-and-butter benefits, well and good; if it did not, too bad; but either way, there were no ideological hopes invested.

Other oral evidence, from Midlands coalfields where there had been a long, pre-1947 history of harmonious industrial relations, predictably presents an even less politicised picture. Coventry Colliery, for example, was held up by one miner as having had 'great sports grounds, great pavilions, they spent money on providing silver bands, a very good cricket team, parks, leisure, it's all part of village life as I was brought up'. At the time of the changeover, his main hope was that benign paternalism under private ownership would continue under public ownership.[3] Overall, a range of expectations and non-expectations obtained at the start of 1947, but few miners seemed to equate nationalisation with workers' control, whatever that might mean.

It was anyway a propitious moment for pragmatism rather than ideology, given that by the time of Vesting Day the government was in serious difficulties over the production of coal – responsible for more than 90 per cent of Britain's energy requirements – and in no great position to resist the implementation of union demands for improved pay and conditions. The previous spring the National Union of Mineworkers had drawn up the 'Miners' Charter', a broad-based wish list (including the modernisation of existing pits, the sinking of new ones, proper training for young miners, and improved social and welfare provision) that had at its core several key demands: average wages not to fall 'below those of any other British industry'; a five-day week without loss of pay; and miners to receive two consecutive weeks' paid holiday. Over the rest of 1946, the response of Manny Shinwell, Minister of Fuel and Power, was essentially to give way – over holidays, the principle of a guaranteed weekly wage and, above all, the five-day week, to come into operation by May 1947. In so doing he overrode the wishes of the fledgling NCB, though such was the parlous state of the industry that arguably he had little choice: not only was there a shortage of manpower (14,000 down on August 1945), but absenteeism rates were still high (running at about 15 per cent) and much-exhorted productivity improvements were barely coming through. Strikingly, the prospect of nationalisation – forced through by the government with what one historian has called 'almost indecent haste' – did as little to improve the situation in the closing months of 1946 as did Shinwell's concessions to the Miners' Charter, so that by the end of the year many factories in the Midlands and north-west were on short-time working because of the lack of coal.

Shinwell himself, for all his bluff and bluster, was a disastrous minister at this difficult time. Hugh Gaitskell, who had drawn the short straw as his Parliamentary Secretary, would observe that 'he walks alone one feels because he has never been able fully to trust anyone', that his usual traits were 'suspicion and aggression', and that 'as an administrator' he was 'hardly a starter' – all fair charges. Working-class and left-wing, Shinwell felt an intense allegiance to the miners, who for so many years had enjoyed a unique position in the labour movement, and he obstinately believed that somehow they would see things through. 'Prime Minister,' he blithely remarked at one point to a sceptical Attlee, 'you should not allow yourself to be led up the garden path by statistics. You should look at the imponderables.'[4]

On Thursday, 23 January 1947 – the day after Anthony Heap noted that 'more and more shops and offices seem to be going in for the new pale blue "fluorescent" system of electric lighting' – snow began to fall in the south-east. It was the start of Britain's most severe and protracted spell of bad weather during the twentieth century. Florence Speed was one of millions who shivered:

24 January. I was frozen today, gas is on at such low pressure. Worked with scarf over my head, mittens on my hands, & a rug round my legs.

25 January. Open spaces look as if sugar has been dredged over them.

28 January. Freeze up continues . . . Thermometer been at freezing point all day. Waste pipe in the bathroom & the geyser frozen.

29 January. Even colder the forecast for tonight, so I've borrowed a balaclava helmet from Fred [her brother] to wear in bed!

30 January. The cuts last night put lights out in the streets. Hyde Park was closed because there were no lights there.

On Sunday the 26th, as the big freeze started to tighten its grip, the annual meeting was held of Oakdale Navigation Lodge, the miners' lodge for Oakdale Colliery in South Wales. 'It was regrettable to hear over the Wireless that Factories were closing down for lack of coal,' remarked the chairman, Sam Garland. 'This was not the fault of the Miners.' Was the importation of Polish miners the answer? Not according to Garland: 'We are in dire need of coal and previously it had been Miners' sons that had filled the pits, changes had come and Miners' sons were looking for a larger life, there were other people's sons who could well do their share before the introduction of foreign labour.' Three days later, the coldest day for more than 50 years, the lights went out not only in London but all over the country; the electricity was off for long spells; gas in most big cities was at about a quarter of its normal pressure; and amid huge snow-drifts transport virtually ground to a halt. 'Wearing my snow boots and fur-lined coat I was not once warm,' grumbled James Lees-Milne. 'All my pipes, including w.c. pipes, are frozen, so a bath or a wash is out of the question. W.c. at the office frozen likewise . . . And we live in the twentieth century. Even the basic elements of civilization are denied us.'[5]

A visitor to London at this miserable time was Christopher Isherwood, over from America for the first time since before the war. Londoners themselves 'didn't seem depressed or sullen' – though 'their faces were still wartime faces, lined and tired', while 'many of them stared longingly at my new overcoat' – and his only criticism of the prevailing stoicism was that 'perhaps the English had become a little too docile in their attitude toward official regulation'. By contrast, he found London's physical shabbiness 'powerfully and continuously depressing':

> Plaster was peeling from even the most fashionable squares and crescents; hardly a building was freshly painted. In the Reform Club, the wallpaper was hanging down in tatters. The walls of the National Gallery showed big unfaded rectangles, where pictures had been removed and not yet rehung. Many once stylish restaurants were now reduced to drabness and even squalor . . . London remembered the past and was ashamed of its present appearance. Several Londoners I talked to at that time believed it would never recover. 'This is a dying city,' one of them told me.

As for the snow, 'it soon assumed the aspect of an invading enemy':

> Soldiers turned out to fight it with flame-throwers. The newspapers spoke of it in quasi-military language: 'Scotland Isolated', 'England Cut in Half'. Even portions of London were captured; there was a night when no taxi driver would take you north of Regent's Park. With coal strictly rationed, gas reduced to a blue ghost and electricity often cut off altogether, everybody in England was shivering. I remember how the actors played to nearly empty houses, heroically stripped down to their indoor clothes, while we their audience huddled together in a tight clump, muffled to the chins in overcoats, sweaters and scarves. I remember a chic lunch party composed of the intellectual *beau monde*, at which an animated discussion of existentialism was interrupted by one of the guests exclaiming piteously: 'Oh, I'm so *cold*!' Two or three of my friends said to me then: 'Believe us, this is worse than the war!' By which I understood them to mean that the situation couldn't by any stretch of the imagination be viewed as a challenge to self-sacrifice or an inspiration to patriotism; it was merely hell.

Such were Isherwood's recollections, published some nine years later, with only a passing reference to English supineness in the face of offi-cialdom. Yet at the time, his visit made a considerable impact upon his friends and acquaintances. 'We realised we had become shabby and rather careless of appearances in our battered surroundings,' recalled his host, the writer and editor John Lehmann. 'That we had become crushed as civilians to accept the ordering about of officialdom. That we had become obsessively queue-forming, and were priggishly proud of it.' Such feelings, induced by Isherwood's 'sharp observation of the altered London', were heightened by the ghastly winter:

> The adrenaline [ie of war] was no longer being pumped into our veins. We endured with misery and loathing the continual fuel cuts, the rooms private and public in which we shivered in our exhausted overcoats, while the snow blizzards swept through the country again and yet again. Were there to be no fruits of victory? The rationing cards and coupons that still had to be presented for almost everything from eggs to minute pieces of scraggy Argentine meat, from petrol to bed-linen and 'economy' suits, seemed far more squalid and unjust than during the war . . .
>
> Worse, still, to my increasingly disillusioned eye, was the kind of mean puritanism that the newly triumphant Labour MPs and their officials appeared to have decided was the proper wear of the day. Too many of them seemed to think there was a virtue in austerity and shabbiness, in controls and restrictions . . .

It was a significant alienation. The metropolitan intelligentsia had mainly welcomed the 1945 election result, but the socialism of daily privation and daily restrictions was not their kind of socialism. Moreover, it was symptomatic, not least in their eyes, that a magazine like *Penguin New Writing* (edited by Lehmann himself) was by this time on a sharply downward spiral in its circulation, having hit a peak of 100,000 in the spring of 1946. This dispiriting trend, Lehmann explained, meant the end of the fond hope, shared by the publisher Allen Lane (founder of Penguin paperbacks), that 'given the right formula an enormous public was now ready to devour what would have been considered almost entirely highbrow fare before the war'.[6]

There was nothing highbrow about the Levenshulme Palais, where Frank Lewis – still working in Manchester, having failed most of his economics exams the previous summer at the University College of South Wales in Cardiff – went on the evening of Monday, 3 February:

2 dances with 'Port Madoc'; she's nice; I'd like to go out with her.
('Wouldn't I with any of them,' repeats a dark hidden voice.) She told
me her nickname was 'Smiler'. She showed me running steps during the
last quickstep at 10 to 11.

I dance with 'Blondex'. Boy, what legs?

I dance with 'Belle Vue', who also taught me running steps.

There was heavy snow that day in the north and Midlands, but Lewis
seems to have been too preoccupied to notice. Not so an anxious Mary
King in her Birmingham suburb. 'Tonight 17,000 employees will be
idle at the Longbridge Austin Motor Works through lack of fuel,' she
recorded that evening. 'Many other firms are in the same plight. It is
a dreadful thing to face.' Two days later, in the context of a weather
forecast of 'more snow, & wintry conditions to continue', her anxiety
deepened: 'One thinks of the shortage of fuel, and home comforts,
such as blankets & sheets, & carpets – the scarcity of food – the difficulty
of transport, and the unemployment of thousands of workers in
factories due to lack of coal & materials. Never in my lifetime have I
known such a period of history . . .'

Finally, on Friday the 7th – the day after Ellen Wilkinson's death
(possibly suicide), barely a week since she had told an audience at the
Old Vic that she wanted Britain to be a Third Programme nation –
Shinwell and his colleagues acted. With sufficient supplies of coal failing
to reach power stations in London, the Midlands and the north-west,
he announced that from the following Monday not only would electricity supplies to industry in these regions be suspended, but householders there would have to make do without electricity daily for three
hours from 9 a.m. and two hours from 2 p.m.

'Somebody has been short sighted somewhere, sometime,' was Mary
King's immediate reaction, and over the weekend much wrath, public
and private, was directed at the hapless Shinwell. Repudiating his
attempt to blame the weather ('Let the Minister look to himself'), and
reckoning that 'never since the Industrial Revolution have we seen a
crisis come in this way', the *Financial Times* declared that the situation
was 'as serious a threat to prosperity, in peace time, as the events which
brought down Mr Neville Chamberlain's Government were to victory
in war time'. The staunchly pro-Tory Glasgow pattern-maker Colin

Ferguson castigated Shinwell's 'crass ignorance' and saw the crisis as
conclusive evidence that the government was 'the silliest set of sneering
gas-bags we've ever been cursed with in this country'; the reasonably
objective James Lansdale Hodson, after noting 'drifts fifteen feet deep
in Northumberland, railways in parts impassable, and queues of
professional women in St John's Wood with buckets at a water-tap in
the road', called Shinwell 'a modern phenomenon – muddling, insouciant,
and a yoke round our suffering necks'. Even Vere Hodgson, not
unsympathetic to the aspirations of the Labour government, accepted
that 'we are in an awful MESS', could not understand why Shinwell
had not resigned and asserted that 'there is not a leader amongst them'.
On Sunday afternoon it did start to thaw in London. But on Monday,
to mark the new restrictions, 'it froze again very hard, so that,' in Lees-
Milne's words, 'the slush is like slippery brick'.[7]

The next 12 days or so, through to about 22 February, were the height
of the crisis, with the weather unremittingly grim and unemployment
rising to more than 1.75 million (compared to just over 400,000 in mid-
January). Government-imposed restrictions were intensified: no electricity for five hours a day across the nation's households; television,
the Third Programme and many magazines suspended; major cuts in
transmission times for the Home and the Light programmes; newspapers
even more severely cut down in size than before because of newsprint
rationing; most forms of external lighting forbidden; and no electricity
to be used in relation to superfluous activities like greyhound racing.
There was also an intense propaganda campaign urging the public to
use, when it could use, as little electricity and gas as possible. Inevitably,
the miners in these weeks came under acute pressure to raise their levels
of production. By and large they seem to have responded, with output
per man-shift being as high during February as at any point over the
previous 12 months, though such weather-induced problems as
inaccessible mines, frozen-solid pithead stockpiles and transportation
difficulties once the coal was ready to leave the colliery could not but
affect overall production. On Sunday the 16th, 'Coal Sunday', many
miners in the South Wales coalfield voluntarily worked a full shift,
winning widespread praise for the 'Dunkirk spirit'.

Could more be done? Sydney T. Jones of Pengam Road,
Penpedairheol, Hengoed, Glamorgan, was probably motivated by public

interest as well as self-interest when the previous week he took his case direct to 'Mr Shinwell':

> I hope you will forgive me for writing to you at this critical time, but it is a matter of the utmost importance in as much as it concerns the very problem with which you are grappling now – the Fuel Shortage.
>
> I am a South Wales miner, and I write to ask – not only for myself – but for several of my butties, that you use your good influence with the Ministry of Transport to get him to restore to us miners the Travel Priority on our local Bus Services, especially those of us who work on the afternoon shifts. I myself, having been home two weeks with flu and bronchitis through having to walk half a mile to the nearest bus stop from the colliery, and waiting about at the end of the queue for the last bus to our village, a mile and a half away, we find at 10.30 p.m. the queue is made up of half-drunks, picturegoers, dance hall riff-raff, and we who have been sweating our guts out at the coal face are left to shiver in the bitter cold wind and hear the bus conductor say – 'Sorry, only three or four' as the case may be. Those types of pub crawlers can get home, but we miners have to walk through the torrents of rain or snow storms across the fields over the mountains to get home about 11.30 p.m., or near mid-night, and then perhaps we have to return in the morning to perform some special job. That means getting up at 4 a.m. to catch the Workers Factory Bus at 5.15 a.m. from the village. So you will see Sir how important it is. Tons and tons of coal is being lost to the nation through miners going to work at (1 p.m.) lunchtime for the afternoon shift and unable to get on the crowded buses through the Priority Ruling having been removed. As you are no doubt aware there are no Collieries, at least, very few are in big towns, and in the Rhymney valley especially miners have to travel miles on buses. So please do your very best to get us to work, and get us home at the end of the afternoon shift. For the day shift it matters not so much; because there are plenty of buses if they miss one. But at 10.30 p.m. at night the last bus from town means everything to us who work on this shift.

Contemporary observers made much of the miners' deep sense of social inferiority, arising out of their bitter, humiliating experiences between the wars; Zweig in his study asserted that this 'inferiority complex' was 'especially strong in South Wales'.[8] If anything, this plea to Shinwell would suggest that things were changing. But in any case, it is undeniably the authentic miner's voice – one obscure, now-forgotten Jones among many obscure, now-forgotten Joneses – and one is grateful it survives.

Few people enjoyed these mid-February days and nights. At Oxford, where the editor of *Cherwell* had just been sacked for publishing a questionnaire that asked female undergraduates if they were still virgins, 'CHRIST ITS BLEEDING COLD' was how the very male (and army-coarsened?) undergraduate Kingsley Amis put it to his friend Philip Larkin. 'Life here is quite impossible,' Evelyn Baring of the merchant bank Barings, probably the most august house in the City of London, reported to a fellow-banker, 'and really no-one would have believed it if they had read it in a novel. From 9 to 12 and 2 to 4 we work in the dim glow of candlelight or nightlight.' The diarists, meanwhile, shivered like the rest:

> *10 February (Monday)*. We walked down Baker St & Oxford St. The sky was heavy, the day grey & dark but the stores inside were gloomier still ... Assistants were straining their eyes trying to write out bills, the darkness was depressing. Coming out onto the streets again the dull light was almost dazzling. (*Florence Speed*)
>
> *11 February*. Go out shopping – much windier & colder – astonishing to see Woolworths, like every other shop, lit by odd gas lamps & candles by cash registers. At 2 pm – sudden plunging into gloom. (*Grace Golden*)
>
> *12 February*. Tonight it is announced that the cuts are to be extended throughout the whole country, Scotland & Wales ... Also that we are to return to a 'black-out' on the streets. Traffic lights will remain ... Yet for all the seriousness of the Country's situation, Ethel & I saw *crowds* – women chiefly! – mob Laurel & Hardy outside The Monseigneur [cinema] at Trafalgar Square this afternoon, to get their autographs ... Hardy – the fat one – is revolting. Huge & grotesque ... Both were hugely delighted at their reception; only moved on when the Policeman said 'Enough'. (*Florence Speed*)
>
> *13 February*. No soap to be bought anywhere, & I feel ready to drop with fatigue by 2 pm. Lily sent me 2 lbs potatoes through the post & I am saving them for Sunday's dinner ... Last night I went to the

Red House to play cards in my fur coat & turban it was so cold there. (*Rose Uttin*)

Penalty now for using current during restricted times, the situation being 'dangerously critical', is a fine of £100 or three months jail ... Yet despite this a woman in a queue in Brixton declared defiantly, 'Well anyway, I'm going to switch on the iron & do my ironing as soon as I get home'. It's because so many haven't played fair – the worst offenders are shopkeepers it is reported – that the penalties have been imposed. (*Florence Speed*)

Gas fire very low, but Ione [her baby daughter] and I managed. Shortage of pennies and shillings announced! ... Down to last nappy but managed to get more dry between 12 and 2 and after 4. We froze up again. (*Judy Haines*)

14 February. Long queues for potatoes ... Reduced clothing coupon allowances. No wonder people steal coupons and clothes ... Black-out so batteries for torches are scarce. (*Gladys Langford*)

16 February. Restrictions and arctic conditions persist ... Several people here ignore lighting regulations and use lamps & radios at forbidden hours. (*Gladys Langford*)

18 February. Yesterday Selfridge's was packed as though there was a bargain sale there. 'Nothing else to do, nowhere to go,' we heard a man say, obviously one of the nearly 3½ millions stood off through the fuel crisis. Today we saw men carrying their wives' shopping baskets. (*Florence Speed*)

19 February. In addition to my usual winter apparel, am now wearing four woollen pullovers (three sleeveless ones under my waistcoat, one with sleeves over it). And yet I still get chilled to the bone sitting in that bleak, unheated office all day. (*Anthony Heap*)

22 February. The weather is atrocious and now gas supplies are threatened. The streets are seas of slush and to cross a wide road means flirting with death. (*Gladys Langford*)

But for Frank Lewis, at the Great Universal Stores warehouse in Manchester, the weather still failed to impinge. 'Getting bloody boring at work, on the bloody shoot [ie chute],' he noted on the 14th. 'If only, too, the British working man didn't do so much bloody grumbling.' And the following Wednesday he went to a 'rag dance' at the

Plaza: 'Bloody awful! Too hot. Terrible women . . . I'll have to take "stronger love measures" to get a girl. I can't go on like this. This sex business is positively getting me down.'[9]

What were other reactions at the height of the fuel crisis and accompanying cuts? Mass-Observation sounded out, between the 10th and 14th, various working-class Londoners:

> I think it's ridiculous for the Royal family to go on such an expensive tour [they had left for South Africa on the 1st] – it should have been put off – the country can't afford it.
>
> Shocking – the position is absolutely shocking. The country is deteriorating rapidly. Thank Goodness I had nothing to do with voting Labour in. They're not the right kind to be at the head of affairs. What with one thing and another life's very trying. And the food – there isn't enough fats to keep oneself fit in this sort of weather. The diet is much too starchy. Oh, I could go on by the hour but what's the good.
>
> Rotten isn't it? Can't be helped though, wouldn't be done unless there was any real need for it. I'm sure everybody is doing their best.
>
> Shinwell? Ha! ha! ha! Don't know much about him, suppose he's doing his best.
>
> They should have warned us that the position was bad. Same as old Churchill did even in the blackest days. Came on the wireless and let us know how we stood, and even if the news wasn't good he somehow gave us confidence. But old Attlee doesn't do that.
>
> It's very bad in our line – the tailoring trade. When we're working on black we're practically working in the dark.

A coalman in Croydon spoke with particular personal experience. 'It's like everything else, the people with a lot of money get all they want,' he explained. 'I delivered half a ton this morning to a house in Purley, their fair ration mind you, but they've already got a stock of about a ton and a half and a couple of tons of coke besides. Now you can't get any coke, but those fellers can, they've got the money see.'

In general, in terms of obeying the restrictions on the use of power – restrictions to some extent based on voluntary compliance – it is clear enough that, as Florence Speed among others complained, not everyone played the game. Nevertheless, in the weeks beginning on 10 and 17 February there were rates of saving of respectively 29 and 28 per cent, ie by comparison with the level of coal consumption immediately before the cuts. Such figures, according to the authoritative history of the fuel crisis, 'attested to the public's willing co-operation with official attempts at enforcement'.[10] This did not necessarily mean, though, that they co-operated with a song in their hearts.

For one child this winter the big freeze was a mixed blessing, for another it was an unmitigated disaster. Roy Hattersley, growing up in a Sheffield suburb, went sledging after school every day – 'tearing downhill on home-made toboggans as we used the public highways as our Cresta Run', for at that time 'there were few motor-cars in Wadsley'. But at night he would leap into bed, still with the socks on that had protected him from 'the freezing linoleum', and huddle under an 'immense weight of sheet, thread-bare blankets, home-made eiderdown and coats carried up from the wardrobe at the bottom of the stairs'. For Bill Wyman (then Bill Perks), growing up in Penge, the atrocious weather meant that his bricklayer father was laid off work and no money came in. 'There wasn't enough food to go round, so he'd hit a couple of us, send us to bed without any dinner,' one of Bill's brothers recalled. '"Get to bed, don't argue!" Then you'd get hit, kicked up the stairs – vroom, that was it . . . And in the house we lived in, you didn't *want* to go to bed. It was freezing cold, really nasty, with ice on the inside of the windows and bedbugs that drove us crazy.'

But for two adults these uncongenial weeks proved the great turning point in their lives. Dirk Bogarde was among the cast (along with other unknowns Kenneth More and Dandy Nicholls) in a new play, *Power Without Glory*, about a working-class London family that opened in late February at a theatre club in Notting Hill Gate. Bogarde, only recently demobbed, played the male lead, Cliff, a neurotic who kills a girl in a *crime passionnel*. The play got rave reviews, with particular praise for Bogarde ('an excellent casual murderer, all egotism and nerves'), and within weeks he had signed a seven-year film contract with Rank. Meanwhile, Elizabeth David found herself stuck in a hotel in Ross-on-Wye, a far cry from Athens, Alexandria and Cairo, where she had spent most of the 1940s. 'Conditions *were* awful, shortages *did* make catering a nightmare,' she recalled years later with only moderate equanimity. 'And *still* there was no excuse, none, for such unspeakably dismal meals as in that dining room were put in front of me. To my agonized homesickness for the sun and southern food was added an embattled rage that we should be asked – and should accept – the endurance of such cooking.' So she began 'writing down descriptions of Mediterranean and Middle Eastern cooking. Even to write words like apricot, olives and butter, rice and lemons, oil and almonds, produced assuagement.' Subsequently, she added, 'I came to realize that in the England of 1947, those were dirty words that I was putting down.'[11]

The weather remained bitterly cold until well into March, but industry gradually got its power back and almost all the temporarily unemployed returned to work. The February restrictions on domestic use of electricity, however, remained in force until the end of April, and significantly, the clear evidence was of a rising trend from late February of covert consumption, suggestive of a general unwillingness to make peacetime sacrifices beyond a certain period. Although there were virtually no prosecutions for breaches of the domestic restrictions, the fact was that those restrictions were backed by legal sanctions; Vere Hodgson was one of the law-abiding millions getting increasingly browned-off. 'We have struggled on all the week with no light and restricted hours of electricity,' she noted on 3 March. 'This is to go on. They have domestic consumers well under their thumb now. We are helpless and we just have to do as we are told.' There were still two atrocious snowstorms to endure – in the south and Midlands on the 4th and 5th, when a train from Wolverhampton to London took 26 hours to complete its journey, and just over a week later in Scotland and the north – but eventually the weather did turn. 'The thaw is here!' exalted Gladys Langford on the 10th, and within a week it had spread from the south of England to elsewhere.[12]

For Erica Ford, the young woman living in the queen of suburbs, Tuesday the 18th was a day of almost sublime, unquestioned normality:

After doing my housework & putting on black suit, Daddy dropped me at Ealing Common [ie station] & I went to Knightsbridge & had look round Harrods. No good. Went up to Leicester Sq. for look at shoes – no good. Had snack lunch at Lyons. Met Gwen 1.30 at Swan & Edgars. Walked up Regent St. She got nice navy costume at Peter Robinson. Had tea Dickins & Jones. I got two-way stretch & sports belt at Lewis's & some Goya perfume.

Got home tired out 6.30. Bussed from town.

But even as she wrote, widespread floods, caused by heavy rain accompanying the thaw, were affecting as many as 31 counties south of the River Ouse, destroying 70,000 acres of wheat and 80,000 tons of potatoes. It was the final supply-shortening, queue-lengthening twist to an unforgettable winter.

To a government already much exercised by absenteeism, the temptation to make permanent the temporary ban on midweek sports meetings was irresistible. Although in the event toned down to a statutory ban only on midweek greyhound racing (the sport that was the particular bête noir of high-minded progressives), with more informal midweek restrictions applying to other sports (including football for the rest of the season), it could hardly have been a less popular initiative. 'Austerity for the sake of it' was the inevitable reaction of the *Daily Express*, while on 18 March a *Daily Herald* reader protested strongly, 'The Government must give us some light in these days of austerity. Football and the dogs have been some of that light.' That evening, as Erica Ford flopped down in Ealing, the limits to people's willingness to continue to prioritise the largely cheerless concerns of the public weal were eloquently shown when a radio broadcast by Attlee on the current situation clashed with a rival attraction. Next day, Mass-Observation asked working-class Londoners between the ages of 30 and 55 whether they had listened to the Prime Minister. Four women are followed by five men:

Yes I heard it. I didn't pay much attention to it, it didn't seem important and certainly wasn't interesting.

Yes I did, oh it wasn't bad – nothing startling was there? – I don't like the way he speaks, as if he is reading from a book.

No, I haven't read the paper today either.

No – I had to go out most of last night – my daughter had a baby you know – a boy, 7 pounds it is.

No, no I didn't – I was listening to the boxing.

No mate I didn't, I heard somebody talking about it a little while ago, don't know what they said – they just mentioned it.

No I didn't, it wasn't advertised much was it? As a matter of fact there was something else on which I wanted to listen to very much – the boxing match.

No, sorry chum I didn't.

I listened to half of it, that's all. I got fed up with it and switched over to the fight . . . I was very disgusted with the result of the fight, the referee must have been 'colour blind'. Ha! ha! ha! It wasn't at all fair – & everyone else seems to think the same thing as well.

The fight in question was the British Empire featherweight championship, at the Royal Albert Hall. Al Phillips of Aldgate won on points against Cliff Anderson from British Guyana – 'an extremely unconvincing decision', reported *The Times*, producing 'a very mixed reception'.[13]

It is debatable, though, how much the government's standing was fundamentally affected by the big freeze. Polling figures by Gallup indicated a sharp short-term rise in dissatisfaction with Attlee and his ministers that was almost wiped out by May. Rather, the events of early 1947 should surely be seen as part of a longer-term continuum, in which *existing* weariness with life in post-war Britain merely deepened – a weariness that in itself did not automatically assume a concrete political form. By the end of March, one of the top hit tunes around, in the dance halls and elsewhere, was 'Open the Door, Richard', a recent number one in the US. 'Wanting a thrill?' asked one of *Melody Maker*'s columnists. 'Get a load of Jack White . . . and see the jam-packed floor crowds lapping up the Astoria maestro's sock version of "Richard", with Sonny Rose at the burlesque end.' Over the next few months, 'Open the Door, Richard' became a great catch-phrase, applicable to almost any kind of restriction in everyday life; Attlee was even advised to 'Open the door, Richard' and replace some of his less thrilling elderly ministers.[14] The political prize was there, in other words, for whoever could find the door's key, real or rhetorical.

'But the same owners and managers are still in charge of collieries, and they are doing the same things' was the answer frequently given to Zweig that summer and autumn as he toured the coalfields and asked what difference the new dispensation had made. 'We see hardly any difference in their behaviour.' Those miners who were members of the new, much-trumpeted Colliery Consultative Committees tended to be particularly disenchanted: 'We have no access to the books; the co-operation on the part of the managers is not genuine ... Our suggestions are completely disregarded and little encouraged ... We have as little to say about the colliery as before.' A further problem was the excessive centralisation. 'Before, we knew where we stood,' a Derbyshire miner explained. 'When we had a grievance the manager could settle it in five minutes, if not on his own responsibility, after a short conversation on the telephone with the Agent. Now we cannot settle anything with the manager. When we come to the manager, he always shifts everything on to the back of the NCB. "I can't do anything without the NCB," he says. But we don't know the NCB ...' Inasmuch as miners did know the NCB, Zweig found, 'irritation and indignation are expressed against the high salaries of officials who have no special qualification'. Furthermore, 'One often hears a certain irritation expressed when the miner is told he is now a partner. "Since the Government took over the mines," a miner said to me, "the popular saying of the managers is, 'It's your pit now,' but it is a mockery, because to most of us it does not matter, or benefit us, whether the mine pays or not." If you mention to the miner that he is a partner, he can be very bitter about it.' All in all, Zweig concluded, 'there can be no denial that at present the miners are disillusioned about the outcome of nationalisation'.

The fact that there were more strikes in the year after nationalisation than in the year before – including a long, high-profile dispute at Grimethorpe that spread across the Yorkshire coalfield – lends credence to the Zweig 'disillusioned' thesis. Yet ultimately it is a thesis predicated on the shaky assumption that most miners had 'illusions' in the first place about a fundamental reordering of social and industrial relations. Moreover, if in reality their aspirations for nationalisation were mainly more modest – focusing in the best 'labourist' tradition on solid, unglamorous, incremental improvements – then it is at least arguable that in the course of 1947/8 these pragmatic hopes started to be realised. 'Working conditions improved markedly almost from the beginning,' Roy Mason, a Yorkshire miner who later became a Labour minister, recalled. 'Training was introduced for newcomers before ever they went down to the coalface. A ban was introduced on young boys going underground before they were sixteen. We had a national safety scheme, with proper standards at every colliery. And for the first time, pithead baths became a standard facility.'[15] There were also improved wages and, despite ministerial and NCB misgivings, the introduction of the five-day week.

So much depends on how one sees the miners – specifically, whether one buys into the somewhat romantic view, prevalent in the 1970s, that they were natural militants who wanted workers' control and had been cruelly betrayed by the stodgy, bureaucratic form that public ownership took. But a rather different narrative starts to emerge if one accepts that the miners, for all their class solidarity and physical courage, were real – and therefore flawed – people: conservative (including about such matters as Polish labour and new forms of mechanisation), usually money-minded, sometimes bloody-minded, always deeply mistrustful.[16] In about June 1948 Mass-Observation surveyed 50 miners and 50 miners' wives in the Doncaster area about their attitudes to nationalisation. Just over three in five expressed 'unqualified approval', mainly on the grounds of the improved wages; just over one in ten expressed 'disapproval', predominantly because 'the old owners of the mines still wielded considerable power'; and among the others, approval was qualified by 'much vocal criticism' about 'the organisation of specific jobs, the alleged increase of officials, and the growth of impersonality in organisation generally'. There were the familiar complaints, echoing Zweig's findings, about remote, overpaid, high-handed 'top hats', but there was no sense of the strong wish to see more consultation of the 'man on the spot' being translated into a desire for the miners to assume strategic control of the industry.

Three pieces of testimony were especially suggestive. The first was by a packer maddened by the impractical *specifics* of nationalisation:

Oh, I don't know what goes on at the Coal Board. I expect it's even worse than down here at the pit. But down here there's far too many non-producers. I can't see the necessity for an 'over-man', a 'deputy', and a 'shot firer' for each district. That's what we've got now in the pit. Before nationalisation we only had one deputy for the same district and we got on all right. They seem to have plenty of money to throw about. They could produce cheaper coal if they got rid of the wasters.

A scientist at one of the pits, himself the son of a miner who had been killed at that pit during the war, presented an unflattering but convincing snapshot: 'The other day I was underground taking samples, and I happened to come to a face where the men didn't know me and they definitely treated me as a spiv – they said so . . . A lot of the miners think if you are not producing coal then you are a spiv . . . The be all and end all is the wage packet and anything likely to affect that is taboo. I am sure they think that my wages are coming out of their pay packet.' The third slice of testimony was by a rank-and-file miner, reflecting what the report found to be a widespread suspicion of the union leaders: 'They're all piss and wind . . . Talk, talk, but when it comes down to doing anything, that's another matter . . . The trouble is especially with the Welsh bastards, they all think in the past and not the present.'[17] With coal in high demand, and with apparently no significant rival source of energy on the horizon, it was a present and immediate future that was looking surprisingly good.

9

Our Prestige at Stake

'How do you feel about unmarried people living together?' was the question that Mass-Observation put to various Londoners in March 1947. 'I think it's perfectly terrible,' replied one middle-class woman in her 50s, 'because the woman always gets the worst of it and it's the beginning of heartbreak.' By contrast, the working-class response was notably non-judgemental:

> I wouldn't do it myself, but I've an open mind on it, and circumstances may have a lot to do with it.
> I suppose it's up to those people themselves – it's up to them entirely.
> I mind my business and I don't care what others do – that's theirs.
> I don't feel nothing.
> Don't know, never thought about it.
> If you love one another, it's all right I suppose.
> I'm not a prude by nature, it's their affair.

Significantly, this unenthusiastic but ultimately pragmatic reaction to sex before marriage was partly repeated – but only partly – when it came to the accompanying question, 'How do you feel about divorce?'

> It depends on the people. If either is to blame they should have a divorce.
> Well, I mean to say, it's a good thing if the couple are unhappy.
> No. A man takes a wife for better or worse, doesn't he?
> I wouldn't grant divorce, they should get on with it.
> I feel very sorry for the kiddies. It's very hard on them but if Mother

and Father can't agree it only makes the children suffer worse – they suffer inwardly.

I think it's an awful thing to happen to anyone – everybody turns away from a divorced woman.

Better to divorce than live unhappily.

I don't like the idea of a divorce – all the publicity and scandal.

In some cases, yes. Marriage is a gamble anyway.

The divorce rate may have been rising – inevitable in the immediate aftermath of war – but across society the stigma remained. Sir Francis Meynell, creator and editor of the long-running, best-selling annual anthology *The Week-End Book*, was from 1946 no longer welcome at royal garden parties on account of his divorce that year, nor from 1947 were two judges who had been discovered by the Lord Chamberlain to have neglected to mention their divorces in their *Who's Who* entries. Divorce law itself had been liberalised in 1937, to the extent that cruelty and desertion had joined adultery as legitimate grounds, but this was still a long way from divorce by mutual consent. 'Would you approve or disapprove if it were made possible to get a divorce simply by agreement between the two parties?' asked Gallup in April 1948. Tellingly, only 27 per cent replied positively, with a bias towards the young and the middle class.[1]

For those visiting the first post-war *Daily Mail* Ideal Home Exhibition at Olympia in March 1947 ('Queues in all directions,' noted a hungry Vere Hodgson. 'We never got a bite.'), the publicity brochure of the furniture-makers James Broderick & Co. left little doubt about woman's place in the overall scheme of things. 'What every newly-wed should know' included a 'Day-to-Day Plan' for new brides:

Monday. Is not essentially a day for laundry. Scour the kitchen after week-end catering activities, check up on rations and shop for vegetables, canned foods and breakfast cereals for a few days ahead.

Tuesday. Manage the light personal laundry, leaving the sheets and bath towels. Get all items dried and ironed during the day whenever possible.

Wednesday. Clean thoroughly bedrooms and bathrooms and use early afternoon for silver cleaning.

Thursday. Change bedlinen, launder 'heavies'. While they dry, clean the lounge. Iron early afternoon.

Friday. Plan meals for week-end, making provision for Monday 'left-overs'. Shop. Give dining room or dining alcove a thorough clean and polish.

Saturday. Keep this free for the family as far as possible. Prepare vegetables for Sunday and manage some cooking in the morning. Then relax.

Sunday. Belongs to you and those who share the home with you. Confine all essential cooking to early part of morning.

'What you wear in the house for the working hours is important,' added a section on appearance. 'Crisp, easily removed gay overalls, smocks, nylon or spongeable plastic aprons look attractive. Wear your hair as you would do for the man-of-the-house's homecoming.'

At this point only about a quarter of married women were in the labour force, and during much of 1947 and 1948, as in 1946, there was considerable pressure from the Ministry of Labour on young married women to return to work. If there was a representative woman's voice in the face of nothing less than a propaganda bombardment, it was surely that of Mary Grieve, editor of the top-selling women's magazine, *Woman*. '"But surely you don't think they will call up women!" said my friend in tones of horror in the middle of our discussion on Britain's dire shortage of manpower,' she reported in February 1947. 'Looking at her shocked face I hardly knew what to say.' Over the ensuing months, Grieve and her columnist Joan Lambert stressed how exhausted the housewife at home already was and called on husbands, industry and government to offer practical help to make it more realistic for married women, particularly if they were mothers, to return to the workplace. In short, 'appeals to women's patriotism are not enough.' And, daringly, 'perhaps what we need is a Mothers' Union affiliated to the TUC!'[2] The suggestion was half tongue-in-cheek, but only half.

It remained clear what most men thought. A snatch of saloon-bar conversation at the Travellers Rest in Aston was overheard in June 1947. Said one man: 'It's all very well asking women to come back into industry but there are plenty of men out of work. It beats me.' His fellow-drinker of mild agreed: 'A woman's got a day's work in the house anyway . . .' As for women themselves, a survey of almost 3,000 of them soon afterwards found that 'apart from small percentages who were either positively in favour of women working or positively against it, the majority thought that women should go out to work only if they can carry out their duties to their homes and families' – that, in other words, 'a woman's first duty is to her home'. Strikingly, less than a third of 'the occupied women' in the survey 'thought that in general women should go out to work'; among 'unoccupied' women, the proportion was less than a fifth.

Yet if there existed – as clearly there did, especially among many women who had worked during the war – a profound desire to get back to (and then stay put in) homemaking normality in familiar surroundings, that was not the exclusive sentiment. 'It's ridiculous to be forced to live like a schoolgirl at the age of twenty-four,' Phyllis Noble wrote in her diary in May 1947. 'The war pulled me out of Lee [a mixed Victorian suburb in south-east London], and now I must make my own road. There is no doubt in my mind that I must get "a room of my own".' She had recently been demobbed from the WAAF, and like many young women – and young men – she had every intention after the war of continuing to broaden her horizons. Later that summer, waiting to start a course to train as a hospital social worker, she went one day to Westminster Abbey in the hope of seeing the Battle of Britain Memorial. 'A long, unpleasant queue put me off,' she noted. 'Odd to see many women (including self) hatless. Such a revolution in so short a time!' Did this sudden hatless-ness presage a new sense of female independence? The emergence by 1947 of Christine Norden (daughter of a Sunderland bus driver and reputedly spotted in an Edgware Road cinema queue) as Britain's first post-war blonde, busty film star only arguably supports the thesis. Either way, the harsh home and/or work dilemma remained, as implacably expounded in the brilliant 1948 Michael Powell and Emeric Pressburger film *The Red Shoes*. Moira Shearer, playing a talented young dancer, is compelled by her lover to choose between giving up her career and giving up her would-be husband. It is a choice she is unable to make, and, in the absence of a third way, she dies.[3]

How did the nation's home-dwellers, whether homemakers or not, spend their free time? Not on the whole in reading, let alone self-improving reading. A Mass-Observation survey in the summer of 1947, carried out among almost a thousand Tottenham residents, revealed that '"reading" was given as the favourite hobby by three in ten of the middle class, by two in ten of the skilled working class, and by one in ten of the unskilled'. Almost half the sample said they never read books at all, but only one in ten went without reading a daily paper (the *Daily Mirror*, the *News Chronicle*, the *Daily Herald* and the *Daily Express* being the most popular), and a mere one in 20 did not read a Sunday paper (with three out of five favouring the *News of the World*). As for magazines, they were preponderantly read by the middle class. Non-readers of books, a group far more working-class than middle-class in composition, were asked to explain their lack of interest:

> None of them subjects is interesting to me. All I like is gangster stories, though there's precious much chance of reading here. Three rooms we got and three kids knocking around. No convenience, no nothing except water. I'm glad to get out of the house I can tell you.
>
> Cos I ain't got no interest in them – they all apparently lead up to the same thing.
>
> I'm not very good at reading, I never was. I've never liked it some'ow.
>
> Too long. I like to get straight into a story. I have started books and I have to read through the first pages two or three times. I like to get stuck straight into a story – there's too much preliminary if you see what I mean.

Less than a quarter of the sample belonged to Tottenham Public Library. 'I don't want to bother' was one explanation; 'I ain't never even thought on it, never mind a reason' another.

Among readers, five preferred fiction to every one favouring non-fiction (in which the two most favoured topics were sport and health). 'I like something I can relax in,' reflected an elderly man. 'Don't like anything that gets me worried and wondering.' Crime and mystery stories were almost twice as popular as any other subject. 'There's nothing to beat a good detective story,' declared a young manual worker. 'Keeps you interested all the way through. When I get into a good murder story I don't hear any of the noise what's going on in the house or anything.' Working-class female readers had, predictably, a penchant for romance:

> My friend is very keen on love stories and when she gets a real good one she brings it in. Some of them are very good and I enjoy a real good cry when I read them ...
>
> My friend lives two doors away and I get books for her too. She likes the same kind of stories as well. It's nice to read about that sort of love and better class people, for you don't notice things as much then. It's a real pleasure to read Ruby M. Ayres' books and I often cry over them.

Ayres was one of Tottenham's six most popular authors – behind Edgar Wallace, Charles Dickens and Ethel M. Dell (a rival purveyor of the old-fashioned love story), ahead of Naomi Jacob (who wrote family rather than love stories) and Agatha Christie.[4] A list of only patchy quality admittedly, but not out-and-out rubbish either, its inclusion of Dickens reminding one that this was a world nearer to the Victorian era than to the early twenty-first century.

Reading (whether of books, papers or magazines) played second fiddle to the wireless in most homes. A survey of domestic evening activities in almost 2,000 households over a wide range of urban dwellings across the country, completed in the spring of 1947, found that whereas the percentage of people reading for half an hour or more was never more than 15 per cent in any two-hour period, there were for equivalent half-hour periods never less than 20 per cent of households with the radio switched on and often more than 30 per cent. The radio was on in no less than 40 per cent of households where school homework was in progress, while the other three most frequent pairs of conflicting activities taking place in the same physical space were radio and reading, radio and conversation, and 'radio and resting'. Given all these and other conflicting activities (including 'between children playing and other people resting' and 'between visitors and meals'), it might be expected that bedrooms were utilised for activities other than sleeping and dressing, but in practice, no doubt partly because of lack of heating, less than 10 per cent were.

Besides, to go upstairs might mean missing *Dick Barton – Special Agent* (15 million listeners a night, a cliffhanger at the end of every episode), or *Twenty Questions* (featuring Richard Dimbleby), or *Down Your Way* (Dimbleby again), or *Variety Bandbox* (making an instant star of Frankie Howerd) or even Benny Hill, who made his radio debut later in 1947. Startlingly, a survey done in June that year of more than 3,000 of the adult listening public found that 77 per cent usually listened while eating each of the three main meals of the day – including eight out of ten for the evening meal, which for two-thirds had taken place by 6.30. Not that these habitual listeners heard much in the way of vigorous airing of the issues of the day, with the BBC in 1947 formally issuing a self-denying ordinance which forbade discussion of any matters either currently being debated in parliament or due in the next fortnight to be debated there. Known as the 'fourteen day rule' or 'fourteen day gag', it was all too typical of an organisation (starting to be known as 'Auntie') that, in the acerbic but just words of one historian, 'shunned controversy and censored itself'.[5]

Similarly symptomatic of the BBC's lack of a hard journalistic edge was the continuing unwillingness to provide regular news bulletins on television. A first generation of television personalities was emerging, including Richard Hearne (aka Mr Pastry) and the bearded cook Philip Harben, famous for using his actual family rations on screen, though programmes could be received only within an expanding but limited radius of about 50 miles from Alexandra Palace, sets were still expensive and difficult to get, and by 1948 a mere 4.3 per cent of the adult population had one in their homes. Even within the BBC, there was little faith in the new medium. In June 1947 R.J.E. Silvey, in charge of audience research and a professed Home Service rather than Light Programme listener, gave three reasons, in addition to 'the extremely high standard of sound broadcasting', why he would not buy a set on his own account if he did not already have a staff set:

The picture itself still seems very primitive. Once the miraculous aspect of television has faded, as it inevitably does, the picture tends to be compared with that of the cinema. The comparison is least odious in respect of television studio productions, but in respect of O.B.s [outside broadcasts] the deficiencies of television are very obtrusive . . . Watching television for as much as an hour is, in our experience, liable to give one the same kind of headache as going to the early cinema did.

For 'people like us' the programmes themselves contain much which is of very little appeal. For example, we just aren't Variety-minded. An occasional little revue is the most in this field which we should ask for from television. In practice, once a fortnight would be the upper limit of our demands for this kind of thing ... Magazine programmes such as *Kaleidoscope* and *Picture Page* seem to us amusing enough if one wishes to demonstrate television to a friend but never of sufficient appeal to warrant switching the set on specially ...

Finally, by no means the least potent factor militating against television in my kind of home is the sheer palaver involved in having to watch it. It means putting the light out, moving the furniture around and settling down to give the programme undivided attention.

But for the less favoured, including Judy Haines in Chingford a few weeks later, the acquisition of a set was exciting enough:

26 July (Saturday). Escott's could get Pye television by Monday!
9 August. Abbé off and put his name down for television. Missed recent good opportunity to buy.
11 September. Had Pye Television Set delivered.
13 September. Abbé had televised cricket while I took Ione to park.
16 September. Television aerial fixed. It took from lunch until nearly 7 o'c.
4 October. Mum and Dad H. came for television variety.

Over in even leafier Ealing, Erica Ford's family got their set early in 1948:

9 February (Monday). It is a Murphy. In the evening we saw television music hall & winter sports. Very good.
10 February. In afternoon looked at television film about Mounties – quite good.
12 February. We saw play 'Gaslight' which was very interesting & so of course knitting remained undone.
29 February. Saw 'Muffin the Mule', a marionette – very good.
1 March. Spent evening looking in & then went off to bed in bit better time [ie than after the previous evening's viewing].

15 March. More knitting & saw television *Dancing Club.* I listened to
play in kitchen, while rest of family saw more television.

That summer, some 900 viewers, predominantly 'suburban, middle
class and middle aged', returned a BBC questionnaire asking about
their television-watching habits. It transpired that an evening rarely
passed in which the owner of a set did not switch on, with no fewer
than 91 per cent saying that it was their habit to watch from 8.30 p.m.
(or earlier) to close-down. Some 16 per cent said they had to make
'frequent' adjustments to the set, and 58 per cent 'occasional' adjustments, in order to get a better picture. As for programme content, the
tone of the replies reflected, according to the BBC's analysis, 'plenty
of enthusiasm for plays – but not "morbid" plays – plenty of prejudice
against dance music, and so on'.[6] All in all, television was hardly yet
the people's medium, but it was clearly starting to be somewhat
addictive for those who had it.

An older addiction was well served on both mediums. Fred Streeter
(former head gardener at Petworth House and almost instantly celebrated for his Sussex burr) emerged as the first regular television
gardener in 1947, the same year that *Country Questions* began (in
April) on the radio at Sunday lunchtime. A direct forerunner of
Gardeners' Question Time, it fielded listeners' queries 'about the countryside', with the celebrated farmer-journalist A. G. Street in the chair
and a panel that featured the West Country's quasi-professional – and
deeply reactionary – countryman Ralph Wightman, the voice from
Piddletrenthide on VE night. The programme's regular listeners may
have included the 400 members of the Bethnal Green Allotments and
Gardens Association. 'Curiously enough they won't go in for competitions,' the group's middle-class-sounding secretary observed in
August 1947 to an investigator into voluntary activities and groups.
'They won't believe they're good enough.' The investigator observed
that the members did not seem to have much contact among themselves:

Yes, that's true. We have no meeting place and it is largely an individual
affair and the Association helps with tools and advice . . . There was a
scheme: we got some waste ground on the Wellington Estate: there were

40 gardening members there who thought it was a grand idea to start a
sort of cultural centre and they're doing very well I think: there's a Mr
H. who lives there and is very keen on it ... I tried to start the same
scheme in three other estates but it did not work. I've come to the
conclusion that you must have the leadership from among the people
themselves, it's no good otherwise.

Elsewhere, the gardening signals were mixed. Contemporary
illustrations of suburban back gardens suggest a new premium being
put on order, often taking the form of a rectangular lawn, a single tree
positioned in the middle, regularly placed square paving stones, and
each plant surrounded by a large amount of soil. But for the many
thousands of married women now staying at home, willingly or otherwise, there was the inspiriting Constance Spry, who started her flower-
arranging school in 1946, wrote prolifically in magazines and, in Jenny
Uglow's words, 'liked boldness, old roses, unexpected wild flowers,
flashes of lime-green – just what was needed after wartime gloom'.[7]
Although the future ultimately belonged to colourful display and dense
planting-cum-foliage, there remained a stubborn puritanical streak in
the British gardening psyche.

The nation's supreme demotic moment in 1947 came soon after the
debut of Street, Wightman et al. On Saturday, 10 May, at the huge
terraced bowl that was Hampden Park in Glasgow, 134,000 (out of
the 500,000 who had applied for tickets) watched Great Britain versus
The Rest of Europe. 'Britain Must Beat Europe: Our Prestige At Stake'
was that morning's *Daily Express* headline about what had, the paper's
Frank Butler declared, 'become known as the Match of the Century'.
Butler was adamant that even a draw 'would be regarded as a moral
victory by the Continentals and leave us the laughing stock of Europe';
among the opposition, he singled out the 'sinister figure' of Parola,
'the sallow-skinned and dark curly-haired Italian centre half, who is
said to be a master stopper'. Moreover, he warned about The Rest of
Europe team as a whole: 'They cleverly avoided revealing any of their
talents to the British reporters who watched them yesterday. All they
showed was some mighty fine acrobatics and high kicking.'

He need not have worried. Stanley Matthews of Stoke City enjoyed
on the right wing an afternoon of mazy dribbles, Chelsea's Tommy

Lawton and Middlesbrough's Wilf Mannion each scored twice, and despite the best efforts of Parola (wearing 'the briefest of briefs') the home team ran out comfortable 6–1 winners. 'Europe is now convinced that the British are bosses of Soccer,' Butler duly wrote, and that evening, in a Glasgow hotel, Matthews signed for Blackpool for £11,500 and a deceptively hedonistic bottle of champagne. By this time the football season was going into overtime because of the many post-ponements caused by the big freeze, and the first post-war Division 1 championship was not settled until mid-June. In a tight finish it went to Liverpool, whose decisive goal in the last match at Wolves was scored by their red-haired centre forward Albert Stubbins. Established that day as a Liverpool icon, he would feature (with a broad grin) almost exactly 20 years later on the cover of *Sgt. Pepper's Lonely Hearts Club Band*.

In the 1940s there were still several professional sportsmen who combined soccer with cricket – among them the gifted, charismatic Denis Compton, who in 1947 experienced a true annus mirabilis. It was not just that he broke all batting records for England and Middlesex, scoring an astonishing 18 hundreds in the course of the season, but the spontaneous, life-affirming way in which he played at such a drab and depressing time. Neville Cardus, finest of English cricket writers, was among those cheering:

> Never have I been so deeply touched on a cricket ground as I was in this heavenly summer, when I went to Lord's to see a pale-faced crowd, existing on rations, the rocket bomb still in the ears of most folk – see this worn, dowdy crowd watching Compton. The strain of long years of anxiety and affliction passed from all hearts and shoulders at the sight of Compton in full sail, sending the ball here, there and everywhere, each stroke a flick of delight, a propulsion of happy sane healthy life. There were no rations in an innings by Compton . . .

Quite early in the season, on 11 June, in the first Test against South Africa at Nottingham, Compton made a match-saving 163. That same day, from the hills above Florence, Dylan Thomas wrote to one of the BBC commentators, 'I hear your voice every day from Trent Bridge . . . You're not only the best cricket commentator – far and away that; but the best sports commentator I've heard, ever; exact, enthusiastic, prejudiced, amazingly visual, authoritative, and friendly.' The recipient was John Arlott, who, in two remarkable years since the war, had stopped being a Southampton policeman and become first a poetry producer at the BBC (working closely with Thomas) and then a cricket commentator and writer. During the 1947 season, he emerged as a nationally known voice and name, his Hampshire burr (what the Head of Outside Broadcasts called 'a vulgar voice') in striking contrast to the conventional, upper-middle-class tones of E. W. Swanton and Rex Alston. For Arlott, at best a mediocre cricketer himself, these immediate post-war years were like a dream; he fell more than half in love with professional cricket as a way of life and with those who played it. 'On a sane and economic level no argument can be adduced for a man becoming a county cricketer,' he wrote soon after the season ended, in a sober assessment of the professional cricketer's many uncertainties and lack of material rewards. 'He is valuable to the student of social history only as an example of the incurable romantic – but it is difficult indeed to deny him sympathy, perhaps even envy.'[8]

During the hot summer of 1947, benefiting from the pre-war Holidays with Pay Act that gave most of the workforce a mandatory and paid one-week annual break, about half the population took a holiday away from home, the overwhelming majority staying within Britain. 'Blackpool: The Holiday Playground of the World' was the title of that premier resort's 1947 brochure, advertising a huge array of hotels, 'boarding establishments' and so on, each invoking a key phrase designed to allure: 'good English cooking', 'separate tables', 'very homely apartments', 'personal supervision', 'central for amusements', 'Vi-spring beds'. Sid Chaplin confined himself to a day trip in June. 'What impressed me most was the number of fish & chip shops, and the high quality of their service,' he told a friend. 'I'm afraid the air isn't very bracing, especially round about ten p.m., when it's full of the stench of stale beer . . . I enjoyed myself in the Pleasure Park, won five woodbines at the rifle stalls and a tin cigarette ash tray . . . Blackpool is a paradise for pleasure.'[9]

Seaside resorts attuned to the urban millions had been flourishing since the late nineteenth century, but the holiday-camp phenomenon was much newer. Although there were other chains – most notably Pontin's and Warner's – the concept became over the years almost synonymous with Butlin's. Billy Butlin's first camp started at Skegness in 1936, to be followed by Clacton two years later; by 1947 he had added Filey, Ayr and Pwllheli. He was certainly on to a winner. In May 1947 W. J. Brown (the Independent MP) went to Butlin's house-warming party at his new home – Dane Court, Bishop's Road, Hampstead – and found 'a magnificent house standing in spacious grounds' and 'furnished most sumptuously', with appreciative guests tucking into 'mountains of lovely food – cold chicken, tongue, crab, salad, asparagus, vegetable salads, and heaven knows what'. Butlin, a driven man, had a flair for publicity; and that summer saw the release of *Holiday Camp*, a sentimental drama introducing the lovable cockney family the Huggetts to the British screen and starring Jack Warner and Kathleen Harrison, with Petula Clark as their 12-year-old daughter. It proved a major box-office success, and Gladys Langford, after going to the Marble Arch Pavilion, thought it 'one of the funniest films I ever saw', though she did add that 'if this be a real picture of a holiday camp, God forbid I should visit one . . . I'd rather live out my life in a basement flat in quietude.'

The idea for the film came from the immensely popular writer (especially in women's magazines) Godfrey Winn, who had been enthused by a brief visit to Butlin's at Filey. Significantly, he depicted the holiday camp as a social melting-pot, where the different classes could come together – on the face of it a fanciful notion, yet it seems that for several years after the war the clientele were as much middle-class as working-class. That did not stop the camps acquiring, in some eyes, a reputation as little better than concentration camps for the proletariat. At a cocktail party in September 1947, a Mass-Observation investigator heard a young middle-class actor from the film being asked if he had gone on location (Butlin's in Skegness) for it. 'My God no, thank heaven,' he replied. 'But a lot of them did – they were there seven weeks – ghastly – it's miles from everywhere and they were stuck.' And as he eloquently added – 'Can you believe it – it's all so hearty and childish they even have "Lads and Lassies" on the Cloakroom doors – Christ!'

Soon afterwards, another Mass-Observation investigator travelled up to Filey in Yorkshire to see a Butlin's Holiday Camp for herself – unfortunately rather late in the season, but the half-empty site still had about 5,000 campers. Her first meal proved a bit of a culture shock – no choice of dishes and being designated to sit with strangers at the same table all week – and then on Saturday evening came the first entertainment, *Butlin Follies of 1947*, a variety show: 'The theatre was packed out, and the audience most appreciative, applauding each turn vociferously.' Next morning, after the daily reveille sung over the tannoy ('There's a new day a tumblin' in') and breakfast, she joined the queue for Sunday papers. 'Standing about outside the shop,' she noticed, 'were small groups of people feverishly looking at the football results and checking on their coupons to see if they had won anything on their Pools that week. Everywhere you walked people were doing the same.' Each day's programme had at least one contest, and on Sunday afternoon it was 'Holiday Lovelies', with the winner getting a loud round of applause at dinner that evening 'when she was asked to stand up so we could all have a look at her'.

Over the next few days, the investigator settled in, on Tuesday evening even enjoying the dancing:

At 10.30 two of the Red-coats disappeared from the Ballroom with a big drum ready for the 'Penny-on-the-Drum' parade. This is a nightly occurrence which everyone appears to thoroughly enjoy. The main idea is that the Red-coats bang the drum as they walk along and gradually collect a long string of campers behind them by singing

'Come and join us
Come and join us
Come and join our merry throng.'

The procession begins in the Regency Bar, works its way all through the camp, through the Viennese Bar and ends up with everybody in the Viennese Ballroom. Everybody is laughing and singing at the top of their voices and the procession winds round and round in the Ballroom and finally breaks up when the orchestra strikes up for the final dance of the evening.

Thursday evening featured the Campers' Concert – 14 items, each 'greeted with vigorous applause' – and on Friday afternoon there was 'Fun and Games' at the giant Bathing Pool: 'Everybody seemed in particularly good spirits ... and felt a special kind of mateyness and comradeship with all their fellow campers.' The camp as a whole was divided into four houses (Gloucester, Kent, Windsor, York); in her concluding remarks on her week's experience, the investigator reckoned that the many inter-house competitions worked as well as they did because there was 'a suspension of disbelief sufficient to give them a sense of communal effort and general mateyness'. The campers, in other words, did not suddenly abandon their critical faculties once they entered this cocooned world of communal pleasures on tap. 'The picture sometimes painted of a set of solemn, suspicious, inhibited people arriving, and a set of slap-happy, healthy, gloriously carefree, 100% Butlinites leaving is distinctly wide of the mark; the vital thing is that some progress is made with everybody, giving a social atmosphere more healthy than the norm.'[10]

———

The summer of 1947 was dramatic and expectant for Glenda Jackson. A labourer's daughter, growing up in Hoylake, she took her 11 plus – only to find that on the day of the results there was a mix-up, involving a long, dreadful period at her girls' primary school being given pitying looks by everyone while those who had passed received multiple congratulations. Eventually, on returning home, she found and read the letter announcing that she had passed. 'I saw adults whom I had known all my life change their attitude to me twice in the space of a very small time,' she recalled. 'Contemptible.'

That autumn, Jackson started at West Kirby Grammar School for Girls, where the expensive, distinctly middle-class uniform requirements included one's own gym outfit, hockey stick and tennis racquet. Albert Finney, a bookmaker's son from Salford and born on the same day as Jackson, also started at grammar school then, as did Bill Wyman, in his case at Beckenham and Penge Grammar School. 'Ninety per cent came from upper- or middle-class homes in the expensive parts of suburban Kent,' Wyman remembered. 'Penge, my home, was definitely the wrong side of the tracks. I was inhibited by what other kids called my "working-class" accent, and a sense of inferiority prevented me from inviting them to my small and spartan home.' Meanwhile, 'local kids in Penge threw bricks at me, knocking my grammar-school blazer and cap (which ...y father could ill afford to buy).' Altogether, it was 'a no-win situation', not least because 'if I tried "talking posh" as they called it when I got home, I was mocked by everyone around me'.

There were, however, significant straws in the wind pointing to a different, potentially less divisive future. At that year's Labour Party conference a resolution from Bristol calling on the minister George Tomlinson to consider 'the rapid development' of common secondary schools, 'in order to give real equality of opportunity to all the nation's children', received unanimous support, while over the next year a handful of local authorities were pushing hard for at least a quorum of comprehensives to be established. The new (but as yet far from universal) egalitarianism was epitomised by the 1948 report entitled *The Comprehensive School* by the National Association of Labour Teachers: 'So long as this stratification of children at the age of eleven remains it is in practice useless to talk of parity in education or of equal opportunity in later life.' After dismissing intelligence tests as 'pseudo-scientific' and intended 'to create an intellectual aristocracy', the report declared, 'It is high time that we forgot the unverified assumption that only a small percentage of our children have sufficient native ability to move on to advanced work of a high standard.'

Three Schools or One? was the title of Lady Simon of Wythenshawe's discussion of the subject that same year. A leading, progressive-minded figure for many years on Manchester's education committee, she here willingly accentuated the drawbacks of tripartism (grammar, modern, technical) and the positives of the comprehensive secondary school. Simultaneously, however, she felt bound to point out that 'middle-class parents will not readily send their children to a school in which they feel that the tone of speech and behaviour will be set by children coming from the poorest homes.' And she made an equally pertinent further point: such parents in this situation would, if they could afford it, look instead to the private sector.[11]

10

The Whole World Is Full of Permits

There was much on the Labour Party's mind by 1947/8 as – following the great burst of legislation since 1945 – it sought to orientate itself for the 1950s. Would it, for instance, tamely line up behind Ernest Bevin's strong pro-American, anti-Communist line? Over Easter 1947, shortly after President Harry Truman had proclaimed his fiercely anti-Soviet Doctrine, denouncing Communism for its inherent expansionism and promising on the part of the free world an 'enduring struggle' against it, three youngish Labour MPs (Richard Crossman, Michael Foot and Ian Mikardo) wrote an almost instantly published pamphlet, *Keep Left*. Critical of Bevin's 'dangerous dependence' on the US, it demanded that British and French Socialists form an alliance sufficiently strong 'to hold the balance of world power, to halt the division into a Western and Eastern bloc and so to make the United Nations a reality'. Within weeks there appeared a counter-pamphlet, *Cards on the Table*, written by Denis Healey on Bevin's behalf and pouring the coldest of cold water on the notion that Britain had anywhere else but the US to turn to if it was serious about wanting to moderate Russia's 'aggressive anti-British policy'.

Over the following nine months, two crucial developments persuaded Crossman et al to turn right. The first was the American initiative (first flagged in June 1947) that in due course became Marshall Aid: large-scale economic assistance to enable Europe's (including Britain's) post-war reconstruction, welcomed almost as much on the Labour left as on its right. The other, in February 1948, was the Communist coup in Czechoslovakia, which was extraordinarily hard to reconcile with a benign reading of Soviet foreign policy. The dramatic events in Berlin during the spring and summer – Russian blockade followed by Western airlift – merely confirmed the point. Benn Levy, briefly a Labour MP after becoming a well-known playwright, spoke in 1948 for many bruised and disillusioned Keep Lefters: 'There is no longer a third choice. We must travel the Russian road or the American road . . . Are we to choose the American alignment which it is widely feared may jeopardise our Socialism, or the Russian alignment which, with the object lesson of Czechoslovakia in mind, we may reasonably believe would end in the loss of our democracy? For better or worse, the choice is made.'¹ Levy did not need to add that that painful, deeply unenthusiastic choice was for the almighty (and more or less democratic) dollar – a choice that from the start precluded neither a continuing visceral anti-Americanism nor a lingering sentimental attachment to the Soviet Union and its stout-hearted people.

As the Cold War set in during 1947/8, so the British Communist Party inexorably hardened its line and narrowed its options. The Labour government was now attacked by it at every opportunity, above all for its subservience to America, while Stalin and the Soviet Union received unstinting, unwavering support, whatever the circumstances and tergiversations. Inevitably, there were defectors. 'I gradually became uncomfortable in the Party and hostile to it,' the playwright Robert Bolt, then a student at Manchester University, recalled of this time. 'I could get no sense out of the people I revered in the Party and no honest answers to the questions I was asking. So I left.' Nor was there much evidence that the shift of approach was striking any great popular chords. Quite the reverse, as the writer (and youthful CP member) Mervyn Jones discovered when he went to Wigan in February 1948 to help the Communist candidate in a by-election:

A few days before the poll, the Communists took power in Czecho-slovakia. It was true that the crisis was provoked by the right-wing parties, who miscalculated their strength; but it was also obvious that the CP would establish a monopoly of power. Up in Wigan, Party leaders, including Harry Pollitt, hastily conferred and produced a leaflet which began: 'Rejoice! Democracy has triumphed in Czechoslovakia!' In the gloom of a snowy morning, I helped to hand it out at the gate of a cotton-mill. The workers littered the ground with it. We polled about 1,300 votes. A Communist candidate today [1987] would be more than satisfied with that figure, but in 1948 it was seen as disastrous.

Overall, the onset of the Cold War could not but affect the temper of British public life. As early as May 1947, Attlee began to chair a Special Cabinet Committee on Subversive Activities; in early 1948 the government established the Information and Research Department (IRD), essentially an anti-Communist propaganda unit; and on 15 March, soon after the Prague coup, Attlee announced that members of the CP and those 'associated with it' would henceforth be forbidden from undertaking work deemed 'vital to the security of the State'. The immediate consequences were dramatic. There began the process of systematically investigating individual civil servants; new academic appointments were more or less closed for Communists or Communist sympathisers; and the BBC summarily dismissed Alex McCrindle, a Communist actor known to millions as 'Jock' in *Dick Barton*. Altogether it was hardly an edifying spectacle; yet whether the Attlee government's quite aggressively illiberal anti-Communism necessarily occupied the moral low ground is arguably another matter. Context, the historian Alan Bullock would remind younger readers almost 40 years later, was all:

> There was a real danger of the Soviet Union and other communists taking advantage of the weakness of Western Europe to extend their power. We know now that this did not follow, but nobody knew it at the time. This was a generation for whom war and occupation were not remote hypotheses but recent and terrible experiences. The fear of another war, the fear of a Russian occupation, haunted Europe in those years and were constantly revived – by the communist coup in Czechoslovakia, by the Berlin blockade.

It was unhistorical, in short, 'to dismiss those fears as groundless because the war and occupation did not occur'.[2]

There were similar heart-searchings over nationalisation. By the summer of 1947, all the public-ownership commitments in the election manifesto had been implemented or were in train – with the exception of the iron and steel industry, always the most controversial of the

1945 promises. Utilities and transport, after all, were publicly owned in many other capitalist countries, while the coal industry in private hands had been generally acknowledged to be in the knackers' yard. But the steel industry, although widely recognised to need a shake-up, was something else. Aneurin Bevan, whose constituency included the Ebbw Vale steelworks, pushed the hardest for early and full nation-alisation, positing it not only as an economic and social good in itself but also as symbolically crucial in demonstrating that Britain's first socialist government with an overall majority had not run out of steam. His opponents included the steelmasters, Lincoln Evans (leader of the steel workers' union) and Herbert Morrison. Eventually, after some heated discussions, including at what was described as a 'very hysterical and steamed up' meeting of the parliamentary party, the Cabinet decided in favour of full nationalisation but not until the 1948/9 parlia-mentary session.

For Morrison, it was a battle lost; henceforth, despite being the principal architect of the way in which nationalisation worked in practice, he was determined to impose an 'enough is enough' line, conscious no doubt that public ownership had never been a great vote-winner in the first place. 'We definitely do not want to nationalise the small man – the shop round the corner,' he told his party's NEC Policy Committee in November 1947. 'We must take care not to muck about with private enterprise, merely for the purpose of being spiteful.' The following May, at the party conference in Scarborough, he similarly insisted that the government should now go slow on nationalisation and instead concentrate on consolidating its existing achievements.

The whole question by this time seems to have touched a raw nerve, whatever the indifference of most workers in the nationalised industries themselves. 'Nationalisation without democracy is not Socialism,' Manny Shinwell told the same conference, 'and we cannot claim that an industry or service is socialised unless and until the principles of social and economic democracy are implicit in its day-to-day conduct.' That was also the view of Michael Young in Labour's research department, but when in 1948 he wrote a party pamphlet on 'industrial democracy', privileging the rank-and-file worker above the union leadership and even flirting with the idea of workers' control, the first edition had to be withdrawn after objections from both Bevan and Morrison. It was a revealing if heavy-handed intervention, for in the end the problem of how to make nationalisation work better would turn not on social liberation from below but on political and economic decision-making from above. Hugh Gaitskell, Shinwell's successor as Minister of Fuel and Power, did not doubt where the sharp end lay, and a diary entry from June 1948 suggests that he was not the only one:

> An argument last night with Nye Bevan at our group dinner about nationalisation. Being, of course, a glutton for power he does not like the present policy of setting up the semi-autonomous Boards. He wants to control and answer for them; in fact to have them under him like departments. There is of course a good deal in what he says. Certainly it is no easy job to try and establish just the necessary degree of control without going too far. Also it is irritating not to be able to keep them on the right lines all the time. On the other hand there would, I think, be even greater dangers if, for instance, the Coal industries were run entirely by the Department. In any case we are now committed in the case of my industries to the principle of the semi-independent Board, and that being so one must give this particular form and relationship a fair trial.[3]

Gaitskell from the right and Bevan from the left were tacitly agreed, in other words, that control of the commanding heights was not for those toiling in the foothills.

———

Even as the decision to defer steel nationalisation was being taken in August 1947, the Labour government was wrestling with what became known as the convertibility crisis. The implacable, inescapable problem was that from 15 July, in accordance with the terms of the American Loan over a year and a half earlier, sterling was fully convertible into dollars. Almost immediately there ensued an appalling drain of dollars from the country, accompanied by a run on the pound. A new round of belt-tightening – and all the attendant criticism – soon became inevitable. 'At dinner we guessed what awful impositions Attlee would announce tomorrow,' noted James Lees-Milne on Tuesday, 5 August, while staying at the Chequers Hotel in Newbury with Harold Nicolson and Vita Sackville-West. 'Harold admits that he foresees no solution to the predicament we are in, and his reason for becoming a socialist is that socialism is inevitable. By joining he feels he may help by tempering it; by remaining outside he can do nothing. He says the sad thing is that no one dislikes the lower orders more than he does.' Next day in the Commons, Attlee duly announced a range of cuts, involving food, petrol and films among other things.

Over the next few days, the political temperature rose with the actual temperature, and Mass-Observation's investigators managed a couple of good 'overheards'. The first was two middle-aged, working-class men on a bus in the City:

Gor blimey Charlie – wot a bloody outlook etc. When are they going to stop cutting things I'd like to know. Still the people wanted em in, didn't they? Now they've got em they've found out a thing or two.

Worse than the war mate ain't it?

At least you knew wot was appening then but yer don't know wot to expect now do yer.

The other was a middle-class man travelling on a Southern Region train to Raynes Park: 'They have got to do these things – after all you must admit they are luxuries. I don't go to the films much so it won't affect me, the cutting down of films. Rounding up the spivs is a good thing – they are a burden on the national effort. They will be doing more drastic things in the winter, you mark my words.'

On the evening of Sunday the 10th, the day after Denis Compton and Middlesex had run riot at The Oval in front of 30,000, Attlee spoke to the nation – 'surely the most colourless politician who ever broadcast', according to Nella Last in Barrow. 'Listen with me to the end,' he asked before seeking to justify his measures, 'and think and talk over what I have said afterwards.' They half-obeyed that injunction at the Royal Clarence Hotel in Exeter, where Lees-Milne heard the speech. 'In the crowded lounge it was received in grim silence,' he observed. 'When over not a soul spoke or made a single comment. Instead, he and she went on with their reading, so typically English. A sign of native phlegm or stupid indifference, who can tell?' In any case, the measures failed to stem the crisis, as over the following week Britain's dollar reserves continued to drain away with alarming rapidity. 'The Government are in these matters, as in all others, worried, nervy, and incapable of reaching decisions,' privately declared one of the Bank of England's executive directors, 'Ruby' Holland-Martin, towards the end of the week.[4]

Finally, on Sunday the 17th, the Cabinet decided there was no alternative but to suspend convertibility. There were three more days of the Fifth Test at The Oval – Compton taking another century off South Africa, while according to *Wisden* 'the terraces presented a dazzling scene with the sun blazing down on the compact mass of people in the lightest permissible summer attire' – before Hugh Dalton on the 20th announced suspension on the radio. 'It is in fact a default,' was the implacable verdict of the *Financial Times*. 'Such a misjudgement of the situation and such precipitate abandonment of the position taken up so recently cannot fail to bring the gravest discredit upon this Government of self-styled planners.' For most people, however, national humiliation probably mattered rather less than the further cuts announced exactly a week later. '"LESS–LESS–LESS" shrieks the "Daily Express" headline this morning,' noted Florence Speed on the 28th – with the weekly meat ration, for example, being cut from 1s 2d to 1s – while Lees-Milne reported himself that day as 'terribly upset by the announcement that the basic petrol ration is to be cut off and all foreign travel to cease'. Yet in Henry St John's office in Bristol, this announcement of the latest cuts 'was freely commented on, but there was no sign of revolt, or any constructive criticism'.[5] Phlegm? Or indifference? A good question, to which perhaps the most plausible answer is that it was a bit of both.

In the short term, the response of the 'self-styled planners' was seemingly to turn to more planning, with Stafford Cripps in September assuming the newly created position of Minister of Economic Affairs, effectively replacing Morrison as planning supremo and enjoying, at least on paper, more clout than the somewhat beleaguered Dalton at the Treasury. On the face of it representing a renewed commitment to centrally directed economic planning, in reality it was the deftest of ploys by Attlee, who in the face of a possible putsch against his leadership thereby neatly detached Cripps from the fellow-plotters Dalton and Morrison. Only weeks later, Dalton was forced to walk the plank after carelessly revealing part of the contents of his Budget speech shortly before delivering it; Cripps replaced him, with his new ministry effectively being subsumed into the Treasury. Over the following year, Cripps proved to be a remarkably effective and dominant Chancellor – arguably the outstanding occupant of No. 11 since Gladstone, certainly since Lloyd George before the First World War. One consequence was a huge boost to the institutional authority of the Treasury, where by this time the out-and-out planners, advocating physical controls (especially over manpower) to achieve a planned economy, were heavily outgunned by the supporters of Keynesian demand management. Indeed, Dalton's ill-fated November 1947 Budget, seeking through fiscal policy to reduce the level of demand, had already made it clear where the Treasury stood; and Cripps, though nominally a committed planner, in practice became increasingly aware of planning's defects and limitations.[6]

Nevertheless, not only did many controls remain in place, but the intellectual shift itself took time to take effect. The influential Evan Durbin, for instance, was hardly a left-winger, yet he was deeply reluctant to abandon socialist planning. Typically, he did not duck the problems, arguing in a 1948 essay that if it was inefficient allocation of manpower that had been mainly responsible for weakening the economy by the time of convertibility, then the only way in which that difficulty could be addressed in a democratically planned manner was through a differential wages policy – given that it was unacceptable to increase significantly the degree of compulsory direction of labour that already existed. Durbin, like everyone else, knew that the stumbling block to his strategy was the trade unions and their deep attachment to free collective bargaining.

Moreover, although the TUC did, through gritted teeth, agree in the spring of 1948 to an informal policy of wage restraint, essentially as a quid pro quo for government efforts to restrain inflation, this agreement neither contained a differential element (such as might stimulate labour mobility) nor implied any endorsement of a wages policy as part of the permanent landscape of a planned economy. 'We shall go forward building up our wage claims in conformity with our understanding of the people we are representing' was how the most powerful union leader, Arthur Deakin of the Transport and General

Workers' Union (TGWU), had put it in 1946, adding that 'any attempt to interfere with that position would have disastrous results'. Nothing had changed fundamentally since then or was likely to change. For all those temperamentally and philosophically wedded to pulling levers from the centre, Keynesian demand management offered a more or less acceptable way out of the planning impasse.

The convertibility crisis also undermined planning in the sense of reconstruction, inevitably leading as it did to a number of major capital-investment cuts. Work on the first wave of New Towns almost ground to a halt, prompting some tellingly patronising, Goldsmithian lines from 'Sagittarius':

> O thou, the city planner's lawful pride,
> With industry and housing side by side,
> Abandon'd ere thy ground-plan was unroll'd,
> Farewell, sweet Stevenage! thou art pigeon-hol'd.
> Here winsome rented dwellings would have been,
> With sun-trap fronts towards th' unlitter'd green,
> Thy Civic Centre, seat of sober pomp,
> Thy glitt'ring Dance-Hall for the modest romp,
> Thy communal canteen and cultural hub,
> Thy decent shop and semi-rural pub.

It was almost as slow-going in the blitzed cities, where large swathes of bomb sites seemed to be settling in for a new duration, while in one, Hull, council elections in November 1947 showed clearly that local people were far more concerned with getting housing as soon as possible than, as they saw it, with watching the local authority engage in expensive, high-falutin' town planning for some distant point in the 1950s – or beyond.[7]

There were even continuing misgivings in Coventry. 'We all wish to see a beautiful and well-planned city rise from the ruins of the old,' one Coventry resident protested earlier that year, 'but you cannot expect people, who are living in overcrowded conditions, with meagre supplies of food and clothing, properly to appreciate the present scheme of transformation in Broadgate. When they see the tons of cement and brickwork, together with the labour personnel involved upon the project, it only seems to widen the gap between their present conditions and the hopes of something better in the near future.' The scheme, though, went ahead, and in May 1948, on a Saturday of blazing sunshine and huge crowds, Princess Elizabeth visited Coventry to declare the redeveloped Broadgate open and lay the foundation stone for its new shopping precinct. 'With your blessing we shall create not only a city of fine buildings, but a happy and prosperous community,' declared Alderman George Hodgkinson, the prime moving force behind Coventry's rebuilding, in his speech of thanks. That day the main local paper was similarly bullish: 'As we look around us we have reason for satisfaction. The old, homely Broadgate we knew was obliterated by bombing. That could never be restored, but in recent months new roads have been constructed, and a garden island has appeared where not so long ago was desolation. Truly Broadgate is a fitting centre-piece for a well-planned city. The foundation stone of the shopping precinct marks the beginning of bigger things.' In sum, Elizabeth's visit 'has given Royal recognition to Coventry's post-war achievements and aspirations'.[8]

Certainly immediate economic difficulties did not stop the activators looking ahead. In 1947 the Labour-run Birmingham City Council, very much under the sway of its dynamic City Engineer Herbert Manzoni, managed to raise a huge loan for the compulsory purchase of five of the city's most run-down areas, more than half of whose 30,000 dwellings were back-to-backs. The move confirmed that in Birmingham, as in other big British cities, there would one day be the juggernaut of large-scale slum clearance. A meeting in April 1948 of the Society of Women Housing Managers tackled the question of how it might work:

Miss Thompson said the breaking up of an old community was a serious thing, as there was often a strong social bond in these areas. The key, she thought, was to get to know the people first, find out the forces making the social cohesion, and try to work in harmony with them.

This point was taken up by Mrs Barclay, president, who said that even when a community was only being moved a short way it seemed almost impossible to re-create the same social bond. The very fact of living in new houses seemed to produce a kind of exclusiveness.

The Danish architectural writer Steen Eiler Rasmussen would almost certainly have agreed with this patient, listening, female approach.

Author of *London: The Unique City*, an instant classic on publication in 1934, he included a solemn warning in his new edition in 1948:

> The evil comes in when architecture is treated as free art, like music and ballet, with the aim of expressing the special mind of its originator. Some so-called modern architects prefer to pose as romantic figures like Beethoven whose countenance seems to reveal the vast profundity obscure. It is good for picture papers and promotes respect for the profession. But as we see today that even music has suffered from over-emphasis of the emotional side it is obvious also that the art of domestic architecture cannot stand a too romantic interpretation.

Instead, as a less hubristic but indispensable goal, 'it must find its justification simply in forming a satisfactory setting to modern life'.

Yet what exactly was 'modern life'? And what in urban terms might be 'a satisfactory setting' for it? 'I have never seen any scientific calculation as to what is the right density either for a town or a part of it,' the minister Lewis Silkin brusquely told a gathering of town planners in July 1948. And he specifically queried those planners' most sacred cow, the concept of the neighbourhood unit: 'The assumption is that by dividing up your population into groups of 10,000 to 20,000 and surrounding them by open spaces, railways and main roads you will get nice little communities living happily and sociably together. On what evidence is that based?' The door was swinging open for a whole new world of applied social research. Or as James Lansdale Hodson had reflected shortly before, 'We remain very ignorant of the state of the nation. Not half enough social scientists are examining what's going on.'[9]

Altogether, the mood by 1947/8 on the non-Communist left was undeniably mixed but still at some fundamental level united. Not everyone might have agreed with Michael Young's nomination of 1960 as a realistic target date for the building of a socialist society, but most would have empathised with the defence of post-war changes made by the central character in J. B. Priestley's *The Linden Tree*, opening in London in August 1947:

Call us drab and dismal, if you like, and tell us we don't know how to cook our food or wear our clothes – but for Heaven's sake, recognise that we're trying to do something that is as extraordinary and wonderful as it's difficult – to have a revolution for once without the Terror, without looting mobs and secret police, sudden arrests, mass suicides and executions, without setting in motion that vast pendulum of violence which can decimate three generations before it comes to a standstill. We're fighting in the last ditch of our civilisation. If we win through, everybody wins through.

Shortly afterwards, in early September, one of Young's colleagues in Labour's research department, the young writer Vincent Brome, had a lengthy, revealing conversation with Bevan. 'Inevitably we spoke of democratic Socialism. We analysed what the Labour Government was trying to do, we examined the difficulties surrounding it, and then, suddenly, he defined Socialism in terms very different from the normal':

Democratic Socialism he said was an instrument for implementing the social conscience, and his case seemed to develop along these lines: – The social conscience expressed itself in thousands of families where children were taught the virtues of compassion and kindness and consideration for others. These beliefs were reinforced by Christian teaching which established fresh links in a long tradition of service as well as self, but when the child left the circle of the family, it found the outer material world largely uninterested in such attitudes. 'Economic necessity quickly frustrated the moral impulse. The very structure of society insisted on disillusionment which led to moral neuroticism . . .

'If you look at some of the points in the Labour Party programme you will see that they are, in a sense, tantamount to an attempt to let society "resolve its guilt anxieties" – or, putting it another way – to do the bidding of conscience . . .'

Many people sympathized with the sick person, everyone wanted the poverty-stricken mother to find a house for her children, but it was assumed by too many that the resolution of these difficulties was entirely the responsibility of the individual concerned. Under Capitalism poor people were thrust back upon their own limited resources and some encountered inordinate hardship. 'But if we do what the Labour Government is doing – transform all these thousands of personal and private headaches into public headaches – we can get something done ... To preach and not to practise, to be obliged by the structure of society to act inadequately or not at all, is to become a moral cripple ... It is to thwart instead of implement the social conscience ...'

There was much more in a similar vein

Brome was impressed. 'Forty minutes and still the phrases came pouring in like Atlantic rollers, full, rich, measured. For a whole hour it went on with hardly a pause, hardly a word from me, and then abruptly he stood up, pleaded pressure of many things and escorted me to the door.'[10]

Anthony Wedgwood Benn – son of a Liberal-turned-Labour peer, in his early 20s, about to come down from Oxford after being a fighter pilot in the war – did not yet have executive responsibilities but in early 1948 he composed his private 'Thoughts on Socialism'. Arguing that pre-war 'poverty and squalor and undernourishment' had made 'a mockery of the price mechanism as a means of translating needs into economic demand', he nevertheless accepted that 'economic efficiency demands a degree of inequality because of the need for incentives'. Even so: 'A certain standard of health, nourishment and housing must be maintained for all. No one else can do it but the state and in Britain a new paternalism is state paternalism: looking after those who cannot look after themselves. This involves interference, but if this interference is democratically controlled we need not fear that an unwieldy bureaucracy will clasp us in its grip.' In short, the answer was democratic socialism, with the emphasis at least as much on the first word as the second: 'We in the English-speaking world have created a wonderful machinery for peaceful change in parliamentary democracy. It has taken 1,000 years ... Socialism is important, I feel certain, but socialism achieved by force is no good.'

Others sounded a wearier, more sceptical note. 'The honeymoon between literature and action, once so promising, is over,' bleakly declared Cyril Connolly, ultimate literary mandarin, bleakly in his magazine in July 1947, some six months after John Lehmann's Isherwood-induced disenchantment:

We can see, looking through old *Horizons*, a left-wing and sometimes revolutionary political attitude among writers, heritage of Guernica and Munich, boiling up to a certain aggressive optimism in the war years, gradually declining after D-day and soon after the victorious general election despondently fizzling out . . . A Socialist Government, besides doing practically nothing to help artists and writers, has also quite failed to stir up either intellect or imagination; the English renaissance, whose false dawn we have so enthusiastically greeted, is further away than ever . . . Somehow, during the last two years, the left-wing literary movement has petered out.

Nor was a society seemingly pervaded by pernickety, pettifogging bureaucracy any more attractive even for a veteran Fabian. 'The whole world is full of permits and control of people,' Lord Passfield (better known as Sidney Webb) lamented two months later in his final letter. 'I am afraid the old ones such as I fall to have to put up with much.' Everything, of course, would be all right so long as the people's party and the people were on the same wavelength. A perceptive observer as well as participant, Gaitskell privately reflected at about this time how often Labour MPs for marginal seats were 'most unrealistic about the Left Wing character of the electorate', and he argued that they made the mistake of 'identifying their own keen supporters – politically conscious and class-conscious Labour men – with the mass of the people, who are very much against austerity, utterly uninterested in nationalisation of steel, heartily sick of excuses and being told to work harder, but probably more tolerant of the Government and appreciative of its difficulties than many suppose'.[11]

Gaitskell's reading of a misalignment between party and people was endorsed in December 1947 by a poll which found that 42 per cent thought the Labour government had so far been 'too socialistic', 30 per cent 'about right', and a mere 15 per cent 'not socialist enough'. For Gaitskell's close friend and contemporary Durbin, such a poll served to confirm that (as he tersely put it in some notes written around 1947/8) 'British people not socialists' and 'the political future is not hopeful'. He had already, in earlier notes, called for 'co-operation between Public Opinion experts and sociological minded politicians' in some 'consumer's research – to find out what our people really want from the State'. Socialists, he now contended,

> must realise that the British people soon tire of any one set of changes – and will soon need a *new emphasis upon the values of personal life* – in a more complex and powerfully unified society.
>   improved communication with them
>   services that deal with personal problems
>   more provision for fun

The fragmentary, unpunctuated nature of Durbin's notes fails to mask the fact that, by this third year of the Labour government, he was working towards a new, potentially very fruitful, more consultative politics that would be predicated on a realistic assessment of the electorate's values and priorities.

None of which meant that Durbin himself made much political headway. 'You will see that God continues to strike heavily,' he had complained to a friend in October 1946. 'Trouble at Edmonton, chest trouble and no job in the Government.' Five months later he was at last given a position, but only as Parliamentary Secretary at the Ministry of Works – one of the less inspiring posts. Nor did the autumn 1947 reshuffle bring any joy. 'I feel a little separated from the consideration of economic policy,' he wrote with understandable disappointment to Attlee. 'I know that I have something to contribute to the Government in this direction.'[12]

The contrast was stark with another economist-turned-politician, Harold Wilson, who in the reshuffle became President of the Board of Trade – at 31 the youngest Cabinet minister of the twentieth century, though in appearance and manner (moustache, incipient paunch, invariable waistcoat, little small talk or sense of humour) middle-aged before his time. It was not quite Pitt the Younger, but it was in its way an equally remarkable advance. The son of an industrial chemist, Wilson in background was solidly northern (mainly Huddersfield), Noncon-formist (Congregationalist) and more middle- than working-class. From grammar school it was a sure-footed ascent: scholarship to Oxford, a top First, fellowship at an Oxford college, research assistant to Sir William Beveridge, wartime work at the Ministry of Fuel and Power that won him an OBE, a seat (Ormskirk) in 1945, a government position from the start, the call to the Cabinet. The appointment received much publicity – almost all of it favourable – and within days the Cotton Board's Sir Raymond Streat was watching Wilson open a textiles exhibition and participate in a conference on the export task ahead. 'I think Wilson made a good impression on my cotton friends and on me personally,' Streat noted. 'He is quick on the uptake – too well versed in economics and civil service work to rant or rave like a soap-box socialist.' A second encounter with the new man followed soon after:

> Harold Wilson reacts too quickly, too smoothly and readily for any impression of particular purpose to emerge. Maybe he hardly gives himself time to identify purpose and if his romantically early start in politics is to lead to the acquisition of the qualities of statesmanship he would possibly be well advised to take himself in hand and leave part of the garden in which such plants could grow ...
>
> He is nice enough as an open-hearted sort of young man and a fond father of a young family to be all right if he does not entirely forget big things by allowing himself to be pre-occupied with a million small ones.

One of Wilson's biographers, Ben Pimlott, has argued that this was somewhat unfair, given that 'a million small things' were at this time the very business of the Board of Trade. But Streat's was still an acute assessment.

What was Wilson's 'particular purpose'? Much has been made of his attachment to Liberalism until the late 1930s and his subsequent lack of a moment of socialist epiphany. Yet what is most striking about his personal-cum-political formation is the cumulatively conclusive evidence that at no stage was he interested in ideas – as opposed to economic statistics, the names and numbers of steam engines, and football and cricket scores. Formidably clever and industrious, he was not (for better or worse) an intellectual. 'Harold Wilson was a rule-governed convergent thinker,' reflected one historian, David Howell, after reading Pimlott. 'He performed according to the rules.'[13] And, unlike the young Gladstone when sent to the Board of Trade, he never complained that he had been 'set to govern packages'.

For the Conservative Party, so crushingly vanquished in 1945, it could be only a long night's journey into day.[14] At its first post-war conference, at Blackpool in October 1946, the mood on the platform was still pessimistic. 'These great, intelligent thoroughbreds, trained from their earliest years to prudent administration and courteous debate, were in their hearts not far from accepting as definitive their electoral defeat,' one observer, the French political scientist Bertrand de Jouvenel, wrote soon afterwards. But on the conference floor there was a much greater sense of defiance – not least (if one accepts her retrospective account) on the part of Margaret Roberts, newly elected President of the Oxford University Conservative Association. The right-wing newspaper proprietor (and wartime Minister of Information) Brendan Bracken reported to Beaverbrook that the delegates 'would have nothing to do with the proposal to change the Party's name' and that 'they demanded a real Conservative policy instead of a synthetic Socialist one.' Although Churchill was initially disinclined to undertake a fundamental review of policy at this stage, in due course a committee chaired by Rab Butler (architect of the 1944 Education Act) was set up.

The outcome was *The Industrial Charter*, published in May 1947 and recognised from the outset as a major policy statement. Less than two years after Churchill's ill-considered 'Gestapo' jibe, the document apparently marked a broad acceptance of the emerging post-war settlement. There would be no denationalisation of the Bank of England or the coal mines or the railways; the new orthodoxy of Keynesian deficit finance – government increasing its spending in order to boost demand and thus employment – was accepted; workers' rights were to be protected; and producers' monopolies and cartels were denounced as vigorously as trade union restrictive practices. One passage particularly caught the prevailing pragmatic tone: 'We Conservatives want to release industry and those who work in industry from unnecessary controls so that energy and fresh ideas may be given their head. But we know that, as things are, there must be some central planning of the nation's work. The world is topsy-turvy. Raw materials are scarce. Stormy weather must be foreseen. There must be a hand on the helm . . .' Altogether, commented the *Spectator*, the document removed any 'excuse for labelling the Conservative Party as at present constituted as reactionary', adding that 'in most cases the difference with Labour is more of degree than of fundamental principle.'

That October, at the party conference in Brighton, the progressive-minded, thoroughly non-grandee (son of an actuary) Reggie Maudling, prospective candidate for Barnet and one of the bright young things on the research side, moved an amendment that the *Charter* be accepted by the party as a whole. Sir Waldron Smithers, the entirely unreconstructed MP for Orpington, protested that 'the party must not allow itself to become infected with the Socialist bug, and it must stick to its principles or perish'. But amid soothing words from Butler (including the phrase 'private initiative in the public interest') and a certain amount of well-rehearsed procedural legerdemain, the Maudling amendment was carried with only three dissenters. It was, the *Spectator* reflected with overall satisfaction, 'a responsible act' that demonstrated 'a positive will to govern on the part of the rank and file'.[15]

In reality, the Tories were not in quite such ideological retreat. Not only did *The Industrial Charter* consistently identify private enterprise as the rightful mainspring of economic activity, but the language almost throughout emphasised the individual at the expense of the collective. 'The ultimate restoration of freedom of choice' for the consumer, 'status as an individual personality' for the worker, and 'a personal incentive to reap a greater reward for greater responsibility' for the manager: all were contrasted, in 'a free and resourceful nation', with Labour's belief that 'the men and women who fought and worked together in the war can now be exalted, controlled and regimented into producing goods, building houses and rendering services in time of peace'. Variety as against uniformity, 'humanising' as against nationalising, giving people 'opportunity' as against orders – this was to be the new, distinctive rhetoric of post-war Conservatism, a rhetoric far removed in the late 1940s from Labour rhetoric, even right-wing Labour rhetoric.

Moreover, although no one in the Tory leadership imagined that there could be a return to the minimalist, 'nightwatchman' state of the nineteenth century, it was far from clear that old-fashioned economic liberalism had been totally banished. 'I do not agree with a word of this,' Churchill memorably told Maudling after being given a five-line digest of the newly endorsed *Charter*; the next most senior Tory, Sir Anthony Eden, was already pushing hard for 'a property-owning democracy' despite the fact that public housing was poised to expand as never before; and a possible Tory Chancellor, Oliver Lyttelton, a hard-money man from the City, was privately contemplating the radical free-market solution of floating the pound. In short, the 'pinks' like Butler (who himself plugged 'co-partnership' essentially as a tactical antidote to nationalisation) and Harold Macmillan (author of *The Middle Way* in the 1930s) were far from having captured the party. A few weeks after the Brighton conference, the somewhat puzzled thoughts of Sir Cuthbert Headlam, a backbencher instinctively sceptical of Keynes et al, were probably representative of much of party opinion:

> I find that this pinkish portion of our party are more prominent but less popular with the rank and file than they used to be. People instinctively dislike their economic planning and plotting and yet can see no alternative to some policy of the kind in present conditions. In this I fancy they are right – the great thing, however, is not to emphasize the necessity for controls so much – if and when we come back into power, it will be time enough to decide how much Govt. intervention in the conduct of industry is required.[16]

There was still, in sum, much to play for – both within the party and, notwithstanding Labour's partial retreat from planning, between the parties.

Not that most people were fussed either way. 'A very large number of people know little about party politics and care little,' declared a Mass-Observation report in the summer of 1947 about public reaction to the *Charter*. 'Any effort at all to obtain interest in a particular political party or policy is immediately confronted with a solid wall of disinterest and disbelief in at least a third of the people of this country' – a state of mind co-existing with 'extreme confusion on any subject even remotely concerned with party politics'. Asked about the differences between the two main parties, most of the survey's respondents were unable to identify any; as for those who did, the analysis rarely went beyond the personal or the non-political. 'The Labour are out for themselves and don't care about the people, but the Conservatives are wonderful, Mr Churchill should be sitting on the throne of Heaven' was a not untypical reply, in this case given by a 55-year-old charwoman. Less than a fifth of the sample, shown copies of the

Charter and other recent political pamphlets, confessed to having ever seen or even heard of any of them. Among those willing to engage with its policies, a worker's charter was generally seen as irrelevant and profit-sharing as impractical. 'It's all right on the outside but it's the inside that counts' was how a Labour-voting baker summed up his response to the pamphlet. 'I just don't trust them, that's all.'

Still, whatever its limitations in terms of popular appeal, there is no doubt that the *Charter* played an important part – if probably more by language than content – in making the Tories once again electoral contenders. For one septuagenarian, obstinately unwilling to stand down even as his finest hour passed into the history books (at this stage mainly being written by himself), this was a gratifying development. 'She told me that her father was very elated by the municipal election results, and was now confident that his party had a following in the country,' Lees-Milne noted in November 1947 after dining with Sarah Churchill. 'Already people in the streets were more respectful to him.'[17]

Ain't She Lovely?

The forces of conservatism were not to be underestimated. In March 1947 Bishop Barnes of Birmingham set out in *The Rise of Christianity* a theology that rejected the evidence of the Virgin Birth, the Miracles and the Resurrection. Over the next year his book sold more than 15,000 copies and generated a huge, wildly varied postbag. 'It is such a brave book,' the actress Sybil Thorndike wrote to him, 'and coming from a priest of the Church it is more than brave. It has been a releasing for me, and I am sure it must have been for many people.' The controversy came to a head in October 1947 when, at a meeting of Convocation, Geoffrey Fisher – Archbishop of Canterbury and uncomfortably aware that a majority of bishops were itching to pass a vote of censure for heresy – explicitly disavowed Barnes. 'If his views were mine,' he added, 'I should not feel that I could still hold episcopal office in the Church.'

Soon afterwards, the *Sunday Pictorial*, noting that 'at the very least the fundamental beliefs of millions are called into question', asked its readers to send in their views. The upshot was a torrent of words (more than three-quarters of a million in one week), with 52 per cent of letters supporting Barnes, 32 per cent against and the rest neutral. Tellingly, his opponents highlighted hypocrisy at least as much as doctrinal impurity. 'Dr Barnes should be expelled from the Church of England for denying the very truths he is paid a large salary to defend,' declared P. G. Thurston of Waterworks Road, Hastings. Ruth B. Hall from Ashford, Middlesex, agreed: 'Resign, man! And at least be honest. At the moment you are taking money under false pretences, in my opinion.' There was, as Mass-Observation's *Puzzled People* survey had shown, a widespread dislike for the established church, seen by many – in a way that had little or nothing to do with theology – as smug and excessively privileged. Barnes himself did not step down. But it was clear that within the church leadership the liberals were in a distinct minority, a minority that did not include Archbishop Fisher, a man of 'benign authoritarianism' (in the phrase of his *Times* obituary) who had earlier been a public-school headmaster and intended to run the Church of England along similar lines.[1]

A few weeks later, Fisher was solemnising the first post-war royal marriage. It had been a contentious choice of husband on Princess Elizabeth's part. In January 1947, before the engagement was announced, a *Sunday Pictorial* poll found that although 55 per cent were in favour of a marriage between her and Prince Philip of Greece (with the stipulation 'if the Princess and Prince are in love'), 40 per cent were against. Many readers felt that she ought to marry a commoner, one declaring that 'the days of intermarriage of royalty have passed'; others saw the marriage as frankly 'a political move'; and plenty echoed the xenophobic view of one household in the Euston Road: 'We, the Russell family – a father and two sons who have served in both wars – say, "Definitely no!" to a marriage with a foreign prince.' Lord Mountbatten, Philip's uncle, was already sufficiently rattled that he had asked the editors of the hostile Beaverbrook press whether they thought opinion would soften if his nephew were naturalised. They had agreed it might help, and Prince Philip of Greece in February duly became Lieutenant Philip Mountbatten, RN.

In July the engagement was at last announced. 'Any banqueting and display of wealth at your daughter's wedding will be an insult to the British people at the present time,' the Camden Town branch of the Amalgamated Society of Woodworkers immediately warned the King, 'and we would consider that you would be well advised to order a very quiet wedding in keeping with the times.' Amid a generally warm press response, the reaction of Florence Speed was probably representative. 'Princess Elizabeth is engaged (official),' she noted, '& judging from the laughing photographs of her taken after a dance at Apsley House last night it is the "love match" it is claimed to be & we are all glad about it.' As for Philip, she added that he was 'the type "easy on the eye", which any young girl would fall in love with'. Although a poll taken soon afterwards revealed that 40 per cent professed indifference to the prospect of the royal wedding in November – typical remarks including 'Feel? What should I feel?', 'I don't care, it doesn't affect me' and 'It's not my business, it's up to them' – by October those actively approving of the marriage were up from 40 to 60 per cent. Even so, James Lees-Milne recorded some disturbing news on 18 November, after dining with Simon Mosley of the Coldstream Guards: 'Says that 50 per cent of the guardsmen in his company refused to contribute towards a present for Princess Elizabeth. The dissentients came to him in a body and, quite pleasantly, gave him their reasons. *One*, they said the Royal Family did nothing for anybody, and *two*, the Royal Family would not contribute towards a present for their weddings.' Moreover, 'when Simon Mosley said that without the Royal Family the Brigade of Guards, with its priv-ileges and traditions, would cease to exist, they replied, "Good! Let them both cease to exist."'

Thursday the 20th was not a public holiday – deemed inappropriate, in the economic context – but there was still enormous interest in the wedding (flower arrangements by Constance Spry). 'How we love the Crown and a wedding!' wrote James Lansdale Hodson next day:

> Our work in the office was put quite out of gear by all the staff listening-in. A newspaper records that Trafalgar Square was so crowded that not a pigeon could find foothold, and I'm told you could shop comfortably in the remoter streets, rows of tempting iced cakes lying untouched. Overnight Londoners brought out their blitz mattresses and blankets and lay on the kerbstone route; hard lying for pleasure now instead of for Jerry, and in the morning women washed in warm water from vacuum flasks before putting on their new make-up.

Not everyone was *quite* bowled over. Finding himself close-up to the happy couple on their way to Waterloo and their honeymoon (at Broad-lands), the journalist John Clarke privately thought that 'she looked to have a great deal too much make-up on', while 'he' (that morning created the Duke of Edinburgh) was 'rather grey-faced and already long-suffering'. The following Monday, dining at the Beefsteak, Sir Cuthbert Headlam was told by the King's Private Secretary, Sir Alan ('Tommy') Lascelles, 'that Philip Mountbatten is a "nice boy", but not much educated – should do all right he thinks for his job'. Later that week, the commercial artist Grace Golden went to a news cinema to see the film of the wedding and observed that 'Princess Elizabeth's charm must lie in her expressions.' But by the New Year there was still undimmed, mainly female enthusiasm to see the wedding dress and presents that had been on display since November. 'Mrs C. and I dragged ourselves out of bed at 7 a.m.,' Vere Hodgson, a staunch royalist, recorded in mid-January, 'and on a cold, wet and windy morning found ourselves in a long queue outside St James' Palace at 9.15 a.m. It was none too soon. At 10 o'clock we were let in with the first thousand.'[2]

There is the odd quasi-intimate diary glimpse of Elizabeth herself. 'She had a very pretty voice and quite an easy manner but is not, I think, very interested in politics or affairs generally,' reckoned Hugh Gaitskell in April 1948 after a quarter of an hour's conversation with her. Soon afterwards, Violet Bonham Carter went to a ball at Buckingham Palace for the King and Queen's silver wedding. 'I have *never* seen Pss E. look better,' she told her son Mark. 'She looked really *pretty* ... She strikes me as being rather "delié" by marriage – with fewer "stops".' The report went on: 'Pss Margaret on the other hand has *none* – as you have always said. Talking to her is not like talking to a "royalty".'

Not long afterwards, on 2 June, the princesses' mother paid a visit to the Lancashire cotton industry. It turned out to be 'a wet day, thoroughly wet, with a raw cold wind', in the words of Raymond Streat, one of the party that met the Queen at Blackburn station and then followed her in the second car of the procession. Early on she visited a mill and talked to the weavers, with Streat struck by 'the positive rapture indicated on the faces of those to whom she spoke'. Lunch at Rochdale Town Hall followed, and afterwards she appeared on the balcony 'and the vast crowd in the Town Hall Square cheered her mightily'. The procession then made its way to Oldham and from there, with the rain still pelting down, to Manchester. During those 7 miles there were 'people all the way on both sides of the road', and 'they surged off the pavement to get a close view of the Queen'. For Streat, it was the culmination of a rich anthropological experience:

Through the windows of our car we heard the voices of the crowd as they looked with fond affection on the receding car of the Queen and expressed their reaction to their immediate neighbours. Many hundreds of times that day I heard the phrase 'Ain't she lovely?' . . . That was the comment of more than three-quarters of the onlookers – just that and nothing more. They had come in curiosity to see a Queen, some no doubt for the first time and wondering what majesty did to a woman: they had seen a sweet and kindly face and shining friendly eyes, a wave of the hand and a little bow in their direction: that was all and their outstanding thought was that 'she' was lovely.

The Firm did not rely on just waves and smiles. Less than a week later, Harold Nicolson went to Buckingham Palace to be sounded out by Lascelles about writing an official life of George V. 'He said that I should not be expected to write one word that was not true,' Nicolson recorded. 'I should not be expected to praise or exaggerate. But I must omit things and incidents which were discreditable.' Nicolson agonised but in the end agreed. And privately he conceded, shortly before getting down to work on the commission, 'I quite see that the Royal Family feel their myth is a piece of gossamer and must not be blown upon.'³

For royalty and subjects alike, at least in theory, there was no getting away from continuing austerity. When Gallup in 1947 asked people what would be their ideal, no-expense-spared meal for a special occasion, their lovingly detailed answer – sherry; tomato soup; sole; roast chicken with roast potatoes, peas and sprouts; trifle and cream; cheese and biscuits; coffee – belonged in large part to the realms of fantasy, certainly in terms of assembling it all on any one domestic table at any one time. By the autumn of that year, following the convertibility crisis, not only had the butter and meat rations been cut again, including the bacon ration halved, but potatoes were on the ration for the first time. In early December, from the vantage point of a Wembley housewife, Rose Uttin summed up a year that had been 'depressing in all ways except the weather':

Our rations now are 1 oz bacon per week – 3 lbs potatoes – 2 ozs butter – 3 ozs marge – 1 oz cooking fat – 2 ozs cheese & 1/- meat – 1 lb jam or marmalade per month – ½ lb bread per day. We could be worse – but we should be a lot better considering we won the war. Cigarettes are 1/8 for 10 our only luxury except for 1 drink on Bridge evenings. Dora [her daughter] became engaged to Mac in October – we did manage a party, but I am wondering how long it will be before they can afford to marry with prices high as they are. One bag coal last week cost 4/10. America & the Labour government say we are producing more – what a joke. They forget to count the lumps of slate & stone in it. Used all the points up by last Wed on oats & mashed potato powder. Hard frost last two nights. Fog yesterday. My dinner today 2 sausages which tasted like wet bread with sage added – mashed potato – ½ tomato – 1 cube cheese & 1 slice bread & butter. The only consolation no air raids to worry us.

Nor was eating out, assuming one could afford it, necessarily a panacea. 'It used to be a treat to have a meal there,' commented Florence Speed in September after a dismal experience at Peter Jones. 'Our lunch costing 3/- was a waste of money,' with the lowlight being 'half-cold at least just tepid fish au gratin'. Or as Lees-Milne, speaking for everyman, put it two months later, 'The food in England is worse than during the war, dry and tasteless, even at Brooks's.'

One food above all became a byword for these straitened, unappetising times. 'A new South African fish on the market – snoek!' noted Speed in October 1947. 'Fred expressed a desire to taste it, so I got a tin when I saw it in Collins. Not cheap – 2/9 a tin.' Fred's reaction went unrecorded, but from the first there seems to have been little enthusiasm for this vaguely mackerel-type fish, seen by the government as the ideal replacement (largely because it came from within the sterling area) for Portuguese sardines. Ten million tins were due to reach Britain, and when in May 1948 there arrived the first large consignment the Ministry of Food celebrated by putting up snoek posters and publicising eight snoek recipes, including a concoction to go with salad immortally called *snoek piquante*. By this time a tin cost only 1s 4½d and took only one point (five less than household salmon) – necessary inducements with so many half-pound tins to get rid of. 'If you have not yet tried the new allocation of snoek, you may be wondering what it is like,' Marjorie Huxley wrote encouragingly soon afterwards in her 'Recipes for the Housewife' in the *Listener*. 'It is rather like tunny fish in texture, but with snoek, it is best not to try serving it as it is, but to break it into flakes and moisten it with some kind of sauce, dressing or mayonnaise.'⁴

Not everything fell victim to the government's – above all Sir Stafford Cripps's – determination to achieve a relentless drive for exports and reductions in unnecessary personal consumption. Cigarettes, for example, stayed off the ration: although their price had gone up sharply (from 2s 4d to 3s 4d for a packet of 20) in Hugh Dalton's penultimate Budget, no minister dared tamper with the working man's inalienable right to smoke, a right barely yet connected with lung cancer. 'All we need to do,' Dalton had reassuringly boomed, 'is to smoke a little slower, make our cigarettes last a little longer, throw away our stubs a little shorter, knock out our pipes a little later; and all this might be good for our health.' Nevertheless, in a thousand and one ways, everyday life remained difficult, perhaps typified by the qualitative as well as quantitative problems involved in that indispensable necessity for almost every household – coal supplies. 'There seems to be more coal dust in the delivery nowadays,' one housewife, Mrs Mary Whittaker, complained in October 1947 on *Woman's Hour*. 'I know we're asked to make briquettes of it, but can you tell me why we get so much of it?'

Housing remained a continuing, high-profile worry, though at least the much-disparaged prefabs (described by Mary King in her diary as 'a blot on the lovely English scenery') were for the time being still going up. Neil Kinnock's family moved in November 1947 to a new two-bedroom prefab on a council estate at Nant-y Bwch. 'It was like moving to Beverly Hills,' he recalled. 'It had a fridge, a bath, central heating and a smokeless grate . . . and people used to come just to look at it.' As for clothing restrictions, Anthony Heap's experience a few weeks earlier was probably typical:

Hopefully hied up to Burton's branch at The Angel, to order one of the fifteen 'made to measure' suits that comprise their present weekly 'quota'. Wanted a grey tweed, but as luck would have it, they hadn't any in this week's 'allocation' of patterns – only blue worsteds. They would, however, try and get me a length next week. In which case, the suit would be ready in about nine months' time! And with that dubious prospect I had to be content.

It was probably even more frustrating for women. 'Proceed early to Marshall & Snelgrove,' Grace Golden noted in January 1948, 'only to learn that they do not change utility garments – I almost burst into tears.'⁵

Gallup revealed that spring that as many as 42 per cent of people wanted to emigrate, compared with 19 per cent immediately after the end of the war. But soon afterwards there were merciful signs that Cripps's strong medicine was starting to work, with a modest petrol ration for pleasure purposes being reinstated from 1 June, together with 12 extra clothing coupons. And in her *The New Yorker* letter a week later, Mollie Panter-Downes optimistically reckoned that such concessions would be 'uplifting in their effect on the public, who are apt to accept controls as a sort of evil forest that has grown up around them and become a tedious but quite natural part of their lives'. Still, Tennessee Williams probably had the right of it. 'I guess England is about the most unpleasant, uncomfortable and expensive place in the world you could be right now,' he wrote not long afterwards to his agent in New York. It was a Sunday, he was staying at the Cumberland Hotel, and on going hopefully to the bar at 2.10 in the afternoon he had discovered that 'there wasn't a drink to be had in all of London until seven'.

Whatever the problems, whatever the sense of monotony and restricted choice, most people *coped*. Take Marian Raynham in Surbiton on a Wednesday in July 1947: 'Had a good & very varied day. Went to grocers after breakfast, then on way home in next door, then made macaroni cheese & did peas & had & cleared lunch, then rest, then made 5 lbs raspberry jam, got tea & did some housework, listened to radio & darned, wrote to Jessie Gould. In bed about midnight.' A key coping mechanism for many women, especially working-class women, was the bush telegraph. 'Round about us we have got a good shopping centre, so we are very fortunate,' explained a miner's widow when asked that year about the effect of rationing on her family budget, 'and I find in getting about you pick up windfalls and swop ideas and hints (for I am not too old to learn).' There was also the indispensable safety valve of humorous grumbling. *Punch* as usual had its finger on the pulse of Middle England, typified by these more or less amusing snippets between October and December 1947:

'Excellent meals *can* be obtained if you know where to go,' says a correspondent. He claims to have found a restaurant where food is fully up to war-time standard.

The Government policy of encouraging large families is emphasized by a recent statement that only in households of six or over is it worth while collecting the new bacon ration weekly.

'What could be better than a comfortable old arm-chair, a cosy little fire, and a good book?' enthuses a reader. We don't know; but no doubt some Ministry or other will soon be telling us.

Since caterers' supplies were cut we hear many people have taken to rations to eke out their eating out.

'Fry your whalemeat with an onion to absorb the oil,' advises a chef, 'and throw away the onion.' As well?

Anyway, there was remarkably little hard, objective evidence to back up the Tory claim that the unappetising austerity diet was actually leading to malnutrition. When the Hunterian Society debated the question in November 1947 at the Apothecaries Hall, nutritionists demonstrated that it was extremely difficult to detect even limited malnutrition. 'The biological system of man was infinitely adaptable to circumstances,' insisted one of them, Magnus Pyke. They did not perhaps go quite as far as Michael Foot had in a recent parliamentary debate – claiming that the children of 1947 were 'healthier, tougher, stronger than any breed of children we have ever bred in this country before' – but their central point was not disproved.[6]

Things looked pretty good to one outsider. Enid Palmer was in her late 20s when in April 1948 – after military nursing service in India and Burma followed by a lengthy stay with her parents in Kenya – she disembarked at Liverpool and caught the train to London. 'The sun shone most of the way – & England looked very pleasant,' she wrote home soon afterwards. 'Little green fields full of apple trees in blossom – sheep and white lambs gambolling about. Children everywhere – dogs all over the place – particularly wire haired terriers like Whiskey. We passed farms – with great English Carthorses pulling loads – and of course the rows and rows of tiny houses with their front and back gardens, washing hanging out.' That Friday evening she reached Addlestone in Surrey, where she was staying with her uncle George, aunt Beattie, cousin Joan and her baby Graham, and 'The Granny'. Uncle George took her on Saturday afternoon to the shops in Woking. 'They are full of nice things,' she reported. 'I eventually bought a pair of blue leather shoes at Dolcis – they cost only 51/- and are beautifully made with a crepe sole. I had to give 7 coupons for them. We walked round Woolworths, it was packed with people.' That evening a trip to the Weybridge Odeon ('comfortable plush seats') was followed by supper back home of 'sardines, tomato & lettuce, bread & margarine & coffee'. All in all, she told her parents, she was impressed:

> I have decided that England is not such a bad place after all. As for the stories one hears about it – they are quite untrue! Everybody looks very well – the children with beautiful rosy cheeks – and what numbers of children – there are crowds of them everywhere. The People are cheerful & happy – everybody is kind & polite & they smile – all the bus drivers & conductors, the railways officials, taxi drivers, porters etc, are polite & pleasant & helpful.
>
> The shops are full of flowers & fruit, sweets, cigarettes, clothes, shoes, everything one could possibly want. The only snag about clothes & shoes is the lack of coupons – one cannot buy them without. Fruit one can buy. There are fine apples, Jaffa oranges, South African grapes. The apples & oranges are 9d a lb. Daffodils are 24 for a shilling. Sweets are rationed – each person is allowed ¼ lb per month. Cigarettes are expensive, and not always easy to get. Other things are plentiful & everything is so much cheaper than in Kenya.

Nor was that all. 'Everybody is well dressed – far better than you or I even are – they may be old clothes but they are smart and well cut ... Few people wear hats or stockings. The commonest working man looks smart in his utility clothing.'

Over the next few weeks, while Palmer waited to go to a maternity home in Colchester to continue her training as a nurse, the honeymoon did not quite last. 'England's countryside is beautiful,' she wrote, 'but there are too many restrictions – everything is crowded & there are queues everywhere.' And: 'Life is narrow and bound by documents.' And again: 'There is one standard topic of conversation in England –

"coupons", "food", "clothes".' She was also rather dismayed by the lack of hygiene, and one day in London, finding herself near Victoria station, she did the enterprising thing:

> I found a public Baths building – after queuing for an hour got a good hot bath for 6d. It was most enjoyable as it was 6 days since I had had one. They are short of coalite here. Today Uncle George said, 'You may have a bath today'. I am afraid he runs this house. I was rather amused at being told when I may have a bath. Nobody else seems to have a bath except Uncle George who has one on Sunday night. Other nights I have a kettle of hot water, heated on the gas.

She also in her letters stopped extolling the abundance of food.

But whatever the objective truth about that, or indeed about the malnutrition question, the crucial, all-pervasive *subjective* reality for most people was that morale generally, and food morale in particular, was low. In the same month that Palmer arrived in England, an official survey asked a representative sample of the population whether they felt they were getting sufficient food to stay in good health. Fifty-five per cent answered 'no', with another 7 per cent doubtful; when a similar survey was conducted two months later, the respective figures were 53 and 9 per cent. '"Something tasty" is the key-phrase in feeding,' Richard Hoggart would memorably write about the working-class Hunslet of the 1950s – but in reality of the 1930s when he was growing up there. 'Something solid, preferably meaty, and with a well-defined flavour.'[7] Given the shortages of anything tasty, especially with the low ration of fats, it was little wonder that almost half of a weary, put-upon population wanted to try pastures new.

Meanwhile, the sense of social malaise if anything deepened. Thirteen million pounds' worth of property was stolen during 1947, more than five times as much as in 1938. 'Newspapers are sprinkled with stories of rascals at work,' noted Hodson in December 1947 – stories that included the *Barnsley Chronicle*'s report of how the town's market had been invaded by 'strapping young men dressed in gaily ribboned slouch hats; the loudest and latest Yankee ties (nude figures painted with luminous paint); fancy overcoats with padded shoulders;

highly-polished pointed shoes'. And all rounded off with 'David Niven 'tashes, cultivated with the aid of a black pencil'. These spivs, 'driven from their holes and corners in London by the manpower hunt, the closer attentions of the police, and income tax officials', attempted to sell toy balloons at 2s 6d, paper flowers at 5s a bunch, and 'worthless glass trinkets at 10s' – '"All very speshull" they whined in their best Cockney accent.' But they got little joy from the Barnsley housewives. 'Why should such fit young men be allowed to carry on like that,' demanded one, 'while my husband is at the coal face risking his life to get coal to keep the likes of those comfortable?'

Soon afterwards, in early 1948, the black market was the subject given by Mass-Observation to its regular panel. 'Do you know of any such dealings in your area? If so, please describe them. (No identification, please.)' More answers than not emphasised their prevalence:

Yes, I do know of such dealings locally. Eggs are sold at from 6d to 1/- each; dead birds at much above the controlled price; milk at 1/- per pint and moreover if one leaves a little extra each week in the empty bottles more milk is forthcoming. Conversely if one stops the tribute the milk stops immediately. No words are used in this little comedy . . . Black market dealings pervade every sphere of life and every commodity. (*Grocer*)

If the Black Market exists as it seems to in the minds of Fleet St then I've not come into contact with it. There's a hell of a lot of a sort of barter going on. Which is very different. (*Commercial traveller*)

My aunt (otherwise a scrupulously honest woman) gets extra supplies of eggs, butter, cheese and fruit from her regular grocer – at fabulously high prices. (*Designer*)

From my experience the focal points in my neighbourhood centre in the local Conservative Clubs. The people who, day in and day out, pour rancorous abuse upon the Government's restrictions are, I find, the very folk who dabble dirtily in this sort of anti-social business. (*Local government officer*)

In common with everyone else in this country I know of such dealings and I would require strong proof to convince myself that we do not, all of us, take part in them. (*Advertising*)

The other day I was in a baker's shop. A woman whispered to the assistant who glanced at me, hesitated, then brought a bag from under the counter (literally) and handed it over. No money passed. I knew at once that about half a dozen eggs had changed hands. (*Pianist and housewife*)

My experience is I don't know anyone who is not in the B.M. (*Steel worker*)

My friends tell me that any number of clothing coupons can be bought at 2/- each; that bus conductors offer nylons to passengers on their buses; I know people who can get all they want in the way of 'points' goods without surrending a point – these they sell. Nearer home, I know a Methodist parson who collects eggs from one of his former 'cures' and who retails them at 6/7 per doz – quite cheap, when one considers that the regular B.M. rate is 10/- per doz. He also can produce silk stockings or marmalade – whichever you want! (*Housewife*)

About the same time, Kenneth Preston was told that the Bishop of Bradford and an ecclesiastical colleague had been overheard 'discussing a 40 pound ham they had secured and which they were going to share between them'. To Preston, a middle-aged English teacher at Keighley Grammar School and the most conscientious of diarists, it was yet one more sign that there was something fundamentally amiss with the post-war world: 'They were paying 10/- per pound for the ham. It is rather shocking to think of one's bishop engaged in black market transactions.'

Most people – respectable and law-abiding – probably shared Preston's dislike of the very fact of the black market, instinctively seeing it as unfair. A Gallup poll in April 1947 found that only 14 per cent thought the authorities were doing enough to stop it. Did that, though, translate into widespread reluctance and/or shame about using it? The Mass-Observation replies in early 1948 suggested, perhaps inevitably, a range of attitudes:

My husband insists that anything one gets over and above the ration is morally a black market transaction. I prefer to call it grey – though I admit he is really right. (*Housewife*)

Generally speaking I feel that the ordinary Englishman leaves such dealings to the selfish who will have this or that no matter who else goes without, and to the shady character who makes his living in the business and has no qualms at all. (*Civil servant*)

A number of my neighbours buy sacks of potatoes ['controlled' rather than rationed between November 1947 and April 1948], onions, oranges when no one else can get them – 'well my dear we pay a bit over the odds but one must have the stuff'. (*Housewife and voluntary social worker*)

I would say that the Black Market is treated as a semi-joke, although a serious one. People feel they are very clever if they can say they have obtained something or other outside the rations or without coupons. (*Sales manager*)

Unfortunately almost everybody I know does these things to a greater or lesser degree . . . I myself must admit that I am not quite without blame myself, where getting things for my family is concerned, although I honestly hope I do less wrong than most. (*Export and production manager*)

I guess we are all human, who wouldn't like some ham, petrol, nylons, all those things that make life worth living (or do they?). No, I think my only dislike in this line is the slimy types who seem to deal in the 'market'. I've no scruples about where the thing comes from really, but some of the slick boys who seem to live by this business get me down. Put it this way. If a Service man came to me and said, 'this rum or whatever it was "knocked off" what's it worth to you?' I'd deal. But when it comes to some flash looking 'won't work' type of Spiv, a guy living on his wits, no fixed abode, no guts, no papers etc, cut me out. If he is a fat cigar-smoking Jew – well I'd rather starve. (*Electrician*)

In fact there is some evidence that by this time – almost three years after VE Day, virtually everyone fed up with continuing rationing – the spiv was becoming a less demonised figure. March 1948 saw the first issue of the *Spivs' Gazette*, a humorous magazine which among other things gave details of the Spivs' Union ('Only genuine spivs, drones, wide boys, eels, butterflies and black marketeers to be eligible for membership . . . All members must wear the official spiv uniform – shoulders to be not less than 46 inches wide . . . Members are not expected to "do" each other – only the public').[8] Put another way, the morality of shared sacrifice no longer seemed quite so compelling as – perhaps – it once had been.

Two developments in 1947/8 pointed the way to a more expansive, acquisitive future. The first took its cue directly from the United States, where self-service shopping had been pioneered in the early 1930s, to the extent that by 1946 almost a third of retail food stores were entirely or partially self-service. The first British experiment along these lines probably took place in a section of the Romford Co-op in 1942, in the context of a staff shortage. The Romford example was soon followed by other London Co-operative Society shops, but it was not until some time after the war that the requisite fixtures and fittings became available for authentic, full-scale self-service conversion. One enthusiast, after a revelatory eye-opening visit to the States, was Tesco's Jack Cohen, the self-made founder of a chain of grocery shops (by this time about a hundred strong) that faithfully obeyed his dictum 'pile it high and sell it cheap'. In 1947 he put his St Albans store on a self-service basis, an experiment that began well but ended after 12 months – partly because the equipment was not yet quite right. Elsewhere, in January 1948 Marks & Spencer introduced at its store in Wood Green, north London, what Kathryn Morrison, the historian of English shopping, has called 'the first full-fledged version of self-service in the UK'. It was only the food department, but in style and layout it was unmistakably on the American model. 'It would appear so far, at least, that shoppers are well pleased with the innovation, several writing to express their satisfaction to the store manager,' reported *Store* magazine in February, though early users were sufficiently cautious that in the first few weeks their number of purchases per visit rarely rose above two or three. About the same time as the M&S initiative, several London Co-ops (including at Upton Park, Barkingside and West Hounslow) were putting entire grocery counters on a systematic self-service footing, while in March one of the more dynamic figures in the co-operative movement, the Portsmouth-based John Jacques, opted for self-service across his domain. Was it the start of an inexorable transatlantic revolution? 'This England of ours is not America,' R. Hardstaff ('Royal Arsenal Grocery Shop Assistant') warned in the *Co-operative News*. 'We live as English, not in the cosmopolitan manner of Americans. The English housewife wants personal service, she likes to shop with salesmen who know and understand her wants and likes.'[9]

The other development was heralded by *Vogue* in the autumn of 1947:

> Fashion has moved decisively in Paris. One has seen changes coming for many months but now they are here, inescapably. Our Fashion Editor sums it up: 'Take last season's round hipline, small shoulder, pulled-in waist, longer skirt, and emphasize each; stress the bosom, stress the *derrière*; add a side-moving hat; and you will have a composite view of the Paris form for the new season.' The skirt may be full – petal-shaped or spreading with unpressed pleats. It may be straight. But either way it descends to anything from fourteen to eight inches from the floor.

From the first, there were opponents of this new, feminine style (largely the work of Christian Dior). 'The ridiculous whim of idle people' was the trenchant view of the Labour MP Bessie Braddock. 'The problem today as it affects British women is to get hold of clothes. They have not agitated for the longer skirt. Their strong feeling is that things should be left as they are. Most women today are glad to get any clothes they can get hold of.' The British Guild of Creative Designers agreed: 'We just have not got the materials. We cannot give way to Paris's irresponsible introduction of the longer skirt.'

For British women, there was a six-month wait before clothes in the new style started to come through to the shops, though in January 1948 there was an early sighting of the soon-to-be-ubiquitous portmanteau term when Panter-Downes noted that 'women's winter coats are being offered at knock-down prices to tempt customers who are gambling on a mild winter and saving their coupons for a spring New Look – Cripps or no Cripps.' The Chancellor was another of the New Look's non-admirers, soon abetted by another Labour MP, Mabel Ridealgh, who in February denounced it as an 'utterly ridiculous, stupidly exaggerated waste of material and manpower, foisted on the average woman to the detriment of other, more normal clothing'. For her as for some other Labour critics, it was not just that the New Look was a needless extravagance at a time of dire shortage of materials, but that it was also a seriously retrogressive step. 'Women today are taking a larger part in the happenings of the world,' she wrote in *Reynolds*

News, 'and the New Look is too reminiscent of a caged bird's attitude. I hope our fashion dictators will realise the new *outlook* of women and will give the death blow to any attempt at curtailing women's freedom.'

Alas for Ridealgh and others, the New Look began in March and April to sweep almost all before it. 'We are selling nothing but New Look clothes, with nipped-in waists and rounded shoulder lines,' reported Marshall & Snelgrove. 'The longer skirt is here, let's face it,' Norah Alexander wrote in her fashion column in the *Daily Mail*. 'You'd think that after all these austere years no one would grudge us this small token of pleasanter things to come . . . Don't let anyone persuade you that it's wanton to covet the sort of clothes they're wearing in the other cities of the world.' A spokesman for the London Model House group, which had tried to persuade the Board of Trade to regulate hemlines, conceded defeat: 'It's impossible to stop the New Look. It's like a tidal wave.' By late April it was popping up in diaries. 'Saw several examples of the New Look, none of which was interesting to me,' sniffed Gladys Langford after a trip to Richmond, where the 'long queues outside all tea-shops' had reduced her to 'orangeade and jam sponge roll at Woolworth's'. But for Grace Golden, standing in a bus queue in Piccadilly was an opportunity to view 'a number of charming "new look" women – the full long skirts quite delightful'. The final, clinching breakthrough came on the 26th, with the outfit worn by Princess Margaret (who a few months earlier had been given a private showing by Dior) to the celebration in St Paul's of her parents' silver wedding anniversary. 'She had fully adopted the tightly waisted, bouffant-skirted, ankle-length New Look,' in the words of a biographer, 'with which she wore – and would always thereafter wear – very high heels and platform soles.' By the end of the year, soon after Mass-Observation had found that 'opposition comes mainly from men over thirty-five', it was estimated that as many as ten million women either had or desired the New Look.[10]

Was the widespread adoption of this new style really such a defeat for female emancipation? 'There was nothing intrinsically submissive about the New Look,' one cultural historian, Angela Partington, has forcefully contended, 'even though it restricted movement and emphasised the curves of the body.'

Its strong colours, severe shapes, and theatrical styling could equally well be read as 'stroppy' and defiant compared to the twee floral prints and sensible cuts of utility styles. The way it was adapted and worn by working-class women transformed it into a hybrid style, 'unfaithful' to the designer's vision, and they appropriated it for working and for relaxing in, as well as for 'dressing up' occasions ... By refusing to keep the functional and the decorative separate, consumers were not only breaking the rules of good design and taste, but using goods to satisfy desires other than those assumed by the marketing industries.

Such assertions may demand fuller empirical testing than is possible, but any argument that gets away from the consumer as a passive, undifferentiated dummy deserves respect.

For at least two women – and their children – the New Look was not unmomentous. In 2002 an interviewer asked David Bailey (brought up 'in a little terraced job in East Ham' with an outside toilet) about his first strong visual memory: "'Going to Selfridges in 1948, where my mother tried on a New Look dress. She couldn't afford it, but tried it on anyway. I remember her twirling around and thinking how beautiful she was, and that was my first fashion picture, I suppose." Taken in your head? "Yeah."' For Carolyn Steedman, born in March 1947 and living in Hammersmith until she was four, an even more graphic early memory was dreaming about her mother. 'She wore the New Look, a coat of beige gaberdine which fell in two swaying, graceful pleats from her waist at the back' – and for Steedman much of the retrospective point of the dream was the fierceness of her mother's desire for the New Look, which in real, impoverished life was too expensive to be attainable. In her memoir, *Landscape for a Good Woman*, she draws a picture of her mother (the daughter of a Burnley weaver) who in two particular respects contradicted the conventional, salt-of-the-earth wisdom about the working class: not only was she politically a Tory, but she had almost overwhelming – and guiltless – material urges, together with powerful resentments if they were not fulfilled. Steedman's remarkable book is, among other things, a plea against the overdeterministic reduction of working-class individuals to flattened figures in a Lowry-type setting, 'washed over with a patina of stolid emotional sameness'. The New Look was, not only for Steedman's mother, a very real as well as symbolic goal.[11]

Even so, there seems little doubt that it was the middle class that *felt* a relatively greater sense of deprivation during these austerity years. In Ina Zweiniger-Bargielowska's words, 'the staples of the middle-class lifestyle – domestic service, ample food and clothes, consumer durables, motor cars, and luxuries such as travel, entertainment and subscriptions – were squeezed by labour shortage and rationing as well as high taxation and rising prices.' Papers like the *Evening Standard* were full of malcontent correspondents. 'Before the war,' complained one in April 1947, 'we could afford to go abroad for holidays. Last year we imposed ourselves upon relatives. We used to play golf, tennis and badminton. How can we afford them now?' Another, a grammar-school master, was only marginally less down-beat: 'We could give up the car; but we cling to it as a last link with comfort and luxury, having surrendered so many other things, including annual holidays, library subscriptions and golf.' By 1948 at the latest, it had become almost axiomatic that it was the middle class that had taken the biggest hit since the war. In a radio talk given in May, four months after the *Economist*'s finding that 'at least ten per cent of the national consuming power has been forcefully transferred from the middle classes and the rich to the wage earners', the economic journalist (and prolific broadcaster) Graham Hutton similarly argued that 'the well-to-do and better-off, the middle classes, have taken the biggest material cuts and sacrifices, as persons or households', whereas 'the less well-to-do have had their material standards raised'.[12]

The obvious temptation – to emigrate – was manfully resisted in Evelyn Waugh's case. At around the time of the cuts following the convertibility crisis, he explained in his diary why he had decided not to decamp to Ireland: 'The Socialists are piling up repressive measures now. It would seem I was flying from them.' But for the veteran travel writer H. V. Morton, the lure of South Africa was irresistible. Not only, he told a friend during the winter of 1947/8, had the Attlee government 'put over more unpleasant measures than any other in history', but England had become a society where 'things moved steadily towards Communism' and 'everything that can be done is being done to pamper the masses and to plunder anyone with capital or initiative'. Soon afterwards, a City banker, Ernest Muriel, was similarly contemplating his sunset years in South Africa: 'A country,' he informed a no-doubt sympathetic correspondent in Cape Town, 'which has many attractions as against Britain, where we are hedged around with so many restrictions and frustrations and where the retired rentier has to pay penal taxation, and, in the Socialist mentality, is looked upon as a cross between a drone and criminal.'

Most stuck it out, including the indomitable 'ladies' for whom Derry & Toms was almost a second home. 'Quite a number of the original upper middle class Kensingtonians survive,' noted the writer John Brophy (father of Brigid) in April 1948:

> All over sixty, now, some over eighty. Most of the men are bewildered and defeated. The old ladies are invincible. Neither rationing, queues, the disappearance of servants, nor heavy taxation and the lowered purchasing power of money gets them down: the unforeseen bad times give them something to talk clichés about. They wear long, rustling skirts, flowered hats, and carry reticules and, in summer, silk sunshades with long handles. The 'New Look' has for the first time in forty years brought them almost within range of contemporary fashion.

These old dears mainly ate their meals in restaurants, where 'they talk[ed] to each other across the small tables as though from mountain top to mountain top. And all banality . . .' They were also, Brophy observed with grudging admiration, 'quite unscrupulous': 'They were born to privilege, and in the days of their decline they fight for it. Given half a chance, any one of them will sail in ahead of the longest bus queue.'[13]

In general it is clear which political party stood to benefit from an increasingly aggrieved middle class. 'Two villages in the Home Counties have each subscribed about £500 for Lord Woolton's Tory fund to fight the next General Election,' Hodson had already noted in January 1948, adding that 'the middle class are rising up.' And that summer, a memo from the Conservative Party's research department set out what it hoped would be the next election's battleground: 'The floating vote is mainly middle class (incomes £700–£1,200 per annum). These people are now finding it impossible to live. The chief fear of the middle-class voter is being submerged by a more prosperous working class. Our whole appeal must be in this direction.' How would Labour respond? Manny Shinwell may have infamously declared in May 1947 that his party did not care 'a tinker's cuss' for any class other than 'the organised workers of the country'; Cripps in his April 1948 Budget may have indulged in a one-off capital levy; but for one of Labour's more thoughtful MPs, Maurice Edelman (sitting, like Richard Crossman, for a Coventry seat), there was a key distinction to make. 'Morrison has spoken of Labour's concern for the "useful" people,' he wrote in the *New Statesman* in June 1948:

> Among the middle class the description 'useful' applies from the white-collar clerk to the working director; it includes Civil Servants, teachers, working shopkeepers, technicians, managers, doctors, journalists and farmers . . . The useful middle classes are an integral part of the Movement.
>
> But there are others among the middle classes whose prosperity and advancement is tied up with a *laissez-faire* economy. Every measure of a planned economy is to them a poisoned draught. Often they owe their careers, started in the working class or the lower middle class, to the competitive nature of business, which has given their commercial aptitude opportunity, and their aggressiveness scope. They include company secretaries, commercial travellers, sales managers and small business men. These, then, are the irreconcilables among the middle classes. Labour's victory is, by definition, their defeat.

In the latter category, Edelman did not even bother to mention the rentiers of Kensington and Cheltenham, of Bournemouth and Budleigh Salterton, the ultimate irreconcilables.

The increasing middle-class sense of being somehow muscled out of the picture by the working class was nicely caught by Gladys

Langford. 'It is very noticeable that nowadays the well-fed, well-clad, sweetly smiling bourgeoisie male & female have disappeared from poster and advertisement,' she reflected in May 1947. 'It is the broadly grinning and obviously unwashed "worker" who appears in more than life size on our hoardings and Tube stations.' The chances are that hostility flowed mainly in one direction, at least to judge by the experience of a friend of Hodson who spent that summer in a hospital ward. 'I hadn't been so close to the working class before,' he told the diarist. 'I didn't find a trace of class antagonism. The chap in the next bed was a Cockney who had three tricks, imitating pheasants, imitating the nurse when she asked "Have a cup of tea?" and creating a rude noise.'[14]

That cheerful chappie was lucky not to be waiting to catch a train from Hungerford station on Tuesday, 6 January 1948. 'A number of prosperous, well-dressed families were collected, who talked loudly about their personal affairs, ignoring the rest of the world and making me ponder the phenomenon of Class, and ask myself how the war had affected it.' Frances Partridge (translator, diarist and member of the Bloomsbury Group) went on:

> When the pressure was on us all, it had seemed as though the relation between master and man, for instance, was suffering a sea-change, and it was a common sight to see a Colonel in a good but worn suit almost cringing to a waitress as he pleadingly enquired 'Do you think I might have a little water?' Today I felt we were in the presence of 'conspicuous padding' – that is to say I was aware that the gentry had reassumed their right to the privileges and support that money gives. Two elderly ladies got into our carriage in the train and drew back their lips from their yellowing teeth with identical snarls of concentration as they pecked about in their handbags. 'Thought for a moment I'd forgotten my handkerchief,' said one. '*Very* nosy day, isn't it?'

The previous day had featured the start, at 4.00 on the Light Programme, of *Mrs Dale's Diary*. Directly replacing the more down-market *The Robinson Family*, each day it told the story of the Dales, a family living in a comfortable house in an outer suburb, Kenton in

Middlesex, though soon moving to a fictitious London locality (Virginia Lodge, Parkwood Hill). Dr Jim Dale had been a GP for 25 years; their son Bob had recently been demobilised from the army; their 19-year-old daughter Gwen worked in an office in town; and there was a cat, called Captain. As for Mrs Mary Dale herself, she enjoyed the services of a domestic help (Mrs Morgan, who seldom stopped talking) and before long came up with a catchphrase – 'I'm a little worried about Jim' – that over the years seeped into the middle-class collective consciousness.

Certainly the two cultures – middle-class and working-class – seldom mixed happily. In the autumn of 1947 the Bristol Empire, situated in the city's east, decided as an experiment to put on eight plays. Those chosen were hardly highbrow, including *Arsenic and Old Lace* and Ivor Novello's *I Lived with You*, but the experiment proved a resounding flop. 'Simply,' explains that theatre's chronicler, 'the Empire audiences did not expect or want to see this type of production, while keen playgoers from other areas of Bristol were not willing to visit the Empire, seen as a working-class home for variety and revue.' Going legit was not a mistake that the London Palladium ever made, though as everywhere the quality could be mixed. 'It was a rotten variety bill, with far too many acrobatic affairs – some of which were positively obscene,' a just-demobbed Kenneth Williams noted in January 1948. 'Sid Field was marvellous, and received terrific and well-merited applause – what camping! I simply roared!'

Field, particularly celebrated for his 'Slasher Green' spiv sketch, was probably *the* variety performer of the late 1940s, but younger ones still had it all to do. A glance at the line-up at the Aldershot Hippodrome a month later reveals Dave and Joe O'Gorman ('celebrated comedians') as top of the bill, with other attractions including Arthur Dowler ('The Wizard of Cod'), Peter Sellers ('Bang On'), Wimpey ('Acrobatic Novelty'), and Cynthia and Gladys ('A Juggling Delight'). Sellers, at this stage an impressionist, was paid £12 10s for his week of twice-nightly appearances, which his friend Graham Stark remembered as a disaster. But on 5 April a star *was* born. 'Wisdom's the name,' the *Daily Express* proclaimed. 'He Woke to Find he had Joined the Star Comics.' Such was the enthusiastic reception for Norman Wisdom's first-night performance at the London Casino. The paper described his act: 'His face is mobile, can be twisted into any shape. He tumbles on the stage, shadow-boxes, tries to play the piano, pulls out a clarinet, tires of it and turns his attention to . . . a vast sandwich. Then he pleads with his audience to follow him in an Eastern song – in gibberish. His props? A stringy tie, an old shirt, and a baggy evening suit, several sizes too large.'[15] Wisdom was 33 (though billed at the time as 27), a former shop assistant, and, like so many of his contemporaries, had begun entertaining while in the army.

At the big football grounds, huge, almost entirely male working-class crowds continued to pour through the turnstiles – in January 1948 the highest League attendance ever, 83,360, saw Manchester United play Arsenal at Maine Road (Old Trafford being still out of commission following bomb damage). Sadly, few Lancastrians ever thought of going to watch Accrington Stanley in the Third Division North and thereby boost the seldom large crowd at Peel Park. Even so, the club by this time had just managed to pay off the mortgage on the ground, and on 10 February a ceremony took place at the Mechanics' Institution. 'The gathering was a happy one to celebrate a happy event,' reported the *Accrington Observer*, 'and the red and white motif was in evidence, from an iced cake bearing the words "On, Stanley, On" to the red and white table flowers.' The main speech was given by Councillor S. T. Pilkington, JP, associated with the club as player, official, director and chairman (for the past 12 years) since 1906. 'He referred to football finance at the present time as being "daft". To pay £20,000 for one player [as Notts County, of all clubs, had recently done for Chelsea's Tommy Lawton], he said was "absolutely silly, crazy finance".' The first match after the ceremony was at home to Wrexham, with a predictable outcome: 'Bad Luck and Bad Shooting beat Stanley.'

Two months later it was the Cup Final, Manchester United versus Blackpool, billed as probably the last chance for the 33-year-old Stanley Matthews to get a winner's medal. But United won 4–2, and years later their winger, Charlie Mitten, recalled a conversation with his opponent that did not exactly focus on the glory aspect (or lack of it): 'I walked off the field with Stan Matthews. He said, "Look at that, Charlie? A silver medal and we get no money." But we never gave much thought to the money side. I said, "Yes, I believe the band get

more than us, Stan." "Yeah," he said. "Bloody disgrace, isn't it?" I
said, "They must have played better than us, that's why."' 'Anyway,'
concluded Mitten with the mellowness of time, 'it was all a bit of a
joke and a laugh.'[16]

There was little inclination yet to abandon cultural hierarchies. 'A
certain Professor Zweig has been doing a little mass-observation in
England all by himself, has had 400 conversations with men earning
between £4 10s od and £6 a week,' noted Hodson in April 1948,
before summarising some of Zweig's findings. Up to half of a wage
could go on tobacco; 3s a week was the usual outlay on football
pools; one in five betted on the dogs; 'real recreational spending' was
'small'; and 'time after time men said, "I have no interests."' Hodson
went on:

> As a picture of Britain I find this decidedly inglorious. Every evening
> I see folk queued up for the cinema. Whatever picture is on, whatever
> drivel it is, the queues are there. Dogs, pictures, tobacco, drink, football
> pools, crooners – what an indifferent lot of pastimes for our people. To
> do a monotonous repetition job you loathe, and to use these anodynes
> to help you forget tomorrow's work! If this is Western civilisation, there
> is a R.A.F. phrase that can be used – we've had it!

A few days earlier Kenneth Preston, on holiday from school, cycled
with his wife and son from Keighley to Nelson. There, after inspecting
the open market ('We always think there is far more food in the
Lancashire shops than here'), they went to a second-hand bookshop:

> Whilst we were having a look round we heard the voices of two women
> in a really incredible conversation. One yelled out to another, who was
> evidently looking at some books, 'Nah! then, don't buy all e' booiks'.
> The other said 'Nay, we don't read much at our 'ouse'. The other replied
> 'No! we don't. I've nivver read a book i'my life'. The other said 'No!
> I often wish I'd read a bit more. You learn stuff from books, don't you?'
> It seems incredible that there could be anyone who had never read a
> book. The woman who said she hadn't, Kath said, would be over fifty.
> These are the folk who vote!!

Attitudes were perhaps not so different in the people's party. Some weeks later, the Labour conference at Scarborough included an eye-opening diversion. 'Paid our first visit to a Butlin Camp [ie at Filey] where the N.U.M. were entertaining us on our last night,' noted Hugh Gaitskell (Winchester and Oxford). 'Very efficient, organised, pleasure holiday making. Everybody agreed they would not go there!'[17]

––––––––

Over the years, the profound cultural mismatch between progressive activators and the millions acted upon would inevitably be played out in some of the most emotive policy areas. In retrospect, two stand out from the late 1940s: crime and race. The first was already becoming the cause of major fractures – not only within elite opinion but also between elite liberal opinion and non-elite illiberal opinion – while the other, even more resonant, was poised to be similarly destructive of any forward-looking, modern-minded consensus.

'More brutal crimes,' recorded an unhappy, almost bewildered Gladys Langford in June 1947. 'Have I been all wrong? Is it that these vicious criminals need flogging and harsh treatment or are they cases for a psychologist?' There were many causes of the increased crime, brutal and otherwise, in immediate post-war Britain – most obviously the pressures and inducements deriving from the rationing of the majority of key everyday requirements – but what was undeniable was that it was happening. During the summer of 1947, the most headline-grabbing case was that of poor Alec de Antiquis, a respectable motor mechanic in his 30s who, as he rode his motorcycle down a Fitzrovia street, was shot dead by fleeing jewellery thieves. The culprits were quickly found (a vital clue being the clothing coupons for a discarded RAF raincoat), and two men were hanged at Pentonville, with the lugubrious Albert Pierrepoint doing the honours. When Cyril Connolly later that year weighed into the government in another disenchanted *Horizon* editorial, one of his main charges was that a regime that did not 'even dare to propose the abolition of the death penalty' bore 'no relation to the kind of Socialism which many of us envisaged'. Yet the fact was that twice already in 1947 the question 'Do you think the death penalty should be abolished?' had been put by Gallup; and each time only 25 per cent had answered 'yes'. Developments in 1948 were unlikely to sway this hardline majority. 'A vast crime-wave is sweeping Britain,' W. J. Brown noted in February. 'And last week a policeman was killed in London.' Indeed, over the year as a whole the number of indictable offences recorded in Britain turned out to be 522,684, almost double the total in 1937.[18]

Unpromising mood music, then, for the abolitionist amendment by Sydney Silverman (Labour MP for Nelson and Colne) to the Criminal Justice Bill being brought forward by Chuter Ede, the Home Secretary. On the day of the debate and vote, 14 April, Cuthbert Headlam on the Opposition backbenches was a sardonic, unsentimental observer of a deep split in the ruling party:

> The H of C (free vote) decided tonight to put the death penalty for murder into cold storage for 5 years which presumably will mean the abolition of capital punishment in English law. The Home Secretary and the Cabinet advised the House that in their opinion this was not the moment to make the experiment – the police and the judges are said to be against the change – but the Comrades as a body were not convinced. Human life is sacred, hanging is no deterrent to murder, other countries have abolished it without any increase of murder – why should not we? All very plausible – all very noble-minded – but what does all the fuss amount to? Chuter Ede gave us figures to show that about 11 or 12 people are hanged every year – that a majority of murder cases are reprieved – that the chance of a miscarriage of justice is very slight . . . We are asked therefore to do away with capital punishment against the advice of responsible authority at a time when criminal violence is on the increase . . . The speeches today were good, bad and indifferent – and each speaker in turn congratulated the one who spoke before him on his high morality and sincerity. There was a deal of sob stuff which depressed me as it always does.

The majority of 23 in favour of an experimental suspension of the death penalty would have been greater if it had been a genuinely 'free vote'. In fact, Attlee on the morning of the debate curtly told his junior ministers that, given the Cabinet's position, they were not to vote for Silverman's amendment. Among those who protested – and in due course abstained – was the rather incongruous pair of Evan Durbin and James Callaghan.

It proved a short-lived triumph for the mainly middle-class Labour backbenchers. Four days later, the *Sunday Pictorial*'s headline was '"Hanging" Vote Worries Public', with the paper's reporters having conducted an intensive two-day inquiry 'all over Britain' which found that 'the majority of the public, while welcoming an end to hanging as the sole penalty for murder, feel it should be kept as protection from the worst criminal types'. Accordingly, 'nine out of ten people favoured degrees of murder, with death for killers in the first degree'. The paper also quoted some representative vox pop:

Criminals will stick at nothing now they know they cannot be hanged. (*Capt. A. E. Tarran, Shadwell, Leeds*)

With this last deterrent gone, no woman will feel safe in London after dark. (*Miss A. Bennett, Martin Way, Merton*)

It is a mistake to remove the only punishment of which armed thugs are afraid. (*Mr T. Ashton, Holloway Road, N7*)

I think Members of Parliament should have their heads examined for coming to such a decision. (*Mr H. Ronson, Deane Road, Bolton*)

How dare the Commons abolish the death penalty without hearing the views of the people they represent! (*Mr T. O'Neil, Wadham Road, Liverpool*)

Now it was up to the Lords. But meanwhile, Gladys Langford noted in early May, '. . . another policeman shot – Forest Gate this time', and later that month another Gallup poll revealed that 66 per cent were opposed to suspending capital punishment for five years and only 26 per cent in favour. The Lord Chief Justice, the uncompromising Lord Goddard, had already made clear his view that criminal law would be respected only if it remained in line with public opinion, and on 2 June (the day the Queen toured the Lancashire cotton mills) the Lords rejected suspension by a crushing 181 votes to 28. At a Cabinet meeting soon afterwards, Attlee – well aware of where public feeling lay – successfully insisted that, for the time being at least, the abolitionist game was up; Hartley Shawcross, no longer the master, left the room in tears.[19]

The summer of 1948 was even more of a defining moment in the centuries-old story of immigration to Britain. For many years the most widely stigmatised 'others' in British society had been the Jews and the Irish, by the end of the war numbering respectively some 400,000 and 600,000 (ie on the mainland). Although it is possible to exaggerate the extent of the prejudice, Jews in particular were demonised, even after the film cameras had entered Belsen and Auschwitz; shockingly, British fascism revived quickly after the war, little impeded by the men in blue. 'I suppose it is perfectly in order for a lousy swine like Jeffrey Hamm [Oswald Mosley's main sidekick] to get up on a street corner in the East End of London and shout, "Down with the Jews. Burn the synagogues. Kill the Aliens," and he gets away with it, but if a person tries to pull him up, what happens?' a concerned local person asked the Home Secretary rhetorically in October 1946. 'The so-called keepers of law and order, the police, go up to this person and tell him he'd better move away before he gets hurt . . . These guardians of the law and order from Commercial Street Police Station openly boast about being members of Jeffrey Hamm's fascist party.' The following year saw anti-Semitic riots in several British cities. These were triggered by lurid headlines about the hanging in Palestine of two captured British sergeants but also involved a widespread belief that it was Jews who were responsible for running the black market – and making a killing from doing so.

There was likewise some persistent anti-Semitism in the higher echelons of society. Frederic Raphael's schooldays at Charterhouse were famously made a misery because of it, while in the City of London the malign legacy survived of Montagu Norman, the notoriously anti-Semitic Governor of the Bank of England between the wars. 'Mr Randell of Bank of England says he is a very pushing individual – German Jew – who established himself here in 1938,' stated (early in 1948) an internal note of the Issuing Houses Association, to which Walter Salomon had applied for his firm to join. 'They don't know a lot about him, but think it would do no harm to let him cool his heels a bit more.' And, damningly: 'His office is full of foreigners.' When the IHA took other soundings, no one denied that Salomon was a man of ability and energy, but – the face not fitting – he did indeed have to cool his heels.[20]

However, the Jew was about to be replaced by the black immigrant as the prime 'other'. At the end of the war, some 20,000 to 30,000 non-whites were living in Britain, and studies were starting to be made of the attitude of whites towards them. Kenneth Little's *Negroes in Britain* – published in 1948 but mainly based on fieldwork done in the late 1930s and early 1940s in Cardiff's Tiger Bay (where Shirley Bassey, seventh child of a Nigerian seaman, was growing up) – concluded hopefully that 'a great deal of latent friendliness underlies the surface appearance of apathy and even of displayed prejudice in a large number of cases,' though he did concede that it was difficult to generalise, given that as yet 'relatively few English people have made close contact with coloured individuals.' The other port with a sizeable number of black immigrants was Liverpool, where Anthony Richmond in the early 1950s examined what became of several hundred West Indians who went there during the war (under an officially sponsored scheme to boost production) and subsequently stayed on. Richmond found that by 1946 at the latest they were encountering considerable prejudice in the workplace from skilled tradesmen who, having served their apprenticeships, 'resented being associated in the minds of English people with the unskilled negro labourer': 'Outside the field of employment there can be little doubt that the area of most intense prejudice against the West Indian Negroes is that of sexual relations,' in that 'men who are accepted in the ordinary course of acquaintance are subjected to serious insults if seen in the company of a white girl', and 'the girl herself is often stigmatised among all "respectable" people'.

A Guyanan at the sharp end of prejudice in 1947/8 was Eustace Braithwaite, who after demobilisation from the RAF struggled, for over a year and despite having a Cambridge physics degree, to get a job: 'I tried everything – labour exchanges, employment agencies, newspaper ads – all with the same result. I even advertised myself mentioning my qualifications and the colour of my skin, but there were no takers. Then I tried applying for jobs without mentioning my colour, but when they saw me the reasons given for turning me down were all variations of the same theme: too black . . .' Eventually, sitting one day beside the lake in St James's Park and watching the ducks, he fell into conversation with 'a thin, bespectacled old gentleman' and related his plight. The stranger told him there were many vacancies for teachers in the East End, and soon afterwards Braithwaite secured a job at an LCC school in Cable Street, scene of the pitched battle between fascists and Communists in 1936. He was the only black teacher in London, and the eventual literary (and cinematic) upshot was *To Sir, With Love*.

Ignorance about black immigrants and where they came from no doubt played its part in shaping indigenous attitudes. A survey of almost 2,000 adult civilians, conducted mainly in May 1948, revealed the following:

What people know	*% of persons*
That native peoples in the Colonies have a lower standard of living than ourselves	67
That Colonial inhabitants are mostly coloured, not white	62
People who can name at least one Colony	49
People who can name at least one food or raw material from the Colonies	37
That the new ground nut scheme is in East Africa	16

'Housewives, unskilled operatives, and people over the age of sixty, are the least well-informed sections of the population,' observed the report, adding that among even the most knowledgeable occupational group, comprising professional, managerial and higher clerical workers, less than two-thirds could explain the difference between a colony and a dominion. The report went on: 'Public opinion is inclined to be complacent about the work that Britain has done in the Colonies. Only 19% think that we have "tended to be selfish in the past" – though this feeling is stronger among the better informed sections of the population than among the more ignorant. In any case, the great majority of people believe that we are doing "a better job now".'[21] These were significant findings. Whatever people's instinctive attitude towards black immigrants, not many believed that Britain morally owed them a favour. The guilt factor, in other words, was still the preserve of a privileged minority.

At the Ministry of Labour (MOL), faced by a serious labour shortage, the need to attract migrants was obvious. But whereas it went out of its way in these years to bring into the British labour market many thousands of white European workers, a high proportion of them Poles, its attitude to Caribbean labour was essentially negative, albeit sometimes covertly expressed. 'Whatever may be the policy about British citizenship,' Sir Harold Wiles, Deputy Permanent Under-Secretary, told a colleague in March 1948, 'I do not think that any scheme for the importation of coloured colonials for permanent settlement here should be embarked upon without full understanding that this means that coloured element will be brought in for permanent absorption into our own population.' The colleague, M. A. Bevan, agreed: 'As regards the possible importation of West Indian labour, I suggest that we must dismiss the idea from the start.' And in May, submitting a report on the question of employing 'surplus male West Indians', the MOL came up with an avalanche of reasons (or what it called 'overwhelming difficulties') why this was a bad idea. There was the major problem of accommodation; Caribbean workers would be 'unsuitable for outdoor work in winter owing to their susceptibility to colds and the more serious chest and lung ailments'; those working underground in coal mines would find conditions 'too hot'; and anyway, 'many of the coloured men are unreliable and lazy, quarrels among them are not infrequent'.[22] That, it seemed, was that.

How did such attitudes chime with questions of British citizenship? The issue had been raised by Wiles in his March 1948 memo, in the knowledge that legislation was in the pipeline for what, following its second reading in May, became by the end of the summer the British Nationality Act 1948. This legislation, distinguishing between citizens of the United Kingdom and Colonies on the one hand and citizens of independent Commonwealth countries on the other, was essentially a response to Canada's recent introduction of its own citizenship and sought to affirm, in the authoritative words of the historian Randall Hansen, 'Britain's place as head of a Commonwealth structure founded on the relationship between the UK and the Old Dominions'. It was not in any sense a measure centrally concerned with matters of immigration; and nor was it really about the colonies. Although in practice it sanctioned what over the next 14 years would be a very liberal immigration regime, it was (again to quote Hansen), 'never intended to sanction a mass

migration of new Commonwealth citizens to the United Kingdom' –
and, crucially, 'nowhere in parliamentary debate, the Press, or private
papers was the possibility that substantial numbers could exercise their
right to reside permanently in the UK discussed'.

Significantly, with cross-party support and little public interest, the
bill's passage was smooth and quick. Inasmuch as politicians considered
the immigration aspect, no one expected the legislation to have more
than a marginal impact. The subsequent recollection of one Tory,
Quintin Hogg – 'We thought that there would be free trade in citizens,
that people would come and go, and that there would not be much of
an overall balance in one direction or the other' – would have applied
equally to Labour.[23] After all, the general expectation was that any
future labour shortage could continue to be met by European labour;
no one anticipated the increasing availability of cheap transportation
from the Caribbean. The act was thus a fine example of liberalism at
its most nominal. Yet by a delicious irony, even as the legislators legislated,
that liberalism was starting to be tested.

On 24 May the *Empire Windrush*, a former German troop-carrier, set
sail from Kingston, Jamaica, with 492 black males and one stowaway
woman. Their destination was Tilbury, and as early as the 26th the London
office of the Ministry of Labour reacted to the news with 'considerable
dismay', predicting that if the men tried to get jobs in areas of worsening
unemployment like Stepney and Camden Town (in both of which there
were quite a few black workers already), 'there will probably be trouble
eventually'. By 8 June the minister, George Isaacs, was emphasising to
MPs that the job-seekers had not been officially invited. 'The arrival of
these substantial numbers of men under no organised arrangement is
bound to result in considerable difficulty and disappointment,' he declared,
adding, 'I hope no encouragement will be given to others to follow their
example.' Over the next fortnight the MOL tried in vain to delay the
Empire Windrush's arrival but did arrange jobs for many of its passengers
– mainly out of London and mainly well apart from each other.

Within the Cabinet the flak for this untoward turn of events was
directed at the Colonial Secretary, Arthur Creech Jones. He was blamed
on the 15th for not 'having kept the lid on things' and was requested,
amid considerable press interest (curious rather than hostile) in the
ship's imminent arrival, to 'ensure that further similar movements either

from Jamaica or elsewhere in the colonial empire are detected and checked before they can reach such an embarrassing stage'. Replying to his critics three days later, Creech Jones did not deny that the men were fully entitled to come to Britain but sought to offer reassurance for the future: 'I do not think that a similar mass movement will take place again because the transport is unlikely to be available, though we shall be faced with a steady trickle, which, however, can be dealt with without undue difficulty.' Fewer than 500 constituting a 'mass movement'? Given that over the previous 12 months as many as 51,000 white European voluntary workers had been placed in one sector alone of the British economy (agriculture), the subtext was almost palpable. Soon afterwards, in a letter sent to Attlee by 11 anxious Labour MPs, there was no beating about the bush:

> This country may become an open reception centre for immigrants not selected in respect to health, education, training, character, customs and above all, whether assimilation is possible or not.
>
> The British people fortunately enjoy a profound unity without uniformity in their way of life, and are blest by the absence of a colour racial problem. An influx of coloured people domiciled here is likely to impair the harmony, strength and cohesion of our public and social life and to cause discord and unhappiness among all concerned.

Accordingly, the MPs suggested that the government should, 'by legislation if necessary, control immigration in the political, social, economic and fiscal interests of our people'. They added that 'in our opinion such legislation or administration action would be almost universally approved by our people'.[24]

This petition to Attlee was sent on Tuesday, 22 June – the very day that the *Empire Windrush*'s passengers disembarked at Tilbury. The *Star*'s report that evening concentrated on '25-year-old seamstress Averill Wanchove':

> She stowed away on the ship and was befriended by Nancy Cunard, heiress of the Cunard fortunes.
>
> Tall and attractive Averill was discovered when the ship was seven days out from Kingston.

Mr Mortimer Martin made a whip round and raised £50, enough to pay Averill's fare and to leave her £4 for pocket money.

Nancy Cunard, who was on her way back from Trinidad, took a fancy to Averill and intends looking after her.

Pathé newsreel film of the new arrivals featured the calypso singer Lord Kitchener (real name Aldwyn Roberts) performing his latest composition, 'London Is the Place for Me', a buoyantly optimistic number which he had started composing about four days before the boat landed. 'The feeling I had to know that I'm going to touch the soil of the mother country, that was the feeling I had,' he recalled almost half a century later. 'How can I describe? It's just a wonderful feeling. You know how it is when a child, you hear about your mother country, and you know that you're going to touch the soil of the mother country, you know what feeling is that? And I can't describe it. That's why I compose the song.'

About half the men, presumably those without jobs already assigned to them, stayed temporarily at Clapham South's wartime deep shelter, run by the LCC. On the first Saturday afternoon, the vicar of the Church of the Ascension, Balham, invited them to a service the next day, to be followed in the evening by tea in the hall. About 80 took up the offer. 'The Jamaicans were charming people,' the *Clapham Observer* quoted W. H. Garland, a representative of the church, as saying afterwards. 'They were churchmen and keen.' The following Saturday – five days after some 40,000 mainly rain-soaked spectators at Villa Park had watched the middleweight Dick Turpin become Britain's first black boxing champion – five of the shelter's residents 'introduced the "Calypso" to Clapham, when they played at the baths at a social held by the Clapham Communist Party'. Under the headline 'Jamaicans Thrill Communists', the local paper went on: 'The chief exponent [Lord Kitchener?] of the calypso was called again and again to the microphone. Some of the verses he sang to the intriguing West Indian rhythm had been given before: others he made up as he went along, poking sly fun at members of the audience.'

Two days later, on 5 July, Attlee replied to his 11 worried backbenchers. 'I think it would be a great mistake to take the emigration of this Jamaican party to the United Kingdom too seriously,' he told them.

'If our policy were to result in a great influx of undesirables, we might, however unwillingly, have to consider modifying it. But I would not be willing to consider that except on really compelling evidence, which I do not think exists at the present time.'[25]

A Change in the Terms of Struggle

Tuesday, 22 June may have been Windrush Day, but *Woman's Hour* that afternoon had cricket on its agenda. 'Yes, I'm one of the awful men you keep switching off,' the cheery commentator Rex Alston told the listeners. 'But please give me a chance this time. I won't keep you more than five minutes – so don't dash off into the kitchen and see if your cakes are burning. I promise you I won't talk about silly mid-on and gully and maiden overs and all the other jargon that must perplex you. All the same, don't tell me that, some time during the week, you won't be bowled over, completely stumped, or even badly caught out!' The occasion for this patronising guff was radio's forthcoming coverage of the England versus Australia Test starting at Lord's two days later. The outcome of the match itself was predictable. England as usual were captained by a well-meaning amateur (Yorkshire's Norman Yardley), and Don Bradman's 'Invincibles' won by the crushing margin of 409 runs.

On Tuesday the 29th, about an hour after the match had finished, the regular 'What's Your Worry?' slot on *Woman's Hour* featured the reassuring voice of Marion Cutler:

It's hard to believe that next Monday will be the much talked about 5th July when both the Health Service and National Insurance Scheme come into force. So today I'll try to clear up some of the points from your questions which have been worrying you – and sure I'm not surprised they worry you . . .

Lately many of you have written to say, 'I'm over age – that's over 60, and too old to join the National Insurance. Does that mean I won't be able to get the free medical treatment and advice under the Health Service?'

No, indeed it doesn't. Let me say once again, joining the National Insurance has nothing to do with what is offered by the Health Service. It doesn't matter what your age is, whether you're married or single, whether you're rich or poor . . .

But I *was* told the other day of one thing that is causing a lot of delay and extra work in getting the Service going.

You know the form E.C.I. which many of you have filled up already and sent in to join the Health Service. In some districts nearly 80 out of every 100 have been returned with the answers to some of the questions left blank. Two spaces in particular – and two important ones – have been left just empty. One is you can't remember, or haven't been told to produce, your Identity Card number, and the other one is you've completely forgotten the day, month and year of your birth.

Well, we've often heard that *not* telling her age has been a woman's weakness, and most of us hope it will be hidden in a birth certificate, or our marriage lines. But alas it has to go down on paper sometimes, and putting it on this Health Service Form is one of the times.

'By next Monday,' Cutler confidently declared, 'it's expected there will be over 14,500 doctors working in the Service, and if you want to you ought to be able to get on the list of one in your district before then – be able to enrol and be accepted as a patient.'[1]

It had been a far from smooth ride to get to this point, with Aneurin Bevan engaged for two years in a fierce war with the British Medical Association (BMA). 'The Act is part of the nationalization programme which is being steadily pursued by the Government,' that body's chairman, Dr Guy Dain, declared in November 1946, the day after the National Health Service Bill had received the Royal Assent. 'What the Minister appears to have done is to have taken the Bill which we had partly fashioned and to have inserted into it the Socialist principles of State ownership of hospitals, direction of doctors, basic salary for doctors, and abolition of buying and selling of practices.' In the event it required some concessions at the margins by Bevan, and no less than three plebiscites of GPs, before an adequate number of doctors were willing to enter the scheme.

Feelings undoubtedly ran high – 'We have not fought and won a war against dictatorship only to submit to it disguised as democracy of the Soviet pattern,' protested J. S. Laurie, a GP in Fitzwilliam, Yorkshire – but there were many doctors, often practising in poorer areas and not always well represented on the BMA, who positively looked forward to a national health service free at the point of delivery. One was probably Gladys Langford's GP in Islington. 'Despite all his trouble on my behalf he utterly refused to accept a fee,' she gratefully noted in May 1948. Another was Mike Leigh's father Abe, practising in Salford. 'He always cursed his private patients and couldn't wait to get rid of them,' the film director recalled. 'When the day came when he had no more private patients, that day was one of celebration as far as he was concerned. He also worked as a visiting factory doctor, mostly around Oldham.' Even so, the more typical GP at this stage was possibly Dr R. P. Liston of Tunbridge Wells. At a BMA representative meeting barely a week before the NHS came into effect, a Scottish doctor argued that it might be necessary to form a trade union to protect the interests of doctors, given that 'clearly we must protect ourselves against the forces of tyranny so latent in a state service'. Liston did not deny the point but insisted that a 'Guild' would be much preferable. For as he added, pressing every middle-class button in the room, 'This word trade union sticks in our gullets.'[2]

During the months leading up to 5 July 1948, there was a torrent of government propaganda – cartoon films, lectures, leaflets and pamphlets, travelling exhibitions, advertisements, broadcasts – explaining and justifying the new welfare arrangements. Press opposition came from predictable quarters, above all Beaverbrook's *Daily Express*, which loudly and insistently banged on that the whole exercise was a waste of taxpayer's money. As for the new dispensation itself (involving a weekly deduction of 4s 11d from the wage-earner, of which only 8½d went to the new health service), there was also a negative note struck by parts of the local press, though more about the insurance than the health aspect. 'The appointed day!' declared the *Falkirk Herald* in its last issue before the 5th:

Not the day appointed for the annual exodus to coast or country, but the day on which the new National Insurance scheme comes into operation.

It will give Falkirk folk on holiday at the seaside something to think about, and the whelks and mussels may remind them that they will be called upon to 'shell' out some more of their hard-earned cash to purchase the much-vaunted cradle-to-the-grave security.

Among the weeklies, the *New Statesman*'s support was hardly surprising – 'That we are doing this undismayed by debt and deficit, dubious international relations and an ageing population is a great tribute to the courage and resilience of our people' – but more telling was the attitude of the tough-minded humorist (and Independent MP for Oxford University, in the last years of that seat), A. P. Herbert. 'July 5th, 1948! Boys, this is going to be a big day,' he began his weekly column in *Punch* at the end of June:

> This column has, at last, obtained a 'Family Guide', with all those delightful Government owls [anthropomorphic drawings, presumably denoting wisdom]: and, being a comparatively elderly column [Herbert was 57], it has suddenly sprung into quite unexpected enthusiasm for the Whole Affair. It had been pretty lukewarm. Indeed, it had been wandering round trying to find out what were the penalties for non-cooperation (there is nothing about *them* in the Family Guide). 'What,' it had muttered darkly, 'would happen if one *declined* to contribute – simply did not stick on the stamps?' But, now that it has read the Family Guide, all that nonsense is ended. Listen, uncountable readers.

There followed from Herbert a broadly sympathetic examination of the new National Insurance arrangements.

But the real plus for the government, in terms of truly uncountable readers, was the sympathetic treatment given by the women's magazines, owing something to personal cajolery by Bevan and other ministers. 'They're a happy family – 8½d a week isn't much to pay to keep them healthy' was *Woman*'s caption on 12 June to a photograph of a smiling quartet (the obligatory father, mother and two small children). And in the accompanying article, Norah Kingswood emphasised that readily available medical treatment under the NHS, free at the point of access, would soon put paid to the grumble she had recently overheard while waiting in the fish queue for her weekend kippers, that

'We'll be paying large sums of money each week and getting precious little back.' At the top end of the market, even *Vogue* was onside. 'The social conscience of the country has been growing steadily,' noted its July issue. 'Progress has been made under Liberal, Conservative and Labour governments. Now we are due to take another stride.' The magazine's editor, the Labour-sympathising Audrey Withers, then had words specifically for her well-heeled readers: 'It has taken a long time to scotch the Class fallacy: to admit that rich and poor are "subject to the same diseases, healed by the same means" – and to ensure that lack of money shall not stand in the way of that healing.'³

One element in society hostile – or at best ambivalent – to the July revolution was the Catholic Church. 'It will be a sad day for England when charity becomes the affair of the State' was the underlying view of Cardinal Bernard Griffin, Archbishop of Westminster; seemingly indifferent to larger questions of national welfare, he managed to nego-tiate the opting-out of Catholic hospitals from the new NHS. Public opinion as a whole was broadly if not overwhelmingly supportive: according to Gallup in March 1948, 61 per cent saw the NHS as a 'good' idea and only 13 per cent as 'bad'. Nevertheless, the apparently mixed feelings of Marian Raynham in Surbiton were probably not unrepresentative. 'Receive leaflet about National Health Service,' she recorded in late April: 'It seems medicine, teeth, glasses, hearing appa-ratus will all be free when July 5th comes, & after paying the insurance of 4 or 5 shillings. Robin is too young & Daddy too old & I am a housewife, so only Ray pays. What with old age pensions, 7/6 for Robin, free school milk & free hearing for Dad & free teeth for me & any new glasses free it seems a crazy world.' Vere Hodgson was, perhaps befitting a voluntary welfare worker, still more sceptical. 'It seems to be all right if we could afford it,' she reflected on the eve of the NHS's start. 'It seems to me just Bankrupt Hospitals being taken over by a Bankrupt Country. You pass on the baby.' Was there fear at this stage about welfare 'scroungers'? It does not come through in the mainly middle-class diaries, but at the start of July the *Liverpool Daily Post* made a front-page attack on 'coloured' stowaways on ships from South Africa who were coming to the city to 'obtain employment, receive dole, a ration book and even free clothing'. And, in a pre-echo of much that lay ahead, the paper demanded that the law be changed, to enable deportation of British subjects and thereby 'curtail the daily increasing numbers' of the uninvited.[4]

There was, by any objective assessment, a huge amount to be done. Earlier in the year, as part of her social-work course, Phyllis Noble spent some time in a Family Welfare Association office in Deptford. She recorded a visit to a poor Irish family living in one of the nearby slums:

> To think such squalor can still exist! Surely I can never forget that smoke-filled room, the mouldy cabbage in the corner, the bowl with the dirty water on the bare boards, the toddler wandering about in threadbare shirt and no shoes. Nor the horror I felt when Mr Doyle said in his heavy Irish accent, but so *casually*, 'There's another behind you' – and I turned and saw a pile of rags on the bare springs of the bed, and hidden in the rags a dirty, tiny baby.

Soon afterwards, a national survey was undertaken of more than 5,000 children, across the social classes, who had been born in the first week of March 1946. The findings were unsensational but important. Maternal efficiency was poorest on the part of the wives of unskilled manual workers, not least because they were often in poor health themselves; a two-year-old from such a family was already virtually an inch shorter than his or her counterpart from a professional and salaried family; there was almost double the relative probability of having had frequent colds over the previous winter; and it was only children of the self-employed who were taken less often by their mothers to child welfare centres.

In practice so much would depend upon ease of access – psychological as well as physical – to the new services. In May, following her Deptford experience, Phyllis Noble went as a student almoner to St Thomas' Hospital. There, at the end of each interview with a patient, she was supposed to ask if the patient could make a donation to hospital funds and, as encouragement, to shake the small tin box that stood on her desk. But at last the much-awaited 5 July beckoned. 'On the final days before the "Appointed Day" in Casualty we joyfully abandoned the little tin boxes,' she recalled. 'It was the symbolic new beginning of a health service that was intended to be free to all.'[5]

On Sunday the 4th there were two starkly contrasting speeches. A radio broadcast by Attlee, after the nine o'clock evening news, summarised and put into historical context the main changes taking place next day; emphasised that 'all our social services have to be paid for, in one way or another', so that only 'higher output can give us more of the things we all need'; expressed the hope that all those who had 'served in the past' on a more voluntary basis would 'still find a field for your generous impulses and public spirit'; and finished with a typically understated peroration: 'Here then is our new scheme of social security for all. I believe that it will increase the health and happiness of our peoples and I ask you all to join in working wholeheartedly for it so that it may bring new strength and well-being to our country.' There was nothing bipartisan about the other speech, given at a Labour rally at Belle Vue and reported thus in *The Times*:

Mr Bevan, Minister of Health, recalled what he described as the bitter experiences of his early life when he spoke in Manchester yesterday. For a time he had to live on the earnings of an elder sister and was told to emigrate. 'That is why,' he said, 'no amount of cajolery, and no attempts at ethical or social seduction, can eradicate from my heart a deep burning hatred for the Tory Party that inflicted those bitter experiences on me. So far as I am concerned they are lower than vermin' . . .

Mr Bevan referred to the launching of the new health service and said that during the next few months there would be complaint after complaint about what they were not able to do. In the past the distress was there, but the complaints were not heard.

'After tomorrow,' Mr Bevan said, 'the weak will be entitled to clamour . . .'

That striking v-word made an immediate impact. 'Had a heated political discussion in the Staff-room, arising out of Bevan's latest exhibition of himself,' Kenneth Preston at Keighley Grammar School noted on the 5th. 'He has been calling Conservatives scum and vermin.'[6] In a prevailing culture that still prized self-restraint above all on the part of its politicians, the gifted and passionate miner's son from South Wales had lapsed – and would never be allowed by his opponents to forget that lapse. The fact that it occurred at the very moment of an unquestionably great achievement only accentuated the piquancy.

The Appointed Day itself was littered with claims and warnings. 'We are leading the whole world in Social Security,' boasted the *Daily Mirror*, adding: 'Our State belongs to the people – unlike so many countries where the people belong to the State – and Social Security converts our democratic ideal into human reality.' *The Times* wondered whether the next generation would be able to 'reap the benefits of a social service State while avoiding the perils of a Santa Claus State' but insisted that 'it would be a grave mistake to overlook the deep feelings and sense of purpose and common humanity which all the new social services are trying, however imperfectly, to express.' A surprisingly sour note came from the *Manchester Guardian*, which – true to its nineteenth-century laissez-faire roots – feared that the state provision of welfare would 'eliminate selective elimination' and thus lead to an increase of congenitally deformed and feckless people. Among the diarists there was grudging acceptance from Anthony Heap ('sounds all right on paper, but how will it work in practice?'), but Cyril Leach, who lived in Harrow and was a senior figure in the insurance world, reckoned that 'it looks like being a fine old muddle'.[7]

Bevan himself, by now in thoroughly benign mood, spent the day in Lancashire. The symbolic keys of a hospital in Manchester were handed over to him; he said that patients in hospitals were 'just human beings wanting help', not members of political parties; and in an afternoon speech in Preston he argued that progress was less 'the elimination of struggle' than 'a change in the terms of struggle'. For some, this momentous day was the day of their birth. They included Lynn Creedy; half a century later, on the NHS's 50th anniversary, she told her story:

I was a home birth. I was born in 41A Victoria Road, Deal, Kent. I was due to be born the day before, but I was born about midday on the fifth, so my father didn't have to pay anything. The midwife was then a lady to be feared; she had a lot of authority. She instructed my father not to let the fire go out in the flat so that she could burn the placenta. Things went on for a while and my father got so engrossed in his cowboy books, which were popular at the time, that he let the fire go out.

'The midwife was not very happy,' she added. 'My mother often reminded him of that...'

For Nella Last in Barrow, it was a typically busy, purposeful day – preparing for the WVS garden party, taking her order to the grocers, getting her hair done, sending a box of new potatoes and some onions to her Aunt Sarah, turning away a hawker selling 'patent' brushes – until soon after tea:

I must have shown the effects of my rush & bustle of the day. My husband said kindly 'would you like to go to a show – have you anything yet to do?' I said 'yes, I've jam to make & fruit to bottle, but all is ready, the fruit would sterilize by itself, & the jam being raspberry only needs 4 minutes quick boil!' ... I said 'I'd love to go for a little run' & he finished 'round Coniston Lake'. It was such a sweet fair night, the top was off the car & I felt akin to my little Shan We [her cat] who lay relaxed on my lap, stretching & flexing his paws at intervals ... I felt the creases all fading out of my tired soul as the peace & beauty of hills & moors came into view. We paused to look at the Lake. My mind was as blank as it's possible for a busy mind to be. I felt I was trying to be one with the rhythm & utter peace. My husband said 'you *shall* lie here if it is in my power – I'd like the same'. I felt startled. I felt it so 'revolutionary'. My queer ideas have so often irked & annoyed that poor dear, try as I would. We smiled at each other. Odd how a shared 'wish' can be so friendly. We were home by 8.30. My bottles had sterilized & my jam soon made – the fruit was 'mashed' with the sugar, & ready for putting on the stove.[8]

Notes

Abbreviations

Abrams	Mark Abrams Papers (Churchill Archives Centre, Churchill College, Cambridge)
BBC WA	BBC Written Archives (Caversham)
Brown	Diary of W. J. Brown (Department of Documents, Imperial War Museum)
Chaplin	Sid Chaplin Papers (Special Collections, University of Newcastle upon Tyne)
Daly	Lawrence Daly Papers (Modern Records Centre, University of Warwick)
Fabian	Fabian Society Papers (British Library of Political and Economic Science)
Ferguson	Diary of Colin Ferguson (Glasgow City Archives)
Ford	Diary of Erica Ford (Ealing Local History Centre)
Gaitskell	Philip M. Williams (ed), *The Diary of Hugh Gaitskell, 1945–56* (1983)
Golden	Diary of Grace Golden (Museum of London)
Haines	Diary of Alice (Judy) Haines (Special Collections, University of Sussex)
Headlam	Stuart Ball (ed), *Parliament and Politics in the Age of Churchill and Attlee: The Headlam Diaries 1935–1951* (Cambridge, 1999)
Heap	Diary of Anthony Heap (London Metropolitan Archives)
Hodgson	Diary of Vere Hodgson (held by Veronica Bowater, literary executor)
King	Diary of Mary King (Birmingham City Archives)
Langford	Diary of Gladys Langford (Islington Local History Centre)
Lewis	Diary of Frank Lewis (Glamorgan Record Office)
Loftus	Diary of Ernest Loftus (Thurrock Museum)
M-O A	Mass-Observation Archive (Special Collections, University of Sussex)
Osborn	Michael Hughes (ed), *The Letters of Lewis Mumford and Frederic J. Osborn* (Bath, 1971)
Preston	Diary of Kenneth Preston (Bradford Archives)
Raynham	Diary of Marian Raynham (Special Collections, University of Sussex)
St John	Diary of Henry St John (Ealing Local History Centre)
Speed	Diary of Florence Speed (Department of Documents, Imperial War Museum)
Streat	Marguerite Dupree (ed), *Lancashire and Whitehall: The Diary of Sir Raymond Streat: Volume Two, 1939–57* (Manchester, 1987)
Uttin	Diary of Rose Uttin (Department of Documents, Imperial War Museum)
Willmott	Diary of Phyllis Willmott

All books are published in London unless otherwise stated.

A World to Build

1 Waiting for Something to Happen

1. M-O A, FR 2263.
2. Heap, 8 May 1945; *Independent on Sunday*, 11 Jul 1999; Langford, 8 May 1945; Harold Nicolson, *Diaries and Letters, 1939–1945* (1967), p 456; M-O A, FR 2263.
3. Nicolson, *Diaries and Letters*, p 457; Langford, 8 May 1945; Vera Brittain, *Wartime Chronicle* (1989), p 265; Heap, 8 May 1945; Langford, 8 May 1945; BBC WA, R9/9/9 – LR/3470; Lewis, 8 May 1945.
4. M-O A, FR 2263; Ursula Vaughan Williams, *R.V.W.* (1964), p 262; Cecil Beaton, *The Happy Years* (1972), p 38; diary of Joan Waley, 8 May 1945; Haines, 8 May 1945.
5. Streat, p 259; Loftus, 8 May 1945; David Rayvern Allen, *Arlott* (1994), p 78; James Lees-Milne, *Prophesying Peace* (1984), p 187; M-O A, TC 49/1/C.
6. *Nella Last's War* (Bristol, 1981), p 280; BBC WA, R9/9/9 – LR/3470; Lewis, 8 May 1945.
7. Joan Wyndham, *Love is Blue* (1986), pp 177–8; *The Noël Coward Diaries* (1982), p 29; Heap, 8 May 1945.
8. M-O A, FR 2263; Ferguson, 9 May 1945; King, 8 May 1945; Streat, p 260; Haines, 8 May 1945.
9. *Hereford Times*, 12 May 1945; *Midland Counties Express*, 12 May 1945; M-O A, FR 2263.
10. Langford, 9 May 1945; St John, 8–9 May 1945; *The Journals of Denton Welch* (1984), p 191.
11. Lees-Milne, p 188; *The Second World War Diary of Hugh Dalton* (1986), p 858; recollections of Michael Burns; Langford, 9 May 1945; Lewis, 9 May 1945; Heap, 9 May 1945; *Fifty Years On* (Radio 4, 23 May 1995); Heap, 9 May 1945.
12. Kenneth Tynan, *Letters* (1994), pp 70–71; M-O A, FR 2263.

2 Broad Vistas and All That

1. The main source for this paragraph is A. H. Halsey (ed), *Twentieth-Century British Social Trends* (Basingstoke, 2000).
2. *Picture Post*, 4 Jan 1941.
3. Richard Bradford, *Lucky Him* (2001), p 52.
4. F.W.S. Craig (ed), *British General Election Manifestos* (1975), pp 123–31; Asa Briggs, *Michael Young* (Basingstoke, 2001), p 69.
5. *Times Literary Supplement*, 14 Jan 2000.
6. John Vaizey, *In Breach of Promise* (1983), p 141; John Singleton, 'Labour, the Conservatives and Nationalisation', in Robert Millward and John Singleton (eds), *The Political Economy of Nationalisation in Britain, 1920–1950* (Cambridge, 1995), p 17.
7. Alan Deacon and Jonathan Bradshaw, *Reserved for the Poor* (Oxford, 1983), p 42;

Nicholas Timmins, *The Five Giants* (2001), p 47; Jane Lewis, *Women in Britain since 1945* (Oxford, 1992), p 21; Jeffrey Weeks, *Sex, Politics and Society* (Harlow, 1989), p 232; *New Statesman*, 6 Feb 1998 (Raymond Plant). Generally on the Beveridge Report, see: Rodney Lowe, *The Welfare State in Britain since 1945* (Basingstoke, 1999), chap 6.1; Timmins, chaps 1–3.

8. Ralf Dahrendorf, *LSE* (Oxford, 1995), p 385; Jim Kincaid, 'Richard Titmuss 1907–73', in Paul Barker (ed), *Founders of the Welfare State* (1984), pp 114–20; Charles Webster, 'Investigating Inequalities in Health before Black', *Contemporary British History* (Autumn 2002), p 86; John E. Pater, *The Making of the National Health Service* (1981), p 78; *Guardian*, 20 May 1994 (Paul Addison).

9. *Times Educational Supplement*, 24 Jul 1943; Gary McCulloch, *Philosophers and Kings* (Cambridge, 1991), p 61; *TES*, 24 Jul 1943.

10. *Financial News*, 22 Jan 1934; Paul Oliver et al, *Dunroamin* (1981), pp 34–7, 46; George Orwell, *Coming up for Air* (Penguin edn, 1962), pp 13, 16; Thomas Sharp, *Town Planning* (1940), pp vii, 54, 57, 109; *Independent*, 19 Feb 2001; *Architectural Review* (Apr 1943), p 86; Gordon E. Cherry, *Urban Change and Planning* (Henley-on-Thames, 1972), p 163; Harold Wilson, *The Governance of Britain* (1976), p 54.

11. F. J. Osborn, 'Space Standards in Planning', in Gilbert and Elizabeth Glen McAllister, *Homes, Towns and Countryside* (1945), p 101.

12. Lionel Esher, *A Broken Wave* (1981), p 31; Patrick Dunleavy, *The Politics of Mass Housing in Britain, 1945–1975* (Oxford, 1981), p 54; *Picture Post*, 4 Jan 1941; *Architectural Review* (May 1942), p 128; Sharp, *Town Planning*, pp 76, 78.

13. Peter Hall, *Cities of Tomorrow* (Oxford, 2002), p 236; Arnold Whittick, *F.J.O.* (1987), p 74; Nicholas Bullock, 'Plans for Post-war Housing in the UK', *Planning Perspectives* (Jan 1987), pp 82, 78; Nick Tiratsoo et al, *Urban Reconstruction in Britain and Japan, 1945–1955* (Luton, 2002), p 6.

14. Junichi Hasegawa, *Replanning the Blitzed City Centre* (Buckingham, 1992), pp 50–52, 77–9; Hasegawa, 'The Reconstruction of Portsmouth in the 1940s', *Contemporary British History* (Spring 2000), pp 49–50; Nick Tiratsoo, 'Labour and the Reconstruction of Hull, 1945–51', in Tiratsoo (ed), *The Attlee Years* (1991), pp 127–31.

15. Gordon E. Cherry, 'Lessons from the Past', *Planning History*, 11/3 (1989), pp 3–7; Tiratsoo et al, *Urban Reconstruction*, p 5; Cherry, 'Lessons', p 5; Brian Chalkley, 'The Plan for the City Centre', in Mark Brayshay (ed), *Post-war Plymouth* (Plymouth, 1983), pp 17–18, 27–8, 30.

16. *Architectural Review* (Jan 1941), pp 31–2; Hasegawa, *Replanning*, p 32; Nick Tiratsoo, *Reconstruction, Affluence and Labour Politics: Coventry 1945–60* (1990), p 13; Tiratsoo et al, *Urban Reconstruction*, p 17. In general on the reconstruction plans for Coventry, see: Tiratsoo, *Reconstruction, Affluence and Labour Politics*, chap 2.

17. *Picture Post*, 4 Jan 1941; Steven Fielding et al, *'England Arise!'* (Manchester, 1995), pp 81–2.

18. Jeremy Nuttall, '"Psychological Socialist", "Militant Moderate": Evan Durbin and the Politics of Synthesis', *Labour History Review* (Aug 2003), pp 238, 241, 243; Stephen Brooke, 'Evan Durbin: Reassessing a Labour "Revisionist"', in *Twentieth Century British History*, 7/1 (1996), p 34; E.F.M. Durbin, *The Politics of Democratic Socialism* (1940), pp 330–31; Jim Tomlinson, 'Planning: Debate and Policy in the 1940s', *Twentieth Century British History*, 3/2 (1992), p 164. In general on Durbin,

in addition to the above, see: Elizabeth Durbin, *New Jerusalems* (1985).

19. *Architectural Review* (Feb 1942), p 40; James Lansdale Hodson, *The Sea and the Land* (1945), p 303; Deacon and Bradshaw, *Reserved for the Poor*, pp 32–4.

20. *The Collected Essays, Journalism and Letters of George Orwell, Volume II* (1968), p 104; M-O A, TC 2/2/J; Vere Hodgson, *Few Eggs and No Oranges* (Persephone edn, 1999), p 334; Mass-Observation, 'Social Security and Parliament', *Political Quarterly* (Jul–Sept 1943), pp 249, 246–7; John Jacobs, 'December 1942: Beveridge Observed', in John Jacobs (ed), *Beveridge 1942–1992* (1992), pp 21–2; Tony Mason and Peter Thompson, '"Reflections on a Revolution"?', in Tiratsoo, *Attlee Years*, p 57; Robert J. Wybrow, *Britain Speaks Out, 1937–87* (Basingstoke, 1989), p 16; BBC WA, R9/9/9 – LR/3163.

21. M-O A, FR 1162.

22. José Harris, 'Did British Workers Want the Welfare State?', in Jay Winter (ed), *The Working Class in Modern British History* (Cambridge, 1983), p 214; Jacobs, 'December 1942', p 21; M-O, 'Social Security', p 253.

23. George H. Gallup (ed), *The Gallup International Public Opinion Polls: Great Britain 1937–1975, Volume One* (New York, 1976), p 75; *Express and Star*, 22 Nov 1943.

24. Hodson, *Sea*, pp 303, 348; Steven Fielding, 'What Did "The People" Want?', *Historical Journal*, 35/3 (1992), pp 627–8; Jacobs, 'December 1942', p 30.

25. Wybrow, *Britain Speaks Out*, p 16; Singleton, 'Labour', pp 21–2; Rodney Lowe, 'The Second World War, Consensus, and the Foundation of the Welfare State', *Twentieth Century British History*, 1/2 (1990), p 175; *The Collected Essays, Journalism and Letters of George Orwell, Volume III* (1968), p 226.

26. Mass-Observation, *The Journey Home* (1944), pp 42, 96, 105, 109–10; M-O A, TC 3/1/F.

27. M-O A, FR 1162.

28. *Architectural Review* (Nov 1941), p 148; Naoki Motouchi and Nick Tiratsoo, 'Max Lock, Middlesbrough, and a Forgotten Tradition in British Post-war Planning', *Planning History* (2004), pp 17–20; *Journal of the Town Planning Institute* (Nov–Dec 1945), pp 1–5.

29. *Architectural Review* (Apr 1943), p 88; Hasegawa, *Replanning*, pp 80–84; Peter J. Larkham, 'Rebuilding the Industrial Town', *Urban History* (Dec 2002), pp 401–2.

30. *Coventry Standard*, 1 Mar 1941; Hasegawa, *Replanning*, p 39; *Coventry Evening Telegraph*, 15/19/21 Dec 1944; Mason and Thompson, 'Reflections', pp 63–4.

31. Mass-Observation, 'Some Psychological Factors in Home Building', *Town and Country Planning* (Spring 1943), pp 8–9; Mass-Observation, *People's Homes* (1943), pp 4–5, 219, 226; *Architectural Review* (Nov 1943), p 144.

32. Mass-Observation, *People's Homes*, p xix; Mrs M. Pleydell-Bouverie, *Daily Mail Book of Britain's Post-War Homes* (1944), pp 19–20; R. E. Pahl, *Divisions of Labour* (Oxford, 1984), pp 321–2; Nick Tiratsoo, 'The Reconstruction of Blitzed British Cities, 1945–55', *Contemporary British History* (Spring 2000), p 39.

33. Tiratsoo, 'Blitzed', p 38; Mark Clapson, *Invincible Green Suburbs, Brave New Towns* (Manchester, 1998), p 58; The Social Survey, *Furniture* (1945), pp 20–21.

34. F. J. Osborn, *New Towns After the War* (1942), p 13; *Picture Post*, 18 Jan 1941.

35. Mass-Observation, *People's Homes*, pp xxiii, 226; Bullock, 'Plans', pp 78, 80; Pleydell-Bouverie, p 19.

36. Dennis Chapman, *A Social Survey of Middlesbrough* (1945–6), pt II, pp 1, 3, 12; pt II, pp 9–10; pt III, pp 14, 24–32; pt IV, pp 1–5, 16.
37. Mason and Thompson, 'Reflections', pp 56–7; Lowe, 'Consensus', pp 177–8; Nicholas Joicey, 'A Paperback Guide to Progress', *Twentieth Century British History* 4/1 (1993), pp 41–4; Harold Nicolson, *Diaries and Letters, 1939–1945* (1967), p 465; *New Society*, 25 Apr 1963; Ross McKibbin, *Classes and Cultures* (Oxford, 1998), pp 527–8; *Picture Post*, 18 Jan 1941; Adrian Smith, 'The Fall and Fall of the Third *Daily Herald*, 1930–64', in Peter Catterall et al (eds), *Northcliffe's Legacy* (2000), pp 179–80.
38. Lesley A. Hall, *Sex, Gender and Social Change in Britain since 1880* (Basingstoke, 2000), pp 139–40; Eliot Slater and Moya Woodside, *Patterns of Marriage* (1951), pp 82–3, 249–54.

3 Oh Wonderful People of Britain!

1. *The Diaries of Sir Robert Bruce Lockhart, Volume Two* (1980), pp 439–40; Langford, 22 May 1945; Haines, 16/19/26 May 1945; St John, 1 Jun 1945; Loftus, 7 Jun 1945.
2. Edmund Wilson, *The Forties* (New York, 1983), p 107; Eric Parker, *Surrey* (1947), pp 105–9; *Author* (Winter 1996), p 137; The Rev. W. Awdry, *The Three Railway Engines* (1967), p 40; *Guardian*, 7 Jun 1995; *Letters for a Life: The Selected Letters and Diaries of Benjamin Britten, 1913–1976, Volume Two* (1991), p 1252.
3. St John, 14 Jun 1945; Keith Waterhouse, *City Lights* (1994), p 170; Humphrey Carpenter, *Dennis Potter* (1998), pp 27–32.
4. Michael Foot, *Aneurin Bevan, Volume I* (Granada edn, 1975), pp 503–4; Edward Pearce, *Denis Healey* (2002), p 54; Austin Mitchell, *Election '45* (1995), p 20.
5. Martin Gilbert, *'Never Despair': Winston S. Churchill, 1945–1965* (1988), pp 32, 49; Haines, 4/5 Jun 1945; Robert Rhodes James, *Bob Boothby* (1991), p 330; Ursula Bloom, *Trilogy* (1954), pp 167–8; Thelma Cazalet-Keir, *From the Wings* (1967), p 124; *Times Literary Supplement*, 9 Jul 2004 (Angus Calder); *News of the World*, 1 Jul 1945; Paul Addison, 'Churchill and the Price of Victory', in Nick Tiratsoo (ed), *From Blitz to Blair* (1997), p 74.
6. Julian Amery, *Approach March* (1973), p 438; Hugh Thomas, *John Strachey* (1973), p 223; *Spectator*, 15 Mar 2003 (Antonia Fraser); John Campbell, *Margaret Thatcher, Volume One* (2000), p 53; *Among You Taking Notes ... The Wartime Diary of Naomi Mitchison* (1985), p 327; Anne Perkins, *Red Queen* (2003), p 78; Simon Hoggart and David Leigh, *Michael Foot* (1981), pp 90–91; Chaplin, 7/3/1, 8 Jul 1945; *Tottenham and Edmonton Weekly Herald*, 22/29 Jun 1945.
7. *Luton News*, 21/28 Jun 1945, 5 Jul 1945.
8. Lord Elwyn-Jones, *In My Time* (1983), p 84; Mitchell, *Election '45*, p 44; Nina Bawden, *In My Own Time* (1994), p 77.
9. M-O A, FR 2270A; Mass-Observation, 'Post-Mortem on Voting at the Election', *Quarterly Review* (Jan 1946), p 59; *The Complete Works of George Orwell, Volume 17* (1998), p 192; Wilson, *The Forties*, pp 109–10; Tony Mason and Peter Thompson, '"Reflections on a Revolution"?', in Nick Tiratsoo (ed), *The Attlee Years* (1991), p 64.
10. *Manchester Guardian*, 4 Jul 1945; Langford, 5 Jul 1945; *The Correspondence of H. G. Wells, Volume 4* (1998), p 523; *Independent*, 30 Jun 2003; Mitchell, *Election '45*,

p 78; Loftus, 5 Jul 1945; St John, 5 Jul 1945; Ferguson, 5 Jul 1945; *News of the World*, 8 Jul 1945; Pathe Newsreel, circa 10 Jul 1945.

11. *News of the World*, 8 Jul 1945; *Nella Last's War* (Bristol, 1981), p 293; James Hinton, 'Militant Housewives', *History Workshop* (Autumn 1994), p 132; Haines, 14 Jul 1945; *Selected Letters of André Gide and Dorothy Bussy* (Oxford, 1983), p 243; *Tottenham and Edmonton Weekly Herald*, 20 Jul 1945.

12. Brown, 2/4, 12 Jul 1945; Osborn, p 88; M-O A, FR 2270B.

13. David Kynaston, *The City of London, Volume III* (1999), pp 508–9; M-O A, FR 2270A.

14. *Lockhart*, p 473; Kenneth O. Morgan, 'Wales since 1945', in Trevor Herbert and Gareth Elwyn Jones (eds), *Post-War Wales* (Cardiff, 1995), p 10; Mitchison, *Among You*, pp 334–5; Selina Hastings, *Evelyn Waugh* (1994), p 495; Walter Allen, *As I Walked Down New Grub Street* (1981), pp 103–4.

15. Tony Benn, *Years of Hope* (1994), p 91; Francis Beckett, *Clem Attlee* (1997), p 198; William Harrington and Peter Young, *The 1945 Revolution* (1978), p 192.

16. A.J.P. Taylor, *Beaverbrook* (1972), p 568; Anthony Howard, '"We Are The Masters Now"', in Michael Sissons and Philip French (eds), *Age of Austerity* (Oxford, 1986), p 3; James Agate, *Ego 8* (1946), p 184.

17. Loftus, 26 Jul 1945; King, 26 Jul 1945; Heap, 27 Jul 1945; *Nella Last's War*, p 298; Haines, 26 Jul 1945; Harrington and Young, *1945*, p 189; Michael Ignatieff, *Isaiah Berlin* (1998), p 134; Peter J. Conradi, *Iris Murdoch* (2001), p 211; Dylan Thomas, *The Collected Letters* (2000), p 624; *The Nightfisherman: Selected Letters of W. S. Graham* (Manchester, 1999), p 51.

18. Pamela Street, *Arthur Bryant* (1979), p 132; John Gale, *Clean Young Englishman* (1988), p 84; *The Noël Coward Diaries* (1982), p 36.

19. Gilbert, *'Never Despair'*, pp 113, 115; Mark Garnett, *Alport* (1999), p 66; *Horizon* (Sept 1945), p 149; *The Collected Essays, Journalism and Letters of George Orwell, Volume III* (1968), pp 446–7.

20. Retrospective explanations include: Henry Pelling, 'The 1945 General Election Reconsidered', *Historical Journal*, 23/2 (1980), pp 399–414; Gary McCulloch, 'Labour, the Left, and the British General Election of 1945', *Journal of British Studies* (Oct 1985), pp 465–89; Geoffrey K. Fry, 'A Reconsideration of the British General Election of 1935 and the Electoral Revolution of 1945', *History* (Feb 1991), pp 43–55; Steven Fielding, 'What Did "The People" Want?', *Historical Journal*, 35/3 (1992), pp 623–39; Stephen Brooke, 'The Labour Party and the 1945 General Election', *Contemporary Record* (Summer 1995), pp 1–21; Michael David Kandiah, 'The Conservative Party and the 1945 General Election', *Contemporary Record* (Summer 1995), pp 22–47.

21. Kandiah, 'Conservative Party', p 106.

22. *Orwell, Volume III*, pp 447–8; *The Times*, 15 Dec 1990; Uttin, 29 Jul 1945.

23. John K. Walton, *Blackpool* (Edinburgh, 1998), p 139; Heap, 29 Jul 1945; *Radio Times*, 27 Jul 1945; Harold Nicolson, *The Later Years, 1945–1962: Diaries and Letters, Volume III* (1968), p 30; Christopher Mayhew, *Time to Explain* (1987), p 88; Gaitskell, p 7.

24. Brown, 1/15, 2 Aug 1945; Lord Taylor of Mansfield, *Uphill All The Way* (1972), p 138; *Lockhart*, p 477; Richard Rose, 'Class and Party Divisions', *Sociology* (May 1968), p 131.

25. *News Chronicle*, 7 Aug 1945; *Radio Times*, 3 Aug 1945; Norris McWhirter, *Ross* (1976), pp 59–60; Heap, 6 Aug 1945.
26. BBC WA, Home Service, 6 Aug 1945; Bloom, *Trilogy*, p 159; Elizabeth Longford, *The Pebbled Shore* (1986), p 226; Joan Wyndham, *Love is Blue* (1986), p 189; Canon L. John Collins, *Faith under Fire* (1966), pp 98–9.
27. Martin Stannard, *Evelyn Waugh: No Abiding City, 1939–1966* (1992), p 151; *Joyce & Ginnie: The Letters of Joyce Grenfell and Virginia Graham* (1997), p 134; *Noël Coward Diaries*, p 37; Frances Spalding, *Vanessa Bell* (1983), p 328; *Letters of J.R.R. Tolkien* (1981), p 116; Ferguson, 8 Aug 1945; Langford, 7 Aug 1945.
28. St John, 7/9 Aug 1945; *Nella Last's War*, pp 302–4.
29. Langford, 14 Aug 1945; *Nella Last's War*, p 305–6; Loftus, 14/15 Aug 1945; *Merthyr Express*, 18 Aug 1945.
30. Headlam, p 475; Haines, 15–16 Aug 1945; Uttin, 15 Aug 1945; Langford, 15 Aug 1945; Heap, 15 Aug 1945.
31. Osborn, pp 92, 95; *Grantham Journal*, 17 Aug 1945.

4 We're So Short of Everything

1. *Tribune*, 14/28 Dec 1945. On the tour itself, see: Ronald Kowalski and Dilwyn Porter, 'Political Football', *International Journal of the History of Sport* (Aug 1997), pp 100–21.
2. *Accrington Observer*, 8/12 Jan 1946; Rogan Taylor and Andrew Ward, *Kicking and Screaming* (1995), p 60; Andrew Ward, *Armed with a Football* (Oxford, 1994), pp 2–9; Heap, 4 Oct 1945; Ford, 21 Sept 1945; Joanna Bourke, *Working-Class Cultures in Britain 1890–1960* (1994), p 186; Ted Kavanagh, *Tommy Handley* (1949), pp 199–200; King, 29 Apr 1946; Kevin Brownlow, *David Lean* (1996), p 203. On *ITMA*, see also Denis Gifford, *The Golden Age of Radio* (1985), p 134; John Gross, *A Double Thread* (2001), p 79.
3. William Glock, *Notes in Advance* (Oxford, 1991), p 40; *Independent*, 4 Aug 1995 (Bryan Robertson); Golden, 12 Mar 1946; Bryan Appleyard, *The Pleasures of Peace* (1989), p 56; *Tatler*, 7 Nov 1945; *Chips: The Diaries of Sir Henry Channon* (1967), p 414.
4. Barry Turner and Tony Rennell, *When Daddy Came Home* (1995), pp 61, 95, 100.
5. Elizabeth Wilson, *Only Halfway to Paradise* (1980), p 22; Jane Lewis, *Women in Britain since 1945* (Oxford, 1992), p 17; Cynthia L. White, *Women's Magazines, 1693–1968* (1970), pp 135–6; *Guardian*, 8 Nov 1999; Janice Winship, 'Nation Before Family', in *Formations of Nation and People* (1984), p 196; Haines, 3 Mar 1946; Heap, 21 Mar 1946; James Lansdale Hodson, *The Way Things Are* (1947), p 278.
6. *The Times*, 18 Dec 2003; *Independent*, 16 Feb 1989; *The Times*, 23 Oct 2000; *Independent*, 26 Oct 2000.
7. Muriel Bowmer Papers (Department of Documents, Imperial War Museum), vol 5, fols 1099, 1118; Barbara Pym, *A Very Private Eye* (1984), p 249; *The New Yorker*, 1 Dec 1945; George Beardmore, *Civilians at War* (1984), p 200; Gerard Mooney, 'Living on the Periphery' (PhD, University of Glasgow, 1988), p 218.
8. M-O A, TC 1/9/B; Brenda Vale, *Prefabs* (1995), p 171; *Pilot Papers* (Nov 1946), pp 28–38.

9. *The New Yorker*, 1 Sept 1945; Bowmer, fol 1090; Heap, 31 Dec 1945.

10. M-O A, FR 2291; Langford, 3 Nov 1945; St John, 8 Nov 1945; King, 9 Nov 1945; Aidan Crawley, *Leap Before You Look* (1988), p 213; Streat, p 325.

11. Haines, 15 Jan 1946; Hinton, pp 132–4; M-O A, TC 67/6/A; Raynham, 13–15 Mar 1946, 2 Apr 1946.

12. Ina Zweiniger-Bargielowska, *Austerity in Britain* (Oxford, 2000), pp 125–6; *The New Yorker*, 9 Mar 1946; Speed, 7/10–11/26 Apr 1946.

13. Sylvia Townsend Warner, *Letters* (1982), p 91; Peter Stead, 'Barry Since 1939', in Donald Moore (ed), *Barry* (Barry Island, 1985), p 450; Quentin Crisp, *The Naked Civil Servant* (Fontana edn, 1977), p 173.

14. John Hilton Bureau Papers (Special Collections, University of Sussex), Box 3, Administrative Files, 28 Sept 1945; *The New Yorker*, 17 Nov 1945; Rupert Croft-Cooke, *The Dogs of Peace* (1973), p 22; Hodgson, 29 Apr 1946; M-O A, D 5353, 5 Sept 1945; Zweiniger-Bargielowska, *Austerity*, chap 4 (incl pp 161, 172); *The New Yorker*, 5 Jan 1946.

15. Bill Naughton, 'The Spiv', *Pilot Papers* (Jan 1946), pp 99–108; Hodson, *Way*, p 159; Turner and Rennell, *Daddy*, p 46.

16. Loftus, 23 Oct 1945; Hodson, *Way*, p 206; Brown, 1/15, 16 Dec 1945; David Hughes, 'The Spivs', in Michael Sissons and Philip French (eds), *Age of Austerity* (Oxford, 1986), p 85; *New Yorker*, 6 Apr 1946; Turner and Rennell, *Daddy*, p 157.

17. Hodson, *Way*, pp 119–20; Reg Green, *National Heroes* (1997), p 144; *New Yorker*, 27 Jul 1946; David Rayvern Allen, *E. W. Swanton: A Celebration* (2000), p 87; Michael Marshall, *Gentlemen and Players* (1987), pp 140–41; *Wisden Cricketers' Almanack, 1947* (1947), pp 193, 412; Lesley A. Hall, *Sex, Gender and Social Change in Britain since 1880* (Basingstoke, 2000), p 147; Nick Tiratsoo, *Reconstruction, Affluence and Labour Politics* (1990), p 50; M-O A, TC 58/1/I.

18. Speed, 6 Aug 1946; M-O A, TC 49/2/C; *Joyce & Ginnie: The Letters of Joyce Grenfell and Virginia Graham* (1997), p 143; Raynham, 8 Jun 1946; M-O A, TC 49/2/C.

19. Asa Briggs, *The History of Broadcasting in the United Kingdom, Volume IV* (Oxford, 1979), pp 197–8, 716, 201.

20. *Coventry Evening Telegraph*, 29 Jun 1946; Hinton, p 135; Haines, 19/20 Jul 1946; Golden, 22 Jul 1946; Speed, 26 Jul 1946; M-O A, TC 67/6/D.

21. Speed, 7/13 Jun 1946; Langford, 19 Aug 1946.

22. Mollie Panter-Downes, *One Fine Day* (Virago edn, 1985), p 174; Angela Thirkell, *Private Enterprise* (1947), pp 188–9; David Pryce-Jones, 'Towards the Cocktail Party', in Sissons and French, *Austerity*, p 203.

23. *Sunday Pictorial*, 7/21 Jul 1946; James Hinton, 'Self-help and Socialism', *History Workshop* (Spring 1988), pp 100–26; *Pilot Papers* (Nov 1946), pp 16–17, 21; *Evening Standard*, 13 Sept 1946.

24. BBC WA, *Woman's Hour*, 7 Nov 1946; Briggs, p 56; Haines, 12 Nov 1946; BBC WA, R9/9/10 – LR/6869.

25. Fay Weldon, *Auto da Fay* (2002), pp 154–5; M-O A, FR 2429A; Hodgson, 24 Nov 1946; Speed, 10 Oct 1946; Langford, 8 Dec 1946; Haines, 19 Dec 1946.

26. Speed, 5 Dec 1946; St John, 15 Dec 1946; Hodson, *Way*, p 299; Mass-Observation, *Puzzled People* (1947), pp 21–2, 42, 51–2, 65, 77, 83–4, 120, 122.

27. Ferdynand Zweig, *Labour, Life and Poverty* (1949), pp 7, 58–64, 127–30, 134–6, 146–7, 152, 154–6, 175.

5 Constructively Revolutionary

1. *Spectator*, 20 Sept 2003 (Raymond Carr); Fabian, G 49/10.
2. Chaplin, 7/3/1, 21 Feb 1946, 12 Jun 1946; *Durham Chronicle*, 21 Feb 1947.
3. Daly, 302/5/8, 302/4/1, 6 Jan 1946, 302/3/1, 23 Feb 1947; *Guardian*, 24 Aug 1979.
4. Heap, 8 Sept 1945; Ben Pimlott, *Hugh Dalton* (1985), p 434; *Like It Was: The Diaries of Malcolm Muggeridge* (1981), p 204; Mervyn Jones, *Michael Foot* (1994), p 141; Kenneth O. Morgan, *Callaghan* (Oxford, 1997), p 60; *New Statesman*, 2 Nov 1946.
5. Brown, 1/15, 14 Feb 1946; Brian Brivati, introduction to Alan Bullock, *Ernest Bevin* (2002), p xiii; Peter Weiler, 'Britain and the First Cold War', *Twentieth Century British History*, 9/1 (1998), pp 127–38; *The Collected Essays, Journalism and Letters of George Orwell, Volume IV* (1968), p 222; Alan Bullock, *Ernest Bevin, Foreign Secretary, 1945–1951* (Oxford, 1983), p 221; *Chips: The Diaries of Sir Henry Channon* (1967), pp 411–12; *The New Yorker*, 20 October 1945; *Tatler*, 5 Dec 1945.
6. Langford, 24 May 1946; Margaret Gowing, *Britain and Atomic Energy, 1945–1952: Volume I* (1974), p 184; Peter Hennessy, *Whitehall* (Pimlico edn, 2001), p 713.
7. Robert Skidelsky, *John Maynard Keynes, Volume Three* (2000), p 470; Bernard Donoughue and G. W. Jones, *Herbert Morrison* (1973), p 353; Richard Toye, '"The Gentlemen in Whitehall" Reconsidered', *Labour History Review* (Aug 2002), pp 197–9.
8. Alec Cairncross, *Years of Recovery* (1985), p 303; Kenneth O. Morgan, *Labour in Power, 1945–1951* (Oxford, 1984), pp 130, 135; Glen O'Hara, 'British Economic and Social Planning, 1959–1970' (PhD, University of London, 2002), pp 4–5.
9. Donoughue and Jones, *Herbert Morrison*, p 354; Stephen Brooke, 'Problems of "Socialist Planning"', *Historical Journal*, 34/3 (1991), p 692; Richard Toye, 'Gosplanners versus Thermostatters', *Contemporary British History* (Winter 2000), p 93.
10. J. D. Tomlinson, 'The Iron Quadrilateral', *Journal of British Studies* (Jan 1995), p 100; Elizabeth Durbin, *New Jerusalems* (1985), p 74; Jim Tomlinson, 'Attlee's Inheritance and the Financial System', *Financial History Review* (1994), p 145; Nicholas Davenport, *Memoirs of a City Radical* (1974), pp 72, 149.
11. Martin Francis, 'Economics and Ethics', *Twentieth Century British History*, 6/2 (1995), pp 240–41; James Lansdale Hodson, *The Way Things Are* (1947), p 135; *Hansard*, 6 May 1946, cols 604–5.
12. *The Times*, 28 Oct 1946; Manny Shinwell, *Lead With The Left* (1981), p 136; Geoffrey Goodman, 'The Role of Industrial Correspondents', in Alan Campbell et al (eds), *British Trade Unions and Industrial Politics, Volume One* (Aldershot, 1999), p 27; Hodson, *Way*, p 174; Tom Driberg, *'Swaff'* (1974), p 223; Michael Young, *Labour's Plan for Plenty* (1947), p 80.

6 Farewell Squalor

1. *The Times*, 30 May 1946; *Financial Times*, 23 Apr 1946; Correlli Barnett, *The Audit of War* (Pan edn, 1996), p 276; Jim Tomlinson, 'Welfare and the Economy', *Twentieth Century British History*, 6/2 (1995), p 219; Tomlinson, 'Why So Austere?', *Journal of Social Policy* (Jan 1998), p 64.
2. Barnett, *Audit*, p 304; Julian Le Grand, *Motivation, Agency and Public Policy* (Oxford, 2003), p 7.

3. Charles Webster, 'Birth of a Dream', in Geoffrey Goodman (ed), *The State of the Nation* (1997), p 120.

4. Rudolf Klein, *The New Politics of the NHS* (1995), pp 26, 17, 20; David Widgery, *The National Health* (1988), p 25; Bruce Cardew, 'The Family Doctor', in James Farndale (ed), *Trends in the National Health Service* (Oxford, 1964), p 157; Wellcome Library for the History and Understanding of Medicine, Archives, GP/7/A.6; Rodney Lowe, *The Welfare State in Britain since 1945* (Basingstoke, 1999), p 176; John Campbell, *Nye Bevan* (1997), p 179; Michael Foot, *Aneurin Bevan, Volume 2* (1973), p 155.

5. Nicholas Timmins, *The Five Giants* (2001), pp 135–6; Joan C. Brown, 'Poverty in Post-war Britain', in James Obelkevich and Peter Catterall (eds), *Understanding Post-war British Society* (1994), p 117; Alan Deacon and Jonathan Bradshaw, *Reserved for the Poor* (Oxford, 1983), p 47.

6. Tomlinson, 'Austere', pp 67–73; David Vincent, *Poor Citizens* (Harlow, 1991), pp 128–9.

7. Andrew Saint, *Towards a Social Architecture* (1987), p 239; Betty D. Vernon, *Ellen Wilkinson* (1982), p 217; Gary McCulloch and Liz Sobell, 'Towards a Social History of the Secondary Modern Schools', *History of Education* (Sept 1994), p 279; Michael Young, *Labour's Plan for Plenty* (1947), p 117; P. J. Kemeny, 'Dualism in Secondary Technical Education', *British Journal of Sociology* (Mar 1970), p 86; D. W. Dean, 'Planning for a Post-war Generation', *History of Education* (Jun 1986), p 107; Barnett, *Audit*, p 302.

8. Brian Simon, *Education and the Social Order, 1940–1990* (1991), pp 104–6; Alan Kerckhoff et al, *Going Comprehensive in England and Wales* (1996), pp 18–19; Vernon, *Ellen Wilkinson*, pp 6–7; Howard Glennerster, *British Social Policy since 1945* (Oxford, 1995), p 62; Martin Francis, '"Not Reformed Capitalism, But … Democratic Socialism"', in Harriet Jones and Michael Kandiah (eds), *The Myth of Consensus* (Basingstoke, 1996), p 43; Ross McKibbin, *Classes and Cultures* (Oxford, 1998), p 234.

9. John Colville, *The Fringes of Power, Volume Two* (Sceptre edn, 1987), p 262; *The Times*, 29 Jun 1946; Dean, 'Planning', p 114; McKibbin, *Classes*, p 246.

10. Fred Grundy and Richard M. Titmuss, *Report on Luton* (Luton, 1945), p 66; Alison Ravetz, 'Housing the People', in Jim Fyrth (ed), *Labour's Promised Land?* (1995), pp 161–2; *Sunday Pictorial*, 21 Jul 1946.

11. Brian Lund, *Housing Problems and Housing Policy* (Harlow, 1996), p 41; Timmins, *Five Giants*, p 145; Steven Fielding et al, *'England Arise!'* (Manchester, 1995), pp 103–4.

12. Bertram Hutchinson, *Willesden and the New Towns* (1947), pts III, VII; *The Times*, 7 Mar 1946; Patrick Dunleavy, *The Politics of Mass Housing in Britain, 1945–1975* (Oxford, 1981), p 229.

13. Nigel Warburton, *Ernö Goldfinger* (2004), pp 126–9; Osborn, p 102; *Coventry Standard*, 31 Aug 1946; J. M. Richards, *The Castles on the Ground* (1946), p 13; Richards, *Memoirs of an Unjust Fella* (1980), p 188; John Betjeman, *Coming Home* (1997), pp 198–9.

14. Garry Philipson, *Aycliffe and Peterlee New Towns* (Cambridge, 1988), p 28; James Landsdale Hodson, *The Way Things Are* (1947), pp 282–3.

15. Andrew Homer, 'Creating New Communities', *Contemporary British History*

(Spring 2000), pp 65–70; Meryl Aldridge, *The British New Towns* (1979), p 33; Colin Ward, *New Town, Home Town* (Stevenage, 1980), pp 10–11; Bob Mullan, *Stevenage Ltd* (1980), p 42.

16. M-O A, FR 2375; Harold Orlans, *Stevenage* (1952), pp 63–7; Jack Balchin, *First New Town* (Stevenage, 1980), pp 10–11; Mullan, *Stevenage Ltd* p 42.

17. Elain Harwood, 'The Road to Subtopia', in Andrew Saint (ed), *London Suburbs* (1999), p 133; Saint, *Social Architecture*, p 58. See also Andrew Blowers, 'London's Out-county Estates', *Town and Country Planning* (Sept 1973), pp 409–14.

18. Simon Berry and Hamish Whyte (eds), *Glasgow Observed* (Edinburgh, 1987), p 234; N. R. Fyfe, 'Contested Visions of a Modern City', *Environment and Planning A*, 28/3 (1996), p 393; Miles Glendinning, '"Public Building"', *Planning History*, 14/3 (1992), p 15.

19. Nick Tiratsoo et al, *Urban Reconstruction in Britain and Japan, 1945–55* (Luton, 2002), pp 40–41; John J. Parkinson-Bailey, *Manchester* (Manchester, 2000), p 189; Percy Johnson-Marshall, *Rebuilding Cities* (Edinburgh, 1966), p 294; Alison Ravetz, *Remaking Cities* (1980), p 24; Peter Mandler, 'New Towns for Old', in Becky Conekin et al (eds), *Moments of Modernity* (1999), p 214; Peter J. Larkham, 'The Place of Urban Conservation in the UK Reconstruction Plans of 1942–1952', *Planning Perspectives* (Jul 2003), pp 295–324.

20. Larkham, 'Place', p 303; David Kynaston, *The City of London, Volume IV* (2001), p 128; Junichi Hasegawa, *Replanning the Blitzed City Centre* (Buckingham, 1992), p 120.

21. *Coventry Evening Telegraph*, 10/13/19 Oct 1945; Phil Hubbard et al, 'Contesting the Modern City', *Planning Perspectives* (Oct 2003), p 388.

22. Tiratsoo et al, *Urban Reconstruction*, p 11; Ravetz, *Remaking*, pp 39, 66; Arnold Whittick, *F.J.O.* (1987), p 91; J. B. Cullingworth, *Town and Country Planning in England and Wales* (1964), p 269; Headlam, pp 505–6; *The Times*, 1 Jul 1948.

23. Edmund Dell, *A Strange Eventful History* (1999), p 74; Alun Howkins, *The Death of Rural England* (2003), p 147; Scott Newton and Dilwyn Porter, *Modernisation Frustrated* (1988), p 117; *Financial Times*, 16 Feb 1991 (Andrew St George); *Independent*, 23 Oct 1999 (Duff Hart-Davis).

7 Glad to Sit at Home

1. Streat, p 310; Anthony Howard, '"We Are The Masters Now"', in Michael Sissons and Philip French (eds), *Age of Austerity* (Oxford, 1986), p 16; James Lees-Milne, *Caves of Ice* (Faber edn, 1984), pp 38, 46; *Independent*, 16 Dec 1991; David Kynaston, *The City of London, Volume IV* (2001), pp 8–9, 19, 24; Ralph Miliband, *Parliamentary Socialism* (1972), p 291.

2. James Lansdale Hodson, *The Way Things Are* (1947), p 309; Martin Daunton, *Just Taxes* (Cambridge, 2002), p 221; Kenneth O. Morgan, *Labour in Power, 1945–1951* (Oxford, 1984), p 185.

3. *The Collected Essays, Journalism and Letters of George Orwell, Volume II* (1968), p 99; *The Complete Works of George Orwell, Volume 16* (1998), p 425; *The Collected*

Essays, Journalism and Letters of George Orwell, Volume IV (1968), pp 220–21; Kenneth O. Morgan, *The People's Peace* (Oxford, 1990), p 108; Osborn, p 108; John Littlewood, *North Hants Golf Club Centenary History, 1904–2004* (Droitwich, 2004), p 65.

4. David Cannadine, *In Churchill's Shadow* (2002), p 236; Lees-Milne, *Caves*, p 94; J. B. Priestley, *Letter to a Returning Serviceman* (1945), p 31; Steven Fielding et al, *'England Arise!'* (Manchester, 1995), pp 137–8.

5. Fielding et al, *'England Arise!'*, pp 139, 152–4; Richard Weight, *Patriots* (2002), pp 185, 190.

6. *Radio Times*, 27 Sept 1946; Fielding et al, *'England Arise!'*, p 147; *Radio Times*, 27 Sept 1946; BBC WA, R9/9/11 – LR/47/1778, 6 Nov 1947; BBC WA, R9/9/11 – LR/47/161, 3 Feb 1947; BBC WA, R9/9/12 – LR/48/596, 16 Apr 1948; *Listener*, 30 Jan 1947; Asa Briggs, *The History of Broadcasting in the United Kingdom, Volume IV* (Oxford, 1979), p 82.

7. Priestley, *Letter*, p 30; Raphael Samuel, 'The Lost World of British Communism', *New Left Review* (Nov/Dec 1985), p 8; Osborn, p 133; Fielding et al, *'England Arise!'*, chap 5.

8. Bertram Hutchinson, *Willesden and the New Towns* (1947), pt IV; *Planning*, 15 Aug 1947, p 72; M-O A, TC 53/2/A; *Listener*, 23 Oct 1947.

9. Dilwyn Porter, 'The Attlee Years Reassessed', *Contemporary European History*, 4/1 (1994), p 98; Sagittarius, *Let Cowards Flinch* (1947), p 24; Speed, 14 Oct 1946.

8 Christ It's Bleeding Cold

1. Hodgson, 1 Jan 1947; William Ashworth, *The History of the British Coal Industry, Volume 5* (Oxford, 1986), pp 6, 3; Bill Jones et al, '"Going from Darkness to the Light"', *Llafur*, 7/1 (1996), pp 103–8; *Durham Chronicle*, 10 Jan 1947; *Coal Magazine* (Jan 1949), p 7.

2. Ferdynand Zweig, *Men in the Pits* (1948), pp 10, 15, 108–11, 142–3.

3. Jones et al, '"Going"', pp 100, 104; Ina Zweiniger-Bargielowska, 'South Wales Miners' Attitudes towards Nationalisation', *Llafur*, 6/3 (1994), pp 73–4, 76; Peter Ackers and Jonathan Payne, 'Before the Storm', *Social History* (May 2002), pp 193–4.

4. W. R. Garside, *The Durham Miners, 1919–1960* (1971), p 395; Mark Tookey, 'Three's a Crowd?', *Twentieth Century British History*, 12/4 (2001), pp 500, 504–5, 495; Gaitskell, pp 28–30; Alex J. Robertson, *The Bleak Midwinter* (Manchester, 1987), p 73.

5. Heap, 22 Jan 1947; Speed, 24–5/28–30 Jan 1947; SWCC (South Wales Coalfield Collection at Archives, University of Wales Swansea), Oakdale Navigation Lodge minutes, MNA/NUM/L/59/A23; James Lees-Milne, *Caves of Ice* (Faber edn, 1984), p 131.

6. *London Magazine* (Aug 1956), pp 45–7; John Lehmann, *The Ample Proposition* (1966), pp 30, 70.

7. Lewis, 3 Feb 1947; King, 3/5 Feb 1947; James Lansdale Hodson, *The Way Things Are* (1947), pp 313, 316; King, 7 Feb 1947; *Financial Times*, 8 Feb 1947; Ferguson, 9 Feb 1947; Hodgson, 9 Feb 1947; Lees-Milne, *Caves*, p 134.

8. Robertson, *Bleak Midwinter*, pp 18, 21, 95–6; Jones et al, '"Going"', pp 101, 108;

SWCC, Penalta Lodge records, MNA/NUM/L/63/D50; Zweig, *Pits*, pp 17–18.

9. *The Letters of Kingsley Amis* (2000), p 116; David Kynaston, *The City of London, Volume IV* (2001), p 18; Speed, 10/18 Feb 1947; Haines, 13 Feb 1947; Langford, 14/16/22 Feb 1947; Heap, 19 Feb 1947; Lewis, 14/19 Feb 1947.

10. M-O A, TC 68/5/B; Robertson, *Bleak Midwinter*, p 116.

11. Roy Hattersley, *A Yorkshire Boyhood* (1983), p 135; Bill Wyman, *Stone Alone* (1990), p 47; John Coldstream, *Dirk Bogarde* (2004), pp 162–7; Artemis Cooper, *Writing at the Kitchen Table* (1999), pp 131–2.

12. Robertson, *Bleak Midwinter*, pp 117–18; Hodgson, 3 Mar 1947; Langford, 10 Mar 1947.

13. Ford, 18 Mar 1947; Susan Cooper, 'Snoek Piquante', in Michael Sissons and Philip French (eds), *Age of Austerity* (Oxford, 1986), p 37; Robertson, *Bleak Midwinter*, pp 122–5; Steven Fielding et al, *'England Arise!'* (Manchester, 1995), pp 161–2; M-O A, TC 25/17/F; *Times*, 19 Mar 1947.

14. Robertson, *Bleak Midwinter*, p 158; Pearson Phillips, 'The New Look', in Sissons and French, *Age of Austerity*, p 127.

15. Zweig, *Pits*, pp 11, 155–60; Roy Mason, *Paying the Price* (1999), p 42.

16. See the stimulating, persuasive analysis in Ackers and Payne, 'Before the Storm', pp 184–209.

17. M-O A, FR 3007.

9 Our Prestige at Stake

1. M-O A, TC 3/3/C; Mary Abbott, *Family Affairs* (2003), p 111; *News Chronicle*, 15 Apr 1948.

2. Hodgson, 10 Mar 1947; M-O A, TC 1/9/F; Janice Winship, 'Nation Before Family', in *Formations of Nations and People* (1984), pp 197–8.

3. M-O A, TC 85/7/B; Geoffrey Thomas, *Women and Industry* (1948), pp 1, 4; Phyllis Willmott, *Joys and Sorrows* (1995), pp 21–2; Willmott, 18 Jul 1947; *The Times*, 22 Sept 1988, *Independent*, 23 Sept 1988; Sue Aspinall, 'Women, Realism and Reality in British Films, 1943–53', in James Curran and Vincent Porter (eds), *British Cinema History* (1983), p 286.

4. M-O A, FR 2537.

5. Phyllis G. Allen, 'Evening Activities in the Home', *Sociological Review* (1951), Section 7, pp 1–15; BBC WA, R9/9/12–LR/48/1261; Anthony Adamthwaite, '"Nation Shall Speak Unto Nation"', *Contemporary Record* (Winter 1993), pp 558–9.

6. BBC WA, R9/21; Haines, 26 Jul 1947, 9 Aug 1947, 11/13/16 Sept 1947, 4 Oct 1947; Ford, 9–10/12/29 Feb 1948, 1/15 Mar 1948; BBC WA, R9/9/12–LR/48/1219.

7. *Radio Times*, 11 Apr 1947; *Independent*, 1 Jun 1990 (Sowerbutts obituary); M-O A, TC 53/2/D; Helena Barrett and John Phillips, *Suburban Style* (1987), p 186; Jenny Uglow, *A Little History of British Gardening* (2004), p 286.

8. *Daily Express*, 10/12 May 1947; Neville Cardus, *Cardus in the Covers* (1978), p 106; *Independent*, 31 Oct 2003; *Daily Telegraph*, 16 Dec 1991 (Arlott obituary); *Pilot Papers* (Dec 1947), p 75.

9. Patrick Slater, *The Demand for Holidays in 1947 and 1948* (The Social Survey, 1948), p 2; M-O A, TC 58/2/F; Chaplin, 7/3/1, 18 Jun 1947.

10. Brown, 1/16, 7 May 1947; Langford, 12 Aug 1947; Colin Ward and Dennis Hardy, *Goodnight Campers!* (1986), p 110; M-O A, TC 58/2/G.

11. Chris Bryant, *Glenda Jackson* (1999), pp 9–10; Bill Wyman, *Stone Alone* (1990), pp 48–9; Brian Simon, *Education and the Social Order, 1940–1990* (1991), p 108; L. S. Hearnshaw, *Cyril Burt* (1979), p 118; Nirmala Rao, 'Labour and Education', *Contemporary British History* (Summer 2002), p 113.

10 The Whole World is Full of Permits

1. Kenneth O. Morgan, *Labour in Power, 1945–1951* (Oxford, 1984), pp 253–4; Giles Radice, *Friends and Rivals* (2002), p 64; Edward Pearce, *Denis Healey* (2002), p 76.

2. Adrian Turner, *Robert Bolt* (1998), p 69; Mervyn Jones, *Chances* (1987), p 114; Steve Parsons, 'British "McCarthyism" and the Intellectuals', in Jim Fyrth (ed), *Labour's Promised Land?* (1995), pp 227–31; Phillip Deery, '"The Secret Battalion"', *Contemporary British History* (Winter 1999), p 20.

3. Bernard Donoughue and G. W. Jones, *Herbert Morrison* (1973), p 403; Morgan, *Labour*, p 121; *Coventry Evening Telegraph*, 17 May 1948; Asa Briggs, *Michael Young* (Basingstoke, 2001), pp 81–2; Gaitskell, p 72.

4. James Lees-Milne, *Caves of Ice* (Faber edn, 1984), p 192; M-O A, TC 25/17/I; M-O A, D 5353, 10 Aug 1947; Kenneth Harris, *Attlee* (1982), p 346; Lees-Milne, *Caves*, p 197; John Fforde, *The Bank of England and Public Policy, 1941–1958* (Cambridge, 1992), p 157.

5. *Wisden Cricketers' Almanack, 1948* (1948), p 227; *Financial Times*, 21 Aug 1947; Speed, 28 Aug 1947; Lees-Milne, *Caves*, p 208; St John, 28 Aug 1947.

6. For a helpful overview of the whole question of planning vis-à-vis Keynesianism in 1947/8, see: Jim Tomlinson, *Democratic Socialism and Economic Policy* (Cambridge, 1997), chap 10.

7. Stephen Brooke, 'Problems of "Socialist Planning"', *Historical Journal*, 34/3 (1991), pp 687–702; Chris Wrigley, 'Trade Union Development 1945–79', in Wrigley (ed), *A History of British Industrial Relations, 1939–1979* (Cheltenham, 1996), p 77; *New Statesman*, 18 Oct 1947; Nick Tiratsoo, 'Labour and the Reconstruction of Hull, 1945–51', in Tiratsoo (ed), *The Attlee Years* (1991), p 137.

8. *Coventry Evening Telegraph*, 9 Jun 1947, 22 May 1948.

9. Patrick Dunleavy, *The Politics of Mass Housing in Britain, 1945–1975* (Oxford, 1981), p 260; *Manchester Guardian*, 19 Apr 1948; Steen Eiler Rasmussen, *London* (1948), p 426; *Journal of the Town Planning Institute* (Jul–Aug 1948), p 151; James Lansdale Hodson, *Thunder in the Heavens* (1950), p 105.

10. J. B. Priestley, *The Linden Tree* (1948), pp 62–3; Vincent Brome, *Aneurin Bevan* (1953), pp 1–3.

11. Tony Benn, *Years of Hope* (1994), pp 125–7; *Horizon* (Jul 1947), p 1; *The Letters of Sidney and Beatrice Webb, Volume III* (Cambridge, 1978), p 465; Philip M. Williams, *Hugh Gaitskell* (1979), p 141.

12. Steven Fielding et al, *'England Arise!'* (Manchester, 1995), p 172; Jeremy Nuttall, '"Psychological Socialist", "Militant Moderate"', *Labour History Review* (Aug 2003), pp 247–8; Stephen Brooke, 'Evan Durbin', *Twentieth Century British History* 7/1 (1996), p 51.

13. Streat, pp 414, 419; Ben Pimlott, *Harold Wilson* (1992), p 111; David Howell, 'Wilson and History', *Twentieth Century British History*, 4/2 (1993), p 180.

14. This account of the Conservative Party's post-1945 remaking of policy owes much to Harriet Jones, '"New Conservatism?"', in Becky Conekin et al (eds), *Moments of Modernity* (1999), pp 171–88.

15. Bertrand de Jouvenel, *Problems of Socialist England* (1949), p 23; Margaret Thatcher, *The Path to Power* (1995), p 48; *My Dear Max: The Letters of Brendan Bracken to Lord Beaverbrook, 1925–1958* (1990), p 58; Conservative Party, *The Industrial Charter* (popular edn, 1947), p 4; *Spectator*, 16 May 1947, 10 Oct 1947; *The Times*, 3 Oct 1947. Also for the Brighton conference, see: Anthony Howard, *RAB* (1987), pp 156–7.

16. Jones, '"New Conservatism?"', pp 177–8, 187; Reginald Maudling, *Memoirs* (1978), p 45; Scott Kelly, 'Ministers Matter', *Contemporary British History* (Winter 2000), pp 38–9; Headlam, p 526.

17. M-O A, FR 2516; Lees-Milne, *Caves*, p 241.

11 Ain't She Lovely?

1. John Barnes, *Ahead of His Age* (1979), pp 402, 410; W. R. Matthews, *Memories and Meanings* (1969), p 310; *Sunday Pictorial*, 19/26 Oct 1947; *The Times*, 16 Sept 1972.

2. *Sunday Pictorial*, 12 Jan 1947; Robert Lacey, *Majesty* (Sphere edn, 1978), p 200; *Times*, 15 Nov 1997; Speed, 10 Jul 1947; Philip Ziegler, *Crown and People* (1978), pp 82–3; James Lees-Milne, *Caves of Ice* (Faber edn, 1984), p 246; James Lansdale Hodson, *Thunder in the Heavens* (1950), pp 61–2; Nick Clarke, *The Shadow of a Nation* (2003), p 19; Headlam, p 533; Golden, 28 Nov 1947; Hodgson, 18 Jan 1948.

3. Gaitskell, p 62; *Daring to Hope: The Diaries and Letters of Violet Bonham Carter, 1946–1969* (2000), p 46; Streat, pp 444–5; Harold Nicolson, *The Later Years, 1945–1962: Diaries and Letters, Volume III* (1968), pp 142–3, 148.

4. Nick Tiratsoo, 'Popular Politics, Affluence and the Labour Party in the 1950s', in Anthony Gorst et al (eds), *Contemporary British History, 1931–1961* (1991), p 53; Uttin, 2 Dec 1947; Speed, 18 Sept 1947, 13 Oct 1947; Lees-Milne, *Caves*, p 239; Susan Cooper, 'Snoek Piquante', in Michael Sissons and Philip French (eds), *Age of Austerity* (Oxford, 1986), p 40; *Listener*, 3 Jun 1948.

5. *Daily Express*, 16 Apr 1947; BBC WA, *Woman's Hour*, 14 Oct 1947; King, 22 May 1948; Martin Westlake, *Kinnock* (2001), p 16; Heap, 17 Oct 1947; Golden, 13 Jan 1948.

6. *News Chronicle*, 19 Apr 1948; *The New Yorker*, 19 Jun 1948; *The Selected Letters of Tennessee Williams, Volume II* (2006), p 198; Raynham, 2 Jul 1947; Melanie Tebbutt, *Women's Talk?* (Aldershot, 1995), p 74; *Punch*, 15/22/29 Oct 1947, 5/12 Nov 1947; *British Medical Journal*, 29 Nov 1947; Ina Zweiniger-Bargielowska, *Austerity in Britain* (Oxford, 2000), pp 222–3.

7. Enid Palmer letters (Department of Documents, Imperial War Museum), 4/14/16/24 Apr 1948; Ina Zweiniger-Bargielowska, 'Consensus and Consumption', in Harriet Jones and Michael Kandiah (eds), *The Myth of Consensus* (Basingstoke, 1996), pp 89, 95; Richard Hoggart, *The Uses of Literacy* (1957), p 37.

8. Christina Hardyment, *Slice of Life* (1995), p 31; Hodson, *Thunder*, p 66; *Barnsley*

Chronicle, 13 Dec 1947; M-O A, Directives for Jan 1948, Replies; Preston, 19 Feb 1948; M-O A, Directives for Jan 1948, Replies; *Spivs' Gazette*, Mar 1948. In general on the black market, in addition to Zweiniger-Bargielowska, *Austerity in Britain*, chap 4, see: Edward Smithies, *The Black Economy in England since 1914* (Dublin, 1984); Mark Roodhouse, 'Popular Morality and the Black Market in Britain, 1939–55', in Frank Trentmann and Flemming Just, *Food and Conflict in Europe in the Age of the Two World Wars* (Basingstoke, 2006).

9. Kathryn A. Morrison, *English Shops and Shopping* (New Haven, 2003), pp 239, 275, 276; David Powell, *Counter Revolution* (1991), p 66; *Store* (Feb 1948), p 20; *Co-operative News*, 17 Jan 1948, 13 Mar 1948; *Dictionary of Business Biography*, Volume 3 (1985), pp 475–9.

10. *Vogue* (Oct 1947), p 37; Pearson Phillips, 'The New Look', in Sissons and French (eds), *Age of Austerity*, pp 129–30, 132–4; *The New Yorker*, 24 Jan 1948; Langford, 24 Apr 1948; Golden, 28 Apr 1948; Theo Aronson, *Princess Margaret* (1997), pp 106–7; M-O A, FR 3095.

11. Angela Partington, 'The Days of the New Look', in Jim Fyrth (ed), *Labour's Promised Land?* (1995), p 252; *Independent*, 14 Jan 2002; Carolyn Steedman, *Landscape for a Good Woman* (1986), pp 12, 28.

12. Ina Zweiniger-Bargielowska, 'Rationing, Austerity and the Conservative Party Recovery after 1945', *Historical Journal*, 37/1 (1994), p 180; Roy Lewis and Angus Maude, *The English Middle Classes* (1949), pp 213–14; *Economist*, 3 Jan 1948; *Listener*, 3 Jun 1948.

13. *The Diaries of Evelyn Waugh* (1976), p 689; C. R. Perry, 'In Search of H.V. Morton,' *Twentieth Century British History*, 10/3 (1999), p 453; David Kynaston, *The City of London, Volume IV* (2001), pp 24–5; John Brophy, *The Mind's Eye* (1949), pp 64–5.

14. Hodson, *Thunder*, pp 16, 29, 83, 216; John Turner, 'A Land Fit for Tories to Live In', *Contemporary European History*, 4/2 (1995), p 193; *New Statesman*, 12 Jun 1948; Langford, 2 May 1947.

15. Frances Partridge, *Everything to Lose* (1985), p 57; Denis Gifford, *The Golden Age of Radio* (1985), p 179; Terry Hallett, *Bristol's Forgotten Empire* (Westbury, 2000), p 155; *The Kenneth Williams Diaries* (1993), pp 20–21; *Aldershot News*, 6 Feb 1948; Roger Lewis, *The Life and Death of Peter Sellers* (1994), p 108; *Daily Express*, 7 May 1948.

16. *Accrington Observer*, 14/17 Feb 1948; Rogan Taylor and Andrew Ward, *Kicking and Screaming* (1995), p 37.

17. Hodson, *Thunder*, p 116; Preston, 9 Apr 1948; Gaitskell, p 69.

18. Langford, 19 Jun 1947; *Daily Telegraph*, 1 Aug 2002 (Higgins obituary); *Horizon* (Dec 1947), p 300; *News Chronicle*, 24 May 1948; Brown, 1/16, 18 Feb 1948; Richard Davenport-Hines, *The Pursuit of Oblivion* (2001), p 298.

19. Headlam, pp 552–3; Kenneth O. Morgan, *Callaghan* (Oxford, 1997), p 85; *Sunday Pictorial*, 18 Apr 1948; Langford, 4 May 1948; *News Chronicle*, 24 May 1948; Fenton Bresler, *Lord Goddard* (1977), p 182; Hartley Shawcross, *Life Sentence* (1995), p 168.

20. David Renton, 'Not Just Economics but Politics as Well', *Labour History Review* (Summer 2000), p 174; Richard Weight, *Patriots* (2002), p 83; Kynaston, *City*, p 223.

21. K. L. Little, *Negroes in Britain* (1948), p 243; Anthony H. Richmond, *Colour*

Prejudice in Britain (1954), pp 76–7; E. R. Braithwaite, *To Sir, With Love* (1959), pp 36–49; G. K. Evans, *Public Opinion on Colonial Affairs* (The Social Survey, Jun 1948), pp ii–iv.

22. Kathleen Paul, 'The Politics of Citizenship in Post-War Britain', *Contemporary Record* (Winter 1992), pp 464, 467; Clive Harris, 'Post-war Migration and the Industrial Reserve Army', in Winston James and Clive Harris (eds), *Inside Babylon* (1993), pp 21–2.

23. Randall Hansen, 'The Politics of Citizenship in 1940s Britain', *Twentieth Century British History*, 10/1 (1999), pp 87–8.

24. David Watson, 'Research Note', *Historical Studies in Industrial Relations* (Mar 1996), p 157; *Hansard*, 8 Jun 1948, col 1851; Harris, 'Migration', pp 23, 24–5; Hansen, 'Politics', p 90; Paul, 'Politics of Citizenship', p 456.

25. *Star*, 22 Jun 1948; Mike Phillips and Trevor Phillips, *Windrush* (1998), pp 66, 70; *Clapham Observer*, 2/9 Jul 1948.

12 A Change in the Terms of Struggle

1. BBC WA, *Woman's Hour*, 22/29 Jun 1948.

2. *British Medical Journal*, 16 Nov 1946, 28 Dec 1946; Langford, 6 May 1948; Michael Coveney, *The World According to Mike Leigh* (1996), p 41; *Star*, 26 Jun 1948.

3. Tom Wildy, 'The Social and Economic Publicity and Propaganda of the Labour Governments of 1945–51', *Contemporary Record* (Summer 1992), pp 45–71; *Falkirk Herald*, 3 Jul 1948; *New Statesman*, 3 Jul 1948; *Punch*, 30 Jun 1948; Janice Winship, 'Nation Before Family', in *Formations of Nations and People* (1984), p 201; *Vogue* (Jul 1948), p 53.

4. *Tablet*, 4 Jul 1998 (Clifford Longley); Steven Fielding et al, *'England Arise!'* (Manchester, 1995), p 172; Raynham, 27 Apr 1948; Hodgson, 4 Jul 1948; *Liverpool Daily Post*, 1 Jul 1948.

5. Phyllis Willmott, *Joys and Sorrows* (1995), pp 42, 64, 66; J.W.B. Douglas and J. M. Blomfield, *Children Under Five* (1958), pp 45–51, 57, 69, 99.

6. Wildy, 'Publicity and Propaganda', pp 64–5; *The Times*, 5 Jul 1948; Preston, 5 Jul 1948.

7. *Daily Mirror*, 5 Jul 1948; *The Times*, 5 Jul 1948; *Manchester Guardian*, 5 Jul 1948; Heap, 5 Jul 1948; diary of Cyril Leach (at Harrow Local History Centre), 5 Jul 1948.

8. *Star*, 5 Jul 1948; *Lancashire Daily Post*, 5 Jul 1948; *The Times*, 23 Jun 1998; M-O A, D5353, 5 Jul 1948.

Acknowledgements

I am grateful to the following for kindly allowing me to reproduce copyright material: Evelyn Abrams (Mark Abrams); Pat Arlott (John Arlott); Ouida V. Ascroft (Florence Speed); Don Bachardy (Christopher Isherwood): Lady Diana Baer (Mollie Panter-Downes); Stuart Ball; Correlli Barnett; BBC Written Archives Centre; Tony Benn; Birmingham City Archives (Mary King); Michael Bloch (James Lees-Milne); The Robert Bolt Estate; Mark Bostridge and Rebecca Williams (Vera Brittain's literary executors, for quotations from her *Wartime Chronicle*); Veronica Bowater (Vere Hodgson); E. R. Braithwaite; Robin Bruce Lockhart (Sir Robert Bruce Lockhart); Michael Burns; Rene and Michael Chaplin (Sid Chaplin); Jonathan Clowes Ltd (*Letters* Copyright © 2001 Kingsley Amis, *Memoirs* © 1991 Kingsley Amis, on behalf of the Literary Estate of Kingsley Amis; Copyright © 1998 Doris Lessing, © 1961 Doris Lessing, © 2002 Doris Lessing, on behalf of Doris Lessing); The Estate of Cyril Connolly (extracts from *Horizon* magazine, copyright © 1945, 1947 Cyril Connolly, reproduced by permission of the Estate of Cyril Connolly, c/o Rogers Coleridge & White Ltd, 20 Powis Mews, London W11 1JN); Renée Daly (Lawrence Daly); Seán Damer; The Dartington Hall Trust Archive; Fabian Society; Margaret Fenton (Frederic Osborn); Howard Ford (Erica Ford); Enid Grant (Enid Palmer); Bill Hamilton, Literary Executor of the Estate of the late Sonia Brownell Orwell, and Secker and Warburg Ltd (extracts from the published writings of George Orwell, copyright © George Orwell); Lord Hattersley; Pamela Hendicott (Judy Haines); David Higham Associates (Arthur Bryant, John Lehmann, Malcolm Muggeridge, Dylan Thomas); Hazel Holt (Barbara Pym); Islington

Local History Centre (Gladys Langford); Jackie Jones (Mervyn Jones); Lynn Jones (Lynn Creedy); P. J. Kavanagh (Ted Kavanagh); Dora L. Kneebone (Rose Uttin); Sir Michael Levey (John Brophy); Alison Light (Estate of Raphael Samuel, for extract from *The Lost World of British Communism*, Verso, 2006); Trustees of the Mass-Observation Archive; Jane Moser (Joan Waley); News International Archive and Record Office (Papers of the John Hilton Bureau); Juliet Nicolson (Harold Nicolson); Jill Norman (Elizabeth David); Angela Partington; The Estate of Frances Partridge (extracts from *Everything to Lose*, copyright © 1985 Frances Partridge, first published in 1985 by Victor Gollancz, reproduced by permission of the Estate of Frances Partridge, c/o Rogers Coleridge & White, 20 Powis Mews, London W11 1JN); PFD (extracts from *The Sea and the Land*, copyright © Estate of James Lansdale Hodson 1945, *The Way Things Are*, copyright © Estate of James Lansdale Hodson 1948, and *Thunder in the Heavens*, copyright © Estate of James Lansdale Hodson 1950, on behalf of the author's Estate; extracts from *The Kenneth Williams Diaries*, copyright © The Estate of Kenneth Williams 1994, on behalf of the author's Estate; extracts from *Love is Blue*, copyright © Joan Wyndham 1986); Mike and Trevor Phillips (*Windrush*); Allan Preston (Kenneth Preston); Alison Ravetz; Marian Ray and Robin Raynham (Marian Raynham); Basil Streat (Sir Raymond Streat); Barry Turner (*When Daddy Came Home* by Barry Turner and Tony Rennell); Roxana and Matthew Tynan (*Letters of Kenneth Tynan*); UCL Library Services, Special Collections (Hugh Gaitskell); University of Wales Swansea, Library & Information Services (South Wales Coalfield Collection); Seymour J. Weissman (Evan Durbin); The Wellcome Library for the History and Understanding of Medicine; Phyllis Willmott; Bill Wyman; Emma and Toby Young (Michael Young); Ina Zweiniger-Bargielowska.

I am indebted, in many different ways, to archivists, librarians, fellow-historians, friends and relatives. They include: Sarah Aitchison; Helen Arkwright; Martin Banham; Nicola Beauman; Elisabeth Bennett; Piers Brendon; Sophie Bridges; Steve Bunker; Peter Cain; Terry Carney; Mark Clapson; Nigel Cochrane; Rob Colls; Fiona Courage; Heather Creaton; Seán Damer; Patric Dickinson; Marguerite Dupree; Joy

Eldridge; Amanda Engineer; Angela Eserin; Alexandra Eveleigh; Robert Frost; Andrew George; Elizabeth Hennessy; Len Holden; David and Val Horsfield; Bill and Gisela Hunt; Caroline Jacob; Harriet Jones; Jacqueline Kavanagh; Bill Lancaster; Valerie Moyses; Jonathan Oates; Erin O'Neill; Stanley Page; Anne Perkins; Andrew Riley; Simon Robbins; Richard Roberts; Richard Saville; Dennis Sherer; Dorothy Sheridan; Emma Shipley; Adrian Smith; John Stevens; David Taylor; Richard Temple; Deborah Thom; Alistair Tough; Jenny Uglow; John Wakefield; Andy Ward; David Warren; Tracy Weston; Yvonne Widger; Melanie Wood; Christine Woodland.

Since 2001 I have been a visiting professor at Kingston University, where I have enjoyed the company and stimulation of Gail Cunningham and her colleagues in the Faculty of Arts and Social Sciences.

The following people kindly read all or part of the various drafts: Julian Birkett; Brian Brivati; Mike Burns; Juliet Gardiner; John Gross; Lucy Kynaston; James Lappin; David Loffman; Sara and Steve Marsh; Glen O'Hara; Dil Porter; Harry Ricketts; Phyllis Willmott. I owe much to their comments, encouragement and often salutary sense of perspective.

My greatest debt, of course, is to those who have been most intimately involved in this project: Amanda Howard for transcribing my tapes; Andrea Belloli for her copy-editing; Libby Willis and Patric Dickinson for reading the proofs; Douglas Matthews for compiling the index; my agent Deborah Rogers and her assistant Hannah Westland; my editor Bill Swainson and his colleagues at Bloomsbury, including Nick Humphrey for his help with pictures, Emily Sweet for putting the hardback to bed, and Arzu Tahsin and Jessica Leeke for their work on the paperback; and, above all, Lucy, Laurie, George and Michael at home. Their belief in me and what I am trying to do has made all the difference.

New Malden, autumn 2007

Picture Credits

VE Day celebrations in Lambert Square, Coxlodge, Newcastle upon Tyne (*NCJ Media Ltd*)

The Tory candidate addresses an election meeting in Bethnal Green, June 1945. Photograph by Kurt Hutton (*Picture Post, Getty Images*)

Aneurin Bevan in Ebbw Vale during the 1945 election. Photograph by Ian Smith (*Time and Life, Getty Images*)

The Haymarket, Sheffield, 1946 (*Local Studies Department, Sheffield Central Library*)

Museum steps, Liverpool, 1946. Photograph by E. Chambré Hardman (*NT/E. Chambré Hardman Collection*)

Mrs Francis, Christmas Street, off the Old Kent Road, 1946. Photograph by Charles Hewitt (*Picture Post, Getty Images*)

The Gorbals, Glasgow, 1948. Photograph by Bert Hardy (*Picture Post, Getty Images*)

'Mr Browning's Winning Team': West Sussex, 1947. Photograph by Marjorie Baker (*Henfield Parish Council*)

England versus South Africa at Lord's, June 1947 (*Reproduced from John Arlott's* Vintage Summer: 1947)

Margate, June 1948. Photograph by Chris Ware (*Picture Post, Getty Images*)

Index

A NOTE ON THE AUTHOR

David Kynaston was born in Aldershot in 1951. He has been a professional historian since 1973 and has written fifteen books, including *The City of London* (1994–2001), a widely acclaimed four-volume history, and *WG's Birthday Party*, an account of the Gentleman v. Players match at Lord's in July 1898. He is currently a visiting professor at Kingston University.

A NOTE ON THE TYPE

The text of this book is set in Linotype Stempel Garamond, a version of Garamond adapted and first used by
the Stempel foundry in 1924. It's one of several versions
of Garamond based on the designs of Claude Garamond.
It is thought that Garamond based his font on Bembo,
cut in 1495 by Francesco Griffo in collaboration with the
Italian printer Aldus Manutius. Garamond types were
first used in books printed in Paris around 1532. Many of
the present-day versions of this type are based on the
Typi Academiae of Jean Jannon cut in Sedan in 1615.

Claude Garamond was born in Paris in 1480. He learned how
to cut type from his father and by the age of fifteen he was
able to fashion steel punches the size of a pica with great
precision. At the age of sixty he was commissioned by King
Francis I to design a Greek alphabet, for which he was given
the honourable title of royal type founder. He died in 1561.

BLOOMSBURY

Smoke in the Valley

Smoke in the Valley, the second book in the series *Tales of a New Jerusalem*, will be published by Bloomsbury in July 2008

'A cracking read . . . evocative and entertaining' *Daily Telegraph*

David Kynaston's *Austerity Britain 1945–51*, the first book in his series *Tales of a New Jerusalem*, was a major *Sunday Times* bestseller in 2007. Here is the second volume from this landmark book covering 1948–51. Continuing his groundbreaking series about post-war Britain, Kynaston presents a breathtaking portrait of our nation through eyewitness accounts, newspapers of the time and previously unpublished diaries. Drawing on the everyday experiences of people from all walks of life, *Smoke in the Valley* covers the length and breadth of the country to tell its story.

'As a portrait of an age which shaped much of modern Britain, it is unsurpassed . . . a plum-duff of a book for both the historian and the general reader' *Guardian*

ISBN: 978 0 7475 9228 0 / Paperback / £7.99

Order your copy:

By phone: 01256 302 699
By email: direct@macmillan.co.uk

Delivery is usually 3–5 working days.
Postage and packaging will be charged.

Online: www.bloomsbury.com/bookshop
Free postage and packaging for orders over £15.

Prices and availability subject to change without notice.

Visit Bloomsbury.com for more about David Kynaston